Voice Over:

The Making of Black Radio

WILLIAM BARLOW

The Making of Black Radio

TEMPLE UNIVERSITY PRESS PHILADELPHIA

Temple University Press, Philadelphia 19122
Copyright © 1999 by Temple University.
All rights reserved
Published 1999
Printed in the United States of America

Text design by Kate Nichols

⊗The paper used in this publication meets the requirements of American National Standard for Information Sciences—Permanence of Paper for Printed Library Materials, ANSI Z39.48-1984

Library of Congress Cataloging-in-Publication Data

Barlow, William, 1943–
  Voice over : the making of Black radio / William Barlow.
    p. cm.
  Includes bibliographical references and index.
  ISBN 1-56639-666-2 (alk. paper).
  ISBN 1-56639-667-0 (pbk. : alk. paper)
  1. Afro-Americans in radio broadcasting. I. Title.
PN1991.8.A35B37 1999
384.54′089′96073—dc21   98-29943

Contents

Preface   vii
Introduction: Shifting Voices   1

Part I. "I'se Regusted": Blackface Radio   13

1. From the Jazz Age to Jim Crow   15
2. The Controversial Phenomenon of *Amos 'n' Andy*   35

Part II. "New World a-Coming": Black Pride Radio   47

3. Brown Bombers and Black Radio Pioneers   49
4. "Destination Freedom"   67

Part III. "Rappin' the Mike": Black Appeal Radio   91

5. Buying Time and Making Rhyme   93
6. The Rise of Black Appeal Radio   108
7. Spin Doctors of the Postwar Era   134

Contents

Part IV. "Rockin' the Pot": Black Counterfeit Radio   155

  8. The White DJ Crossover Crusade   157

  9. The Rock-and-Roll Rebels   176

Part V. "Burn Baby Burn": Black Power Radio   195

  10. "A Change Is Gonna Come"   197

  11. Microphones in the Riot Zones   212

  12. The FM Frontier   226

**Part VI. "Payin' the Cost to Be the Boss":
Black-Owned Radio**   243

  13. Bridging the Ownership Gap   245

  14. Entrepreneurs with Attitude   264

  15. Blackgrounding Public Radio   279

Afterword: Talking Drums   294

Notes   299

Index   319

Photographs follow page 164

Preface

ost writers, even cultural critics and scholars, tend to write about subjects that intrigue them, and I am no exception. This project and my other books have grown out of my own experiences of black radio, initially as a listener and more recently as a music programmer. My first encounter with black radio, in Columbus, Ohio, during the mid-1950s, was memorable for the level of culture shock involved. At the time, I was a fairly typical "army brat"; my father was a career officer and a West Point graduate. We moved to Columbus after being stationed in Heidelberg, Germany, for three years. While in Heidelberg, I attended a small, all-white grade school for military dependents and listened to sports and pop-music programming on the Armed Forces Radio Service (AFRS). My favorite radio show was the *Friday-Night Hit Parade*. Spike Jones and Johnnie Ray were my early pop idols; I even took to imitating Ray's famous tearjerker "Cry" at local school talent contests. By the time I left Heidelberg, Pat Boone's version of "Tutti Frutti" was the *Hit Parade*'s top-ranked record, and white buck shoes were the latest fashion statement among my peers.

In Columbus, my cultural milieu changed drastically. Although still living on an army base, I attended an interracial junior high school where I first met black teens and became friends with some of them, especially on the basketball court. One of those new friends was "Moon" Mullins, the point guard on the school team. Mullins introduced me to black radio in the person of "Doctor Bop," the DJ of choice among black youth in Columbus at the time. Doctor Bop was a rhyming and signifying verbal trickster: "This here's Doctor Bop on the scene with a stack of shellac in my record machine!" His local evening music show was notable for its vernacular pyrotechnics and raucous R & B discs by such artists as Little Richard, Shirley and Lee, Chuck Berry, LaVerne Baker, Bo Diddley, James Brown, Hank Ballard and the Midnighters. Both the music and the language were a revelation to me. I had never heard black rhythm-and-blues records, only the counterfeit "cover versions" played on the *Hit Parade;* needless to say, I liked the black originals much better than the sanitized counterfeits. Hearing Little Richard's original recording of "Tutti Frutti" after a steady diet of Pat Boone's cover version alerted me to a racial paradox in popular music that I had never been consciously aware of and opened my ears to a segregated genre of black music.

Doctor Bop's inventive use of the black vernacular unmasked for me another facet of racial masquerading on the airwaves. Like many "war babies" of my generation, I listened to *Amos 'n' Andy* on network radio in the late 1940s; I also remember hearing Beulah on AFRS while living in Germany in the early 1950s. Understandably, I thought these caricatures were real black voices—until my encounter with Doctor Bop. His novel refiguring of black dialect had the effect of flushing out the impostors, once I'd made the connection. Little did I know that, almost thirty years later, these sort of racial contradictions in radio broadcasting would become a major focus of my writing.

In the late 1950s and early 1960s, while finishing up high school in Harrisburg, Pennsylvania, I became a jazz fan. This new development of my musical tastes was facilitated by Sid McCoy, a velvet-voiced black DJ broadcasting on WCLF-AM in Chicago; his late-night show *The Real McCoy* could be heard in Harrisburg. The jazz artistry of Miles Davis, John Coltrane, Thelonious Monk, and the Modern Jazz Quartet, as well as the vocal styling of Billie Holiday, Dinah Washington, Joe Williams, and the lesser-known Bill Henderson, was a revelation, and I listened to *The Real McCoy* religiously. The show inspired me to begin collecting jazz LPs and to seek out live jazz venues in both Harrisburg and New York City (which was three hours away by car).

By the time I got to San Francisco in the late 1960s, the Bay Area was a hotbed of radical political and cultural insurgencies: student sit-ins and strikes, the rising Black Panther party, massive and militant antiwar protests, the emerging youth counterculture. New media sprang up in the forms of a local "underground" press and radio outlets. The radio experiment took place on two marginal FM commercial stations: KMPX and, later, KSAN. An eclectic staff of renegade DJs and radical journalists crafted a counterculture-oriented "free-form" music, talk, and information format that was an overnight sensation. I was a student activist at San Francisco State, living in the Haight-Ashbury district, when underground radio hit the airwaves in the Bay Area, and it soon became essential listening for all of us involved in the student movement and the local counterculture.

While neither largely black-staffed nor black-formatted outlets, San Francisco underground radio emulated black radio in a number of important ways. Most of the white disc jockeys associated with KMPX and then KSAN during their underground heyday had started out as R & B jocks on AM radio in the previous decade; consequently, their musical tastes and playlists included the soulful sounds of Aretha Franklin, Otis Redding, Donny Hathaway, and Sly and the Family Stone, as well as the contemporary rock of the Beatles, the Rolling Stones, Jimi Hendrix, the Grateful Dead, Santana, and Jefferson Airplane. The most prominently featured jazz DJ in KSAN's underground lineup was Roland Young, an outspoken black musician and cultural revolutionary, who hosted a late-night show that explored the frontiers of jazz and world music. KMPX and KSAN also had similarities in mission to black radio: like the pioneering African American staffs on black-oriented radio in the 1950s, the San Francisco underground radio programmers made listeners' concerns, as well as community involvement and outreach, a cornerstone of their programming philosophy.

Although the San Francisco underground radio experiment was short-lived, it made a lasting impression on me. In effect, the experience transformed me from a listener to a programmer. By the early 1970s, I was involved in the newly emerging "community" radio movement; at the time, I was a graduate student in the History of Consciousness program at the University of California, Santa Cruz. While living in Santa Cruz, I was active in efforts to start two noncommercial FM stations, KUSP and KCSC. My first stint as a disc jockey occurred on KUSP, where I was also part of a staff collective. Later, I moved on to become KCSC's first manager and to host a music show on that station. During this period, I also embarked on a major research project focusing on the cultural history of the blues, which would eventually evolve into my Ph.D. dissertation and then the book *Looking Up at Down: The Emergence of Blues Culture.*[1] Quite naturally, my radio shows began to reflect my interest in the blues; I used them to explore the history of the music and to interview blues musicians, especially the older ones. By the time I left Santa Cruz in the late 1970s, I was hosting blues shows on KCSC and on KPFA-FM, the Pacifica radio network's flagship station in Berkeley, California. My shows on KPFA highlighted historic blues recordings from the pre–World War II era.

As fate would have it, my move to Washington, D.C., in 1977 coincided with the launching of the Pacifica network's fifth radio station, WPFW-FM, in the nation's capital. Unlike the other Pacifica outlets, WPFW was a black-staffed and black-formatted community station; its mission was to serve the needs of the city's large African American population. As a Pacifica and community radio veteran, I was asked to participate in putting WPFW on the air, and I was assigned a music show in the original program schedule. Initially, I hosted a Saturday-night mix of blues, jazz, and soul music called *Gumbo,* but after a few months in that time slot, I moved over to Monday nights to host *Blue Monday,* a show that focused exclusively on the blues. For the next twelve years I produced and hosted *Blue Monday,* acquiring the nickname "Doctor Blues" in the process. From Doctor Bop to Doctor Blues, my black radio odyssey had come full circle.

WPFW celebrated its twentieth year on the air in 1997. I still host a weekly music show on the station, but since the early 1990s I have been a world music programmer, part of a team of DJs hosting a weeknight music strip called *Rhythms of the World.* My Tuesday-night show focuses primarily on the musics of the African diaspora outside the United States. Over the past two decades, hundreds of people, mostly African Americans, have passed through WPFW as station managers, program directors, paid staff, and volunteer programmers. Many of these WPFW comrades have shared their extensive knowledge of black music and culture with me, as well as their perceptions and memories of black radio. We have also struggled collectively to maintain a financially strapped black community radio station in a highly competitive urban market.

The specific concerns of this project grew out of an earlier chapter on black radio that I wrote for *Split Image: African Americans in the Mass Media.*[2]

While working on the chapter, two things soon became apparent. The first was the small number of scholarly articles, books, and dissertations on African Americans' portrayal and participation in radio broadcasting since the 1920s. The subject largely had been ignored by researchers and scholars in all the relevant fields of study—including media studies, cultural studies, and even African American studies. Some of this can be attributed to the lack of scholarly attention given to radio in general, studies of which pale in comparison to the material published on cinema, television, popular music, and the print media. Moreover, where the history of radio has been documented, as in Erik Barnouw's classic three-volume study of broadcasting in the United States, scant attention is given to African Americans' role in the enterprise.[3] But in addition, black radio has always been, first and foremost, a local medium; it has never had the national exposure accorded to the better-known black film and television releases, with national distribution outlets. For these reasons, black radio has remained uncharted and, for the most part, undocumented as a historical terrain.

My second discovery while working on the *Split Image* chapter was that black radio had played a far greater role in the shaping of urban black culture—and the popular culture as a whole—than I had first surmised. Especially since the late 1940s, when it emerged as African Americans' most ubiquitous means of mass communication—surpassing the black press—black radio has been a major force in constructing and sustaining an African American public sphere. It has been the coming-together site for issues and concerns of black culture: language, music, politics, fashion, gossip, race relations, personality, and community are all part of the mix. Moreover, black radio has been omnipresent on both sides of the color line, part of a shared public memory that dates back to the 1920s and has deep roots in the broader popular culture. The point was brought home to me repeatedly whenever I discussed the project with colleagues, students, friends, and casual acquaintances: nearly everyone, black and white, had favorite stations, favorite disc jockeys, and fond memories of listening to black radio—especially while growing up.

After the publication of *Split Image,* I spent the 1990/91 academic year in residence at the Schomberg Center for the Study of Black Culture in New York City, on a National Endowment for the Humanities fellowship. With the support of Howard Dodson, the director of the center, and his dedicated staff, I was able to conduct an extensive search for print material on black radio in radio trade publications, the black press, and the mainstream press. I also listened to a wide range of vintage black radio programs (docudramas, DJ airchecks, soap operas, news, talk and public affairs shows, etc.), and I continued to interview people who had worked or still worked in black radio. These oral histories, which I began collecting while working on the *Split Image* chapter, would become the backbone of my research.

Oral testimony was crucial to the project because the written material and recorded programming I uncovered on black radio showed significant historical gaps; probing the public memory was the only way to reconstruct the missing history. Yet I also had a methodological rationale for pursuing this line of research. I wanted the project to privilege the local and grassroots nature of black radio—to tell the story from the bottom up, and to do so as much as possible in the words of those who were involved. To do this, however, I needed to interview a large pool of subjects, especially in key urban areas where black radio has had a major historical impact. Needless to say, just getting the interviews on tape was an enormous logistical task.

Luckily, my research dovetailed with a similar project initiated by Jacqui Gales Webb, a talented producer with the Smithsonian Institution in Washington, D.C. Webb's proposal for a thirteen-part radio series on the history of black radio was funded in 1994 by the Corporation for Public Broadcasting. She assembled a team of producers and researchers, including Portia Maultsby, an ethnomusicologist at Indiana University; public radio producers Sonja Williams and Lex Gillespie; Eric Gordon, a research consultant; and myself as the series' historian. Working together, we developed a blueprint for the series. Over the next year, we interviewed about 150 people we had targeted for interviews and conducted our research for the series. *Black Radio: Telling It like It Was* was released in 1996; it subsequently won both the Dupont (Columbia University) and the Peabody (University of Georgia) Award for the year's best radio documentary series. As for my book project, I now had access to a large enough pool of oral testimony to proceed with organizing and writing the manuscript.

A Howard University Faculty Research Grant enabled me to pull together all the research and write the first draft of the book. Howard was also important to the project in other ways. My colleagues in the School of Communications gave me much-appreciated support and encouragement, as well as valuable feedback. In particular, I thank Jannette Dates, dean of the School of Communications; Bishetta Merritt, chair of the Department of Radio, Television and Film; and fellow faculty members Abiyi Ford, Judi Moore Latta, Abbas Malek, Paula Mantabane, and Sonja Williams. Howard students also proved a valuable resource while working on the project. We regularly discussed and debated the history of black radio in my class on "African Americans in Broadcasting"; in addition, the students kept me up to date on current listening trends among black youth throughout the country. And last but not least, Howard has two radio stations that have been on the air since I arrived on campus in 1980: WHUR-FM, a fifty-thousand-watt commercial station with an "urban-adult" format, and WHBC, a student-run cable outlet with a hip-hop format that is heard only on campus. Over the years, I have been able to monitor the programming, observe the internal operations, and interact with the staffs of these stations. This sort of ongoing access has furthered my understanding of the black radio enterprise from two very different perspectives, and it has proved a valuable asset to the study.

My publisher, Temple University Press, likewise played a pivotal role in bringing this project to fruition. Janet Francendese, my editor, was a constant source of encouragement and critical feedback while I was working on the manuscript; her grasp of the subject and eye for detail were invaluable to my work. I also thank Herman Gray at the University of California, Santa Cruz, and Gilbert Williams at Michigan State University, both of whom reviewed the manuscript and made valuable suggestions on how to strengthen it. Their input is greatly appreciated.

During the final stages of organizing and writing this book, a new and complicated theme emerged. I was struck by how much racial crossover had taken place on the airwaves—both white Americans "sounding black" and, to a lesser degree, black Americans "sounding white." My research had uncovered constant references to this dual phenomenon, especially when discussing with interviewees the period from the 1930s to the 1960s. But this recurring theme was problematic; what did it mean to "sound black" or "sound white" on the air during those decades? These designations are obviously cultural markers that have as much to do with who is making the observation as with whom that person is referencing. Furthermore, there were and continue to be a multitude of vernaculars on both sides of the color line; standard American English is always in flux, under siege, and

being contested. Nevertheless, the documentation indicates that these verbal masquerades, which I characterize in this book as "racial ventriloquy,"
have played a prominent and contradictory role in the history of black radio, especially during the early decades. As a cultural historian, I couldn't
hide from these data; at the very least, I had to try to make sense of the phenomenon for the readers. Consequently, I included the material and
theme in the larger historical framework, thus giving weight to the contradictions as well as the continuities in the making of black radio.

All the cross-cultural experiences I've described here have been invaluable to this project, as they have enriched my understanding and appreciation of African Americans and their culture. However, my long immersion
in African American music and my long-term association with WPFW have
ironically resulted in some confusion about my racial identity. It is not unusual for both black and white listeners who have heard me on the air to be
surprised by my skin color when they meet me in person; this was especially
true during my tenure as Doctor Blues. My affiliation with Howard University and published work on black music and culture undoubtedly contribute
to the assumption that I am black, but being identified with WPFW seems
to play a larger role. (To some degree, this assumption rests on the still widespread prejudice that a white person's interest and involvement in African
American, Latino, or Asian American culture are insincere, illegitimate,
and even irrational.) No doubt, some of the confusion stems from the music I play on my shows, but I suspect that how I sound on the air also influ-
ences how I am perceived racially—not that I try to "sound black" or to fool
my listeners, but I do spend a lot of my time conversing with African Americans on a daily basis (and for that matter, listening to black radio stations).
I also tend to incorporate the new jazz and hip-hop parlance of my colleagues and students into my conversational speech; in particular, this has
proved an effective teaching technique.

At a recent party for WPFW staff and volunteer programmers, I was
talking with the *Drive Time Jazz* crew, five veteran jazzologists whose collective wisdom defines the station's jazz canon. In the course of our conversation about white crossover jocks on black radio outlets, I confided in
them that some listeners assume I am an African American and then asked
them, quite earnestly, if I "sounded black" on the air. They all looked at
me for a moment, then cracked up laughing. The verdict, so to speak, was
unanimous.

Introduction: Shifting Voices

> Language, for individual consciousness, lies on the
> borderline between oneself and the other. The word in
> language is half someone else's. It becomes "one's own" only
> when the speaker populates it with his own intentions, his
> own accent, when he appropriates the word, adapting it to
> his own semantic and expressive intention. Prior to this
> moment of appropriation, the word does not exist in a
> neutral and impersonal language (it is not, after all, out of a
> dictionary that the speaker gets his words!), but rather it
> exists in other people's mouths, in other people's context,
> serving other people's intentions: it is from there that one
> must take the word, and make it one's own.[1]
>
> —Mikhail Bakhtin

In his groundbreaking history of African American humor, *On the Real Side* (1994), Mel Watkins uses the term *racial ventriloquy* to characterize the mimicry of black speech patterns by white radio entertainers: "Following a pattern established by minstrelsy and blackface actors on stage and screen, whites played Negro roles in nearly all the early radio shows. In the beginning, when programs were not broadcast before a live audience, this new electronic medium made the pretense much easier. The deception depended entirely on mimicking black dialect and intonation. Thus radio had introduced a new phenomenon: racial ventriloquy."[2]

Radio certainly enhanced the possibilities and the practice of racial ventriloquy. As an invisible "theater of the mind," it was the ideal medium for such voice impersonations. But these verbal transgressions were hardly a new phenomenon in popular culture; that characteristic applied more to radio broadcasting in the early twentieth century. The roots of racial ventriloquy go back to the antebellum era and are intertwined with the rise of slavery. Moreover, the verbal mimicry took place on both sides of the color line, usually as part of a more complex code of cultural crossover practices. In her recent book on the subject, Susan Gubar refers to this phenomenon as "racechange: The term is meant to suggest the traversing of race boundaries, racial imitation or impersonation, cross-racial mimicry or mutability, white posing as black or black passing as white, pan-racial mutuality."[3] Gubar also uses the term *racial ventriloquism* in her discussion of the uses of black rhythms and dialect in the poetry and prose of modern literary figures such as Carl Sandburg, Carl Van Vechten, e. e. cummings, William Carlos Williams, and William Faulkner. Their indulgence in the practice of racial ventriloquism attests to its resilience and influence in American culture.

The Masks of Minstrelsy

It was during the antebellum period that racechanges and racial ventriloquy first became fashionable in both white popular culture and black slave culture. In the beginning, white males in blackface mimicked the song, dance, dress, customs, and creolized speech patterns of African slaves for fun and financial gain; in the process, they created America's first culture industry—blackface minstrelsy. At the same time, black slaves were known to have enjoyed "puttin' on" the highfalutin airs of their white owners, parodying their dress, dance, and mannerisms as well as mimicking their English diction.[4] This curious transgressing of the racial divide, played out in the white popular culture and the slave folk culture, would go through several reincarnations in the generations to come. But in terms of magnitude and impact, it was the white-initiated racechanges that carried the day; with few exceptions, they set the tone and defined the parameters of the discourse for the society as a whole.

The practice of "blacking up" began during the Elizabethan era in England. White actors applied burned cork to their faces in order to caricature African subjects; in most instances, they also parodied the slaves' creolized West Indian dialect to round out the impersonations. One of the earliest blackface characters to emerge on the American stage was "Sambo," who appeared as a comic foil in Boston and New York theatrical productions in the late 1780s. A forerunner of the urban-dandy stereotype, Sambo's dress was gaudy, his manners pretentious, his intelligence lacking: "Sambo tinks himself a pretty fella. He sing well, he dance well. Can't tink so pretty well." Sambo's rudimentary West Indian dialect was in sharp contrast to the highbrow English used by the play's white characters.[5] As with blackface parodies in general, racial ventriloquy was employed here to give voice to the caricature; it was, in effect, the audio dimension of the stereotype.

Blacking up and racial ventriloquy were integral to the rise of blackface minstrelsy in the early 1800s. The minstrel show, based in the urban North, was the nation's first homegrown performance tradition, and it would dominate American popular entertainment for the rest of the century. The first wave of blackface characters to capture the public's fancy were initially identified with popular minstrel songs—in particular, "Jim Crow" (1828) and "Zip Coon" (1834). As popularized by Thomas "Daddy" Rice, Jim Crow was a ragamuffin plantation "darky" who performed a song-and-dance routine that bordered on the grotesque. Rice's Crow was a servile simpleton. He wore dirty and tattered clothing; rags tied around his dilapidated shoes, his toes protruding; a battered straw hat over a coarse, black wig; and burned cork on his face. His dance routine, full of awkward gyrations and clumsy footwork, was accompanied by the following nonsense verse:

> Weel about, turn about.
> And do jis so
> Eb'ry time I weel about
> And jump Jim Crow.[6]

The stereotypical counterpart to this plantation buffoon was the urban dandy Zip Coon, popularized by George Washington Dixon in the mid-1830s. Dixon's Coon was a pompous blackface pretender who vainly tried to imitate the dress, deportment, and speech of the nation's white urban elite. His high opinion of himself even led to presidential aspirations:

> I tell you what will happen den, now bery soon
> De Nited States Bank will be blone to de moon

> Dare General Jackson will him lampoon
> And de bery nex President will be Zip Coon.
> Now mind wat you arter, your turnel Kritter Crockett
> You shant go head without Zip, he is de boy to block it
> Zip shall be President, Crockett shall be vice
> An den dey two togedder will had de tings nice.[7]

By the 1830s, the West Indian dialect of the colonial-era Sambo had been replaced by the native dialects of Jim Crow and Zip Coon. The unprecedented popularity of these caricatures on the new and robust urban theater circuit gave birth to the antebellum blackface minstrelsy craze. At first, individual blackface acts such as Daddy Rice's Crow and G. W. Dixon's Coon were in great demand; but in the 1840s, a number of minstrel troupes were formed, and they soon eclipsed the solo acts in popularity. These troupes (Virginia Minstrels, Ethiopian Serenaders, Christy Minstrels) created the first blackface minstrel extravaganzas—full evenings of stage entertainment based on parodying black song, dance, speech, and behavior. The standard minstrel lineup included a couple of musicians on banjos and fiddles; two comic end men named Tambo and Bones; and eventually a middleman, the "Interlocutor," who served as master of ceremonies. The strait-laced and supercilious Interlocutor was routinely ridiculed by Tambo and Bones; these minstrel end men, who often resembled Jim Crow and Zip Coon, also played the tambourine and bones rhythm makers on the musical numbers.[8]

The standard minstrel show had three parts. The opening act featured minstrel songs and mockery performed primarily by blackface urban dandies. The second part highlighted blackface novelty acts, such as the cross-dressing "Negro wench" spectacles and comic monologues known as "stump speeches." The finale was usually a narrative skit with song and dance, set on a mythical Southern plantation populated by happy-go-lucky blackface slaves. The minstrel show, in effect, linked together the plantation buffoon and the urban dandy, presenting them as two sides of the same coin.

Blackface minstrelsy's penchant for racial ventriloquy was most evident in the stump speeches. This kind of lowbrow comic oratory customarily burlesqued the futile attempts of blackface characters to speak like educated and urbane whites on topics as varied as bankruptcy ("Definition of the Bankrupt Laws"), the steam engine ("Locomotive Lecture"), and the blues ("A Brief Battering of the Blues"). "Lectures Darkly Colored" by the so-called Professor Julius Caesar Hannibal is a typical antebellum example: "Ihah come from way down in ole Warginna whar I studded edicashun an' siance all for myself, to gib a corse of lectures on siance gineraly, an' events promiscuously, as dey time to time occur. De letter ob invit I receibed from de comitee from dis unlitened city, was full ob flattery as a gemman ob my great disernment, edicashun, definement and research could wish."9 Much of the humor in these monologues was based on crude malapropisms, trite puns, pomposities, non sequiturs, and slovenly pronunciation, but the blackface minstrels also went to the source when crafting their interpretations of black dialect. The most acclaimed practitioners, from Daddy Rice to Virginia Minstrels leader Dan Emmett, purposely sought out black people in order to learn their vernacular. Emmett, in particular, was known for his "close contact with the Negro" and reportedly spent countless hours rehearsing his dialect routines.[10]

During its antebellum heyday, blackface minstrelsy attracted a huge audience among young white working-class males in the North and Midwest. New York City was the mecca of blackface entertainment, but New Orleans and San Francisco were also important hubs of minstrel activity. Paradoxically, blackface minstrelsy did not have a large following in the antebellum South, and it was even banned in some Southern cities by the 1850s. Politically and ideologically, minstrelsy was closely aligned with Jacksonian democracy; hence it supported territorial expansion, white supremacy, and slavery. This final viewpoint was expressed in the blackface minstrels' propagation of the plantation myth, which reproduced the white slave owners' rationalization of slavery as benign, paternal, and racially desirable. In addition, minstrelsy's propensity for sarcastic blackface caricatures—from Sambo to Tambo and Bones—tended to justify race oppression. Historian Joseph Boskin has argued that these stereotypes enabled whites to keep black men in their place at the bottom of the social hierarchy: "To make the black male into an object of laughter, and conversely, to force him to devise laughter, was to strip him of masculinity, dignity, and self-possession. Sambo was, then, an illustration of humor as a device of oppression, and one of the most potent in American popular culture. The ultimate objection for whites was to effect mastery: to render the black male powerless as a potential warrior, as a sexual competitor, and as an economic adversary."[11]

The response to blackface minstrelsy by public figures is noteworthy. The nation's leading literary pundits—for instance, Walt Whitman and Mark Twain—touted minstrelsy as America's first native performing art. In his autobiography, Twain lamented: "If I could have the nigger show back again in its pristine purity and perfection I should have little further use for opera." He was particularly impressed by the quality of the racial ventriloquy: "The minstrel used a very broad negro dialect; he used it competently and with easy facility and it was funny—delightfully and satisfyingly funny." In stark contrast, Frederick Douglass considered blackface minstrel troupes "the filthy scum of white society, who have stolen from us a complexion denied to them by nature, in which to make money, and to pander to the corrupt taste of their white fellow citizens."[12] In Douglass's mind, blackface minstrelsy crassly commodified race, thereby furthering a process of degradation set in motion by slavery. From Twain's vantage point, the "nigger show" carnivalized race, transforming it into the funny bone of American culture.

In his recent study *Love and Theft: Blackface Minstrelsy and the American Working Class,* Eric Lott has characterized these two poles of the debate over antebellum minstrelsy as the "people's culture" position (Mark Twain) and the "racial domination" position (Frederick Douglass). He goes on to point out that both perspectives continued to resonate in the discourse on the subject throughout this century but that the racial domination, or "revisionist," position eventually became the "reigning view." In Lott's interpretation, however, blackface minstrelsy itself was not "univocal" but rather a site of conflicting and contradictory articulations of race, "blackness," and slavery. For example, he shows that the popular "Uncle Tom" minstrel shows in the 1850s articulated proslavery, moderate, and anti-slavery viewpoints, depending on who was involved in the productions. Lott summarizes his findings as follows: "My study documents in early blackface minstrelsy the dialectical flickering of racial insult and racial envy, moments of domination and moments of liberation, counterfeit and currency, a pattern at times amounting to no more than two faces of racism, at others gesturing toward a specific kind of political or sexual danger, and all constituting a peculiarly American structure of racial feeling."[13]

Blackface entertainment languished during the Civil War. The call to arms forced many troupes to disband, and while the conflict continued, blackface impersonators all but vanished from the minstrel stage. A few groups survived by leaving the country; the Christy Minstrels, for instance, relocated to Havana, Cuba. After the war, however, some of the veteran performers returned to the stage in blackface. Dan Emmett, perhaps the best-known minstrel to resume his stage career as a blackface specialist in Negro dialect, remained active through the 1880s. Yet, while the blackface tradition showed some continuity after the Civil War, it no longer dominated minstrelsy as it had during the antebellum period. There was now competition from other ethnic stereotypes, such as the Asian and the Native American. In addition, the minstrel productions were more lavish, their social commentary was much broader, and women were now included in the entertainment as dancers, singers, and comics.[14]

But while the blackface tradition was losing favor on the established minstrel theater circuit, it was finding a new home in the postbellum South. There, a revival of the antebellum minstrel show became linked to the rise of a "cult of the Confederacy," whose adherents no doubt found solace in the blackface stereotypes and the plantation myth. This convergence opened up a new circuit of venues for blackface acts: at veterans' halls, fraternal lodges, public parks, college campuses—wherever festivities honoring the Confederacy were held. As a result, the South helped spawn a new generation of blackface entertainers, who learned their trade performing at these grassroots venues. Born during Reconstruction, the cult of the Confederacy would continue to thrive well into the twentieth century, providing blackface minstrelsy with a solid base of support.[15]

Another important factor influencing the postbellum blackface tradition was the influx of African American entertainers into minstrelsy. During Reconstruction, black troupes (Georgia Minstrels, Callander's Colored Minstrels, Haverly's Colored Minstrels) and individual performers (James Bland, Sam Lucas, Billy Kersands) emerged as stars on the minstrel stage. White and black audiences flocked to the shows of these "genuine" Negro entertainers; the Georgia Minstrels initially billed themselves as the "Only Simon Pure Negro Troupe in the World." But paradoxically, the authenticity of the black minstrels was masked by burned cork, and their stage acts re-created the antebellum blackface stereotypes and plantation myths—in effect, giving them renewed credibility. To a large degree, this recycling of plantation material was orchestrated by the white entrepreneurs who owned and managed the urban theaters, the music publishing firms, and even the black minstrel troupes; they were reluctant to part with successful blackface minstrel formulas. Furthermore, African American entertainers had little autonomy. Minstrelsy was the only venue open to them, and they lacked the power to negotiate for their artistic and racial integrity, because the white owners hired the talent and demanded compliance with the blackface legacy. Black performers had to fetishize their own race to gain access to the minstrel stage.[16]

The careers of black minstrelsy's most famous entertainers, from James Bland and Billy Kersands in the 1870s to Bert Williams in the early 1900s, offer clear, if disheartening, illustrations of this protracted dilemma. Bland, the most talented African American tunesmith of his generation, routinely wrote nostalgic "darky songs": "Carry Me Back to Old Virginny," for example, told the story of an elderly ex-slave longing for his former master and life on the plantation. Kersands, perhaps the greatest black minstrel showman of all, was best known for his ostentatious deportment, dialect jokes, and huge grinning mouth—all prominent features of the recycled Coon stereotype in the postbellum era. Williams, the most gifted humorist of his generation, also relied heavily on dialect jokes and continued to entertain white audiences in blackface long after other African Americans refused to do so. All three men found success in accommodating antebellum minstrel stereotypes and thereby became locked into demeaning performance styles. They also added a new twist to the racial ventriloquy cycle: black entertainers imitating white impersonations of African Americans.[17]

New Medium—New Voices

Radio came of age during the twilight of blackface minstrelsy and helped prolong its slow demise. The first racial ventriloquists to take to the airwaves in the 1920s were white entertainers such as Freeman Gosden and Charles Correll (*Amos 'n' Andy*) and Moran and Mack (*Two Black Crows*); they pioneered the showcasing of blackface dialect comedy on radio. During the next decade, these race impersonators, along with many more of their ilk, were major attractions on the national radio networks, and they also proliferated on local outlets. Their radio shows recycled many of the previous century's most demeaning blackface stereotypes (Jim Crow, Zip Coon, Mammy), with little regard for the racial implications of their humor. (See Part 1.) For their past, the first African Americans to break the color line in radio broadcasting in the 1930s were announcers and disc jockeys who sounded white on the air. Black radio pioneers such as Jack Cooper (Chicago), Eddie Honesty (Hammond, Indiana), Ed Baker and Van Douglas (Detroit), and Bass Harris (Seattle) followed the lead of the industry's leading professional announcers with respect to their use of the English and their style of announcing. Their voice masking was motivated by a desire to achieve parity with their white counterparts in broadcasting, but in addition, they sought to distance themselves from the blackface dialect that was so pervasive on the airwaves at the time and to attract black and white middle-class listeners. (See Part 2.)

During the postwar era, changes in the radio industry sparked a second wave of racial ventriloquy on the nation's airwaves. In this instance, white disc jockeys who "crossed over" to play popular black music (jazz, R & B, soul) on their shows also tended to imitate the vernacular and speech patterns of the era's leading African American DJs. The new generation of black "personality jocks" was fashioning an innovative and playful style of radio announcing based on the use of common black urban street slang and folklore. (See Part 3.) White DJs from Alan Freed in the early 1950s to Wolfman Jack in the 1960s copied and, in most cases, exaggerated this style on the air in order to sound black and outrageous to their racially mixed teenage audience. In some respects, these impersonations were a form of flattery, but they also involved a good deal of parody. The numerous white DJs who crossed over to black vernacular and music formats were both cultural rebels and voyeurs; they transgressed the color line while indulging their racial fantasies. (See Part 4.)

For their part, the majority of African American disc jockeys in the postwar era sought to reverse and undermine the racial ventriloquy cycle by privileging contemporary black vernacular in their announcing styles. The exception to this trend occurred only when black announcers and DJs managed to secure employment at white radio outlets; in these instances, they were invariably expected to sound white. But given the lingering segregation in the radio industry during this period, only a small number of African Americans were hired by white stations. Then, in the wake of the civil rights movement, segregation began to break down in both the radio industry and society at large. By the late 1960s, black disc jockeys who crossed over to white rock formats were no longer required to mask their voices (a prime example being Frankie Crocker in New York City). At this juncture, the youth counterculture was incorporating black urban slang into its own "hippie" vernacular; racial ventriloquy was, in effect, giving way to racial hybridity in the popular culture and on the airwaves.

While racial ventriloquy played a major role in the early portrayal of African Americans on radio, its importance has diminished considerably over the past few decades. Since World War II, the history of black radio has become increasingly woven into the fabric of the broader African American struggle for racial equality, political empowerment, economic prosperity, and cultural self-determination. In the postwar era, African Americans working in radio mounted their first sustained challenges to Jim Crow employment practices in the broadcast industry. They also produced the first black radio docudramas to counter the corrosive blackface stereotypes still featured on the networks, and black entrepreneurs purchased their first radio stations. During the civil rights movement in the 1950s and 1960s, African American disc jockeys, talk-show hosts, and radio newscasters played a critical role in facilitating the flow of information about civil rights issues and activities. They helped mobilize people for demonstrations and marches, provided a forum for civil rights leaders such as Dr. Martin Luther King Jr., and, in the case of the DJs, boosted the morale of listeners by playing "message music" on their shows. By this time, radio had become the omnipresent mass medium in the black community; a huge majority (over 90 percent) of African Americans owned radio receivers and listened to black-formatted stations on a daily basis.

During the urban riots in the mid-1960s, African American personality jocks stayed on the air around the clock in an effort to contain the civil unrest. They kept their listeners up to date on the latest news from the riot zones, opened up the microphones to community leaders, and urged people to exercise caution and restraint. After Dr. King's assassination, there was a movement among the more militant African Americans in the radio industry to extend the "Black Power" cultural agenda to broadcast programming, especially on the newly emerging FM stations. Although these efforts eventually collapsed, while in progress they accounted for some groundbreaking programs and left their imprint on black radio formats nationwide. (See Part 5.)

Black Power militants also made station ownership a major issue for African Americans involved in the radio industry. By the mid-1970s, a coalition of black media activists and entrepreneurs was pressuring the broadcast industry and the federal government to open up more opportunities for people of color to purchase their own broadcast outlets. At the time, African Americans owned less than 1 percent of the nation's radio stations. As a result of this offensive, the number of minority-owned stations increased steadily in the late 1970s and continued to do so well into the 1980s. From the late 1980s to the end of the twentieth century, however, this trend has reversed, mostly due to ownership deregulation by the Federal Communications Commission (FCC). In the 1990s, the number of black-owned stations has declined; overall, they make up less than 3 percent of the nation's total. (See Part 6.)

Voice Over chronicles the rise of black radio in the twentieth century, from its prewar roots in racial ventriloquy, to its postwar contributions to the African American freedom struggle, to its current status as the most popular mass medium in the black community, as well as that community's most vital source of information and culture. Along the way, the book documents the role black radio has played in extending the popularity and influence of black music nationwide, helping shape the always-changing urban black vernacular, mobilizing African Americans around political and cultural issues, and galvanizing a sense of community among African Americans—especially at the local level. But first and foremost, *Voice Over* is the untold story of the people involved in the making of black radio—the unheralded programmers, producers, entertainers, entrepreneurs, and activists who devoted their careers and much of their lives to creating an African American presence on the airwaves. The reconstruction of their collective history, told in their own words whenever possible, is the major objective of this study.

PART I

" I'se Regusted": Blackface Radio

AMOS: What's de difference between a Democrat an' a Republican, Andy?

ANDY: Well, one of 'em is a mule an' de other one is a elephant. Dat's the way I gets it.

AMOS: I don't know either to be a Democrat or a Republican.

ANDY: Well, where wha' your ancestors?

AMOS: My aun' didn' have no sisters.

ANDY: No, no, your ancestor, your . . . never mind. I believe you ought to be a Democrat 'cause you look more like a mule than anythin' I know. . . .

AMOS: . . . Now tell me dis. How many votes does it take to elect a presiden'?

ANDY: Well, one of 'em has got to have de majority and de other one has got to have de pleurisy.

AMOS: Both of 'em is bad, isn' dey? My grandpa had de pleurisy, but I ain't heard of nobody havin' dat other thing.

—*The Amos 'n' Andy Show,* September 27, 1928

1

From the Jazz Age
to Jim Crow

he 1920s, commonly referred to as the Jazz Age, was a watershed
decade in American history. In the years between the end of World
War I and the onset of the Great Depression, the character of the
nation's urban life, popular culture, and race relations changed dramatically. The transformation of urban life came about through the
confluence of several social forces: rapid industrial growth, improved
transportation, the commercial development of new communications
technologies, and a population boom. During World War I, European immigrants in industrial cities were joined by unprecedented numbers of
rural white and black migrants, who came to work on the war-industry assembly lines. After the war, the assembly lines retooled to mass-produce
consumer goods, the industrial workforce continued to expand, and the
nation's country-to-city migrations accelerated.

Mass production also fueled mass consumption, paving the way for a
consumer-driven culture in the 1920s. Both radio and race were interwo-
ven into this new cultural formation, but in very different ways. Radio became the nation's first broadcast conduit for mass entertainment and mass
advertising, reaching millions of listeners on a daily basis by the end of the
decade; in the process, it fostered the fusion of the commercial and the
popular in American culture. Race, by contrast, became a major symbol in

the new consumer culture, as evidenced by the widespread popularity of jazz and blackface entertainers during this period. Cultural icons as diverse as Freeman Gosden and Charles Correll (*Amos 'n' Andy*), Al Jolson (*The Jazz Singer*), and Bert Williams (*Ziegfeld Follies*) made racial caricature the centerpiece of their art. In addition, the musical luminaries of the era, such as Paul Whiteman, Sophie Tucker, Bessie Smith, Duke Ellington, and Jimmie Rodgers, were inspired by the emergence of jazz and blues as the country's latest popular music craze—which they also helped promote. Whiteman even called himself the "King of Jazz," as did New Orleans cornetist and bandleader Joseph "King" Oliver. Clearly, race was not only a popular draw but also a contested commodity in the Jazz Age culture—and both sides of the color line were engaged in its reproduction.

For the most part, African Americans' introduction to the consumer-driven culture of the 1920s took place in Northern urban centers. During World War I, the black population in the North increased by almost 80 percent, from 900,000 to 1.6 million. Another 350,000 African Americans joined the armed forces, and many of these soldiers resettled in the North after the war. This upsurge in black migration was a consequence of complex social and economic factors, sometimes described as "push" and "pull" factors. Rigid segregation and a moribund plantation economy in the South pushed black migrants north. In 1920, 7 million African Americans, mostly agricultural workers, still lived in the rural South; the vast majority were very poor and had no prospects for a better life.[1] Pulling them to the urban North were plentiful jobs in factories and service, higher wages, and the possibility of moving up the economic ladder. While by no means absent, segregation in the North tended to be less repressive and pervasive than in the South. Segregation was codified in law in the Southern states, but African Americans in the North had the right to vote, hold public office, and organize politically; in comparison with Southern blacks, they were more likely to own their own homes and businesses. Representing the epitome of racial progress, the *New Negro*, a term coined in the black press, was constructing the new black metropolises. Places like Harlem in New York City and Chicago's Southside, centers of the political and cultural ferment taking place among African Americans in the 1920s, lured thousands of Southern blacks (not to mention crowds of white cultural tourists).

Harlem headquartered both Marcus Garvey's Universal Negro Improvement Association (UNIA)—the organization behind his "Back to Africa" movement, which claimed 4 million black followers in the 1920s—and the era's most important black arts movement, the Harlem Renaissance. Chicago's Southside was the birthplace of the Brotherhood of Sleeping Car Porters, the first independent black labor union in the country, organized by A. Philip Randolph in 1925. It was also the stronghold of a black political machine that elected Oscar DePriest to Congress in 1929, making him the first African American congressman in three decades. And the Southside was the home of the nation's largest black newspaper, the *Chicago Defender,* which was in the forefront of the crusade to bring African Americans north to the "promised land" of freedom and opportunity. During the Jazz Age, these vibrant communities formed the twin capitals of a new and prosperous black entertainment industry, their streets honeycombed with clubs, speakeasies, cafés, cabarets, dance halls, and theaters that showcased the greatest black entertainers of the era.

At the national level, black entertainment was dominated by the Theater Owners' Booking Association (TOBA) and the "race" record companies, which specialized in recording black music. The TOBA, a network of predominantly white-owned vaudeville theaters, catered to black customers by regularly featuring black entertainers. At the height of its success in the mid-1920s the association included more than fifty theaters, employing hundreds of African American performers who played for an estimated weekly audience of thirty thousand. The TOBA vaudeville shows featured a wide variety of black entertainers—comedians, dancers, singers, and musicians. The star attractions were comics such as Flournoy Miller and Aubrey Lyles, dance dynamo Bill "Bojangles" Robinson, and legendary blues divas Ma Rainey, Bessie Smith, Ida Cox, and Mamie Smith. Wages and working conditions were notoriously poor in the TOBA—African American entertainers routinely referred to it as "Tough On Black Asses." But while exploiting black talent, the TOBA also created an economic base for it to develop and mature. Consequently, the era's most important African American entertainers spent their formative years on the TOBA circuit, where they honed their skills—and paid their ducs.[2]

Finding a Voice on Vinyl

In this explosion of black pop culture, race record companies emerged in the early 1920s, two decades after the birth of the record industry; up to that point, only select black entertainers, such as comic Bert Williams and bandleader James Reese Europe, had been given the opportunity to make commercial recordings. But the pioneering record labels never completely ignored African American popular music—if only because a sizable segment of the record-buying public found it fashionable. Instead, the fledgling record industry relied on Tin Pan Alley's diluted renderings of black songs or, in some cases, resorted to the technique of "covering." This practice was accomplished by paying white artists to make cover versions of popular songs written by African Americans—for example, Sophie Tucker's rendition of W. C. Handy's "Saint Louis Blues," which sold over a million copies after its 1917 release.[3]

Until the post–World War I era, the record labels ignored black consumers and potential black recording artists. Mamie Smith's recording "Crazy Blues," for the Okeh Record Company in 1920, changed all that. That pioneering disc sold two hundred thousand copies in less than a year, alerting the record industry to the existence of a large new market among African Americans. Initially, smaller record labels such as Okeh in New York and Paramount in Chicago took the lead in recording black artists and selling their discs to the black community. To do so, they set up separate divisions within their companies, each with its own catalog, advertising budget, distribution network, and personnel. This practice of segregating popular music along racial lines was duplicated by the larger labels, such as Columbia and Victor, when they belatedly ventured into the new African American market. By this time, the record industry had adopted the term *race records* when referring to the discs made by black artists. In the 1920s, the word *race* was often used in the black press as a progressive term for African Americans; it was symbolic of black pride and solidarity. This did not go unnoticed by the record labels, which employed the term in their marketing strategies.[4]

At the peak of its prosperity in the 1920s, the record industry netted $128 million in yearly sales—a high-water mark that would not be repeated until after World War II. During this period of growth, the race-record segment of the industry was also expanding rapidly. In the mid-1920s, it was estimated that African Americans were purchasing 6 million discs annually. By the end of the decade, close to eight thousand race records had been released: about five thousand blues titles, two thousand jazz titles, and one thousand religious titles. Among those recorded were the greatest black musicians of the era: vaudeville blues singers Bessie Smith, Ma Rainey, Mamie Smith, Ida Cox, Sippie Wallace, and Alberta Hunter; rural blues pioneers Charlie Patton, Henry Thomas, Blind Lemon Jefferson, Leroy Carr, Blind Blake, Big Bill Broonzy, and Lonnie Johnson; early jazz innovators Louis Armstrong, Jelly Roll Morton, Sidney Bechet, Coleman Hawkins, and Fats Waller; jazz bandleaders Joseph "King" Oliver, Fletcher Henderson, Bennie Moten, and Duke Ellington; gospel luminaries Blind Willie Johnson, the Mitchell Christian Singers, and the Norfolk Jubilee Singers.[5]

Like the TOBA, the race-record labels exploited black artists: not only by paying them less than their white counterparts but also by cheating them out of their royalties. Yet race records also documented the music of an entire generation of African Americans at a critical historical juncture. In addition, jazz and blues made significant inroads into the pop-music mainstream during this period. As a result, numerous black songwriters and musicians came to the forefront of the music industry as innovators and trendsetters, if not yet as producers or owners.

Radio Samples the Jazz Age

Much like the record industry, radio broadcasting in the United States rapidly expanded in the 1920s. As the decade opened, radio had only a handful of stations broadcasting regularly; its experimental programming reached small audiences, and no one had yet heard commercial advertising on the airwaves. By the end of the decade, nearly one thousand stations filled the air, two national networks (NBC and CBS) had formed, millions of loyal listeners regularly tuned in, and broadcast advertising drove the industry. In sharp contrast to the record companies, neither the networks nor the independent local stations (all white owned) targeted black consumers during this period; instead, they broadcast to the general public, which they defined as the mainstream white majority. Figures from the 1930 census reveal that 14.4 percent of the black urban households and only .03 percent of black rural households in the nation owned a radio receiver. The vast majority of African Americans did not have regular access to a radio. This blackout was never a 100 percent proposition, however; there were even a (very) few African American broadcasters. Still, much like the entertainment industry, radio began to produce shows based on those commercial outgrowths of black culture that appealed to its white audience. In particular, the major broadcasters turned to Tin Pan Alley for their musical fare, showcasing its watered-down cover versions of jazz and blues originals, and resurrected the century-old blackface minstrel tradition—in effect, making radio its last refuge.[6]

The first full decade of radio broadcasting in the United States coincided with the fabled Roaring Twenties, a period of significant cultural upheaval on both sides of the color line. In white America, middle-class "flappers" and "flaming youth" openly revolted against the repressive moral codes at the foundation of their parents' strait-laced culture. These young rebels turned to African American culture, particularly music, dance, language, and humor. Jazz, blues, dances like the Charleston and the black bottom, black slang, and jokes all became fashionable with this subgroup of "white Negroes" and symbolic of their generational revolt against the established social order.

This sort of expropriation of African American culture was hardly new and rarely benign. Since slavery, American popular culture had been infused with black innovations in music, dance, and comedy. These infusions both enriched the cultural mix and encouraged the cultural rebellion of disaffected segments of the white population—most noticeably, bohemian fringe elements in the nineteenth century and middle-class young adults from the 1920s on. More often than not, a misguided and condescending dilution of the original African American song, dance, and humor, tailored to the white mainstream, made the fortunes of white entrepreneurs, entertainers, and tunesmiths. The African Americans who created these art forms and styles could do nothing about the theft of their material; most remained in obscurity, and the few who managed to gain entrance into the white-controlled entertainment industry were often forced to compromise their art and even their integrity in the process. Bert Williams performing in blackface on Broadway comes to mind, as does Duke Ellington playing "jungle music" for the white patrons of the Cotton Club in New York City. In the 1920s, these racial expropriations and restrictions played a decisive role in determining the form and the context of black participation in the entertainment industry—which now included a new medium called radio broadcasting.

A major source of radio programming during the Jazz Age was live and recorded music. Initially, broadcasters favored phonograph records as a cheap and ready-made solution to the problem of what to offer listeners on the airwaves. But in 1922, the American Society of Composers, Authors and Publishers (ASCAP) began to demand that radio stations pay an annual fee for the use of recorded music that had been copyrighted by ASCAP members. The station owners responded by forming their own trade organization, the National Association of Broadcasters (NAB), which took the lead in opposing the fee demands. While a number of the better-financed stations eventually cut a deal with ASCAP, especially after a federal court upheld the legality of the music organization's position, the NAB remained steadfastly opposed to the yearly license fee, and most NAB members refused to include ASCAP songs in their programming. This impasse contributed to an upsurge in live music broadcasts from the fledgling radio industry.[7]

In the 1920s, most live music broadcasts on radio featured either potted palm, concerts or popular big-band dance performances. *Potted palm,* an industry term for classical and semiclassical concert music played by amateur musicians who volunteered their services to the stations, provided broadcasters with an inexpensive alternative to ASCAP-controlled music. But as the radio industry moved toward network and commercial broadcasting at the end of the decade, the novelty of these performances—and of the medium itself—had worn off. Dance music's popularity was rising, and stations showcased large, professional dance bands in remote broadcasts from hotel ballrooms, dance halls, and nightclubs. Some stations hired dance orchestras for live weekly broadcasts from their studios, while others scheduled regular appearances by product-sponsored dance bands such as the Cliquot Club Eskimos, the A & P Gypsies, the Ipana Troubadours, and the Lucky Strike Orchestra. The musicians in these various dance orchestras tended to be white members of the American Federation of Musicians (AFM), which was one of the most segregated unions in the American Federation of Labor (AFL). The white AFM locals had control over most of the major theaters, amusement parks, hotels, and cabarets; hence it was easy for them to extend their domain into radio, once it became a national fixture. Consequently, no African American musicians played in these the early radio bands.[8]

For the most part, the popular dance music associated with the Jazz Age had black roots. Yet the pioneering African American dance bands—James Reese Europe's and Fletcher Henderson's in New York City; Erskine Tate's, Ferdinand "Jelly Roll" Morton's, and Joe "King" Oliver's in Chicago; Bennie Moten's in Kansas City; and Kid Ory's in Los Angeles—that had first injected big-band jazz into the cultural mainstream were seldom heard on radio in the 1920s. Instead, the airwaves regularly featured the commercially successful white dance bands of the era, such as those led by Ben Bernie, Vincent Lopez, B. A. Rolfe, and Paul Whiteman (the self-proclaimed King of Jazz), giving their popularity an added boost. The same tendency held true for radio vocalists during the Jazz Age. Much of the popular vocal music of the day, including the songs written by Tin Pan Alley tunesmiths, was rooted in jazz or blues, but the singers who achieved stardom on radio in the 1920s were predominantly white interpreters of black song—the best known being Al Jolson, Rudy Vallee, Eddie Cantor, and Sophie Tucker. Meanwhile, the decade's greatest African American vocalists—luminaries such as Louis Armstrong, Bessie Smith, Ma Rainey, Leroy Carr, and Florence Mills—were rarely heard on radio; nor were hundreds of black artists who recorded for race-record labels in the 1920s, who still were not represented in ASCAP's catalog.[9]

Yet, despite this pattern of musical expropriation and racial exclusion in the industry, some African American musicians managed to appear on radio during the Jazz Age. The most notable performed live in the studios of local stations or were featured on special remote broadcasts from hotels, nightclubs, and dance halls in urban centers such as New York, Pittsburgh, Chicago, Atlanta, and Los Angeles. In 1921, jazz pianist Earl "Fatha" Hines and vocalist Lois Deppe were the first African Americans to perform on KDKA, Westinghouse's pioneering station in Pittsburgh. The broadcast created something of a sensation in the local black community. According to Deppe, "A lot of people had crystal sets, and there was a radio buff on Wylie Avenue who had a loudspeaker sticking out his window. The street was all blocked with people and we were just mobbed when we came back."[10]

The first African American jazz band to reach the airwaves on the

West Coast, Kid Ory's Sunshine Orchestra, performed on a short series of remote broadcasts from the Plantation Club in Los Angeles in 1922. Atlanta's premier radio station, WSB, broadcast a live concert from the 81 Theater in 1923, featuring vaudeville blues diva Bessie Smith; the *Atlanta Constitution*–owned station also aired weekend broadcasts showcasing the Morehouse College glee club as well as local black church choirs, gospel quartets, and jubilee singing groups. Perhaps the best-known African American musician associated with radio broadcasting in the 1920s was Deford Bailey, the diminutive blues harmonica player regularly featured on the famous Grand Ole Opry show, broadcast out of Nashville, Tennessee.[11]

From all indications, the most hospitable radio stations to African American performers in the 1920s were in New York City and Chicago, the major urban centers for black music and entertainment during the same period. The first African American to be heard on the airwaves in New York appears to have been comedian Bert Williams, who was featured on WHN early in 1922. At the time, Williams was performing in blackface on Broadway in the *Ziegfeld Follies*. The songwriting duo of Noble Sissle and Eubie Blake were featured on at least three New York stations (WJZ, WHN, WEAF) in 1923—no doubt due to the success of their black musical *Shuffle Along*. Other notable New York radio debuts by African American performers included Florence Mills on WHN in 1923; Sam Wooding's dance band on WJZ in 1924; and a Paul Robeson reading from Eugene O'Neill's *The Emperor Jones,* broadcast locally in 1925. In addition, New York stations did numerous remote broadcasts from local nightclubs and dance halls such as the Club Alabam, the Plantation Club, the Savoy Ballroom, and the Roseland Ballroom, all of which featured black jazz orchestras. Fletcher Henderson's pioneering big band, featuring trumpeter Louis Armstrong, was broadcast periodically from the Club Alabam and then the Roseland Ballroom between 1924 and 1928. Chick Webb's band was heard on remote broadcasts from the Savoy Ballroom in the late 1920s.[12]

Duke Ellington's orchestra topped all the others during this period; between 1927 and 1930, the band performed live on more than two hundred radio shows over the New York airwaves. At the time, Ellington's manager, Irving Mills, negotiated appearances for the Duke and his orchestra not only in radio but also in film—and at a time when very few African

Americans were granted access to these entertainment industries. For his efforts, Mills took one-half of Ellington's profits, and he automatically owned 50 percent of everything Ellington wrote while under contract. The arrangement reflects the racial exploitation that was so pervasive in show business during the Jazz Age.[13]

A number of African Americans living in New York City during this period were involved in radio projects that went well beyond the occasional black music and comedy broadcasts. In the fall of 1927, Floyd J. Calvin produced the first radio program devoted to "Negro journalism." The hour-long show was sponsored by the *Pittsburgh Courier* and broadcast on WGBS. In the late 1920s, actor-writer Carlton Moss launched a weekly African American drama series, *The Negro Hour,* on WJZ. The series was short-lived, but its dramatic group evolved into the highly acclaimed Lafayette Players, which continued to be involved in black radio drama throughout the 1930s. In 1929, the Harlem Broadcasting Corporation, the first independent African American radio venture of its kind, was founded. The company operated its own radio studios on the corner of Lennox Avenue and 125th Street. It also leased broadcast time on WRNY, a local radio outlet, and ran an artist bureau for African American radio talent. *A Rise to Culture,* a radio extravaganza produced by Harlem Broadcasting in 1930, was staged at a local auditorium; more than one hundred performers, including W. C. Handy, donated their talents to the event.[14]

In Chicago, the city's premier African American comedy team, Flournoy Miller and Aubrey Lyles, were heard on the local airwaves doing their popular vaudeville routines as early as 1922. The same year, the first black dance band to broadcast locally was Clarence Jones and his Wonder Orchestra, which was heard on Chicago's KYW, a Westinghouse station. In 1924, Jimmie Wade's Moulin Rouge Orchestra was featured as part of WBBM's opening-day broadcast ceremony; the station was the first in the country to adopt a jazz format. WBBM broadcast more African American jazz bands during the 1920s than any other station in Chicago, even though it was white owned and, in terms of audience, white oriented. As was the case in New York City, remote broadcasts from local hotels and nightclubs were also standard fare on radio in Chicago. Pittsburgh native Earl "Fatha" Hines's orchestra was heard live on WEDC from the Grand Terrace Hotel in the mid-1920s, while Jimmy Noone's dance band was broadcast from the Platinum Lounge on WWAE. Other black jazz ensembles of note featured on local remote broadcasts included big bands led by Erskine Tate, Luis Russell, and Lil Hardin Armstrong—one of the few African American women involved in jazz in the 1920s.[15]

In addition to jazz, black religious music and the blues were heard on Chicago's airwaves during this period. As early as 1923, KYW aired the city's most renowned African American mass choir, the eighty-voice Mundy Choristers. During the rest of the decade, Mundy's choir was often featured on special Sunday broadcasts, along with many other African American religious groups. Blues musicians who performed on Chicago's airwaves in the 1920s included boogie-woogie piano legends Pinetop Smith and Albert Ammons, as well as the pioneering urban blues guitarist and vocalist Lonnie Johnson. In 1929, Jack Cooper, the first successful black disc jockey in the country, debuted his initial radio program—also called *The Negro Hour*—on WSBC, a local radio outlet. During the next decade, Cooper emerged as Chicago's most important African American radio entrepreneur.[16]

Generally speaking, more African Americans were engaged in radio programming during the Jazz Age than during the Great Depression. This was due, in part, to the abundance and the diversity of local radio outlets in the early days of broadcasting, before the advent of commercial networks. Local stations in the 1920s, especially those situated in large urban markets, were much more likely to feature black entertainers than the network operations of the next decade. One researcher identified no fewer than eight hundred local radio broadcasts that showcased African American talent between 1920 and 1930.[17]

Another factor encouraging black participation in radio during the Jazz Age was the existence of a relatively large and prosperous black entertainment industry, which collapsed in the 1930s. Both the TOBA vaudeville circuit and the race-record business were essential to the success of African American performers in the 1920s, often paving the way for local radio appearances. The collapse of these enterprises during the early years of the depression, however, tended to marginalize black entertainers—both in the music industry and throughout show business in general. Further, the sale's of race records and the number of TOBA venues fell off dramatically in the 1930s, and African Americans continued to be routinely excluded from participating in both the commercial radio and the film industries. In the case of radio, the lack of black voices on the airwaves tended to discourage black listenership, which did not increase much during the depression years. Consequently, it was relatively easy for the two dominant commercial networks—NBC and CBS—to overlook African Americans and employ blackface imitators.

Jim Crow Jams the Networks

Between 1927 and 1934, the period spanning the enactment of the emergency Federal Radio Act (1927) and the passage of the landmark Federal Communications Act (1934), the country's broadcasting system became network dominated and advertising driven. Over these years, commercial radio also emerged as the most pervasive mass medium in the United States. African Americans paid scant attention to these developments; radio was still a costly novelty to much of the black population, and as a group, they had no real stake or say in its development. Nonetheless, the networks' commercial juggernaut would create serious obstacles for African Americans seeking employment in the broadcast industry or access to the nation's airwaves. Racial barriers minimized black involvement in broadcasting during the time of the industry's greatest growth and prosperity.

The expansion of network broadcasting and the rapid proliferation of network affiliates was simply astonishing. In a seven-year period (1927–1934), the number of stations signed up with NBC or CBS rose from about fifty to almost three hundred, by 1934, all but three of the nation's fifty-thousand-watt, clear-channel outlets—the most powerful stations in the country—were part of a network. As a result, the networks virtually controlled the airwaves, especially during the prime-time evening hours. According to one study, by the mid-1930s, stations owned or affiliated with NBC and CBS were responsible for 97 percent of the nation's nighttime broadcasting.[18]

Commercial advertising drove the rapid expansion of the networks during this period and quickly emerged as the economic linchpin of the broadcast industry. As 1927 began, advertising financed only 4.3 percent of the country's radio stations; by the mid-1930s, all of the networks' primetime shows supported by advertising and produced by the same advertising agencies that made the commercials. The revenues generated by radio advertising translated into huge profits for the networks. In 1934 alone, NBC and CBS earned nearly $75 million in national advertising revenues, a remarkable figure during a period of deep economic depression and sharp declines in other major entertainment industries, such as music and film. In hindsight, it is clear that national advertising not only accelerated the networks' growth but also bankrolled their eventual transition to television broadcasting.[19]

As they rose to the pinnacle of power in the radio industry, both NBC and CBS followed what amounted to a Jim Crow policy with respect to the employment and portrayal of African Americans. Neither network hired blacks as announcers, broadcast journalists, or technicians, and certainly no blacks became producers or executives in the national operations. None of the network affiliates was black owned, nor were any of the independent stations. During the 1930s, the few African Americans working in radio were the musicians, comics, and entertainers sporadically heard on the network airwaves.

For the most part, black radio characters were created by white entertainers schooled in blackface minstrelsy—Gosden and Correll (Amos and Andy) being only the most prominent of these "Negro dialect" specialists. The few African American actors and actresses hired by NBC and CBS were invariably cast in similarly stereotypical comedy roles, thus reinforcing the airwaves blackface legacy. The same pattern of cultural exclusion and expropriation dominated public-affairs and popular music programming. The live musical broadcasts tended to showcase the most commercially successful white swing bands and vocalists of the era, virtually ignoring the black innovators who shaped the music's major stylistic variations. The public-affairs shows on network radio routinely avoided racial issues and rarely included black participants in their public forums.

These Jim Crow policies reflected the nation's troubled race relations and the particular needs of network broadcasting. Network policy makers understood that they could not gain mass appeal by upending social conventions or taking controversial stances, especially on race matters. Both networks adopted employment practices in line with the exclusionary membership policies of the three key labor unions involved in the entertainment side of the industry: the American Federation of Musicians (AFM), the American Federation of Radio Actors (AFRA), and the Radio Writers Guild (RWG). Only the AFM existed during the formative years of network broadcasting (1926–1934); the AFRA and the RWG were organized later in the 1930s. The AFM was divided into segregated local unions, and almost all the musicians' jobs on network radio were controlled by the white locals. The other two unions admitted no black members until the years of the second world war, and then only a token few. Thus, the unions in tandem with the networks systematically excluded African Americans from employment opportunities in the radio industry.[20]

The commercial sponsors of network programming hewed to a similar line. In general, sponsors were extremely reluctant to bankroll programs with African Americans in leading roles, fearing that their products would become black identified and unappealing to white consumers. As one advertising executive explained: "Pillsbury flour is one of our biggest accounts. If it gets out that we were pushing Negro talent on a Pillsbury program, the next thing you know, it would be branded a 'nigger flour' and it would never move."[21] Network sponsors and the advertising firms that did their bidding tended to invest in radio shows that avoided racial characters—and issues, for that matter. When they agreed to sponsor a network series with black subjects, they preferred white actors or actresses in those roles.

Finally, the emergence of Jim Crow on network radio owed something to explicit racial policies in the South. The networks' Southern affiliates, in line with the region's segregationist social order, refused to allow African Americans access to the airwaves and threatened to boycott any network programs that violated their color line. For the networks and their sponsors, who now depended on a national audience, the threat was a significant deterrent.

Obviously, the policies of the unions, networks, sponsors and ad agencies reinforced one another, and all were geared to the notion that radio's purpose was to deliver an audience of white consumers to the advertisers. At its most crass level, programming offered pleasant interludes between commercials.

Stereotypes and Stumbling Blocks

Network radio's penchant for lily-white melodramas and blackface comedy shows had the overall effect of seriously limiting the range of African American characters heard on the airways. Though the appearance of Amos and Andy on the nation's airwaves was a defining moment in the early history of radio broadcasting—the show quickly attracted an unprecedented 40 million loyal listeners, transformed its obscure creators into radio's first national megastars, and ushered in the "golden age" of commercial broadcasting—as the routine quoted in the epigraph to this part illustrates, the thrust of the series' blackface comedy was to portray African American males as bumbling ignoramuses. The buffoonery of the characters, for the most part, was based on their inability to speak or comprehend standard American English. Moreover, the characters demonstrate that they are woefully deficient in their knowledge and understanding of American politics. Hence lurking behind the frivolous blackface comedy routine is the notion that the typical African American adult is unfit to participate in the political process of debating the issues, voting, running for office, belonging to a political party, and so forth—because for him or her to do so would be tantamount to making a mockery of American democracy.

While Amos and Andy and their progeny dominated black male images on commercial radio until World War II, black women were invariably stereotyped as Sapphires or Mammies. The two best known, Aunt Jemima and Beulah, were portrayed as portly and jovial domestics by white actresses and even a white actor. Aunt Jemima, her grinning, full face framed with a red polka-dot bandanna tied around her head, had already become a nationally recognized trademark for a pancake flour made by Quaker Oats. In the mid-1920s, the company obliterated the line between commerce and entertainment. Quaker's advertising agency hired a white actress, Tess Gardella, to portray Aunt Jemima—in blackface—for a media campaign that included a number of record releases on the Victor label, a cameo role in the Broadway musical *Showboat,* and, ultimately, a morning radio series on CBS. On this daily broadcast, Aunt Jemima entertained her listeners with breakfast recipes, minstrel songs, housekeeping hints, and pancake commercials. The program was a fixture on network radio for the next two decades, during which time the role of Aunt Jemima passed on to two more white actresses—Harriet Widmer in 1935 and Vera Lane in 1943. It was not until 1947 that a black woman, Edith Wilson, was hired to play Aunt Jemima.[22]

Beulah was the brainchild of Marlin Hurt, a white radio comedian who first played the character on NBC's *Showboat* variety series in the late 1930s. The bossy, wise-cracking maid soon moved on to *The Fibber McGee and Molly Show,* where she became radio's most popular Mammy. This success enabled Hurt to create his own network comedy series, *The Marlin Hurt and Beulah Show,* with Beulah now cast as his maid. Although Hurt died in 1946, Beulah flourished in the fantasy world of broadcasting, and after a few more years on network radio, she moved over to network television. At this point, an African American assumed Beulah's role—Hattie McDaniel, the black actress best known for her Mammy roles in such Hollywood films as *Gone with the Wind.* During the postwar era, Beulah was often cited, along with Amos and Andy, as a prime example of racial stereotyping in the mass media. When asked about being typecast, McDaniel responded: "I don't know about you, but I'd rather play a maid for $500 a week than work as a maid for $50 a week."[23]

The few African Americans who penetrated the networks' racial barriers found poor working conditions and little prospect of carving out a career in broadcasting. The three major network radio series with enormously popular black hosts failed during this period. Timid sponsors were partly to blame. In 1933, *The Ethel Waters Show* was canceled a few weeks into the series after NBC's Southern affiliates threatened a boycott and Amoco withdrew its sponsorship. NBC's *Quizzicale,* starring Cab Calloway, was also jettisoned soon after its debut, due to the lack of commercial sponsorship. Calloway later remarked: "It was impossible for Negroes to get a regular commercial sponsor in those days." In 1937, Fleischmann's Yeast sponsored *The Louis Armstrong Show* on CBS. The weekly variety program, featuring Armstrong singing pop standards and doing comedy skits instead of showcasing his prodigious jazz talents, was geared toward a white audience. The sponsor stayed its course, but the show could not compete with the popular *Jack Benny Show,* in the same time slot on NBC, and was dropped after thirteen weeks.[24]

Another disconcerting, if not downright insulting, radio industry practice involved tryout requirements for African American performers. Candidates for black roles in comedy or variety series had to demonstrate that they could speak "Negro dialect" as defined, and in some cases even taught to them, by white entertainers and scriptwriters. As a result, African Americans were routinely rejected for black radio roles because, as one frustrated actress stated, "I have been told repeatedly that I don't sound like a Negro." The few black entertainers actually hired for roles endured a ridiculous ordeal of instruction. Lillian Randolf, for instance, spent three months working on her racial accent under the tutelage of James Jewel, the white originator of *The Lone Ranger* radio show, before she was finally hired for a role in his *Lulu and Leander* series on WXZ in Detroit, Michigan. Johnny Lee, a black comic on *The Slick and Slim Show* on WHN in New York City, complained: "I had to learn to talk as white people believed Negroes talked in order to get the job." This situation persisted well into the 1940s. Actor Frederick O'Neal, who portrayed a character in the *Beulah* radio series during the war years, recalled: "After I appeared on the Beulah program several times, the producer insisted that I use more dialect in my speech." And as late as 1947, Wonderful Smith, a popular African American comedian with *The Red Skelton Show,* was fired by the series producers because, in Smith's words, "I had difficulty sounding as Negroid as they expected."[25]

By far the most well known and financially successful African American on network radio in the late 1930s was Eddie Anderson, who played Rochester on NBC's *The Jack Benny Show.* Rochester was not only Benny's trusted chauffeur and valet but also a razor-toting, whiskey-drinking, crap-shooting womanizer. This clever and, at times, contradictory mix of the faithful servant and the urban Zip Coon produced an updated minstrel character tailor-made for the national white listening audience. As Jack Benny's comic foil, Rochester was allowed to be smart and sassy with his boss even as he also mothered Benny, a die-hard bachelor. This led one historian to suggest that "the pair became, in fact, the oddest racial couple in American culture. They shared intimacies and domestic arrangements on radio and television that went far beyond the typical employer–employee association. In developing a symbiotic relationship, they reflected subtle changes occurring in American society that would ultimately alter the stereotype of the black male."[26]

For his part, Eddie Anderson was so myopically focused on the relative complexities of his own role that he did not see racial stereotyping as widespread in radio broadcasting. Ignoring the lack of diverse black characters, he defended radio's images in a rather self-serving way: "I don't see why certain characters are called stereotypes. The Negro characters being presented are not labelling the Negro race any more than 'Luigi' is labelling the Italian people as a whole. The same goes for 'Beulah,' who is not playing the part of thousands of Negroes, but only the part of one person, 'Beulah.' They're not saying here is the portrait of the Negro, but here is 'Beulah.'"[27]

Toeing the Color Line

The radio networks avoided racial issues on their public-affairs shows. Rarely did any of the four leading panel discussion programs in the 1930s—*America's Town Meeting of the Air* (CBS), *The University of Chicago Roundtable* (NBC), *People's Platform* (CBS), and *America's Forum on the Air* (NBC) address the serious racial issues of the day. Subjects such as segregation in the South and racial stereotyping in the mass media were totally off limits. Rarely were any prominent African Americans heard discussing national issues on these public-affairs forums, although this would change somewhat during World War II.[28]

The news commentaries were by far the most popular public-affairs offerings on network radio during the depression years. Broadcast news commentators such as Floyd Gibbons, H. V. Kaltenborn, Gabriel Heater, and Walter Winchell became nationally recognized media celebrities in the 1930s; their power to focus public attention on particular issues often rivaled that of the nation's political leaders. In this realm, as well, the networks employed no black journalists. Moreover, only a small minority of progressive white commentators spoke out about the pervasive racial injustices and bigotry still plaguing American society. For example, H. V. Kaltenborn alone protested against the judicial lynching of the so-called Scottsboro Boys in Alabama, during that infamous 1934 trial.[29] The networks blacked out controversial racial incidents and issues on their public-affairs programming throughout the decade, sometimes resorting to extreme measures.

Bald-faced censorship was one. For example, NBC's long-running Sunday gospel series featuring the Southernaires, a popular black gospel choral group, always had a guest speaker, usually a member of the clergy. Guests were routinely asked to submit a copy of their remarks to the show's producers, who would then "blue-pencil"—edit out—anything they deemed controversial. Early in 1938, the president of the National Association for the Advancement of Colored People (NAACP), Major Arthur Springarn, publicly challenged this policy. After his own written remarks were extensively blue-penciled by NBC producers, Springarn went on the air and, disregarding his censored script, delivered a blistering attack on segregation and racism in the United States. NBC abruptly canceled the guest-speaker segment of the series.[30]

Swing-band music, enormously popular in the 1930s, also fell under the distorting influence of the networks' Jim Crow policies. As local and independent broadcasting declined during the decade, the networks emerged as the chief and, in many regions, the only radio outlets for swing. Both NBC and CBS showcased remote late-night swing broadcasts from hotels and ballrooms around the country, in effect holding the power to make or break swing musicians through their booking policies. The lion's share of their live swing broadcasts during the Great Depression showcased white dance bands and vocalists. Featured repeatedly in these shows, Guy Lombardo's Royal Canadians and the Casa Loma Orchestra, as well as the dance bands of Artie Shaw, the Dorsey Brothers, Harry James, Glenn Miller, Kay Kyser, Ozzie Nelson, and Benny Goodman (the so-called King of Swing), saw their popularity with radio audiences parlayed into a greater demand for appearances and records. White vocalists, too, enjoyed a considerable career boost from their network appearances; the Andrews Sisters, Mildred Bailey, the Boswell Sisters, Helen O'Connell, Dinah Shore, Kate Smith, Bing Crosby, and Frank Sinatra became stars with the help of radio.

The networks' most popular live swing broadcasts with sponsors, such as the *Fitch Bandwagon* on NBC, maintained a rigid color line when hiring musicians. These commercially driven shows were assigned the prime-time slots in the schedule and were heavily promoted. When black musicians did perform on network radio in the 1930s, they appeared as guests on a handful of variety shows with liberal credentials, including *The Rudy Vallee Show* and *Shell Chateau*. Some were also featured as part of the networks' sustaining-time programming, which had no commercial sponsors and was produced in house. Duke Ellington, Fats Waller, Art Tatum, and

Maxine Sullivan all hosted network sustaining-time programs for brief periods of time, and the gospel groups Wings over Jordan and the Southernaires were regularly featured as part of the networks' Sunday programming. Appearing from time to time on the "integrated" variety shows were African American groups and artists, including the Mills Brothers, the Golden Gate Jubilee Quartet, Chick Webb's Orchestra, Cab Calloway, and Paul Robeson. This pinch of pepper in a bowl of salt was just enough liberal tokenism to help forestall accusations of racial prejudice in the industry.[31]

The 1930s proved to be network radio's halcyon years. NBC and CBS dominated the airwaves, and the airwaves dominated the public imagination and popular culture. But radio's golden decade was also marred by the broadcast industry's pervasive discriminatory practices and demeaning stereotypes. With the notable exception of the *Amos 'n' Andy* protest of the late 1920s and early 1930s (discussed in Chapter 2), racism in broadcasting went unchallenged during the depression era. But just as major technological, social, and political changes had ushered in this golden age, new changes on the same scale would bring about transformation. The outbreak of World War II, another massive wave of black migration, and the advent of television reshaped the broadcast industry, eventually making radio the most ubiquitous mass medium in the black community.

2

The Controversial
Phenomenon of
Amos 'n' Andy

A s radio broadcasting embarked on a golden age, becoming the "national pastime" of the American populace, it also became a sanctuary for the revival of blackface minstrelsy. This paradoxical development put African Americans in a position of little influence with respect to both their portrayal and their participation in the popular new electronic media. Radio had initially been heralded as force for democracy; broadcasting would unite the entire nation over the airwaves and give voice to the citizenry in all of its diversity. Then, in the late 1920s, the emerging commercial networks promised to elevate American culture to new heights of excellence through the presentation of original and quality programming to the public, free of charge. The stage seemed to be set for African Americans to enter the broadcast mainstream. Instead of showcasing the popular black entertainers and actors of the era, however, the radio networks began to feature white performers who specialized in "Negro dialect." By this time, the blackface tradition had lost much of its credibility and was no longer in great demand on the vaudeville stage and in Hollywood films. While African Americans in these entertainment venues were still presented in stereotypical roles, the characters were more often than not played by black performers, rather than by white imitators. On network radio, however, African Americans were excluded in favor of blackface entertainers, who gave new life to what Mel Watkins has characterized as "racial ventriloquy." This revival of nineteenth-century blackface dialect stereotypes largely grew out of the spectacular success of *The Amos 'n' Andy Show* on NBC.

The Emergence of Gosden and Correll

The voices behind Amos and Andy belonged to Freeman Gosden and Charles Correll, a little-known vaudeville comedy duo who specialized in blackface humor. Gosden, as the so-called expert on Negro dialect, wrote the early scripts and was the voice behind most of the leading characters in the show, including the women. Born in 1899, he was a native of Virginia with close emotional ties to the cult of the Confederacy. His father had proudly served under Colonel John S. Mosby, the legendary "Gray Ghost" who had led daring guerrilla raids against Union troop positions and supply lines in northern Virginia during the Civil War. Freeman was born and raised in Richmond, the former capital of the Confederacy. Even at the turn of the century, the city clung tenaciously to its Civil War heritage and heroes: in the 1890s, a large statue of Robert E. Lee was unveiled adjacent to Monument Avenue, the city's major thoroughfare, and Confederate president Jefferson Davis's body was returned to Richmond for reinterment. Lavish ceremonies accompanied both events and attracted huge crowds, including thousands of Confederate veterans dressed in their old Civil War uniforms. In 1908, when the city unveiled new monuments dedicated to Jeff Davis and General J. E. B. Stuart, about twenty thousand Southern veterans converged on Richmond for weeklong festivities. Young Freeman was on hand for this celebration with his father, and it made a lasting impression on him. When his father died, an obituary saluted the elder Gosden as a "gallant Confederate soldier," while his tombstone simply read: "Served under Colonel Mosby."[1]

Like many white Southerners of his generation who were drawn to the cult of the Confederacy—including *The Birth of a Nation* filmmaker D. W. Griffith—Freeman Gosden was also fascinated by blackface minstrelsy at an early age. While growing up in Richmond, one of his close childhood friends was a black youth nicknamed Snowball (Garrett Brown), who lived for a time in the Gosden household. The two boys often performed minstrel routines for Freeman's convalescent father. Later in his career, Gosden credited Snowball as an important source of the humor that went into the *Amos 'n' Andy* radio scripts and also modeled a character from the series, Sylvester, on him. While still in his teens, Freeman Gosden joined his first blackface troupe, a fairly typical example of the growing number of amateur and semiprofessional minstrel groups springing up not only in the South but all over the country. Most of these troupes based their stage shows on the antebellum blackface tradition. Gosden's group performed for local civic organizations, such as the United Daughters of the Confederacy, during their annual conventions and fund-raising events. Troupe members were usually paid modest amounts for their services.[2]

After serving in the U.S. Navy during World War I, Freeman Gosden launched his career as a professional entertainer by going to work for the Joe Bren Company, a Chicago-based theatrical company that staged fund-raising shows for fraternal and civic groups including the American Legionnaires, the Elks, the Kiwanis, and the Shriners. As one of the company's traveling directors, Gosden went from town to town organizing the shows with local talent. It was on one of his first assignments in North Carolina that he met his future blackface comedy partner Charles Correll, who also happened to be employed by Joe Bren.[3]

Unlike Freeman Gosden, Correll had grown up in the North, where he had little contact with African Americans. He was born and raised in a working-class family in Peoria, Illinois. His father was a construction foreman, who encouraged his son to follow in his footsteps. But young Charles was more attracted to vaudeville, in part because it offered an escape from the drudgery of his father's vocation and lifestyle. Correll's first venture into blackface humor came as a teenager, when he secured a role in a local "Tom show"—a burlesque of Harriet Beecher Stowe's *Uncle Tom's Cabin*, staged by amateur white actors who blacked up for the performance. Correll moved on to play the piano in nickelodeons while developing his skills as a soft-shoe dancer. Then, in the early 1920s, while employed by the Joe Bren Company, he met his future radio compatriot Gosden. The two shared a mutual interest in blackface humor and soon became good friends. By 1924, they were rooming together in Chicago and trying to develop a vaudeville act.[4]

A year later, Gosden and Correll were performing regularly on two Chicago radio stations—singing popular Tin Pan Alley tunes on WEBH's live Friday-night broadcasts from a local hotel, and doing blackface comedy routines for a weekly Joe Bren minstrel show on WLS. They were not paid for either show but figured the exposure would be payment enough, if it helped them get ahead in show business. Their first major breakthrough on radio came in 1926: WGN, owned by the *Chicago Tribune,* hired them to develop a nightly "radio comic strip." They centered the new show, *Sam 'n' Henry,* on two black Southern migrants. Gosden later explained that they had chosen black characters because "blackface could tell funnier stories than whiteface comics."[5] Sam and Henry, two poor and uneducated farm laborers from rural Alabama, had moved north to Chicago in pursuit of the American Dream. Thwarted at every turn, their numerous get-rich-quick schemes invariably ended in disaster, and their gullibility routinely set them up to be fleeced by urban con artists. Conceived as comic foils, Sam was a meek and sentimental simpleton, whereas Henry was a domineering and conniving braggart.

To African Americans living in Chicago, the content and the characters of the *Sam 'n' Henry* serial were reminiscent of comedy routines and characters originally developed by the popular local black vaudeville team of Flournoy Miller and Aubrey Lyles. The team was a star attraction at the Pekin Theater in Chicago throughout the 1920s and the featured act in two of the decade's most highly acclaimed black musicals, *Shuffle Along* and *Runnin' Wild,* which were staged both in New York and in Chicago. Gosden and Correll undoubtedly became familiar with Miller and Lyles's stage act while living in Chicago in the early 1920s. Their liberal use of the originators' material in the *Sam 'n' Henry* series and, later, in *The Amos 'n' Andy Show,* led many African Americans in Chicago (and later, those in Harlem) to think that Miller and Lyles were performing on the airwaves. Flournoy Miller would later sue Godsen and Correll for using his vaudeville stage material, but without success; comedy skits and characters could not be copyrighted. For their part, Gosden and Correll never denied that they had "borrowed" some of their material from Miller and Lyles—it was a common practice throughout show business. As if to make amends, they even hired Miller as a consultant to their radio and television series years later.[6]

Another probable source of the blackface humor in *Sam 'n' Henry* was Octavus Roy Cohen, a white Southerner who billed himself as "the Negro's

O. Henry." Cohen authored a series of crude Negro-dialect stories on the trials and tribulations of "Florian Slappey," a gullible rural buffoon who migrates to Birmingham, Alabama, in search of fortune and fame. There, he gets caught up in the frivolous machinations of the city's pretentious black "sassietie" (society)—a group obsessed with aping the mannerisms and mores of the white social elite. Most of the characters in the Florian Slappey stories are members of the "Sons and Daughters of I Shall Arise," a fictional black order that Cohen also crassly burlesqued. In general, Cohen's lowbrow caricatures of black urban life cast African Americans in the worst possible light, portraying them as lazy, illiterate, venal, licentious, and supercilious—totally insulated from, and out of touch with, the highbrow white cultural mainstream they supposedly were seeking to emulate.[7]

Like Florian Slappey, Sam and Henry are black country bumpkins from Alabama. The first episode in the radio series has the duo riding a mule cart to Birmingham, where they board a train destined for Chicago. Once settled on the Southside, Sam and Henry join a fraternal order much like the one in the Florian Slappey stories; in this case, it is called the "Jewels in the Crown." The similarities in location, plot, and character suggest that Gosden and Correll also borrowed material from Cohen for their initial series. Moreover, like Flournoy Miller, Octavus Cohen was later hired by Gosden as a writer for *The Amos 'n' Andy Show* during its twenty-year run on network radio.[8]

Amos and Andy on the Airwaves

The transformation of *Sam 'n' Henry* into *Amos 'n' Andy* came about as the result of a better offer from a competing station, WMAQ, owned by the *Chicago Daily News*. Because WGN, which had broadcast the show for two years, still owned the rights to the *Sam 'n' Henry* title, the new show was called *Amos 'n' Andy*, but it retained the characters, the locale, and the story line of its forerunner. The move was a tremendous break for Gosden and Correll; their nightly radio series was now being recorded for syndication on other stations around the country. Within a year and a half, the growing national popularity of the newly syndicated show caught the attention of NBC, who offered the comedy team a $100,000 yearly contract. Now set in Harlem rather than in Chicago's Southside, *Amos 'n' Andy* debuted on NBC's "blue" network on August 29, 1929; it was broadcast from 6:00 to 6:15 P.M. every evening except Sunday. In a matter of months, the blackface comedy serial would become the most listened-to radio show in the land.[9]

Amos and Andy, like Sam and Henry, were offspring of the antebellum minstrel caricatures Jim Crow and Zip Coon. Amos (and his predecessor Sam) was cast in the Jim Crow mold: simple-minded, timid, gullible, superstitious, and naive. In contrast, Andy (and Henry) was a recycled Zip Coon: pretentious, lazy, boisterous, and philandering. The story line of the serial revolved around the duo's misadventures as proprietors of the "Fresh Air Taxicab Company of America, Incorpulated," and their membership in a supercilious fraternal order called the "Mystic Knights of the Sea." The leader of the lodge, the infamous "Kingfish," a blustering and shiftless Coon caricature even more outlandish than Andy, would eventually become prominently featured in the show, along with his wife, Sapphire, a bossy, shrewish Mammy figure. In the convention of these well-known blackface stereotypes, Gosden and Correll's comedy relied heavily on malapropisms and tortured syntax. Some of duo's favorite sayings— "I'se regusted," "Ain't dat sumptin'," "Holy mackerel"—eventually became common household slang.[10]

At the height of its unprecedented popularity, in the early years of the Great Depression, just over 50 percent of the national radio audience— about 40 million people—routinely listened to *The Amos 'n' Andy Show*. The first network radio series to develop such a massive listenership, the show had a major influence on the serial formats developed for network broadcasting in the 1930s. *Amos 'n' Andy* also sparked a boom in the sale of radio sets and generated a wide variety of profitable spin-off products, including comic strips, phonograph records, toys, a candy bar, and a feature-length film (*Check and Double Check*, 1930). Gosden and Correll, in effect radio's first superstars, became the highest-paid entertainers in broadcasting and were in such great demand that they were invited to perform at the White House for President Herbert Hoover.[11]

The comedy team's popularity spawned a host of imitators, flooding the local and network airwaves with ludicrous caricatures: *Anaesthetic and Cerebelum* on KGW, Portland, Oregon; *Honeyboy and Sassafras* on KSAT, Fort Worth, Texas; "Watermelon and Cantaloupe" on *The Corn Cob Pipe Club*, WEAF, New York; *Slick and Slim* on WHN, New York; *Lulu and Lean-*

der on WXYZ, Detroit; *Buck and Wheat* and *The Two Black Crows* on CBS; *Aunt Jemima* on NBC; "Moonshine and Sawdust" on NBC's *The Gulf Show;* and "Molasses and January" on NBC's *Showboat*. Few of these blackface radio acts lasted long; one that did, Pick Malone and Pat Padgett, the white comedy team that started out as Molasses and January on NBC, held onto its popularity for the rest of the decade. In 1939, the Crosley Rating Service listed *Pick 'n' Pat*—the duo were now using their own names and broadcasting on the CBS network—among the top five comedy shows on the airwaves, ahead of even *Amos 'n' Andy*. This spinoff comedy team continued to rely on crass blackface dialect jokes and skits as the mainstay of their act after they made it big on their own.[12]

Taking Offense—Taking the Offensive

The spectacular success of *The Amos 'n' Andy Show* among white audiences created an enormous controversy among African Americans, especially those living in urban areas where the program was more accessible. Not since the release of D. W. Griffith's film *The Birth of a Nation* (1915) had a mass-media cultural product become the object of so much scrutiny, debate, and protest in the black community. However, there was a crucial difference in African Americans' reactions to the feature film and the radio series. The condemnation of Griffith's movie for its negative portrayal of black people and its glorification of the Ku Klux Klan was uniform among African Americans, but *Amos 'n' Andy* had both ardent supporters and determined detractors.

The opposing camps coalesced around two of the nation's leading African American weekly newspapers and their respective founders: Robert Abbott's *Chicago Defender* and Robert Vann's *Pittsburgh Courier*. Although the *Defender's* circulation had fallen off since its high-water mark of 280,000 in 1920, the press run was still well over one hundred thousand copies, making it the most widely read black newspaper in the country. The *Courier* had become the *Defender's* chief rival for national readers by the end of the 1920s, at which time it had a circulation of over fifty thousand. By the time the *Amos 'n' Andy* controversy began, Robert Abbott had become the most prominent black newspaper publisher in the United States and particularly well known for his fiery editorial crusades on behalf of racial pride and progress. Nevertheless, Abbott counted Gosden and Correll among his personal friends and was generally supportive of their radio series. Beginning in 1927, the comedy team appeared at *Defender*-sponsored charity events in Chicago's black community.

In return, the newspaper printed glowing accounts of these appearances and applauded the success of *Amos 'n' Andy* on network radio. Despite the *Defender*'s long-term support for the comedy team, considerable local opposition to the show—especially among Chicago's black clergy—developed once *Amos 'n' Andy* gained a national audience. Bishop W. J. Walls, respected leader of the city's African Methodist Episcopal Zion Church and the first to speak out, began condemning the radio series from the pulpit in 1929, then attacking it in the black press a year later. Deploring Gosden and Correll's "crude" and "moronic" characterization of African Americans, Bishop Walls regarded the show a "dangerous text" that worked to undermine the racial progress made by black migrants in urban America since World War I.[13]

Soon after Bishop Walls publicly criticized the show, Robert Vann launched a full-scale editorial offensive against it. Like Walls, he vehemently objected to Gosden and Correll's demeaning portrayal of African Americans, but he was also indignant that two white comics were getting rich and famous for their caricatures of black people and humor. Vann's editorial barrage also noted that the show's theme song ("A Perfect Song") was the theme D. W. Griffith had first selected for *The Birth of a Nation,* and that many of the radio show's comic routines were taken from Miller and Lyles. In 1931, Vann intensified his campaign against *Amos 'n' Andy.* Using "self-respect" as a rallying cry, he initiated through the *Courier* a national petition to drive the series from the airwaves. Responding to Vann's crusading call for black ministers to preach a sermon on self-respect, on October 25, hundreds of African American preachers all over the country supported the petition campaign. Vann also urged his readers to overwhelm the press with letters protesting the radio series and to boycott Pepsodent toothpaste, the show's sponsor on NBC.[14]

Confident that the crescendo of black public outcry against *Amos 'n' Andy* and support of the *Courier*'s petition campaign would continue to build, the newspaper soon increased its goal—from one hundred thousand to 1 million signatures. Indeed, November 1931, the *Courier* had collected 740,000 signatures and had enlisted the NAACP to present them to the Federal Radio Commission (FRC). Robert Vann marked the occasion by boasting: "There is little doubt in the minds of some of the ablest lawyers that the Radio Commission will rule that Amos and Andy propaganda is harmful to a portion of the citizenry of the United States." When the *Defender* sponsored another local charity event featuring the comedy team, a front-page *Courier* story referred to its rival as the "Chicago Surrender, World's Greatest Weakly," and accused it of insulting the thousands of African Americans who signed the *Courier*'s petitions. At the same time, Vann and his associates tried to broaden the protest against *Amos 'n' Andy* by encouraging a wide variety of black civic, fraternal, and religious organizations to endorse the petition campaign. By the end of the year, endorsements came from groups as diverse as the National Association of Colored Waiters and Hotel Employees, the National Baptist Convention, and a number of national black fraternal organizations such as the Elks, the Knights, and Daughters of Africa.[15]

For their part, Gosden and Correll never discussed the protests but addressed the controversy by using their star status to cultivate goodwill among African Americans. They continued to appear regularly at charity events in Chicago's Southside and Harlem, where they posed for publicity photos with African American celebrities and children. On one such occasion, the *Defender* reported that Gosden told the audience "how much he loved Race people." Gosden and Correll used their new influence in the entertainment industry to secure employment for prominent African American performers that they had befriended. They chose Duke Ellington's orchestra for a musical role in their feature film *Check and Double Check* and tapped Bill "Bojangles" Robinson, as well as Cab Calloway and his band, as headliners in the 1930 NBC special *Harlem Salutes Amos 'n' Andy*.[16]

In the end, Gosden and Correll rode out the controversy on the strength of their continuing popularity. The protest movement against *Amos 'n' Andy* fell apart in 1932. Early in the year, the FRC dismissed the *Courier*'s petitions and refused the NAACP's request for public hearings on the controversy. Furthermore, the Pepsodent boycott had no evident impact on the show's sponsor or on NBC. Disillusioned, the organized opposition to *Amos 'n' Andy* melted away; Vann's *Pittsburgh Courier* moved on to other issues and campaigns. For its part, the blackface comedy series remained a staple of network broadcasting for years to come.[17] Throughout the 1930s, *The Amos 'n' Andy Show* held onto its millions of loyal listeners and its celebrity status in the popular culture. Even the rich and powerful expressed their admiration—Presidents Herbert Hoover and Franklin Roosevelt, industrialist Henry Ford, FBI director J. Edgar Hoover, and Louisiana governor Huey Long (who appropriated the "Kingfish" nickname in an obvious gesture to enhance his political appeal). Clearly recognizing the show's uniqueness, British literary giant George Bernard Shaw, after his first visit to the United States, told the press: "There are three things which I will never forget about America—the Rocky Mountains, Niagara Falls, and Amos & Andy."[18] This widespread recognition solidified the show's standing as a cultural force and the foremost radio comedy.

The Stereotypes Solidify

Even though the comedic formula of *The Amos 'n' Andy Show* was not altered in the 1930s, its lineup and story line shifted. The series' early plots largely revolved around the doings of Amos and Andy—their romantic interests, financial problems, and their membership in the Mystic Knights of the Sea. But by the middle of the decade, Amos and Andy moved to the sidelines as George "Kingfish" Stevens; his wife, Sapphire; and a simpleton called "Lightnin'" came to center stage. Lightnin' and Kingfish, also cast in the Jim Crow and Zip Coon molds, had none of the redeeming qualities of Amos and Andy. While Amos may have been naive, slow-witted, and gullible, he was also hard-working, trustworthy, and respectful of women. During the early years of the depression, Amos was even held up as a model of thrift and diligence in the face of economic adversity. And while he was notable for his aversion to work, philandering ways, and get-rich-quick schemes, Andy was never mean spirited or venal. The friendly flimflam man's pranks were harmless and amusing, and his own misfortunes elicited a good deal of sympathy from the radio audience.[19]

Lightnin' and Kingfish, in contrast, were strictly one-dimensional blackface stereotypes, more preposterous and more predictable than Amos and Andy. Lightnin', a radio version of film comedian Stepin Fetchit's slow-motion buffoon, was the show's comic foil. Kingfish, a bombastic and conniving dandy who thrived on others' misfortune, became the chief protagonist in the series, along with his domineering and manipulative spouse, Sapphire. The story line of the show now revolved around the Kingfish's absurd bunco operations—everything from impersonating an African king in a scam to fleece his lodge members, to selling bogus deeds to the Brooklyn Bridge—and his ludicrous marital squabbles with Sapphire and her mother. The show's namesakes now were relegated to cameo appearances, with Amos as an occasional walk-on and Andy as a bamboozled victim of Kingfish's chicanery.[20]

Gosden and Correll made these changes in the show as part of a calculated effort to maintain their national audience in the highly competitive field of radio comedy—and to a certain extent, they were successful. While no longer ranked first after 1932, *The Amos 'n' Andy Show* remained among the top programs on network radio throughout the New Deal era and World War II, making it the longest-running series in the history of radio broadcasting.

African Americans who listened to network radio during this period were quite familiar with *The Amos 'n' Andy Show;* some had fond memories of it, others did not. New black listeners usually believed at first that the cast was made up of black comedians. Undoubtedly, all African Americans had mixed emotions about the series. In varying degrees, they found it both humorous and offensive. This ambivalence was aptly summarized by a longtime black listener who also worked in the radio industry: "Historically, black folks have always been caught in a very knowing type of schizophrenia. You could laugh at it, and yet you resented it because it misrepresented you. One line instantly comes back. They put the buzzer to the office in reverse. So Andy would say—'Buzz me Miss Blue and come in here.' It was utterly ridiculous. It was that kind of comedy. You laughed at it, yet you understood clearly the misrepresentation of you as a black person."[21]

New Deal reformer James Fly, while serving as FCC chairman, once referred to the National Association of Broadcasters (NAB) as "dead mackerel in the moonlight—it both shines and stinks at the same time."[22] The same could be said about *The Amos 'n' Andy Show.* Its contributions to the growth and development of commercial broadcasting—and by extension, to the shaping of the nation's mass-media popular culture—were considerable. The show pioneered the serial format on network radio, thereby becoming the precursor of the soap operas and sitcoms that have been a central component of radio and television programming up to the present. In addition, *Amos 'n' Andy* had a widespread and uncanny populist appeal; it was the first radio program in the country to attract a mass audience on a regular basis—one that, by all accounts, cut across class, race, and gender lines. The show's record-setting attraction and longevity elevated it to the status of a cultural icon. The series was hailed as a national treasure and a touchstone for Americans from all walks of life.

But the fabled comedy show also enhanced the use of racial ventriloquy on the nation's airwaves, resurrecting nineteenth-century blackface caricatures that became more outlandish as the series progressed. It also had a ripple effect on radio comedy in general, spawning numerous imitators. Taken together, these stereotypes had a far-reaching influence on the perceptions of race in American society. For almost two decades, they held a virtual monopoly on radio's depiction of African Americans; there were no competing audio images of black people, especially on the networks. The national radio audience, a big slice of the American public at the time, was treated to a steady diet of blackface stereotypes at a time when the nation remained rigidly segregated, by law and by custom; when African Americans were experiencing widespread discrimination in employment, housing, education, health care, and criminal justice. By portraying black people as one-dimensional buffoons, radio provided white listeners with a convenient rationale for the plight of African Americans and for their status as second-class citizens.

Much like D. W. Griffith's *The Birth of a Nation,* Gosden and Correll's *Amos 'n' Andy Show* helped fan the flames of white supremacy in the popular culture. Griffith made use of cinematic "historical facsimiles" and bestial Negro stereotypes to portray African Americans in the worst possible light; yet his film was praised by President Woodrow Wilson, who proclaimed: "It is like writing history with lightning. And my only regret is that it is all true."[23] Gosden and Correll fused racial ventriloquy with radio comedy and also won the applause of presidents. The major difference between the two cultural milestones was that one was fictional race history while the other was fictional race humor—and the humor proved to be far more enduring.

PART II

"New World a-Coming": Black Pride Radio

And Louis missed with a left swing, but in close brought up a hard right uppercut to the jaw, and again a right to the body, a left hook, a right to the head, and again a right to the body, a left hook, a right to the head, a left to the head, a right—Schmeling is going down, but he held to his feet, held to the ropes, looked at his corner in helplessness, and Schmeling is down! Schmeling is down! The count is four, its—and he's up, and Louis a right and left to the head, a left to the jaw, a right to the head, and Donovan (the referee) is watching carefully. Louis measures him, a right to the body, a left hook to the jaw, and Schmeling is down! The count is five, five, six, seven, eight, the men are in the ring, the fight is over on a technical knockout. Max Schmeling is beaten in one round!

> —NBC broadcast, heavyweight
> championship fight between
> Joe Louis and Max Schmeling,
> June 18, 1938

3

Brown Bombers and
Black Radio Pioneers

n the evening of June 18, 1938, millions of African Americans all over the country huddled around radio sets to listen to the heavyweight world championship fight between Joe Louis and Max Schmeling. The matchup pitted the reigning champ, known to his loyal fans as the "Brown Bomber," against the only man ever to have defeated him. Two years earlier, the German Schmeling had scored a twelfth-round knockout over Louis, capturing the title. Louis subsequently regained the championship belt, but only after Schmeling had relinquished it. Hence the rematch was an opportunity for Louis to avenge his only loss.

Perhaps more important, however, this championship fight had manifold symbolic implications, both in the United States and on the world stage. On the domestic front, boxing was the only major sport in which black athletes could compete professionally against whites. Joe Louis's rise to the pinnacle of the boxing world thus represented an important victory for all African Americans, proving that given a fair opportunity, black athletes could excel in professional sports. Louis was an enormously popular hero among African Americans during the years he fought for or defended the heavyweight title. Not since the heyday of the legendary Jack Johnson had a boxing champion generated so much fanfare in the black community.

On the international stage, the Louis-versus-Schmeling rematch was generally perceived as a symbolic test of strength between two major world powers inching toward belligerency. Schmeling's 1936 victory over Louis had given Adolf Hitler and his followers something to crow about, just a few months after Jesse Owens had scored his spectacular triumphs in the Olympic Games in Berlin. With the growing threat of war in Europe, the Louis–Schmeling rematch was portrayed as a mythical showdown between American democracy and German fascism and, more specifically, as a test of racial supremacy. Schmeling's victory would reaffirm the master-race theories of Hitler's Third Reich. Louis's victory would strike a blow for America's democratic ideals—and inspire pride throughout the African diaspora.

The championship bout, staged before a sold-out crowd in Yankee Stadium, was broadcast live on NBC, with blow-by-blow commentary by Glen McCarthy. Almost midway through the first round of action, Joe Louis unleashed a fusillade of devastating head and body combination punches. The fight was over in less than three minutes.

Joe Louis's stunning first-round victory set off spontaneous celebrations in black enclaves all over the country; wherever there were radio receivers, there was instant jubilation. Bursting with racial pride, African Americans poured into the streets, cheering, shouting, and dancing for joy. Louis had avenged his only loss and dignified his race in the process. That this moment of athletic victory could ignite a nationwide celebration—a spontaneous experience shared and remembered by so many people—testifies to the power of radio. Listenership was notably on the rise among African Americans, and they hungered for black heroes on the airwaves.

Jack Cooper: "Fly in the Buttermilk"

Jack Cooper is the undisputed patriarch of black radio in the United States. His innovations and achievements in the broadcast industry prior to World War II set the stage for the rapid proliferation of "Negro-appeal radio" in the postwar years. Almost single-handedly, Cooper demonstrated that radio programming produced by African Americans could attract a sizable urban listening audience. His remarkable radio career spanned four decades, from the mid-1920s to well into the 1950s. During this period, his major accomplishments included being among the earliest of the black vaudeville performers to write and star in his own radio comedy skits (WCAP, Washington, D.C., 1925); producing and hosting the first successful weekly radio show featuring African Americans (*The All-Negro Hour*, WSBC, Chicago, 1929); pioneering the modern disc jockey format (WSBC, 1931); launching the first successful black radio production company (Jack L. Cooper Presentations, 1932); and creating the first successful black advertising firm specializing in radio (Jack L. Cooper Advertising Company, 1937). In addition, Cooper was responsible for groundbreaking programming in the areas of news, public affairs, and music. As a result of his tireless labors and entrepreneurial genius, he was able to build a black radio empire in Chicago, establishing a foothold for African Americans in the commercial broadcast industry.

Yet Jack Cooper was also a proverbial "fly in the buttermilk"—the first black broadcaster to forge a successful career in the radio industry. And like most minority members trying to move up the economic ladder, he adapted to the dominant (white) culture accordingly. In Cooper's case, the adjustment led to the birth of an African American school of racial ventriloquy on the airwaves—one that emulated the white professional announcers and commentators on network radio. In aspiring to sound like these white models of broadcast decorum, he perfected an on-air delivery that was virtually the same as theirs. Conspicuously absent was any hint of "Negro dialect" or the use of black vernacular speech in general. Cooper undoubtedly chose this verbal strategy to prove that a black broadcaster could be as civil and well spoken as his white competitors in the industry; for him, racial pride and uplift were at stake. In contrast to Gosden and Correll's degradation of black vernacular speech, Jack Cooper's racial ventriloquy was a dignified rendering of standard English as practiced by white professionals—and ultimately, an exercise in cultural assimilation.

Cooper's life reads like a black version of the Horatio Alger odyssey, in which hard work, self-reliance, and perseverance overcome poverty, discrimination, and the lack of formal education. He was born on September 18, 1888, the last of ten children in what would soon become an impoverished single-parent home. At the age of ten, he quit school and went to live with a foster family in Cincinnati, Ohio, so he could work at the local racetrack. As a teenager in Cincinnati, he also worked as a newsboy and a bellhop, and he trained to become a successful amateur boxer, eventually winning the Ohio Negro welterweight title.

In the early 1900s, Cooper embarked on a career in show business, working as a dancer and comic on the TOBA circuit. He married a showgirl and eventually led his own vaudeville troupe, the Cooper and Lamar Music Company. Lamar (his first wife's stage name) wrote the music for the troupe and served as its musical director. For his part, Cooper wrote and performed in the comedy routines, acted as master of ceremonies, and managed the business end of the operation. During this period, he also managed at least two TOBA theaters in the South and wrote for African American newspapers in Memphis, Tennessee, and Indianapolis, Indiana.[1]

Jack Cooper's flair for journalism inadvertently led him into radio broadcasting. In 1924, as the *Chicago Defender*'s assistant theater editor, he covered the black entertainment world and wrote a weekly column, "Coop's Chatter," extolling the virtues of hard work, self-help, and race pride. A year later, the *Defender* sent him to Washington, D.C., to open the paper's new office. Late in 1925, the producer of a local Washington variety show on WCAP hired him to write and perform comedy skits in Negro dialect. He broadcast these scripts three times a week, handling all the voice parts himself for five dollars a show; late in life, Cooper would boast that he was "the first four Negroes on radio." The job opened up a new career path for the veteran journalist and showman, but it also imposed limitations that were consistent with the racial status quo in the industry and the society. Cooper's comic routines were restricted to the dialect humor demanded by his white employer, locking him into the blackface minstrel tradition—much like his contemporary Bert Williams. And because WCAP broadcast from a segregated downtown hotel, Cooper had to ride the service elevator to get to his studios. He soon grew tired of these restraints and quit his job at WCAP; but the experience marked a major turning point in his career.[2]

Returning to Chicago in 1926, intent on establishing radio as a black enterprise that appealed to African Americans, Cooper developed a proposal for *The All-Negro Hour*—a weekly variety show featuring black entertainers. Still working for the *Defender,* he shopped the proposal around to local stations but found no takers. In 1929, he approached Joseph Silverstein, Chicago's father of "ethnic radio" and the owner of WSBC, a low-power (250 watt) operation that shared its frequency (1260 AM) with two other local stations. Silverstein had replicated the format found in other large urban centers that catered to the needs of foreign language–speaking immigrants. Operating on the margins of the radio industry, these stations adopted a brokerage system of airtime allocation. Entrepreneurs from the various ethnic enclaves in large cities like Chicago, where immigrants were a quarter of the population, bought blocks of airtime for foreign-language broadcasts; they bankrolled these programs with advertising revenues raised from business operations in their respective communities. The growing number of African American residents in Chicago made Cooper's proposal a logical candidate for this format, especially since WSBC's limited signal could cover the Southside, where the black population was concentrated.[3]

The All-Negro Hour premiered on WSBC on Sunday, November 3, 1929, at 5 P.M. with a black vaudeville revue showcasing fast-paced comedy routines and upbeat musical numbers. Many of the original members of this troupe became mainstays of the early weekly show. Cooper himself was centrally involved in all aspects of the production: he wrote the scripts, announced the acts, performed in the comedy skits, and sang as one of the two "Black Diamonds" that opened and closed the program. The following lyrics from the closing theme song convey the aims and the tone of the initial broadcasts; notice the absence of dialect:

> We're two Black Diamonds direct from Dixie
> Where the corn and cotton bask in the sun,
> We hate to leave you, we hope we've pleased you
> And you've really enjoyed our fun.
> We aim to chase your blues, and kill old gloom
> And fill your life with glee
> When we appear on WSBC
> The two Black Diamonds direct from Dixie.[4]

Cooper originally modeled *The All-Negro Hour* on the conventional black vaudeville show, minus the dancers; undoubtedly, he was drawing on his many years of experience on the TOBA circuit. But in a few months, he began to modify the format to appeal to a broader listening audience. First, he developed a religious component for the show: a segment hosted by the popular singing preacher D. E. Milton and featuring a guest church choir from the local community each week. Religious music had no place on the vaudeville stage, but it seemed appropriate on Chicago's premier black radio program, especially since it was broadcast on Sundays. The segment became so popular that Cooper was soon producing several on-going religious shows, many of them live broadcasts of Sunday church services. These programs showcased the city's best gospel artists, including a young Mahalia Jackson.[5] By opening up the local airwaves to the city's black churches, Cooper won the support of the black clergy, who in turn recruited their congregations as listeners and even as participants. As a result, Cooper gained a new audience base, and his Sunday broadcasts became a source of pride for Chicago's black churchgoers.

In another format change, Cooper abandoned the TOBA-style comedy routines in favor of the radio comic strip just as the *Amos 'n' Andy* craze was sweeping the country. In 1930, he launched no fewer than three radio comedy serials as part of *The All-Negro Hour: Luke and Timber,* the misadventures of two Southern migrants in Chicago; *Mush and Clorinda—The Alabama Sunflowers,* a humorous look at a husband-and-wife vaudeville team; *Horseradish and Fertilizer,* a romantic comedy also set in Chicago. Cooper wrote, directed, and acted in all three serials, the last of which ran for twelve years on a succession of local stations.

On the surface, these shows appear to be *Amos 'n' Andy* imitations, especially *Luke and Timber.* They have all the external trappings of blackface humor on radio—the Southern black dialect, the ludicrous names, the clash of rural and urban cultures. But as historian Mark Newman has pointed out, Cooper's radio comic strips were created by a black humorist, performed by an all-black cast, and broadcast to a black audience. Futhermore, his characters did not use malapropisms, nor were they as one-dimensional as the blackface radio stars. *The Amos 'n' Andy Show,* as well as most of its progeny, had just the opposite racial orientation: created by white interlopers, an initially all-white cast, and broadcast to a predominantly white listening audience. Jack Cooper was, in fact, highly critical of Gosden and Correll for these very reasons; furthermore, he felt their show undermined race pride and progress. Consequently, the radio serials on *The All-Negro Hour* were not only black alternatives to *Amos 'n' Andy* but also examples of authentic African American satire and self-parody. From Cooper's perspective, they were the real comic voices of black America, and Amos and Andy were the impostors. Moreover, these audio comic strips were presented along with other kinds of entertainment, such as the religious broadcasts, so the soundscape of black life on Cooper's shows was much broader than anything that came before it. In addition to the comedians were ministers, gospel singers, jazz musicians, and a professional-sounding master of ceremonies.[6]

The most far-reaching programming innovation that Jack Cooper initiated on *The All-Negro Hour* was the disc-jockey format. It came about almost by accident. In Cooper's original vaudeville revue format, the music was broadcast live; the pivotal musician was a pianist, who backed up the various vocalists on the show and provided musical continuity between the segments. But in early 1932, the show's female pianist demanded a pay raise, and when Cooper balked at her demands, she walked out on him just before a scheduled broadcast. Cooper's on-the-spot solution, both pragmatic and ingenious, is described by his third wife, Gertrude, who was an eyewitness: "He got a barrel and set some little record player on it and held a mike to it. And that's the way he carried the show for that night. And that was his start in the record business. And of course, after that the station got equipment."[7]

Jack Cooper wasn't the first radio broadcaster to play records over the airwaves; in fact, the practice was widespread in the early days of broadcasting, before the commercialization of the radio enterprise. But early in the 1920s, when ASCAP began to charge stations a hefty annual fee for the privilege of playing records on the air, station owners responded with live music broadcasts of material not protected by ASCAP. This trend continued for the rest of the decade. When Cooper switched from live music to discs on that fateful Sunday in 1932, he unwittingly became the precursor of a national trend that would mushroom after World War II. Ironically, he was able to make this historic format shift because of the availability of race records, which Jim Crow practices largely excluded from the ASCAP catalog. Cooper could play popular black jazz and gospel recordings on the air free of charge, whereas he had to pay musicians to play live on his show. When his audience declared themselves more receptive to race records than to his live music lineup, *The All-Negro Hour* new disc-jockey format replaced all the live secular music segments in the show, as well as two of the three comedy serials. It was also at this point that Cooper's professional broadcast voice and diction totally dominated his programs.[8]

From the outset of his career in broadcasting, Cooper's ambitions reached well beyond *The All-Negro Hour*. He envisioned a black radio enterprise that would ultimately control all the components of its own operation—from scripting and producing to distribution and advertising. One of his first major projects was to establish a black-owned radio broadcast and production facility independent of WSBC. Using his popular radio show as leverage, Cooper struck a deal with the Metropolitan Funeral System Association, a trade organization for black funeral-home owners; in return for a percentage of the profits, the group put up the money for a studio complex that would become Cooper's base of operations for the next two decades. Building a black advertising base for his enterprise was more difficult. Especially during the depression years, local black businesses were reluctant to advertise on an untested commercial medium, forcing Cooper to rely almost exclusively on ad revenues from white businesses catering to African Americans. Even when he set up his own radio advertising agency in 1937, white entrepreneurs continued to be his major clients. But by then, he had embarked on a new and more profitable money-making venture to keep his operation afloat: selling radio airtime directly to black customers—from disc jockeys to preachers, businesses to churches or civic groups.[9]

Cooper's adoption of the brokerage system for his radio enterprise resulted not only from his advertising dilemma but also from his unrelenting efforts to expand and diversify programming. He began to buy more and more airtime. By 1938, he controlled seventeen hours of WSBC's weekly broadcast schedule and was looking to other local stations for more. At the zenith of his broadcast activity in the late 1940s, Cooper was purchasing over forty hours of weekly airtime on four different Chicago stations: WSBC, WHFC, WAAF, and WBEE.[10] He divided the broadcast hours between programs produced in house by Jack L. Cooper Presentations and paid for with ad revenues generated by the Jack L. Cooper Advertising Company, on the one hand, and programs developed by aspiring African American broadcasters, religious and secular, who bought time, on the other. The brokered arrangements invariably more than doubled his initial investment. As a former employee explained: "You see, Jack bought 20 hours a week just over WSBC. He bought it for roughly $600 a week at $30 an hour. He would sell the time for $15 for a 5 minute slot, and 'one spots' for as much as $5 and $10 apiece. So you can see the money that he was making because all of his time was sold out."[11]

The steady expansion of airtime also enabled Cooper to diversify his programming considerably. After the demise of *The All-Negro Hour* in 1936, Sunday-morning and -evening broadcasts were almost exclusively religious in nature. They included gospel disc-jockey shows such as *Song of Zion,* educational programs such as *Know Your Bible,* and remote broadcasts of Sunday services from local black churches. Beginning in the mid-1930s, during the summer months, a Sunday-afternoon time slot was devoted to baseball. Cooper brokered a deal with the Chicago American Giants, the local black professional team, to broadcast their Sunday games live from Comisky Park; his pitch-by-pitch coverage of the games made him the first African American sportscaster on the airwaves. In addition to the baseball broadcasts, he did a series of live interviews with such black sports heroes as Jesse Owens, Joe Louis, and Leroy "Satchel" Paige from his radio studios.[12]

Jack Cooper's weekday lineup was dominated by jazz disc-jockey shows, most of which were hosted by his own stable of protégés. Many of these employee-trainees went on to successful careers in broadcasting; among the best known are Oliver Edwards, Eddie Plique, Manny Mauldin, William Kinnison, and Gertrude Roberts Cooper—the boss's third wife. The daughter of a local minister, Trudy Cooper hosted her first radio show in 1938; over the next three decades, she was prominently featured on four different local stations and became the city's most celebrated black female broadcaster. All of Jack Cooper's disc-jockey protégés tended to follow his lead with respect to musical selections and on-air presentation. Like their mentor, they took a decidedly professional approach to their work on radio. Cooper's jazz format showcased the discs of well-established black and white swing bands and vocalists, scrupulously avoiding the more pedestrian and often risqué vaudeville and urban blues recordings. His announcing privileged standard American English over the black vernacular, a preference he shared with the most educated and affluent African Americans. In effect, Cooper and his team became the voice of the urban black bourgeoisie and a symbol of racial uplift. Their disc-jockey format would dominate black radio programming in Chicago until the aftermath of World War II.[13]

When Cooper focused on news and public affairs, he also developed some groundbreaking programming models. In the early 1930s, he initiated a long-running, late-evening news roundup, at first in conjunction with the *Chicago Defender* (*Defender Newsreel*) and later with the *Pittsburgh*

Courier. The *Defender Newsreel* was the first black newscast of its kind in the Midwest; it focused on events and issues that were of particular interest to African Americans. During the postwar years, Cooper organized a mobile news team to cover fast-breaking stories of interest to the local black community. With its remodeled van equipped with a small radio studio and a mobile transmitter, the team broadcast live from the scene of traffic accidents, fires, crimes, news conferences, political rallies, and demonstrations. At its high point, the mobile unit provided on-the-spot news coverage for four different Chicago radio stations which carried Cooper's broadcasts.[14]

Of Cooper's public-affairs programs, *Search for Missing Persons* had the highest profile. Launched in 1938, with the cooperation of the Chicago Police Department, the weekly show was credited with locating more than twenty thousand African Americans separated from family and friends during the massive World War II–era migrations to Chicago. *Listen Chicago,* however, was the most critically acclaimed public-affairs program. A weekly roundtable discussion on social issues and problems of interest to African Americans, it was renowned for the diversity of viewpoints it brought to the airwaves. Cooper's popular public-affairs offerings also included *Situations Wanted,* a weekday segment of job listings; *Our Community Marches On,* a program on local black accomplishments hosted by well-known social worker and activist John M. Ragland; *Your Legal Rights,* a call-in show hosted by a team of black lawyers; and *Social Security for You and Your Family,* an educational feature highlighting the benefits of New Deal legislation as it related to African Americans.[15]

At the height of his broadcast activity in the 1940s, Cooper commanded the largest black radio operation in the country. During this period, he was responsible for more than fifty radio programs, broadcast on four different Chicago stations; his production and advertising companies employed scores of African Americans as writers and announcers, as well as technical and sales personnel; and he was earning close to $200,000 a year from his various radio enterprises. In 1947, *Ebony* magazine named him the "Dean of African American disc jockeys."[16] In the course of his two decades on the radio in Chicago, he had become a living legend—not only in his adopted hometown but throughout black America.

The Strange Radio Career of Paul Robeson

In the years leading up to World War II, Paul Robeson emerged as one of black America's the most visible and vocal cultural figures. His pioneering achievements as an athlete, scholar, stage and film actor, and concert vocalist, coupled with his charismatic personality and good looks, created a formidable public image. At a time when black males in the mass media were routinely depicted as comical Coons or shuffling Toms, Robeson was a refreshing alternative, especially for African Americans. Here was a serious actor who undertook dignified dramatic roles, a classically inclined vocalist who paid homage to the folk music of his ancestors, and an outspoken political activist who waged a lifelong struggle against racial discrimination—both at home and abroad. This unique combination of personal magnetism and race advocacy not only endeared Robeson to the black populace but also won him international acclaim as a champion of oppressed people everywhere. More than any other person of his generation, Paul Robeson came to symbolize black pride, progress, and resistance to white domination.

Robeson scored his first major triumph on network radio as the featured vocalist for the premiere broadcast of "Ballad for Americans" on November 5, 1939. Produced for CBS's experimental series *The Pursuit of Happiness,* under the direction of award-winning radio dramatist Norman Corwin, "Ballad" was a patriotic anthem of epic proportions that celebrated the history of American democracy. With lyrics by poet John Latouche and music by composer Earl Robinson, the ten-minute dramatic tone poem had sentiments that appealed to American citizens of all political persuasions. It applauded the nation's prowess and potential but did not excuse its racial oppression:

> Our country's strong, our country's young
> And her greatest songs are still unsung.
> . . . .
> Man in white skin can never be free
> While his black brother is in slavery.

It celebrated the nation's ethnic and religious diversity:

> I'm just an Irish, Negro, Jewish, Italian
> French and English, Spanish, Russian
> Chinese, Polish, Scotch, Hungarian
> Latvian, Swedish, Finnish, Canadian
> Greek and Turk and Czech and double check American.

> And that ain't all, I was baptized
> Baptist, Methodist, Congregationalist
> Lutheran, Atheist, Roman Catholic
> Amish, Jewish, Presbyterian
> Seven Day Adventist, Mormon, Quaker
> Christian Scientist and lots more.

But the piece also criticized venal behavior, racism, and chauvinism:

> Out of the cheating, out of the shouting
> Out of the murders and the lynching
> Out of the windbags, the patriotic spouting.

In a final crescendo of patriotism, "Ballad" reaffirmed national pride:

> Deep as our valleys, high as our mountains
> Strong as the people who made it
> For I have always believed it
> And I believe it now
> And you know who I am
> America![17]

The radio premiere of "Ballad for Americans" took place two months after war broke out in Europe. Introduced by Norman Corwin, Robeson's booming baritone voice, complemented by a large choir and the CBS Symphony Orchestra, stirred the studio audience and listeners across the country. At the conclusion of the performance, the audience rose to give Robeson and company a thunderous fifteen-minute ovation, and hundreds of listeners jammed the network's switchboard for hours to register their approval. In the afterglow of the broadcast, Corwin congratulated Robeson on "making radio history." CBS rebroadcast the popular program on New Years Day; the Victor label then recorded it for commercial distribution. The recording topped the pop charts in 1940, with close to 1 million copies sold. Almost overnight, Paul Robeson was thrust into the national spotlight as a spokesman for American democracy. "Ballad" composer Earl Robinson, well aware of the discrimination Robeson had encountered in the radio industry and the society at large, commented on the "tremendous irony" of the situation: the man whose voice was chosen to represent America's most cherished ideals was still a second-class citizen in the country he championed.[18]

Prior to 1939, Paul Robeson had made only two cameo radio appearances—on variety shows in the early 1930s, to sing spirituals. On a third program, *Shell Chateau,* hosted by Al Jolson and aired during the fall of 1935, Robeson sang the obligatory black folk song, and played the part of a fictional African chief in a scene loosely adapted from his forthcoming film *Saunders of the River* (1937). In this dramatic vignette, Robeson's impassioned plea for peace, reminding his people of the horrors of war and the benefits of living in harmony with one's neighbors, succeeds in averting tribal warfare. This portrayal on network radio of a wise and dynamic African leader was well ahead of its time, given the pervasiveness of Jim Crow in broadcasting during this period, and it went largely unnoticed— a mere blip on the national soundscape. In terms of radio during the 1930s, Robeson's distinct baritone voice was much better known to European audiences than to U.S. listeners. His major European concerts were routinely broadcast by the host countries, and the national radio services in England, France, Spain, and the Soviet Union interviewed him extensively during his visits.[19]

With the phenomenal success of "Ballad," and with war enveloping Europe, Robeson suddenly found himself in great demand for radio and public appearances. During 1940, his concerts became major cultural events; about 160,000 people came to hear him sing in Chicago's Grant Park, and his sold-out concert at the Hollywood Bowl in Los Angeles set an attendance record. That year he was the featured vocalist on a broadcast of the *Kraft Music Hall,* a popular CBS program hosted by Bing Crosby, as well as the producer and host of a special tribute to the International Brigades that fought for the Loyalists in the Spanish Civil War. (He called his program *Five Songs for Democracy*.) In addition, Robeson starred in yet another rebroadcast of "Ballad" as part of a CBS special titled *All God's Children*. In 1941, he was featured on a broadcast of NBC's sustaining-time series *Freedom's People,* which documented the contributions of African Americans to the nation, and he participated in a radio special in honor of actor Canada Lee, delivering a stirring tribute to Lee and to African American cultural achievement in general.[20]

The pace of Paul Robeson's domestic radio appearances quickened after the United States declared war on the Axis powers. He was also enlisted by the federal government for a series of international propaganda broadcasts on shortwave radio, which were heard in Europe, Africa, and the Middle East. Although Robeson energetically participated in these special broadcasts on behalf of the war effort, he did not lessen his forceful criticism of racial injustice in American society. Because of his dedication to both causes, he emerged as a leading advocate of African Americans' "Double V" campaign, a grassroots effort calling for victory over both fascism abroad and racism at home. As one of the campaign's most visible and outspoken champions, Robeson, in a nationally broadcast speech given at the influential *Herald Tribune* Forum in 1943, proclaimed: "The disseminators and supporters of racial discrimination and antagonism appear to the Negro and are, in fact, first cousins if not brothers of the Nazis. They speak the same language of the master race and practice, or attempt to practice, the same tyranny over minority people."[21] By this time in his radio career, Robeson was in more demand as a speaker than as a vocalist or actor. While other celebrities supported the war effort in a variety of ways—pitching war bonds, entertaining the troops, or serving in the armed forces—he was notable for using his star status to promote democracy and racial equality both at home and abroad.

Robeson sometimes appeared as one of many guest celebrities offering words of encouragement for the war effort, but on many of the wartime broadcasts, he was the major attraction. He was chosen to headline NBC's special broadcast of the mammoth "Labor for Victory" rally, held in Yankee Stadium during August 1943, which organized labor called for in response to a Detroit race riot two months earlier. As a respected African American leader, longtime friend of the labor movement, and early supporter of the Congress of Industrial Organizations' (CIO's) drive to organize black and white industrial workers into the same unions, Robeson was the logical candidate to reconcile the smoldering racial tensions in the domestic workforce. Commenting on the riot, he acknowledged it was a serious setback for race relations and the war effort, but he also stressed the necessity of racial cooperation on the home front in achieving victory over the fascists and full democracy in the United States. As the principal speaker on a special program commemorating the 135th birthday of Abraham Lincoln (a government-sponsored and -produced tribute, broadcast in Europe and Africa over shortwave radio in February 1944), Robeson praised Lincoln's unwavering wartime resolve to preserve the Union and free the slaves, and he urged listeners to follow the example of the martyred American president in the current struggle.[22]

Near the end of World War II, Paul Robeson was hopeful that the proposed formation of the United Nations would create a new international forum for the peaceful resolution of conflicts among nations and ethnic groups. To support the effort, he appeared on the CBS special *Word from the People* on April 24, 1945, celebrating the opening of the United Nations Conference in San Francisco; the program was written and produced by "Ballad" director Norman Corwin. In addition, Robeson was the principal speaker at a series of "Win the Peace" rallies, held around the country at the end of the war to marshal public support for the United Nations and to protest against U.S. intransigence in the growing political rift with the Soviet Union.[23]

But diplomatic relations between the two postwar superpowers degenerated into a cold war, and the distraught Robeson threw his support behind the 1948 maverick presidential candidacy of Henry Wallace, former vice president in the Roosevelt administration. Standard-bearer of the newly formed Progressive Party, Wallace ran on a platform favoring cordial relations with the Soviet Union. Robeson turned down the vice presidential spot on the ticket, but he campaigned tirelessly on Wallace's behalf and was a prominent member of the Progressive Party's inner circle. During the campaign, Robeson appeared in a series of radio broadcasts on behalf of Wallace and the Progressive Party. These broadcasts marked his last hurrah on network radio. Wallace made a dismal showing at the polls, and in the context of postwar prosperity and complacency, Robeson's radical political views became increasingly controversial. His career went into a tailspin.[24]

Early in 1949, Robeson traveled to Europe for a series of concerts and speaking engagements. The leading U.S. newspapers covered his speeches in Paris and Moscow, taking his remarks out of context and sensationalizing them. He was reported as supporting the Soviet Union's view that the United States was to blame for the cold war and as saying that African Americans would not fight in a war against the Soviet Union. The mainstream press pilloried him for these remarks. The House Un-American Activities Committee (HUAC) of the U.S. Congress held a public hearing to determine whether African Americans supported such a position but did not ask Robeson to testify; instead, HUAC's chief witnesses included a black FBI informer and baseball star Jackie Robinson, the first African American to play in the major leagues. The FBI informer falsely claimed that Robeson was a member of the Communist Party and had ambitions of becoming the "black Stalin" of the United States. Robinson's comments were more judicious, but in the end, he, too, felt compelled to distance himself from the remarks attributed to Robeson—a stance that made the headlines in most of the country's leading newspapers.[25]

The HUAC hearings had a disastrous effect on Robeson's career. Job offers in theater and film dried up, speaking engagements were often canceled due to anti-Communist opposition, and his concert fee plummeted from $2,000 to $300 per performance. Moreover, the federal government confiscated his passport, making it impossible for Robeson to work in Europe—or even in Canada. In a matter of months, the media had so demonized him as a "Red menace" that his appearances in some places provoked violent protests. The most publicized incident took place in Peekskill, a small town on the Hudson River about fifty miles north of New York City. A Robeson concert scheduled to take place near Peekskill on August 27, 1949, had to be canceled after a mob of anti-Robeson protesters attacked the concertgoers; dozens had to be hospitalized. A week later, twenty thousand Robeson supporters returned to Peekskill for a rescheduled concert. They were met by about eight thousand angry demonstrators, many of whom were World War II veterans, as well as by about one thousand state police. Amid high tensions, the concert took place without incident; but when concertgoers attempted to leave in their cars and rented buses, local vigilante groups attacked them. In the melee, vehicles were overturned and set on fire, 150 people were injured seriously enough to require medical treatment, and twenty-five "union guards" protecting

Robeson were arrested by the state police. The "Peekskill Riot" received national press coverage, most of which blamed the violence on outside "Red agitators." The news media vilified Robeson for his role in the incident, and he was denounced on the floor of the U.S. Congress as a "communist agent provocateur."[26]

The coup de grâce to Paul Robeson's career in broadcasting came a few months after the Peekskill violence, in February 1950, when he was invited to appear on NBC's *Today with Mrs. Roosevelt* as part of a panel discussion on "the role of the Negro in American political life." When word of the invitation got out in the press, the network's headquarters was deluged with angry phone calls protesting Robeson's inclusion: NBC canceled his appearance on the program and banned him from ever speaking or performing on the network. Thus Robeson became the first American to be publicly blacklisted by a major broadcast network. In just a decade, he was transformed from the voice of American democracy to, as one of his adversaries put it, "the voice of the Kremlin." His career, his health, and ultimately his peace of mind were ruined.[27]

Paul Robeson was a casualty of the country's drift to the right after World War II. As the cold war gained momentum, his association with left-wing causes isolated him from the political mainstream—and to some extent, from the black community. During World War II, his support for the Soviet Union, an ally, was acceptable; at the same time, his attacks on racism were usually launched in the context of promoting racial harmony on the home front and thus were more tolerable. But in the postwar period, Robeson's unwavering defense of Communism and of the Soviets' cold war policies made him an easy target for Red-baiters; he was discredited in the public eye and marginalized politically. Robeson's downfall, however, was also orchestrated by the federal government and the mass media—perhaps, in part, as payback for his past political and racial transgressions. The government used FBI harrassment, the HUAC hearings, and the passport seizure to punish and intimidate him; the leading newspapers misrepresented his pronouncements and sensationalized his misfortunes; the major networks blacklisted him. All this was played out in the press and on the airwaves as a cautionary soap opera, a warning to others on the left—in the entertainment industry and in the black community—of the perils of siding with the Communists in the cold war.

The Robeson controversy put African Americans on the defensive, and as his troubles mounted, his stature among them lost some of its luster. In the war years, as a prominent spokesman for democracy, the war effort, and the Double V campaign, Robeson was a source of pride among African Americans and enjoyed enormous popular support. But as the cold war set in, monopolizing his political energies, Robeson lost a segment of his widespread black support. Coverage of him in much of the black press tended to recycle the mainstream media accounts of his unpopular left-wing stands, and a number of African American civil rights leaders, politicians, entertainers, sports celebrities, and labor leaders distanced themselves from him politically and personally. Stigmatized by the negative attention and stripped of his heroic cultural status, Paul Robeson faded into history as a tarnished symbol of race pride and progress.

4

"Destination Freedom"

During World War II, both the federal government and the radio industry adopted new social policies regarding African Americans. Although U.S. propaganda followed the lead of the European democracies in pointing to Hitler's megalomania and the Nazi theory of Aryan racial superiority as the root causes of the war, race relations in the United States were not, in actual practice, consistent with democratic theory or the nation's self-image. The South was still in the grip of an apartheid-like separation of the races, and in the North, racial discrimination barred African Americans from a wide range of housing, employment, and schooling opportunities, as well as social services.

In the years leading up to the war, the federal government itself continued to maintain a segregated workforce and armed forces. After the war started, however, the government greatly needed African Americans' unqualified support for the war effort—for both manpower and propaganda purposes. Political agenda setters in the black community, such as labor leader A. Philip Randolph, recognized a rare opportunity for big-ticket socioeconomic gains. In 1941, Randolph threatened to mobilize one hundred thousand African Americans for a march on Washington, D.C., if the government did not end discrimination against black workers in the war industries and the federal workforce. Partly to avoid international embarrassment,

President Franklin Delano Roosevelt issued the last-minute Executive Order 8802, banning racial discrimination in the defense plants and the federal bureaucracy. An important victory for African Americans, this move emboldened the advocates of the fledgling Double V campaign, a progressive black initiative linking victory over fascism abroad with victory over racism at home. Some saw the executive order as an indication that the Roosevelt administration, pressured by the looming world war, was willing to make significant changes in federal Jim Crow policies within the civilian workforce. The military, however, remained totally segregated.[1]

Orchestrating Racial Harmony on Wartime Radio

During the New Deal era, the Roosevelt adminstration had developed a mutually beneficial relationship with the radio networks. The networks gave the White House free access to the airwaves anytime it wished; in return, the White House took a hands-off attitude toward the regulation of commercial radio broadcasting. President Roosevelt immediately took advantage of the networks' part of the deal. In his first ten months in office, he or his surrogates spoke on radio 150 times. From 1934 to 1940, Roosevelt averaged seven major radio speeches a year. These well-crafted addresses to the American people were tailor-made for the networks. Each speech was twenty-five minutes long, topical, and aired during the prime-time evening hours. A small number of these presidential speeches were designated as "fireside chats," which became famous for their common-sense discussion of government and Roosevelt's trademark opening: "Dear Friends." Throughout the decade, the White House regularly used network radio to shape the president's public image and to popularize New Deal policies—a first in American politics.[2]

When World War II broke out in Europe, the White House moved quickly to incorporate radio into the federal government's preparations for all-out warfare. The Department of War was given the responsibility for coordinating international and domestic propaganda efforts; it set up the Office of War Information (OWI) to handle the international dimension of the project. The OWI made radio broadcasting the centerpiece of its propaganda campaign. It recruited a talented staff from the radio and advertising industries and organized two separate international broadcast networks. The first, a shortwave operation broadcast in several different languages to populations around the globe, would eventually link together dozens of shortwave stations, employ hundreds of skilled radio workers, and broadcast thousands of hours of programming. After the war, it evolved into the Voice of America. The second OWI-created network, Armed Forces Radio Service (AFRS), was designed to entertain the troops overseas. Its broadcast format mixed popular disc-jockey music shows, recycled network programs, and special AFRS productions such as *Command Performance,* a weekly variety show featuring show business luminaries in live broadcasts from Hollywood. By 1945, the AFRS was linked to more than eight hundred stations, located wherever American troops were stationed abroad.[3]

Domestic propaganda initiatives in support of the war mobilization at first were orchestrated by the War Department's public relations office. Race relations were a top priority. Radio was enlisted in the public relations office's "intergroup strategy" to promote racial harmony on the home front by means of government-produced programs and special wartime broadcasts by the commercial networks. With America's entry into the war, various federal agencies were directed to develop radio shows that addressed the race issue in a progressive manner and showcased African Americans in a positive light. One such program was *Men o' War,* a patriotic weekly musical revue produced by the U.S. Navy, with an all-black cast of sailors stationed at the Great Lakes Naval Training Center in Illinois. Initially a statewide broadcast, the series moved to CBS as a sustaining-time program in 1943 and remained on the air there until the end of the war.[4]

Perhaps the most ambitious radio production that a government agency undertook during the war years was *Freedom's People,* an eight-part series produced by the Federal Radio Education Committee in the U.S. Office of Education with "the aim of prompting national unity and better race relations." It was developed by Dr. Ambrose Caliver, a specialist in Negro education, in consultation with a team of black scholars that included Howard University professors Sterling A. Brown and E. Franklin Frazier. Each program told "the story of the American Negro" by highlighting African Americans' contributions to the nation in the areas of military service, music, science, sports, industry, education, arts, and theater. The series' all-star cast was a virtual Who's Who of black America: A. Philip Randolph, Joe Louis, Paul Robeson, W. C. Handy, George Washington Carver, Fats Waller, Canada Lee, Cab Calloway, Dorothy Maynor, Jesse Owens, Todd Duncan, Walter White, Josh White, Count Basie.

Freedom's People debuted on NBC ten days after the bombing of Pearl Harbor. The first show sought to "dramatize Negro participation in past wars." The thirty-minute special included a short docudrama, *The Battle of Henry Johnson,* about a World War I African American soldier decorated for valor. In addition, musician and composer Noble Sissle, along with Colonel West A. Hamilton, commanding officer of the 366th Infantry Division, reminisced about James Reese Europe's famous black military band, which had been attached to Hamilton's unit during World War I.[5]

The War Department also made a number of friendly interventions into network broadcasting during the war years. In early 1942, members of the department's public relations unit began to approach network executives and producers about the development of radio programming that would simultaneously support the war effort and rehabilitate the image of African Americans. Two of the networks' leading soap opera producers, Frank and Ann Hummert, responded to the urging of the War Department's experts by inserting a number of exemplary black characters into their most popular daily soaps. Among these new black role models was Franklin Brown, a young, clean-cut military enlistee, whose appearance in *Our Gal Sunday* served as a springboard for an ongoing discussion of African Americans' loyalty to their country and devotion to God. In *The Romance of Helen Trent,* the black hero was a dedicated and well-mannered medical doctor who rescued the heroine from a life-threatening situation and then became her "Negro friend." The saintly doctor went on to work as the staff physician at a defense plant. His presence in the story line generated an ongoing discussion of "the capabilities of the Negro, his unflagging loyalty to his country, and his patience with persecution."[6]

The federal government's overtures to the networks led, inadvertently, to the broadcast of *An Open Letter on Race Hatred,* the landmark radio program on domestic race relations during the war years. *Open Letter* responded to the 1943 Detroit race riot, an outbreak of racial violence that left six whites and twenty-nine African Americans dead, hundreds injured or arrested, and close to $1 million in property damage. While the local police aggressively "pacified" black looters on Hasting Street—killing seventeen African Americans in the process—white mobs were allowed to attack black citizens indiscriminately on Woodward Avenue, the city's racial dividing line. The violence ended with the arrival of federal troops, dispatched to Detroit by President Roosevelt.[7]

The bloodshed in Detroit shocked the nation. In its immediate aftermath, NAACP leader Walter White organized an effort to broadcast a special radio program on the causes and consequences of the riot. Among his recruits were William Robson, an award-winning radio dramatist with CBS, and Wendell Wilkie, the 1940 Republican Party presidential standard-bearer. Wilkie was especially instrumental in getting CBS to broadcast the show; at the time, he was in the national spotlight for the recent publication of his best-selling book *One World,* which championed the cause of worldwide peace and brotherhood. CBS, however, monitored the project closely. Network president William Paley himself reviewed three separate versions of the program before approving it. *Open Letter* scriptwriter William Robson recalled that the CBS kingpin ordered him to make a number of changes in the show before sanctioning a final revision.[8]

Even the edited version of the script was a tour de force in radio docudrama. In the opening statement, the CBS announcer solemnly warned the listening audience:

> Dear Fellow Americans: What you are about to hear may anger you. What you are about to hear may sound incredible to you. You may doubt that such things can happen today in this supposedly united nation. But we assure you, everything you are about to hear is true. And so we ask you to spend thirty minutes with us, facing quietly and without passion or prejudice, a danger which threatens all of us. A danger so great that if it is not met and conquered now, even though we win this war, we shall be defeated in victory; and the peace which follows will be for us a horror of chaos, lawlessness, and bloodshed. This danger is race hatred.[9]

The program then launched into a blistering condemnation of racism in American society, by linking the white gangs of "kluxers, cowards, and crackpots" that had wantonly attacked African Americans in Detroit to the "gangs of German youth armed with beer bottles and lead pipes" whose assertion of "mob rule" had put Adolf Hitler in power. At the conclusion of the broadcast, Wendell Wilkie stated bluntly:

> Two-thirds of the people who are our allies do not have white skins. And they have long hurtful memories of the white man's superior attitude in his dealings with them. Today the white man is profess-ing friendship and the desire to cooperate and is promising op-portunity in the world to come when the war is over. They wonder. When the necessities of war cease to make cooperation valuable to the white man, will his promises mean anything? Race riots in De-troit, Los Angeles, and Beaumont, Texas, do not reassure them. . . . Fascism is an attitude of the mind, an attitude which causes men to seek to rule others by economic, military, or political force or through prejudice. Such an attitude within our borders is as serious a threat to freedom as is the attack from without. The desire to de-prive some of our citizens of their rights—economic, civic, or po-litical—has the same basic motivation that actuates the fascist mind when it seeks to dominate peoples and nations. It is essential that we eliminate it at home as well as abroad.[10]

An Open Letter on Race Hatred won the prestigious Peabody Award for broadcasting excellence in 1943. The same year, *Time* magazine praised it as "one of the most elegant programs in radio history."[11]

In addition to such special noncommercial broadcasts and the soap operas, the networks opened up their public-affairs programming to African Americans. After more than a decade of neglect, the most presti-gious public-affairs forums on network radio began to broadcast frank dis-cussions on race relations and the status of black America. NBC's *America's Town Meeting on the Air* led the way. In 1942, it broadcast a roundtable dis-cussion on African Americans' contributions to the war effort that fea-tured only black participants—a network first. The program revisited the issue of race over the next three years, in broadcasts that always included at least one prominent black spokesperson; poet Langston Hughes, labor leader A. Philip Randolph, author Richard Wright, concert vocalist Mar-ian Anderson, and civil rights leader Walter White appeared on the show as panelists during the war years. Likewise, CBS's renowned public-affairs forum *People's Platform* began to utilize interracial panels in addressing formerly taboo topics, such as "Is the South Solving Its Race Problem?" broadcast in December 1944.[12]

Both networks also produced a variety of special public-affairs offerings that boosted the war effort in one way or another and, in the process, occasionally valorized African Americans' role in that endeavor. For example, NBC's much ballyhooed *The Army Hour*, which each week documented the experiences of American troops in the field, featured programs on African American units in all three armed services. CBS's award-winning series on ethnic diversity in the armed forces, *They Call Me Joe*, included a show on a black serviceman, and CBS produced *The Negro in the War*, a 1945 radio documentary on the wartime contributions made by black soldiers, factory workers, and journalists. Also in 1945, NBC broadcast *Too Long, America*, a public-affairs program on the racial barriers that African Americans in the workforce encountered, narrated by Hollywood film star Edward G. Robinson and concluded by New York City mayor Fiorello LaGuardia.[13]

The radio campaign to present positive and humane images of African Americans broadened to include the AFRS, which, among other things, was dedicated to countering Axis broadcast propaganda, some of which targeted black troops stationed abroad. Axis propaganda focusing on African Americans was somewhat inconsistent in its messages but broadly aimed at promoting racial animosity. Nazi broadcasters such as "Axis Sally" denigrated black servicemen, calling them subhuman cowards and slackers, in order to fuel white racism among American troops. In contrast, the Japanese propaganda broadcasts of the notorious "Tokyo Rose" often made sympathetic overtures to black troops by playing the popular race records of the era and condemning their segregated, second-class status in the armed forces; here the tactic was to nurture racial antagonism by encouraging the disaffection of African American servicemen.[14]

In response, the AFRS not only included black military personnel in its broadcast operations but also developed special programs targeting African American troops stationed abroad. A few of the African Americans in the armed forces who had experience in radio broadcasting, such as Wonderful Smith, were assigned to the AFRS. Smith worked as a disc jockey on a station in Calcutta, India, and was surprised by the amount of latitude he was given in producing the show. Prior to the war, on *The Red Skelton Show*, Wonderful Smith had regularly appeared in a stereotypical role that required him to speak in a blackface dialect. Now, with the AFRS, he was allowed to use his own voice, develop his own comic monologues, and choose his own records. Wartime radio seemed to be changing the racial rules dramatically.[15]

The Hollywood entertainment division of the AFRS produced two major weekly wartime variety shows that prominently featured black entertainers: *The Mildred Bailey Show* and *Jubilee*. *The Mildred Bailey Show*, hosted by the well-known female jazz pianist and vocalist, featured an interracial lineup of guest jazz artists in live jam sessions. Among those who appeared regularly on the show were bandleaders Benny Goodman, Count Basie, Paul Whiteman, and Tommy Dorsey; pianists Teddy Wilson and Mary Lou Williams; drummer Gene Krupa; swing fiddler Stuff Smith; and vibraphonist Red Norvo (Bailey's husband). Late in the war, the series was taken over by CBS, which continued to produce it for both the AFRS and the company's network outlets.[16]

Jubilee, a weekly program that originated in 1942 with primarily black talent, featured black comedy and a wider variety of African American music than the jazz-oriented *Mildred Bailey* series. During the war years, *Jubilee* showcased the most popular African American entertainers in the country: jazz bands led by Louis Armstrong, Lionel Hampton, Count Basie, and Jimmy Lunceford; the International Sweethearts of Rhythm, a female swing band with a large following among black servicemen; vocal harmony groups such as the Mills Brothers, the Golden Gate Quartet, the Ink Spots, the Delta Rhythm Boys, and the Charioteers; popular female vocalists such as Ella Fitzgerald, Dinah Washington, and Lena Horne; comedy stars such as Eddie "Rochester" Anderson, Butterfly McQueen, Wonderful Smith, Eddie Green, and Ernest Whitman (who often served as master of ceremonies); popular male vocalists such as Nat King Cole and Louis Jordan; blues legend Leadbelly (Huddie Ledbetter); Hollywood film star Hattie McDaniel; and the ubiquitous Brown Bomber, Joe Louis.[17]

Typical of a *Jubilee* production is the 1943 broadcast featuring Lena Horne and Eddie Anderson. The show begins with master of ceremonies Ernest Whitman introducing the Tiny Bradshaw Orchestra, which performs the upbeat "Hit That Jive Jack," with Tiny on vocals. Next up are the Charioteers, who sing "A Slip of the Lip Can Sink a Ship" after the vocal group's leader, Wilfred Williams, dedicates the song to the GIs overseas. Whitman then introduces the female star of the show, Lena Horne, who sings a sultry "Shoo Shoo Baby"; she is joined by Eddie Anderson to perform a comedy skit promoting their upcoming film, *Broadway Rhythm*.

Then they sing a novelty tune called "Solid Potato Salad" and wish the troops in the field a fond farewell. After a comedy monologue by Whitman, the show concludes with "Rockaway" by Tiny Bradshaw and his band. The AFRS continued to produce and broadcast *Jubilee* well into the postwar era, but in time, the balance of talent shifted from black to white entertainers.[18]

While most of the AFRS's network entertainment programs were produced by its Hollywood division, the War Department's Information and Education Division, based in Washington, D.C., produced a variety of public-affairs and educational programs for distribution on the AFRS, some of which dealt with African Americans in the military and on the home front. For example, the Information and Education Division's radio unit produced *U.S.S. Booker T. Washington,* an AFRS special commemorating the maiden voyage of the navy's first all-black destroyer. It also created a program on the USS *Campbell,* an all-black Coast Guard cutter that destroyed six Axis submarines, which was broadcast as part of the AFRS's *Man behind the Gun* series.[19]

As the war drew to a close, the acceptance of this sort of black programming in the AFRS began to diminish. In 1945, the American Negro Theater produced a radio program called "The Story They'll Never Print" for the AFRS series *This Is the Story.* The script for the show relied on case studies of factory integration conducted by the Urban League, dramatizing how black and white workers could coexist in the same factory without racial antagonism. The program cleared all the censorship hurdles in the War Department, but the colonel in charge of program distribution at the AFRS branch in Hollywood destroyed the master copy of the show, with the explanation that "no nigger-loving shit goes out over this network!"[20] The incident suggests that racist attitudes had not actually diminished in the military. Radio's wartime focus on African Americans and on the need for racial harmony would not survive the peace.

Retrenchment and Red-Baiting in Postwar Radio

Commercial radio slowly returned to business as usual when the war ended. With respect to race relations, the industry largely reverted to the pre–World War II status quo. The token number of African American programs aired by the networks only generated controversy. In February 1946, CBS produced an extravaganza in honor of National Negro Newspaper Week; the integrated lineup included Frank Sinatra, Rex Ingram, Dr. Charles Drew, Joe Louis, Jackie Robinson, Ella Fitzgerald, the Ink Spots, Paul Robeson, and a special message from President Harry Truman. The majority of CBS's Southern affiliates refused to broadcast the show. In the summer of 1946, NBC launched *The Nat King Cole Show,* and at about the same time, CBS introduced *Night Life,* featuring a black master of ceremonies named Willie Bryant and live broadcasts from Harlem. The latter show's racially mixed cast prompted more protests from the network's Southern affiliates and was dropped from the schedule. Similar problems beset *The Nat King Cole Show,* which lasted only three months before NBC pulled the plug. Later in the decade, the upstart Mutual Broadcasting System aired a four-part series titled *To Secure These Rights;* the program dramatized the findings of President Truman's Commission on Civil Rights. A bloc of Southern stations affiliated with Mutual refused to broadcast the series, and a coalition of Southern politicians demanded and received rebuttal time on the network. Other short-lived black radio ventures on the networks included a Mahalia Jackson gospel show on CBS and *The Jackie Robinson Show* on the fledgling ABC network. A lack of commercial sponsors and resistance from Southern broadcasters again forced the programs off the air. Meanwhile, *Amos 'n' Andy* expanded into a half-hour comedy serial, and the characters of Beulah on *The Fibber McGee and Molly Show* and Rochester on *The Jack Benny Show* continued to thrive. In effect, blackface comics were reinstalled as the dominant radio portrayals of African Americans.[21]

In the face of this postwar retrenchment, African Americans and their allies in the radio industry continued to protest against racial discrimination and stereotyping in commercial broadcasting. The more blatant stereotypes, such as Aunt Jemima, became the targets of angry criticism and threatened product boycotts. In May 1946, the Twelfth Annual Conference of the Ohio State University Institute for Education by Radio featured a panel discussion on African Americans in radio broadcasting. One panelist, *Open Letter* scriptwriter William Robson, criticized the typecasting of African Americans as "Uncle Toms and Aunt Jemimas" because it reinforced "white racial supremacy." A second panelist, *Billboard* magazine editor Lou Frankel, stated candidly: "Radio is not contributing a damn thing to better race relations. With few exceptions, radio still handles the Negro in the same old Uncle Tom, crap-shooting minstrel tradition."[22]

But by the end of the 1940s, rising domestic cold war tensions were adversely affecting the struggle against racial barriers and stereotyping in the radio industry. The networks carried live HUAC's series of controversial hearings on suspected Communist subversives in the Hollywood entertainment industries. In the aftermath of these hearings, a small cadre of ex-FBI agents began to compile dossiers on suspected Communist sympathizers in broadcasting and film. In a newsletter and then in a 1950 book titled *Red Channels,* they listed these individuals and cited their alleged pro-Communist activities. The list was virtually a roll call of the most progressive people in the entertainment industries, especially those most active in the struggles for civil rights and racial equality: radio producer Norman Corwin, conductor Leonard Bernstein, composer Aaron Copland, director-actor Orson Welles, playwright Lillian Hellman, actor Phillip Loeb (who was cited for sponsoring the End Jim Crow in Baseball Committee), and radio dramatist William Robson. Loeb and Robson soon could find no employment in their professions. Many of those cited in *Red Channels* were as good as blacklisted by the networks, which were imposing loyalty oaths on their employees.[23]

Red Channels also cited distinguished African Americans in show business who were in the forefront of the struggle for racial justice, and their careers suffered accordingly. Cited along with Paul Robeson were Langston Hughes, Lena Horne, actor Canada Lee, writers Theodore Wald and Shirley Graham, radio producer Michael Grayson, jazz pianist Hazel Scott, actress Freddie Washington, and folksinger Josh White. Distraught by the damaging accusations, White appeared as a "friendly" witness at the HUAC hearings in order to distance himself from the leftist cultural politics of Robeson and Lee, both of whom he specifically condemned.[24]

Cold war Red-baiting increased the risks for African Americans who criticized the persistence of racism in the radio industry. Many refused to bow to the threat of the blacklist—a doubly significant term in this situation. In New York, the Committee for the Negro in the Arts sponsored a conference on "Television, Radio and the Negro People" in June 1949. The committee's report to the conference documented the exclusion of African Americans from radio industry jobs as executives, producers, directors, technicians, and commentators. In addition, it criticized the continuing stereotypical portrayal of African Americans on network radio. The report concluded: "The truth about the American Negro is not held a fit subject for radio. The Negro is isolated and misunderstood and not allowed to communicate. Radio today has posed for each of us the question: Is the greatness and humanity of Negro America, of Crispus Attucks, Frederick Douglass, Marian Anderson, Paul Robeson and Jackie Robinson, to be presented over the radio channels forever in terms of Amos 'n' Andy and Beulah?"[25] A month after the conference, actor Canada Lee echoed the criticism of the committee report in an interview printed in *Variety* magazine. Lee might have been alluding to accusations in *Red Channels* when he stated that an "Iron Curtain" prevented African Americans from entering the field of broadcasting, resulting in blackface stereotypes dominating the portrayal of African Americans on network radio while their real life stories and characters were ignored.[26]

Black Radio Drama and
Docudrama: *New World a-Coming*

An outspoken critic of Jim Crow in the radio industry, Canada Lee also was a central figure in one of the most provocative and innovative black radio series of the wartime and postwar eras. *New World a-Coming*, adapted from journalist Roi Ottley's popular book of the same name, premiered in 1944 on WMCA, a New York City outlet not affiliated with a network. The weekly program was broadcast from 3:00 to 3:30 P.M. on Sundays and sponsored by a Harlem civic group. Ottley wrote the early scripts and also narrated a few; Michael Grayson produced and directed the series; Duke Ellington wrote the theme song; and Canada Lee served as narrator for much of the series and acted in many of the dramatic productions.[27]

In its thirteen-year history, *New World a-Coming* featured a wide spectrum of programming—from dramas to documentaries, from live broadcasts of famous entertainers to special tributes to prominent black leaders. The radio documentaries usually dealt with local or race issues; approaches and topics varied. Specific programs on housing, hospitals, and health care in Harlem, as well as more generalized soundscapes such as

"Harlem: Anatomy of a Ghetto," were mixed with special programs on black orphans, nurses, and churches in the metropolitan area and even a groundbreaking exposé of the plight of Puerto Ricans in New York City, which won the coveted Peabody Award for broadcasting excellence. Other documentary-oriented programs in the series included "Hot Spot U.S.A.," a look at housing discrimination in industrial centers, and "Apartheid in South Africa," another Peabody Award winner. In "The Story of Negro Music," Canada Lee's narration traces the evolution of African rhythms and native songs into slave spirituals and secular music, which in turn evolved into ragtime, blues, and jazz. The music on the program was performed by a local gospel choir and an all-star jazz band featuring pianist Art Tatum and vocalist Billie Holiday.[28]

Most of the factual stories told on *New World a-Coming* could aptly be described as "docudramas," in that all the historical events depicted in the series were dramatic reconstructions of the past. In the 1930s, the CBS-sponsored series *March of Time,* produced by *Time* magazine, had pioneered this practice of restaging history for public consumption over the airwaves. The technique was fairly common in radio broadcasting when *New World a-Coming* began to use it in the mid-1940s. The series' "Story of the Vermont Experiment," for example, is a docudrama on a church project that placed black youths from Harlem in the homes of white families in rural Vermont for a few weeks in the summer. The project was hailed in New York's black press as a model for building good race relations. In the radio broadcast, the two ministers responsible for the project, Adam Clayton Powell in Harlem and Richard Lowe in Vermont, played themselves; they restaged a series of conversations with each other that highlighted the birth and evolution of the experiment. In addition, a series of short vignettes dramatize the interactions between the black youths and their hosts. Apprehensions are expressed on both sides of the color line, but race barriers are soon broken down and new bonds of friendship and mutual understanding begin to emerge. At the conclusion of the program, narrator Canada Lee proclaims: "The Vermont Experiment is a significant development in the progress of good race relations in this country, a milestone on the road to a New World a-Coming!"[29]

In addition to the fact-oriented docudramas, *New World a-Coming* broadcast a number of fictional docudramas that focused on current social problems. Much of the program "Negroes in the Entertainment

Industry" is devoted to this sort of dramatization. After an introduction that critically alludes to the underemployment of African Americans in the performing arts, the program presents a fictional sketch of a young black musician named Sonny, whose ambition is to become a concert pianist. Forced to join a dance band to make a living, he endures low pay, long hours, and racial discrimination while traveling with the band on the road. Returning home, he considers quitting music and going to work as an elevator operator, like his father. But in the end, his mother admonishes him: "Get some fight back in you!" As the theme music rises to a crescendo, Canada Lee states: "Sonny's story is the story of thousands of Negroes in the entertainment field today. Traditionally, it was supposed to offer real opportunities for Negroes, but the specter of race prejudice pursues the Negro entertainer wherever he turns. What an irony it is, when much of the music that identifies America to the world rose from the voices of American black men." To emphasize the message of the dramatization, pianist Hazel Scott is introduced. She recounts how, as a young girl, she also had ambitions to be a concert pianist but was eventually forced to play jazz on the nightclub circuit in order to survive. As if to prove her point, Scott proceeds to play a jazzy version of a Rachmaninoff composition, to end the show.[30]

In addition to the docudramas, *New World a-Coming* experimented with serious dramatic productions, especially those dealing with race relations. Some were based on original radio scripts, while others adapted plays, novels, or short stories—for instance Dorothy Parker's short story "Arrangements in Black and White" and Howard Fast's epic novel about the Reconstruction era, *Freedom's Road,* which was presented in two parts on successive Sundays. Parker's story, scripted for radio by Roi Ottley, is a cautionary tale for white folks on race relations. The action takes place in a fashionable East Side penthouse in New York City, where a renowned black concert vocalist, Walter Williams, is giving a private concert. A frivolous white guest, Mrs. Burton, asks the hostess of the recital to introduce her to Williams, in the process revealing an appalling naïveté with respect to African Americans and their culture. After meeting the famous vocalist, Mrs. Burton exclaims to the hostess: "I haven't any feeling at all because he's a colored man. Wait until I tell Burton [her husband] that I called him mister!" There is a sharp musical sting; then the narrator concludes:

Yes, she called him mister. Obviously, there's nothing world shak-
ing about this, and you may rightly say I know no such person. But
this woman, like thousands, is the victim of the popular miscon-
ceptions about Negroes. Too often has she seen Negroes in motion
pictures and radio caricatured as lazy buffoons, naive children, and
faithful servants enchanted by their white masters. Thus, when the
races meet much embarrassment follows, for well-intentioned
meetings may hurt, even anger Negroes. Today's presentation was
offered as a sort of guide of what not to do in similar circumstances.
The truth is people like Mrs. Burton become fewer in number as
democracy is extended in American life.[31]

One of the original dramatic scripts produced for *New World a-Coming,*
titled "The Mammy Legend," deconstructs this centuries-old black female
stereotype. Narrator Canada Lee introduced the show by stating: "If there
is one thing that irritates Negroes today it is the Mammy legend, often ro-
manticized in song and story. Yes, of course the Mammy did exist once.
For at least two centuries she was an institution of the Old South. But today that Mammy has become largely a fiction, a museum piece of slavery
days. Yes, it is true that Mammy doesn't live here anymore. Yet you still
hear people say. . . ." White voices follow in a collage, making stereotypical remarks about black female maids and domestics. Lee's comment that
the persistence of such racist attitudes can lead to conflicts between employers and employees frames a story about one such maid, Martha, and
her white employers, the Milburns. Martha has worked for the Milburns
for ten years and has practically raised their son, Junior; her own son,
Charlie, is in military training to be a pilot. When Charlie visits unexpectedly, he gets into a discussion with the Milburns and their guests about segregation in the armed forces. Charlie's view that segregation is antidem-
ocratic and therefore incompatible with the country's professed ideals
makes his white audience uneasy. After Charlie leaves, Martha overhears
Mr. Milburn telling one of his guests that Charlie's "radical" ideas will get
him into trouble in the "real world" and lecturing Junior about the perils
of "mixing with colored people." The father is obviously upset by Junior's
admiration of Charlie during his brief visit. This lesson so angers Martha
that she confronts the Milburns about indoctrinating their son with their
racial prejudices. Although Mr. Milburn apologizes, Martha quits and

goes to work in a parachute factory. In the last scene, Junior visits her in her new apartment. Delighted to see him, she invites him, saying: "In my house, friends are always welcome!"[32]

New World a-Coming also broadcast a number of tribute extravaganzas for famous people and special events, modeled after those produced by Norman Corwin. During the war years, Corwin's productions included a tribute to D day forces and a memorial for President Roosevelt. Postwar tributes on *New World a-Coming* focused on African Americans and their achievements. For example, "Tribute to Canada Lee" was staged during the actor's celebrated portrayal of Bigger Thomas in the Broadway adaptation of Richard Wright's controversial novel *Native Son*. The show was produced in conjunction with the Mutual Broadcasting System, which offered it to member stations nationwide. Paul Robeson, as master of ceremonies, hosted the entertainment, which began with a short comedy skit by Hattie McDaniel and Eddie "Rochester" Anderson, broadcast live from Hollywood. (It is interesting that Anderson agreed to appear on the show, despite Lee's public criticism of Rochester as a degrading stereotype.) The broadcast also featured Bill "Bojangles" Robinson tap-dancing on the air, music by Duke Ellington and his orchestra, W. C. Handy playing the "Saint Louis Blues" on his trumpet, a congratulatory telegram from Joe Louis, and a segment from the stage version of *Native Son*. Even Richard Wright was on hand to praise Canada Lee's many accomplishments, Lee himself came forward at the end of the program to thank everyone.[33]

For his part, Robeson gave a short keynote address and sang a song that he said he wrote for the show "in the spirit of Native Son":

Jim Crow

Lincoln set the Negro free
Why is he still in slavery?
Why is he still in slavery?
Jim Crow.

This is the land we call our own
Why does the Negro ride alone?
Why does the Negro ride alone?
Jim Crow.

When it's time to go to the polls
Why does the Negro stay at home?
Why does the Negro stay at home?
Jim Crow.

Freedom for all it is said
Freedom to suffer until he's dead
Freedom to suffer until he's dead
From Jim Crow.

If we believe in liberty
Let's put an end to slavery
Let's put an end to slavery
From Jim Crow.[34]

Even when staging what was essentially a black radio variety show, *New World a-Coming* sustained a critical edge in confronting racial discrimination and stereotyping. It consistently broadcast programs that viewed race relations in American society through the prism of African American history and culture. But the series reached only local listeners in New York City. The rest of the national radio audience had few alternatives to the networks' standard fare of Amos and Andy, Beulah, and Rochester.

Richard Durham's *Destination Freedom*

The other critically acclaimed black radio series in the postwar era to utilize the docudrama format was *Destination Freedom*. Also a half-hour program broadcast on Sunday afternoons (over NBC-affiliated WMAQ in Chicago), it ran from June 1948 to October 1950. The talented creator and writer of the show, Richard Durham, had worked as an editor for the *Chicago Defender* and *Ebony* magazine. He had also written radio scripts for two Chicago-based productions: *Democracy USA,* a 1946 series on famous African Americans who had made contributions to the struggle for democracy at home and abroad, and *Here Comes Tomorrow,* a soap opera set in Chicago's Southside ghetto. But Durham's greatest achievement in radio was the consistent quality of the scripts he wrote for *Destination Freedom*. All 105 scripts were meticulously researched dramatizations of black history and culture, focusing on the struggles and achievements of a broad range of African American leaders: lawyers, preachers, doctors, soldiers, scholars, politicians, entertainers, authors, athletes, and artists. To dramatize these "real-life stories," Durham worked with the W. E. B. Du Bois Theater Guild, a local group of socially conscious actors that included Oscar Brown Jr., Janice Kingslow, Wezlen Tilden, Jack Gibson, Fred Pinkard, and Studs Terkel. The *Defender* sponsored the first thirteen docudramas; the remainder were sustaining-time programs sponsored by WMAQ, the same station that had launched the *Amos 'n' Andy* serial two decades earlier.[35]

Thematically, *Destination Freedom* resonated to the political and social conflicts that were at the heart of the black experience in America up to the cold war. The plots brought to life the horrors of Southern slavery, Jim Crow segregation, lynching, and disenfranchisement from the perspective of the victims. Racial discrimination in education, employment, housing, transportation, and public accommodations received critical attention in Durham's scripts, as did the struggles to overturn these injustices. In most instances, the heroes in the historical docudramas were achievers and activists who found themselves constantly at odds with the racism entrenched in American society. The sagas depicted such figures as Crispus Attucks, holding firm to his convictions in the face of entrenched Revolutionary-era racial bigotry; Frederick Douglass, challenging the cultural and legal basis of slavery ("We will have no peace until all men are free in public opinion as well as law!"); and Ida B. Wells, arguing that lynching was not a "moral" issue but "a matter of murder for money and jobs." All of Durham's scripts illuminated the clash between democratic ideals and the brutal realities of race in the United States, investing every story with compelling tension and psychological depth.[36]

Richard Durham's efforts to reconstruct the heroic dimensions of the black experience in America reinforced the radical message in his radio plays. His quest for an authentic history of African Americans led him to the writings of W. E. B. Du Bois, Carter G. Woodson, and John Hope Franklin. Du Bois and Woodson also proved valuable protagonists for two of Durham's more provocative docudramas. The script "Searcher for History" dramatized Du Bois's contributions to the struggle for racial equality and to scholarship on black history. Du Bois sought to illuminate the past because "only in the light of truth and publicity can we begin to dissolve discrimination and race hatred." Likewise, Carter G. Woodson, as a "Recorder of History," worked to "uncover the treasures of Negro life so that America's goal of equality and justice may be strengthened by the knowledge of their struggle for freedom in the past."[37] In both episodes, a true understanding of the past opened the way for a brighter future.

The panorama of African American history gave Durham a rich assortment of heroic figures as dramatic subjects. In particular, it enabled him to venerate an array of leaders of African descent who were in the forefront of the rebellion against slavery: Frederick Douglass, Harriet Tubman, Gabriel Prosser, Crispus Attucks, and Denmark Vesey, as well as the liberators of Haiti, Henri Christophe and Toussaint L'Ouverture. The Denmark Vesey docudrama focused on the cadre of revolutionaries who plotted the Charleston, South Carolina, slave insurrection: Vesey, who had purchased his own freedom; Rolla Hand, a trusted house servant of a prominent white Charleston family; Paul Poyeus, the major black preacher in the city; and Gullah Jack, an African conjurer with a loyal following among the field slaves working on the plantations around Charleston. Durham's script brings this diverse group to life, with each individual contributing something different to the cadre and taking on a specific role in advancing the plot. Their common cause and strong bonds with one another are symbolic of their solidarity against slavery: none is free until all are free. Denmark Vesey summarizes the insurrection's credo at his trial, when he tells the judge who has just condemned him to death:

> My treachery began when I read the Declaration of Independence. It said all men were created equal. It grew when I read that black Crispus Attucks died to help the colonies become free. Did he die just to free white men or all men? Then I read what Ben Franklin, Tom Paine, Lafayette, and Jefferson had said, and their words warmed my blood. They wanted their revolution to make all men free and equal. But they stopped with some men free and some men slaves. I took up where they left off. I found my price when I was a slave. I paid it. If my life is the price I pay to be free—take it. But until all men are free and equal—the revolution goes on.[38]

Destination Freedom championed the cause of freedom and equality not only for all men but also for all women. Years before either civil rights or women's rights was placed on the postwar national agenda, Richard Durham was agitating for both in his docudramas. Alongside Crispus Attucks, Denmark Vesey, Frederick Douglass, and W. E. B. Du Bois in his dramas were Harriet Tubman, Sojourner Truth, Ida B. Wells, Mary Church Terrell, Mary McCleod Bethune, Marian Anderson, Katherine Durnham, and Gwendolyn Brooks. These black women, oppressed because of their race and their sex, developed a double political consciousness. As Sojourner Truth says to her captors as they prepare to burn her at the stake for her opposition to slavery: "Where half the world is servant to the white man—there is no peace. . . . Burning me will not burn out the right women have to be free, to choose their own ways of life, to be their own masters!"[39] Mary Church Terrell, a prominent feminist and civic leader in the early 1900s, also articulates this crucial synthesis of race and gender consciousness when addressing a hostile crowd of white women, in a program called "The Long Road":

> Women! Since when have we needed cowards in bedsheets and masks with shotguns to safeguard our persons and our homes? The only protection women need is protection by equality under the law. Equality of opportunity and the right to share the benefits of this land alongside men. Equality to choose an associate without fear of intimidation by bigots and the hissing of cowards. That's why I'm staying in the South and getting Negro and white women together—to find their freedom together. In the right to vote and the right to work will freedom be found—for once a white woman bows down to white masculinism, she is ready for slavery.[40]

In some instances, *Destination Freedom* made common cause with the anticolonial struggles of people of color in other countries. African Americans' struggle against racism and exploitation in the United States made them kindred spirits with those in Africa and Asia who were fighting for liberation from foreign domination. In fact, Durham perceived African Americans as a "universal people," able to join together with and inspire the downtrodden all over the planet. The longevity of their ordeal in the New World, as well as their resilience in the face of constant oppression, made them ideal advocates for the struggling masses everywhere. In Durham's words:

> It so happens that there has come to be created in America a people whose emotional fabrics and repeated experiences bring them very close to becoming in this Atomic Age the universal people. While some leaders may have difficulty identifying their lives with this mainstream—a Negro personality undergoing the experiences of segregation and sharecropping it is instantly recognizable to the 500,000,000 Chinese people who have undergone the same experience under imperialism for three hundred years. A Negro character confused by the caste system in the land of his birth is instantly identifiable to the 450,000,000 Indians in Asia and the 150,000,000 Africans in Africa, with Burmese Malayans, with the Jewish people whose identical struggle has led to the creation of a new nation, and with millions of Europeans and white Americans who also want to uproot poverty and prejudice.[41]

Richard Durham's *Destination Freedom* elicited popular and critical acclaim during its two years on WMAQ, winning praise from the governor of Illinois, Adlai Stevenson, and the noted producer Norman Corwin, as well as an award from the Institute for Education by Radio at Ohio State University. By 1950 and the start of the Korean War, however, the black focus of the program had become a casualty of the political conservatism of the times. After Durham and the Du Bois acting troupe left the series, whose name was unchanged, a fictitious "Paul Revere" became the host for programs dramatizing stories on white American war heroes such as Nathan Hale and Dwight David Eisenhower.[42]

Undoubtedly, the militant African American characters and heroic themes of *Destination Freedom* violated the network's sense of what was politically correct for the time. From the series' inception, Durham struggled with his NBC supervisors over the portrayal of his characters and the direction of his plots. He defined his purpose in a written introduction to the series: "To break through stereotypes—shatter the conventions and traditions which have prevented us from dramatizing the infinite store of material from history and current struggles for freedom."[43] His supervisors wanted a different approach, and initially, they tried to assign several script proposals to in-house NBC staff writers. Durham asserted that the program's concept and script proposals were copyrighted by him and threatened to take them elsewhere if he were denied authorship and control over the final product. When the staff director assigned to the program by NBC attempted to change the character of Crispus Attucks in the very first production, Durham responded with a lengthy and passionate justification of his characterizations. Arguing for the representation of black agency in history, he demolished the conventional portrayals of African American heroes:

> What I as a writer am striving to accomplish with certain major Negro characters . . . [is] to portray Negro people as they actually are; as I know them, see them, live with them, as I know they think, react and feel in certain positions, and not as they are portrayed or characterized (or sub-characterized) in movies and on the radio in general. . . . A Negro character will be rebellious, biting, scorning, angry, cocky, as the occasion calls for—not forever humble, meek, etc., as some would like to imagine him. . . . White people have cushioned themselves into dreaming that Negroes are not self-assertive, confident, and never leave the realm of fear and subservience—to portray them as they are will give a greater education to the audience than a dozen lectures on the subject. . . . [The Negro's] role in society and history has been so distorted—so much based on illusion, chauvinism, and conjecture—so much a part of the psychological need of a good many whites for some excuses to carry on untenable attitudes—that the first point in the series was to bring up some little known facts of history which would give the audience a new insight on people in general. . . . Attucks picked his own destination, others didn't pick it for him. . . . Your Attucks had somewhat the approach of an intelligent pullman porter. Not the biting, fighting hero which would have carried the audience with him—at least the Negro audience. In other words, these characters are leaders, initiators of historical movements—not accidents. In most cases they were in their time leaders of white groups as well as Negro groups—as was the case with Attucks or Frederick Douglass. For instance, to present Harriet Tubman as a sort of refined version of Aunt Jemima would be

criminal. To present her as a sort of religious fanatic would be far-fetched. To present her as so many Negro women are—dauntless, determined, who have a healthy contempt for people who live by race prejudice and who are quick to recognize and extend a warm hand to other humans, would be an honest, but for radio, a radical approach. . . . Negroes in general believe that their complete, full scale emancipation is inevitable. No amount of demands for abnormal subservience, segregation, or denials can stop it. They take equality as a matter of fact—as most people take the fact that two times two equal four.[44]

Perhaps Durham unwittingly predicted the program's shift away from African American subject matter when he identified his approach as "radical" for radio. The political climate of cold war America was not hospitable to radicals, black or white.

Like *New World a-Coming*, the quality, acclaim, and relevance of *Destination Freedom* did not bring it in reach of a national audience; it was aired only locally. In common with other radio shows in major urban centers during this period, it also struggled to survive against competition from television. As commercial television became widely available, cataclysmic changes occurred in the programming formats and the economic structure of the radio industry. The networks abandoned the production of radio programs in a rush, in order to establish themselves in television. Taking with them radio's most popular entertainers and the national advertisers, the networks (with the help of the advertising industry) reorganized the national radio market into a nationwide television market. The established advertising agencies retained their consumer and customer bases, transferring them to a new medium. If the radio stations affiliated with the networks could not afford to switch to television broadcasting, they were left without their major source of programming and advertising revenues. Local stations suddenly had to find new sources of programming, new advertisers, and new audiences. Although these rapid changes devastated the national scope of commercial radio broadcasting in the short run, they also created the conditions in which the first black-oriented radio stations could be established. It was an unexpected opportunity for black broadcasters and entrepreneurs, long denied a role in the industry.

PART III

"Rappin' the Mike": Black Appeal Radio

From the top of the hill stroll the mellow frames,
threaded on down and nobody be lame.
There's Sue from Vine Nine, Rocket Kitty and O'wee Fine,
Dottie Dee, Mabel and Jan, the Martin Sisters with their
    terrible tan.
. . . .
Yes the Gators are sliddin' in, draped in their mud fronts,
so sharp and fly don't nobody grunt.
Zig zag pockets on one button rolls,
bolero jackets strictly for strolls.
All the cats are hipped to the tip and draped on down,
here are a few of the crazy cats who came to town.
There's Daddy Rabbit with the do-rag habit,
and Ice Cube Slim in his pork pie brim.
My man Jivin' Joe with Charlie the Blowtop,
check out Frantic Fred and Heavy Hiphop,
. . . .
The stash begins to rock, the band starts hopping,
the real gone Gators hit the floor and start bopping.
Now if there's no rootin' and tootin'
won't be no cuttin' and shootin'.
Don't start no slippin' and slidin'
won't be no ambulance ridin'.

          —Lavada Durst (Doctor Hep Cat),
           aircheck, KVET, Austin, Texas

5

Buying Time and
Making Rhyme

During the fall of 1948 in Austin, Texas, listeners who tuned in to station KUET's new late-night disc jockey were no doubt shocked to hear the unfamiliar voice and diction of "Doctor Hep Cat," rapping about the sporting crowd on hand for a local black dance concert. His sudden appearance on the airwaves, along with the emergence of numerous other African American DJs, heralded a new era in the development of black radio nationwide. Before this new era—that is, until the late 1940s—ethnic radio stations operating in large urban centers such as Chicago and New York City provided African Americans with their only broadcast outlets. At first, the time-brokered programs that black entrepreneurs created on these stations were exercises in racial uplift and assimilation; the hosts aspired to sound like the professional broadcast announcers of the day, and they played only the more refined and sophisticated jazz records during their shows. Jack Cooper had pioneered this style of announcing and the accompanying jazz music format in Chicago on WSBC in the early 1930s. By the end of the decade, his model had been adopted by several local protégés and had spread to outlets in nearby Hammond, Indiana, and Detroit, as well as to Washington, D.C., Philadelphia, New York City, and Seattle. To say that these disc jockeys were pioneers rather than revolutionaries in no way trivializes what they accomplished.

The Earliest Black Disc Jockeys

Among the pioneers of the 1930s, Eddie Honesty became a fixture on WJOB in Hammond; his daily music show, *Rocking in Rhythm,* featured discs by the popular swing bands of the era—black and white. Honesty, the son of a Memphis college professor, was educated at Howard and Fisk Universities. He broke into radio as an engineer in Chicago, before moving on to the Hammond station. Like Jack Cooper, Eddie Honesty used standard American English on the air; a number of his fellow black DJs remember him as sounding white. His playlists tended to favor "the better type of jazz," as one of his colleagues observed, while avoiding "suggestive blues."[1]

In the Detroit radio market, two black entrepreneurs were brokering airtime on separate stations by the late 1930s. Ed Baker on WJIB, like Jack Cooper, launched his own advertising agency to boost his on-air sales. By the mid-1940s, he employed a staff of twelve and was the second-highest-paid African American radio announcer in the country. Van Douglas on WJBK, a Virginia native, migrated to Detroit in the 1930s and majored in speech at Wayne State University. In addition to his daily jazz show on WJBK, he was employed from time to time as a professional announcer to read commercial copy.

Out on the West Coast, the first black radio show host was Bass Harris, whose two-hour daily afternoon program premiered in 1933 on KING in Seattle, Washington. The son of a local minister, Harris was known for his relaxed, baritone vocal delivery and his ability to ad-lib commercials. His playlists featured the popular swing-band hits of the era, and initially, as much as half of his audience was white.[2]

On the East Coast, WDAS in Philadelphia began to broadcast special African American programs on a brokerage basis as early as 1930. By the end of the decade, the station's most successful black music show was the *Negro Swing Parade,* hosted by African American disc jockeys who played race records. The program was profitable enough to sponsor live remote broadcasts from local clubs that showcased black musicians. In New York City, two radio outlets—WCNW and WMCA—were in the forefront of brokering time slots for African American programs. During the war years, WMCA was the home of *New World a-Coming* and also featured a weekly black music show,

Tales from Harlem, hosted by Joe Bostic. During the same period, WCNW broadcast a daily program hosted by blues guitarist Henry Copeland.[3]

In the nation's capital, the pioneering African American disc jockey was Hal Jackson, who broke the color line in local broadcasting on WOOK in 1937. A native of Charleston, South Carolina, Jackson moved to Washington, D.C., in his early teens, after both his parents passed away. He lived with family friends while working his way through high school and then Howard University—busing tables at various hotels and cleaning the latrines in Union Station. With a college degree, he went to work as a sports editor for a local black weekly and as the play-by-play announcer for the Homestead Grays, a Negro League baseball team. Early in 1937, Jackson approached WINX, a powerful AM outlet owned by the *Washington Post,* about broadcasting some of the Homestead Grays' local games—and was laughed out of the station. At the time, WINX was a lily-white operation, like all the other radio outlets in town.

The incident stiffened Jackson's resolve to gain access to the city's segregated airwaves. He hired a white advertising agency to broker a time slot for him on WOOK, the city's only ethnic radio station. On the day of his first broadcast, Hal Jackson walked into the WOOK studios with Dr. Mary McCleod Bethune, head of the National Council of Negro Women, and Dr. Charles Drew, a prominent Howard professor; they were to be the first guests on his show. Jackson had also lined up a number of black businessmen to sponsor his radio debut. Caught off guard and faced with such an imposing delegation from the local black community, WOOK's management didn't resist, and Hal Jackson launched Washington, D.C.'s first regular African American–hosted radio program.[4]

Within six months of his breakthrough broadcast in the nation's capital, Jackson had brokered time slots on two nearby Maryland stations, in Annapolis and Baltimore, and was quickly emerging as the region's leading black radio announcer. His program *The House That Jack Built* was primarily a disc jockey–driven operation, similar to those developed by Jack Cooper and other African American radio pioneers. His playlist was shaded toward swing and pop: "I did everything—Peggy Lee, Ella Fitzgerald, the big bands—Duke and Count, Billie Holiday and Sarah Vaughan, Nat King Cole. I had a thing that I called 'The House That Jack Built'—and I'd say, 'Hi, this is Hal Jackson, the host that loves you the most, from The House That Jack Built. . . . Let's go out on the terrace this afternoon and see who is waiting for me. Oh, it's Nat King Cole!' "[5] Jackson was the major black DJ on the Washington airwaves throughout the 1940s. At the end of the decade, he moved on to New York City, where he continued his long career in radio.

Most of the black radio disc jockeys who broke the color line in broadcasting before the second world war relied on an upscale form of racial ventriloquy. Their on-air presentations resembled those of the industry's standard-bearers. Being the first African Americans regularly on the airwaves in their respective locales, they quite naturally aspired to sound just as "professional" as the high-profile, veteran announcers—who were, invariably, white males. Modeling themselves on their white predecessors—especially with respect to voice and diction—in their efforts to sound "colorless," they consciously avoided the use of black slang or oratory. For the same reason, their playlists tended to favor the mainstream jazz artists of the swing era, while ignoring the blues—a musical tradition with a large following among the African American masses. In effect, these black radio pioneers were middle-class reformers who took an entrepreneurial and assimilationist approach to racial progress. Theirs was no small accomplishment: they not only broke the color line, but their ongoing success on the airwaves also helped undermine its Jim Crow rationale. To cross over into the white cultural mainstream, however, they found it necessary to mask their voices and censor their musical selections.

In the South, neither ethnic radio stations nor black disc jockeys gained even a foothold in the broadcast industry, which continued to employ an all-white workforce until World War II. Early in the 1940s, however, regional white business establishments that catered to a black clientele began to sponsor live music shows oriented toward their customers. For the most part, these programs featured local African American entertainers. One of the first and most influential was *King Biscuit Time,* aired on KFFA in Helena, Arkansas. The show was launched in 1941 as a vehicle to promote King Biscuit flour (produced and sold by the Interstate Grocery Company); it featured a white announcer, Sonny Payne, and the legendary black blues musician Rice Miller, soon to be better known by his radio name "Sonny Boy Williamson." Miller was a masterful blues harmonica player and songwriter, well known throughout the Mississippi Delta for his distinctive style and flamboyant showmanship. He organized a small blues band that included guitarist Robert "Junior" Lockwood and drummer Peck Curtis, and they played on KFFA five days a week at noon-time, when most of the Delta's field hands were taking their lunch break, and then traveled to evening engagements in the region.[6]

At first, Miller and his band were not paid for the broadcasts; instead, they were regularly allowed to announce their upcoming gigs. Later in the decade, they were paid modestly. *King Biscuit Time* became a huge success with black listeners in the rural mid-South. It developed such a large following that the Interstate Grocery Company began to market a new product—Sonny Boy Corn Meal. Each bag had a large picture of a smiling Rice Miller, harmonica in hand, sitting on a giant ear of corn. *King Biscuit Time* went on to enjoy a lengthy association with KFFA, even though Miller had moved on by the late 1940s. By then, a growing number of similar programs in the South showcased African American blues and gospel performers. Invariably, these live music shows were sponsored by local white businessmen hoping to sell their wares to black consumers. This development proved to be a milestone in Southern broadcasting; for the first time, the profit motive seemed to outweigh the need to maintain the color line on the airwaves—a trend that would gain momentum in the postwar years.[7]

The Postwar Radio Revolutionaries

By the late 1940s, a new wave of black disc jockeys began to emerge on the nation's airwaves. They were, in part, the product of the massive World War II urban migration, and they gave voice to an apparent generational shift taking place in African American culture as a whole. During the war years, more than 1 million African Americans living in the rural South migrated to urban and industrial centers, mostly in the North and on the West Coast. In addition, many of the 1 million African Americans who served in the armed forces relocated in urban areas when they returned to civilian life. By the end of the war, the cities with the largest black population increases were Chicago (an increase of 100,000), Los Angeles (75,000), New York City (70,000), and Detroit (50,000).

This tide of black migration, coupled with unprecedented urban growth and prosperity, reinvigorated African American culture, leading to radical developments in music, dance, language, and fashion. The postwar period witnessed the birth of bebop jazz, rhythm and blues, new styles of jitterbug dancing, zoot suits, conked (straightened) hair, and the adoption of porkpie hats; it ushered in the era of the urban black hipster, sporting a new ghetto vernacular and a rebellious new lifestyle. Moreover, the postwar prosperity sparked a resurgence in the moribund African American entertainment industry. In particular, the number of independent race-record labels rose considerably, and a new "chitlin circuit," linking together black music venues around the country, emerged from the ashes of the old TOBA. These developments set the stage for the dramatic rise of a younger generation of African American DJs. In 1947, only sixteen black DJs were on the airwaves throughout the United States; just two years later, that number had risen to over one hundred.[8]

"The Ole Swingmaster": Al Benson

The prototype for this new wave of postwar black disc jockeys was Al Benson, who broke into radio as a preacher in 1945 on WGES in Chicago. Benson was born Arthur Bernard Leaner in Jackson, Mississippi, in 1910. Before migrating north, he attended Jackson Normal College in his hometown and worked as an entertainer in regional vaudeville shows. In the mid-1930s, Leaner moved to Chicago, where he founded a storefront church for Southern black migrants. To support himself and his religious calling, he worked as a cook on the Pennsylvania Railroad, then as an interviewer for the Works Progress Administration (WPA), and finally as a probation officer for Cook County. In addition, he was a Democratic precinct captain for Congressman William Dawson, leader of Chicago's black political machine during the Great Depression and the war years. The Reverend Arthur Leaner was still using his original name when he made his premiere radio broadcast on WGES in 1945. The fifteen-minute Sunday-evening program featured a sermon by Leaner and gospel music by a local vocal group. Only after WGES refused to allow the good Pastor to sell advertising in his brokered time slot, because of the religious nature of the program, did he decide to switch to a secular disc-jockey format—a transition that triggered his name change.[9]

As Al Benson—"the Ole Swingmaster"—Leaner was an overnight sensation in the Chicago radio market. He began his rapid ascent to fame and fortune late in 1945, with a weekly one-hour show on WGES. Two years later, he was broadcasting twenty hours a week on both WGES and WJJD (another local outlet). In 1948, a *Chicago Tribune* poll named Benson the most popular disc jockey in the city; he received more votes than Jack Cooper and any of the city's leading white DJs. In 1949, Al Benson won the *Chicago Defender*'s annual "Mayor of Bronzeville" contest by a huge majority, making him the most revered African American public figure in the city. One of his many fans from the postwar era explained his popularity this way: "Oh I liked the musicians and athletes, but they were distant. You would see them and feel proud, but Al Benson was with us fifty-two weeks out of the year, talking that talk on the air and then walking that walk out on the streets. Yes sir, he was the main man!"[10]

Benson's phenomenal appeal on the airwaves undoubtedly stemmed from his black-identified style. He was the first radio announcer in the Chicago market to speak with a black Southern accent and use black street slang on the air, and he was the first local disc jockey to feature the popular—and previously taboo—urban blues hits of the era on his shows. He also proved to be the consummate radio pitchman. Prior to his career in broadcasting, Benson had worked closely with migrant and working-class African Americans in Chicago, in both a religious and a social service capacity. He was well aware of their daily lives, as well as their dreams and aspirations. Equally important, he spoke to them in their own vernacular—"native talk," as he called it.

This was Benson's key to building a large following among Chicago's black population. Increasingly, the black community was composed of working-class Southern migrants, who readily identified with Benson's thick Mississippi Delta accent—no doubt enhanced by his habitual consumption of whiskey while on the air—and with his folksy use of black urban slang. This personal bond between "Ole Mushmouth," as many of his fans referred to him, and his audience led to his ascendancy as the nation's first African American "personality jock." Moreover, it was a radical departure from the professional-sounding and middle class–oriented shows produced by Jack Cooper and his associates. As one native Chicago disc jockey explained: "Jack Cooper would be considered more highbrow than Benson. Benson was, you know, let's get down—down and dirty. Let's do it in the alley. He'd be talking that talk—talking stuff, you know. And Jack Cooper's thing was that he wanted to conduct it on a more dignified plane. But he did not communicate with the people like Benson did.

Benson came on the scene and just turned on the town. Everybody was listening to Al Benson and talking about him. He just had a charisma, a magical kind of charisma."[11]

Al Benson's playlists proved as revolutionary as his native talk. Almost single-handedly, he pioneered the transition to a rhythm-and-blues format on Chicago's airwaves. "R & B," an amalgam of electrified urban blues, gospel vocal styles, and swing-band instrumental arrangements, emerged as a new African American musical genre in the 1940s, reigniting the race-record business. Especially popular among black urban migrants and teenagers, by the end of the second World War, R & B was outselling jazz in the race-record market; but it was getting little airplay on the networks or in the local radio markets, even among the handful of black disc jockeys on the air. In Chicago, Jack Cooper's big-band jazz format continued to dominate the "black appeal" programming. Moreover, he and his protégés refused to play R & B releases on the air because of their "suggestive" lyrics and "lowlife" cultural connotations. Al Benson changed this situation dramatically. In consultation with two of his nephews who operated a Southside record store, he learned not only that R & B discs were selling better than their jazz counterparts but also which new releases were in the greatest demand locally. These were the records that he would feature on his shows. Before long, Benson not only played the latest R & B hits but could make or break a new disc in the Chicago market simply by deciding for or against adding it to his playlist.

By the end of the 1940s, Al Benson was the most powerful disc jockey in Chicago, and a force to be reckoned with in the resurgent race-record business. In the words of one record-label executive: "Benson totally revolutionized the whole radio industry . . . he was the main reason why so many independent black record companies featuring rhythm and blues and even gospel artists grew. Can you imagine a disc jockey sitting in front of a mike six days a week for ten hours a day for four years? Nobody else had ever done it up till then, and none—black or white—has done it since."[12]

The final component of Benson's unprecedented success story was his prodigious talent as a pitchman, on and off the air. His business associates, such as former WGES owner Elizabeth Hinzman, generally remembered him as "the greatest salesman that I have ever known." Many of his local sponsors, especially clothing and furniture stores, reported huge profits as a result of his personal endorsements. National sponsors such as Budweiser, Ace Beer out of Canada, and California Swiss Colony Wine made substantial inroads into Chicago's African American consumer market by hiring the "Ole Swingmaster" as their local spokesman. Benson promoted his products with highly unorthodox tactics. One coworker recalled that he would develop a hit list of the local clubs that did not carry an alcoholic beverage he was pushing; then he'd visit those clubs with a group of his friends and order a round of that beverage for the house. When the chagrined bartender admitted the club didn't carry Budweiser or Swiss Colony, Benson would announce that he would take his business elsewhere and return only if his beverage of choice was in stock. More often than not, the ploy succeeded.[13]

Benson was well aware of the central role advertising played in his success on the airwaves. In his own words: "I soon learned that the way to stay on radio was to find and sell sponsors. . . . Whenever I sold sponsors on my show, I would have no problem selling their products to my audience because they believed in me. I used to say, 'And that's for real' to let my audience know that what I was selling them was good merchandise and no crap. I would throw sponsors off my show if I felt that they were selling shoddy merchandise or ripping off my listeners. I found out early that I couldn't help my sponsors unless I had listeners. The two things went hand-in-hand."[14] Benson was so successful as a radio pitchman that he changed the way business was conducted with respect to black appeal radio. Like Cooper and his disciples, Benson began his radio career brokering airtime on local stations. But when the popularity of his show skyrocketed, Benson was able to negotiate a new deal (initially with WGES) that gave him a commission on the advertising he attracted to the station and free airtime as long as he continued to attract sponsors. This new financial arrangement cut his overhead to almost nothing. Even more significant, it eventually led to the end of time brokering in black appeal radio, removing a major obstacle facing aspiring African American DJs.[15]

Al Benson's career in radio reached its zenith in the 1950s. As the new decade began, he broadcast a total of ten hours a day on three different Chicago stations (WGES, WJJD, WAAF). Further, all his shows originated from his own radio studio, which was located in his house. He now brokered some of his own airtime to a select group of novice black disc jockeys, whom he took under his wing. The spectacular success of these radio ventures enabled Benson to expand his role in the entertainment field. In 1951, he became the first African American in Chicago to host his own weekly television variety show, featuring both local and national R & B acts. A year later, he launched his own label, Parrot Records, to record Chicago blues artists such as J. B. Lenior and Snooky Pryor. But by far his most lucrative business venture was the staging of a series of R & B concerts at the Regal Theater on Chicago's Southside during the 1950s. These shows, which featured the country's hottest R & B performers, attracted as many as 125,000 fans a week. They also raised Benson's profile as Chicago's most flamboyant black impresario. He took to wearing tailor-made suits in bright red, orange, green, or blue and riding around town in his chauffeur-driven white Cadillac convertible. As his nephew George Leaner recalled: "There was a period when Al held those shows at the Regal, with all the big showbiz acts, that people came to see him as much as they came to see the acts. And he would always do it up just like showbiz folks. He would change his costumes four or five times during the show and really was the star. He would bring the house down in those flashy suits he wore."[16]

Throughout the 1950s, Benson not only was Chicago's leading black showman but also was in the forefront of the struggle against racial discrimination. When an important racial issue was in the news, Benson more often than not gave his opinion on it in the course of his daily broadcasts. For example, when a black family who moved into an all-white neighborhood in Cicero, a Chicago suburb, had their apartment firebombed by a white mob, Benson immediately condemned the violence; then, on the air, he raised money for the destitute family. As a result, Benson was the target of a number of threats on his life, which he reported to the FBI. On at least two other occasions, the FBI was called in to protect him after he received death threats linked to his public pronouncements on racial injustice and bigotry. His activism extended far beyond his radio broadcasts. He was personally involved in integrating a number of Chicago's most prestigious nightclubs, and he often spoke on behalf of local black political candidates at rallies and fund-raisers. Undoubtedly, his most famous political protest occurred on the eve of the 1956 presidential election, when he chartered an airplane and flew over his hometown, Jackson, where he dropped five thousand copies of the U.S. Constitution in order to "wake up the citizens of Mississippi."[17]

By the time Benson retired from broadcasting in the early 1960s, he was a millionaire—and he had transformed the soundscape of black appeal radio. In the Chicago region, he was the major inspiration for younger black disc jockeys, many of whom emulated Benson's down-home street talk and R & B musical format. Next to him, the three most popular DJs on WGES in the 1950s were Sam Evans, McKie Fitzhugh, and Richard Stams—the "Clown Prince of the Disc Jockeys." Stams's *Open the Door Richard* show mixed R & B with such black comics as Moms Mabley and Pigmeat Markham and was especially appealing to black teenagers; McKie Fitzhugh broadcast from his well-known Southside nightclub, the Disc Jockey Show Lounge; and Sam Evans was successful enough on the airwaves to stage large R & B shows in the city. On WOPA, a rival black appeal outlet in nearby Oak Hill, Illinois, Big Bill Hill and Purvis Spann also emerged as popular down-home DJs in the 1950s. Both Hill, the son of an Arkansas sharecropper, and Spann, who hailed from Itabena, Mississippi, were strong proponents of Chicago's electric blues, popular among Delta migrants; and both acknowledged Al Benson as their role model. During his career, Benson also trained a number of "satellite jocks" to work in some of the time slots he controlled, and he sponsored a yearly disc-jockey contest as a recruiting device. Among those who won the contest and went on to successful careers as DJs were Vivian Carter, Lucky Cordell, Sid McCoy, and Herb Kent ("The Cool Gent"). Jesse Owens, the Olympic gold medalist, also broke into the broadcast profession under Benson's tutelage in the 1950s.[18]

Rhymers and Signifiers: Daddy-O Daylie and Doctor Hep Cat

Al Benson's crucial influence on the rise of black appeal radio extended well beyond Chicago. Many of the black DJs who entered the field during his early heyday in the late 1940s were familiar with his achievements and tended to follow the trail he blazed with respect to the R & B format, the use of black urban slang, and the sales pitch. Among these newcomers were Jesse "Spider" Burke, a college graduate in electrical engineering who debuted in 1948 with an hourly late-night show on KXLW in Saint Louis; James Early, the "Bluest Voice on the Delta," who was Mississippi's first black DJ on WROX in Clarksdale, beginning in 1947; Ramon Bruce, a former pro football player, who hosted the popular *Ravin' with Ramon* on WHAT in Philadelphia, which drew up to a thousand fan letters a week in 1947; and Willie Bryant, the "Mayor of Harlem," who launched his late-night R & B show *After Hours* on WHOM in New York City in 1949.[19]

This new wave of African American disc jockeys introduced "rhyming and signifying" to the nation's airwaves. A mainstay of the black oral tradition since slavery, *signifying* is the art of humorous verbal warfare, in which the combatants employ a range of devices—from ridicule to cockiness—in order to humiliate their adversaries and enhance their own status. These verbal barbs and boasts are often embellished by rhyming the words at the ends of the sentences. Perhaps the best-known example of signifying is "the dozens," a folk game of verbal insult that belittles by making derogatory remarks about an adversary's family—particularly the mother. Folklorist Roger Abrahams has characterized the dozens as "mother-rhyming," a cultural practice he not only traced back to slavery but also found among a number of West African peoples.[20] The continuing presence of these forms of verbal combat in the black oral tradition suggests that each new generation of African Americans has adopted them to their own circumstances, in the process changing the content but leaving the form and the intent mostly intact.

From all indications, the first black DJs prominently to feature rhyming and signifying—without the obscene content—on the airwaves were Holmes Bailey (Daddy-O Daylie) in Chicago and Lavada "Doctor Hep Cat" Durst in Austin, Texas. Both men were hired as disc jockeys in 1948 because of their mastery of the latest street slang, or "jive talk," and because of their ability to speak in rhymes. Bailey initially gained notoriety as a rhyming bartender; according to fellow Chicago DJ Sid McCoy:

> Daddy-O's whole thing was rhyme. He was the precursor of today's rappers because back when he did his radio show—he did it in rhyme. And he developed that thing as a bartender. People would come from miles around to be at his bar—all the celebrities liked to hang out with Daddy-O. He would get up there with a glass and pour that drink and he'd be rhyming all the time that he was making that drink. He would wrap the glass in a napkin, and at the end of a couplet he would set the glass down. Then he'd take the ice and throw it up in the air and catch it behind his back. He was fantastic. Everybody loved him.[21]

Holmes Bailey embarked on his radio career when the owner of the bar where he worked offered to sponsor him as a disc jockey on WAIT, a local Chicago outlet. A jazz aficionado since his youth, Bailey jumped at the opportunity to play his favorite music on the air. His nightly show debuted on WAIT late in 1948. For the occasion, he created the hip pseudonym "Daddy-O Daylie"; the name stayed with him for the rest of his days in radio. In addition to introducing rhyming to the local airwaves, Daddy-O Daylie was the first DJ in the Chicago market to prominently feature bebop jazz recordings on his show, which he called *Jazz from Dad's Pad.*[22]

Bebop was a radical new genre of modern jazz, created by young black musicians in rebellion against the musical conventions and culture associated with swing. By the mid-1940s, swing dance music was dominated by white jazz orchestras—much to the detriment of their black counterparts. Members of the younger generation of musicians coming up through the ranks of the African American swing bands created an archetype for jazz improvisation that was virtually inaccessible to white jazz veterans (or novices, for that matter). Moreover, these young rebels fashioned a unique jazz vernacular for their cultural subgroup; in effect, they created a new vocabulary to go with their revolutionary new music. Daddy-O Daylie was a leading proponent of the bebop revolt and a major innovator of its hipster idiom; bebop trumpeter and figurehead Dizzy Gillespie credits him with popularizing both the music and the black vocabulary associated with it. Daddy-O remained a fixture on Chicago's airwaves throughout the 1950s and 1960s, building a large and devout following among the modern jazz lovers in the city.[23]

Lavada Durst was born and raised in Austin, Texas, where his father worked as a bricklayer and his mother as a nursemaid for wealthy white families. After graduating from the local black high school in the 1930s, Durst went to work as director of athletics at the Rosewood Recreation Center in Austin—a job he held for thirty-five years. During his tenure at Rosewood, he coached and mentored two future pro football legends: the Detroit Lions' Dick "Night Train" Lane and the Dallas Cowboys' "Hollywood" Henderson. To supplement his regular job income, Durst also played the piano and sang the blues at weekend house parties, and he was employed as the public-address system announcer for the local Negro League baseball games at Disch Field in Austin. It was his novel play-by-play commentary, often set to rhyme, that led to his career as a disc jockey.

In the summer of 1948, Durst's baseball rhymes caught the attention of a white spectator, John B. Connally Jr., the owner of local radio station KVET and an up-and-coming Texas politician who would eventually be elected governor. After the game, Connally sought out the rhyming announcer and offered him a job as a DJ on his station. Durst was given the newly created late-night airshift and adopted the radio name Doctor Hep Cat for his first show. Six nights a week, from 10 P.M. to midnight, he played R & B discs and talked the latest hipster idiom, set to rhyme:

> Jumpin' Jills and jivin' Cats,
> upstate Gates in Stetson hats,
> lace your boots and tighten your wig,
> here's some jive. Can you dig?
> I'm Doctor Hep Cat, on the scene,
> with a stack of shellac in my record machine.
> I'm hip to the tip, and bop to the top.
> I'm long time coming and I just won't stop.
> It's a real gone deal that I'm gonna reel,
> so stay tuned while I pad your skulls.[24]

Lavada Durst was the first black disc jockey not just in Austin but, apparently, in the entire state of Texas. Initially, KVET's all-white staff belittled and ostracized him, refusing him entrance into the station during daylight hours. Nevertheless, his novel R & B show prospered, and by the early 1950s, Doctor Hep Cat was the hottest DJ in the Austin market—and had developed a considerable crossover appeal. In addition to his sizable local black audience, he had legions of devoted white listeners among the students attending the University of Texas in Austin. Interest in his show was so widespread among college students that he published a booklet called *The Jives of Dr. Hep Cat*, which contained a selection of his on-air rhymes and a glossary of "jive talk" for beginners. Throughout the 1950s and well into the next decade, Doctor Hep Cat ruled the late-night airwaves in Austin. He retired from radio in the early 1970s to become a minister in a local church.[25]

Only a decade separated radio's flamboyant performers of black vernacular speech from the professional-sounding pioneers. Yet, like swing and bebop, the two groups of DJs sounded radically different from each other, and they represented different social tendencies among African Americans. Disc jockeys like Doctor Hep Cat, Daddy-O Daylie, and Al Benson were not assimilationists; they were black populists, broadcasting the music and speech of common black folk. Their intent was not to lift up the race but to celebrate its unique grassroots cultural expressions. This radical shift, driven by class and generational differences, set the stage for the birth of black appeal radio stations in the postwar era.

6

The Rise of Black
Appeal Radio

The coming of a new and growing wave of African American disc
jockeys on the nation's airwaves was linked to a chain of events
that ultimately led to the emergence of the first "black appeal" stations in the country. Instead of earmarking a percentage of their airtime
for black-oriented shows, these local outlets committed their entire
broadcast schedules to programming by and for African Americans. For
the most part, this transition—unthinkable prior to World War II—was
economically driven. During the postwar years, the radio industry's control over national programming, advertising, and listenership collapsed
when the major networks focused on television. Radio again became a
local and laissez-faire enterprise, in which stations had to fend for themselves amid increasingly cutthroat competition. In these circumstances,
the black radio consumer could no longer be ignored—especially in urban markets, where African Americans constituted a substantial percentage of the total population. Ironically, the first radio stations to
switch over to black appeal formats were located in the South, and all
but one were white owned. As with programs like *King Biscuit Time,* the
dictates of the local Southern marketplace prevailed over the customs of
segregation.

A Black Appeal Beacon: WDIA

The first major breakthrough for a black appeal station took place in Memphis, Tennessee, where African Americans made up 40 percent of the population in the postwar era. Like most large industrial and commercial centers in the South, Memphis prospered and grew considerably during the war years; business was profitable and jobs plentiful. At the same time, the city continued to maintain a rigid color line and tolerate a corrupt political machine, run by E. H. "Boss" Crump, a wily segregationist who lorded over local politics and vice from the 1910s to the 1940s. In spite of the backward machine politics, however, the economic climate in Memphis remained bullish in the postwar period, especially in the field of broadcasting. Television was still out of most families' reach, and radio prevailed as the most popular, profitable, and ubiquitous broadcast medium. While the networks were preoccupied with bringing TV on line, in Memphis, radio again was becoming accessible to entrepreneurs and open to format innovations.[1]

In the middle of 1947, two white Memphis business associates, John Pepper and Bert Ferguson, launched WDIA—a low-power, 250 watt daytime operation. It was the city's sixth AM radio station. Pepper was the scion of a wealthy Memphis family with extensive business interests in the Mississippi Delta. A graduate of Duke University, he had owned a radio station downriver, at Greenville, Mississippi. After serving as a naval pilot during World War II, he returned to his hometown ready to start another radio station. He recruited an old friend and fellow radio enthusiast, Bert Ferguson, as a partner in the project. Ferguson, another Memphis native and a college graduate who served in the navy during the war, had worked for Pepper at the Greenville station. Pepper put up most of the $48,000 to start WDIA, while Ferguson applied for the FCC license and then managed the station's day-to-day operations. WDIA signed on the air June 7 with a country-and-western music format; but business was slow, and within a year the struggling newcomer switched to a classical music format. Late in 1948, with the station still in the red and on the auction block, Ferguson convinced his reluctant partner to try black appeal.[2]

While an announcer and engineer for WBHQ in Memphis in the late 1930s, Ferguson had engineered the late-night remote broadcasts of the city's traditional *Midnight Ramble,* a local African American vaudeville review staged exclusively for white folks at a Beale Street theater every Thursday evening. These broadcasts were hosted by the master of ceremonies of the *Midnight Ramble,* Nat D. Williams, one of Beale Street's favorite sons. Ferguson was impressed by Williams's rapport with the white audience and by the unique crossover appeal of the weekly broadcast. Not only was it popular among white listeners, but as he learned from Williams, the *Midnight Ramble* show was also a source of pride in the local black community. Almost ten years later, Williams was Ferguson's first choice for hosting a daily show on WDIA. It was a brilliant stroke that changed the station's fortunes and established a formidable black community institution.[3]

Ferguson and Pepper were aware of the political and economic risks in their venture. As Ferguson later recalled: "The atmosphere was such, with Crump running everything, and we could see him saying, 'Look, we don't want any nigger radio station in town.'"[4] To avoid opposition from the city's hard-line segregationists, WDIA moved gradually and without fanfare toward an all-black format, in the hope that the changes would go undetected.

"Product identification" was their major economic worry. At the time, the rule of thumb in the advertising end of the radio business was that black appeal shows imposed an undesirable racial image on the sponsor's product; the products thus identified with Africans Americans would be shunned by whites. Conventional wisdom dictated that only advertising for products and services sold exclusively to the black population made sense on black appeal shows. Ferguson and Pepper couldn't afford to lose the few regular white sponsors they had on WDIA, but they also saw great potential in the untapped African American market. As Ferguson put it: "The Negro market has become too important to be overlooked or ignored any longer in this day of strong competition for the consumer dollar—and the Negro's money has the same golden color as anyone's!"[5] Applying the same strategy they used with the politicians, WDIA's owners proceeded cautiously, saying nothing to the sponsors about the format changes taking place. The station produced its first black appeal program and began to cultivate a new audience among African Americans. The hope was that once the ratings were up, the advertisers would go along with the changes.

The Radio Genius of Nat D.

WDIA's first African American disc jockey, Nat D. Williams, was short in stature and almost blind; nonetheless, he was a towering visionary in the Memphis black community—a virtual Renaissance man. His remarkable career as an educator, newspaper columnist, showman, promoter, producer, and radio broadcaster spanned four decades, from the 1930s to the 1960s, and was full of pioneering achievements. Born in 1909 in a house on Beale Street—the fabled hub of African American cultural and social life in Memphis—Williams was raised by his mother, a dancer in local vaudeville revues, and his grandmother, who nurtured his lifelong love of learning. Throughout his life, Nat D. was plagued by terrible eyesight and wore thick glasses; friends gave him the nickname "3-D" in the 1950s. Yet, despite his poor vision, Williams graduated from high school with honors and earned a degree in history at Tennessee Agricultural and Industrial (A & I) College, a black college in nearby Nashville. He worked a short time as a journalist in New York City, then returned to Memphis in the early 1930s and took a job teaching history at Booker T. Washington High School. Long before the standard high school texts had any mention of it, he was including material on African Americans and Native Americans in his U.S. history classes. His popular lectures on famous black and American Indian historical figures who were in the forefront of their people's struggles against white domination were memorable eye-openers to the legions of students who passed through his classes.[6]

Williams was a formidable newspaper essayist. His weekly column in the *Memphis World,* called "Down on Beale Street," belongs to a tradition in American journalism that dates back to Frederick Douglass and even Tom Paine. The columns were outspoken in their advocacy of political rights, economic opportunity, and racial pride for African Americans. Williams was particularly concerned with the color line in American society and wrote some of his most elegant and provocative columns condemning it. He published the following in 1946:

Too long and too deeply has consciousness of color pervaded our lives. It sinks into the souls of our saints, tainting their saintliness. It seeps into the minds of our children, making them old before their time. It rides into the consciousness of our young men, warping their dreams. It shackles the minds of our scholars, making them intellectual eunuchs. Too long has it been drummed into my ears and seared on my consciousness that the Negro woman's bed is the playground of the world. The Negro press, stage and screen glorify only the Negro woman who has white features. The nation's press and movies portray the typical Negro woman as Aunt Jemima, despite the counteracting refinement of a Madame Bethune or Marian Anderson. I hope to see the day, black as I am, when men will not be afraid to be fair, when they can welcome justice in their courts; allow truth a real hearing in their schools, churches and homes; and make the lust for gold and power secondary to the urge for service and human welfare. I hope I can live to see the day, black as I am, when colored folks here in the United States will have a common ideal rather than a common misery.[7]

In another column, written early the same year, Williams wrote candidly about his color: "I'm black, Jack, black as a hundred midnights in a cypress swamp. But may I remind you, I ain't mad about it. This black is all right with me, it hasn't cost me a dime. I pay only for ignorance—not my blackness."[8] Over the years, Williams's columns in the *Memphis World* were periodically reprinted in the *Pittsburgh Courier* and the *Chicago Defender;* as a consequence, he gained a national reputation as a champion of racial justice.

In his role as a Beale Street impresario, Williams emceed the *Midnight Ramble* and was also the driving force behind the legendary Amateur Night at the Palace Theater, initiated in the late 1930s. Every Tuesday evening, aspiring musicians, dancers, comics, vocalists, and fans from Memphis and the surrounding rural counties would converge on the Palace Theater on Beale Street, to compete for the amateur title or to cheer for their favorite contestants. Among those who won the coveted title over the years were future R & B luminaries B. B. King, Bobby "Blue" Bland, Al Hibler, Johnny Ace, Rufus Thomas—and a young, white farm boy named Elvis Presley. Nat D. was involved in producing an entertainment extravaganza and parade for the popular "Memphis Cotton Makers' Jubilee," a yearly event held simultaneously on both sides of the city's color line—whites called it the "Memphis Cotton Carnival"—which was similar to Mardi Gras in New Orleans. He also produced and hosted an annual musical fund-raiser for

Booker T. Washington High School, using student talent. These local entertainment ventures increased Williams's stature in the city and provided him with an unexpected bridge to radio broadcasting.[9]

Tan Town Jamboree, Williams's original show on WDIA, premiered on October 25, 1948, at 3 P.M. At the start of the broadcast, the novice radio host made a gaffe that became his trademark on the air; as he recalled, "When he [the cue man] pointed his finger at me, I forgot everything I was supposed to say. So I just did what became typical of me. I laid out for dead. I just started laughing 'cause I was laughing my way out. And the man said, 'The people seem to like that,' and we made it standard. So ever since then, Nat has started his program laughing and closed his program laughing."[10]

Williams's booming baritone laugh, along with his folksy rapport with his listeners, became the focal point of his DJ personality. He would open his show with his raucous laugh and then the rhyme "Well, yes siree, its Nat D. on the Jamboree, comin' at three on AM seventy-three. Now whatchu bet?" In a similar vein, he sprinkled his radio discourse with folk witticisms: "Worryin' is just like a rockin' chair, lots of movement, but you ain't getting nowhere."[11] Like Daddy-O Daylie and Doctor Hep Cat, Nat D. was one of the early black disc jockeys in the country who incorporated rhyming and signifying into his style of broadcasting. In spite of his educational position, he chose to speak like a Beale Street sage.

The musical format that Williams pioneered on WDIA was a dramatic shift from the classical music it replaced. He described the transition as follows: "We came up with the idea of giving them some blues. Only thing is, the only black record the station had was 'Stomping at the Savoy'—which became my first theme song—and it was by a white writer. We started scrounging around and finally got some records by blues artists like Fats Waller and Ivory Joe Hunter and then we had to clean them up. Some of these records were—well—suggestive. And the way I cleaned them up was, when it got to be suggestive, I'd just start laughing and talking. First thing you know, it caught on. The listeners were ready for a different sound."[12]

Initially, however, white listeners were hostile. Outraged callers demanded: "Get that nigger off the air!" There were even a few bomb threats. One irate woman admonished: "If John Pepper's grandfather could see what's going on here now, he would turn over in his grave!"[13]

(Pepper's grandfather was a Delta plantation and slave owner during the Civil War.) Black listeners, by contrast, were elated and flooded the station with letters praising the show. The African American response was so overwhelming that in a matter of weeks, Williams was doing two additional shows: *Tan Town Coffee Club* in the mornings and *Nat D.'s Supper Club* in the evenings. The station was becoming a black appeal outlet.

Williams had no illusions about his employers' motives. In his *Memphis World* column, he openly discussed the proposition with his readers: "They are businessmen. They don't necessarily love Negroes. They make that clear. But they do love progress and are willing to pay the price to make progress. One of the most neglected markets in the Mid South is the Negro market. And that's true because so many white businessmen take the Negro for granted."[14] In a different literary vein, Williams's column forecast the financial breakdown of the color line:

> 'Mongst all this talk
> 'Bout integration
> As collud folks balk
> 'Gainst segregation
> Looms one bodacious tho't:
> It's called dollar-gration![15]

Yet, while Nat D. clearly recognized the untapped potential of the African American market, at no time in his radio career did he make any effort to exploit it as an entrepreneur. Instead, he approached the endeavor as a race activist, much as he approached his entertainment projects. Unlike Jack Cooper and Al Benson, Williams did not make a fortune in radio broadcasting; for the most part, he and his family continued to live on his modest teacher's salary. Nevertheless, his impact on the development of black appeal radio would be as far-reaching as that of Cooper and Benson.

WDIA's transition to an all-black format, which took a little less than a year, was orchestrated by Nat D. Williams with the advice and consent of General Manager Bert Ferguson. Williams was the mastermind behind most of the new programs that debuted on the station in the wake of *Tan Town Jamboree*'s surprising breakthrough. Shows included religious broadcasts, public-affairs offerings, women's programming, gospel music shows, and more R & B shows. In addition, Williams was the major conduit for most of of the African Americans who came to be employed by WDIA as on-air staff. Ferguson was more than willing to go along with these recommendations after he discovered the station's ratings were skyrocketing. In the spring of 1949, WDIA jumped from last to second in the Memphis radio market, attracting 17 percent of the local listening audience; by the fall of 1949, it was number one in the market, with 28 percent of listeners regularly tuning in. Simultaneously, WDIA completed its transition to a totally black format.[16]

WDIA's Sunday broadcast schedule converted to black appeal programming early in the transition period. Most of the day was given over to a variety of religious offerings. Three live fifteen-minute segments featured the city's most acclaimed African American gospel quartets: the Spirit of Memphis, the Southern Wonders, and the all-female Songbirds of the South. In addition, a series of remote broadcasts of religious services featured prominent black churches, including the Baptist congregation of Dr. Herbert Brewster, the city's leading African American minister and one of the country's foremost gospel composers. Finally, Nat D. hosted a Sunday-morning Bible class for WDIA's younger listeners, as well as a roundup of local church news and community affairs announcements.[17]

Williams's most ambitious and controversial public-affairs show was *Brown America Speaks*. The thirty-minute Sunday-afternoon roundtable forum, featuring some of the city's leading black citizens and hosted by a more somber Nat D. Williams than appeared on the blues programs, premiered on September 11, 1949, at 4:30 P.M. It quickly became known for candid discussions of racially charged subjects, such as the segregation of the city's public facilities, job and wage discrimination in the workforce, and police brutality in the black community. *Brown America Speaks* won an award for public-service excellence in 1950 from Ohio State's Institute for Education in Radio and Television. It also generated a good deal of hate mail. Williams's daughter recalled that her father would receive a regular barrage of these letters on the Tuesday after the Sunday broadcasts, regardless of the topic, and that many were routinely written by the same irate white listeners. Nat D. also had a hand in initiating such WDIA public-affairs offerings as *Good Neighbors,* a thirty-minute Sunday-evening program that weekly highlighted a "good neighbor" who was making a positive contribution to the black community, and *Workers Wanted,* a biweekly listing of local employment opportunities for African Americans.[18]

A Legacy of Talent

Among the early African American recruits Williams brought to the station's airwaves were talented colleagues from Booker T. Washington High School. Some, like Maurice "Hot Rod" Hulbert and A. C. "Moohah" Williams, would go on to become well-known disc jockeys in their own right. Hulbert, like Williams, was a product of Beale Street. His father owned a popular nightclub on the downtown entertainment segment of the strip and was commonly known as the "mayor" of the street; Maurice Hulbert thus grew up in a black show business milieu. By the time he graduated from high school, he was working as a bandleader and master of ceremonies for local Beale Street musical productions. His stage presence and savvy caught the eye of Nat D., who successfully lobbied the principal at Booker T. Washington to hire Hulbert as the musical director of the school's annual student talent showcase and fund-raiser. When Ferguson indicated to Williams that he was looking for additional black DJs, Hulbert was one of the first individuals Nat D. suggested for the job. After an interview, he was hired to host an early-afternoon R & B show called *The Sepia Swing Club.*[19]

On a spring day in 1949, at two in the afternoon, the *Sepia Swing Club* debuted on WDIA with "Hot Rod" Hulbert, the "high-octane pilot" of a radio rocket ship, at the helm. Playing jet-engine sound effects in the background, he shouted out greetings to the city's African American neighborhoods—"Orange Mound, Hollywood, New Chicago, Binghamton, Willett Bottom, Sutherfield"—as he blasted off into the airwaves. Hot Rod also rhymed his pronouncements and peppered his discourse with the latest black street slang. Within months, he rivaled Williams in popularity and was asked to launch two other music shows. As the dignified Maurice Hulbert Jr., he hosted *Delta Melodies,* a weekday early-morning gospel show; later in the morning, as the smooth "Maurice the Mood Man," he played romantic ballads for housewives on *Sweet Talking Time.*[20]

As one of WDIA's black appeal pioneers, Hulbert was no stranger to racial prejudice during his early months on the airwaves. He vividly recalled an encounter with a sponsor, a white man who owned a local furniture store:

> The sales manager thought I should meet the owner and see the store so I could talk about the products better. . . . So he took me out and when he introduced me, I put out my hand to shake his hand and he didn't raise his hand. And I looked at my hand and I looked at him and I reached in my back pocket and pulled out my handkerchief, wiped my hand, put my handkerchief back in my back pocket and stuck out my hand again. And he still didn't shake my hand. So I looked at him. And I didn't say anything, I just turned and walked away.[21]

A few months later, after Hulbert had boosted the furniture store's sales in spite of the insult, the owner had a change of heart and readily shook his benefactor's hand.

On another occasion, Hulbert agreed to sit in for Williams on *Brown America Speaks*. As he recalled:

> Well, *Brown America Speaks* was really outta my line . . . but anyway, I did the program. And being proud of my blackness, I went into a thing that was a poemlike thing. And I did it with humility and passion. And I said, 'We helped fell your lumber, we breast-fed your babies, cooked your food. Ruling powers of this country, won't you give us justice now? We helped you build your railroads, we helped you fight your wars. Ruling powers of this nation, won't you give us justice now?' And it went on and on. . . . I was really feeling it. And after it was over, white people called the station and complained. So that's how I learned that we had white listeners. And they complained so badly, I never did that show again. At all . . . I think Bert Ferguson and John Pepper thought I was a little too far out at that point in time.[22]

Nevertheless, Hot Rod Hulbert's radio career flourished. In the fall of 1950, his exceptional ratings caught the attention of Jake Emory, co-owner of WITH in Baltimore, Maryland. Emory lured Hulbert away from WDIA with a fat salary increase. By the end of 1951, Hot Rod's rocket-ship show on WITH made him the top black disc jockey in the Baltimore market.[23]

A. C. "Moohah" Williams, a Memphis native and high school biology teacher, used his spare time to serve as the director of the Teen Town Singers, the city's best-known black teenage vocal ensemble. Two of the group's alumni, Carla Thomas and Issac Hayes, would become associated with Memphis's Stax Records in the 1960s. Like Nat D., A. C. Williams was a graduate of Tennessee A & I, where he picked up the nickname Moohah— an American Indian word for "mighty." At the urging of Nat D., Moohah was hired in June 1949 to host a Saturday-morning program on WDIA called *Teen Town Jamboree,* featuring the Teen Town Singers. His role at the station soon expanded to include hosting *Moohah's Matinee,* a Saturday-afternoon jazz program. He also launched *Wheelin' on Beale,* a weekday country-blues show, and *Saturday Night Fish Fry,* a three-hour Saturday-evening R & B cele-bration. In addition, in the early 1950s, Bert Ferguson hired Moohah as a promotional consultant. His job was to be WDIA's liaison to the local black community; as such, he was the first and only African American employed as part of WDIA's management team during the station's heyday.[24]

Undoubtedly, the most famous WDIA alumnus recruited by Nat D. Williams was Riley B. King, who would become the internationally re-nowned B. B. King, "King of the Blues." Back in 1949, the young Missis-sippi Delta farmhand aspired to become a radio blues star like Sonny Boy Williamson. When King walked into the WDIA studios and asked Nat D. for an audition, Williams liked what he heard and offered the novice blues guitarist a spot on his show. King's guest appearances on *Tan Town Jam-boree* led to his own regular fifteen-minute weekday segment. Bert Fergu-son later hired him to promote a tonic medicine, Peptikon, on a live Saturday-afternoon broadcast, and King soon composed a popular blues jingle for it:

> Peptikon it sure is good
> Peptikon it sure is good
> Peptikon it sure is good
> You can get it anywhere in your neighborhood.[25]

When Hot Rod Hulbert left for Baltimore, King was named the new host of the popular *Sepia Swing Club.* By this time, King was known on

WDIA as the "Beale Street Blues Boy"—a nickname that would later be shortened to "B. B." WDIA launched King's career in the music industry; he made his first blues recordings in the WDIA studios, and members of the station's white management team worked as his booking agents for a period of time in the early 1950s. But as his music career gained momentum, B. B. had less and less time to devote to radio. He left WDIA in 1953 to work full time as a bluesman.[26]

In the 1950s, gospel music was quite popular among local black listeners, and it was prominently featured in WDIA's program schedule. A number of gospel disc jockeys achieved celebrity status as broadcasters on the station. Among the earliest and most colorful were the Reverend Dwight "Gatemouth" Moore, Brother Theo "Bless My Bones" Wade, and Ford Nelson. Moore was yet another Beale Street product; a native of Memphis and former student of Nat D. Williams, he started as a bluesman. After winning the famous Amateur Night contest on Beale Street, "Gatemouth," as he was called by his fellow entertainers, moved to Chicago to pursue a career as a blues vocalist. During a nightclub appearance on the Southside early in 1949, the rising star experienced a religious conversion. According to Moore, when he went on stage that night, he completely forgot his entire blues repertoire—the only thing he could sing was "Shine on Me," an old gospel favorite. The audience thought he had lost his mind, but Gatemouth took it as a religious sign and embarked on his second calling as a minister of the Lord. He was groomed for his new vocation by the Reverend Clarence Cobb, Chicago's most successful black radio preacher, and developed a preaching style every bit as flamboyant as his mentor's.[27]

During a visit to his hometown late in 1949, the newly ordained Moore was approached by Nat D. about doing a gospel show on WDIA; he jumped at the offer. His weekday show, *Light of the World*—named after his gospel signature piece, "Jesus Is the Light of the World"—debuted on the station in October 1949 in the 1 to 2 P.M. time slot. Moore soon became notorious for his unorthodox religious high jinks, which he enthusiastically promoted over the airwaves. On one occasion, he sold tickets to his own funeral, to be held in W. C. Handy Park on Beale Street. When the fateful day arrived, a curious crowd gathered around a coffin bearing Rev. Moore, laid out in his Sunday best. At the announced time of his death, Moore leaped up out of the coffin and preached an inspired sermon, "You

Must Be Born Again."[28] On another occasion, Gatemouth proclaimed on the airwaves that he was going to walk on water, just as Jesus had. On the appointed day, a large crowd gathered on Beale Street and followed Moore down to the Mississippi River. Stopping at the edge of the river, he reached down and touched the muddy water and addressed the gathering; "Children, the water is troubled today, and Rev. Moore cannot walk on troubled waters!"

Gatemouth Moore was WDIA's leading gospel disc jockey for almost two years. During this period, his ubiquitous on-air invocation—"I'm grateful, children, I'm grateful!"—became a popular expression not only among the city's black churchgoers but also with the denizens of Beale Street's nightlife. Moore left Memphis late in 1951 for better pay at WEDR, a black appeal outlet in Birmingham, Alabama; there, he continued to work as a gospel DJ and promote his unique brand of religious salvation.[29]

With the departure of Moore and Hulbert, Ford Nelson and Brother Theo "Bless My Bones" Wade emerged as the city's most popular gospel disc jockeys. Nelson, a well-known Beale Street pianist who played in B. B. King's local band, was initially hired, on Nat D.'s recommendation, to host a live, fifteen-minute weekday blues show on WDIA. But his urbane and authoritative announcing style made him the leading choice to replace Hulbert in the morning gospel slot, a change that occurred in the spring of 1951. Nelson's gospel show, also called *Tan Town Jubilee,* followed Nat D.'s *Tan Town Coffee Club* in the morning lineup. Within a few months, he was also hosting *Highway to Heaven* and becoming known as the station's "dean of gospel music."[30]

In stark contrast to Ford Nelson's erudite gospel presentations were the down-home religious homilies of Brother Theo Wade. During his initial broadcast on WDIA, he spilled a cup of hot coffee in his lap and fervently shouted out over the airwaves: "Bless my bones!" The declaration stuck like flypaper and became his radio name. At the time of his debut as a disc jockey, Brother Wade was also the mentor and manager of the Spirit of Memphis, the city's most popular religious quartet, and the major producer of gospel concerts in the mid-South. His shows featured such national gospel luminaries as Mahalia Jackson, Sister Rosetta Tharpe, and the Soul Stirrers and filled the local Memphis baseball stadium with nearly twenty-five thousand loyal fans. As Memphis's most famous gospel producer, Wade put his contacts with gospel performers around the country to good use on WDIA; his programs always featured the latest popular gospel releases, as well as live appearances by the recording artists. In addition to a two-hour early morning show, *Delta Melodies,* Wade hosted an hour-long program, *Hallelujah Jubilee,* from 8 to 9 P.M. On the weekends, he was the voice and mind behind *Jubilee Roll Call,* the region's first top-ten gospel countdown show, broadcast on Saturday afternoon, and he hosted a two-hour live version of *Hallelujah Jubilee* on Saturday evenings, which became the radio showcase for local gospel talent.[31]

Like Al Benson in Chicago, Brother "Bless My Bones" Wade was a legendary radio pitchman; but WDIA restricted the black air-staff commissions on a sales pitch to solicitations for call-in purchases. Wade became a master of such folksy commercials. Whether he was selling baby chicks or Jesus tablecloths, the telephone switchboard at WDIA lit up when he made his pitch. As Nat D. quipped: "Wade could sell an Eskimo a refrigerator—and then sell him the ice to go with it!" Bless My Bones Wade remained a fixture on WDIA's airwaves for two decades. Toward the end of his reign, he was hailed as the mid-South's "GOP" (Grand Old Poppa) of gospel music.[32]

A Woman's Place Is on the Air

Another dimension of WDIA's unique black appeal format were the programs by and for African American women. The first, *Tan Town Home-makers,* aimed at middle-class black housewives, debuted in August 1949. *Homemakers* was broadcast from 9 to 10 A.M. on weekdays and hosted by Willa Monroe, the reigning diva of Memphis's African American social elite. Monroe's lover, Robert Wright—a wealthy bandleader and show business entrepreneur who owned the city's premier black nightclub, the Brown Derby—had given her a twenty-room mansion, where she lavishly entertained their many friends. One of those in Monroe's social set was Nat D. Williams, and her guest appearances on his shows led directly to her being hired at WDIA. *Tan Town Homemakers* was a mix of soft ballads by such female artists as Eartha Kitt, Sarah Vaughan, and Dinah Washington; Willa's favorite recipes and homemaker hints; "women's news" from the society pages of the local black newspaper; and interviews with other local African American women of prominence. Monroe was an overnight sensation on WDIA. According to the spring 1950 ratings, 40 percent of the Memphis listening audience tuned in to her show. She was in such great demand among her female fans that she held office hours to accommodate their requests for homemaker counseling. The startling success of the *Homemakers* show paved the way for more women's programming on the station.[33]

The next wave of African American women heard on WDIA in the early 1950s included two teaching colleagues of Nat D. Williams, Gerry Brown and Carlotta Stewart Watson, as well as Star McKinney and Martha Jean Steinberg. Gerry Brown won the station's first female disc-jockey contest in 1950 and was hired as hostess for a ballad-dominated R & B show called *Nite Spot,* on weeknights from 9 to 10 P.M. Brown ended her radio career when she married nearly a year later. Carlotta Stewart Watson, who used the name Aunt Carrie on the airwaves, produced and hosted *Spotlight,* a fifteen-minute weekday-morning call-in show that focused on advice for love and family problems. Star McKinney, hired as the station's "society editor" in 1950, soon started hosting a weekend society news segment. The reigning beauty queen of the Cotton Makers' Jubilee, McKinney also teamed up with Robert "Honeyboy" Thomas for the Saturday-morning show *Boy Meets Girl,* which featured the romantic ballads of black crooners and chanteuses, such as Nat King Cole and Dinah Washington.[34]

By far the most successful and popular black female DJ to emerge on WDIA in the 1950s was Martha Jean Steinberg, who took on the radio name "Martha Jean the Queen." The Memphis native was married to a local musician, trumpeter Luther Steinberg, and was active in the local African American community as a fashion show producer before joining the station. After placing second in WDIA's disc-jockey contest, Martha Jean was recruited to cohost a Sunday-evening show with Nat D. Williams. He was the "old-timer" who preferred the swing-era recordings of Duke Ellington, Fats Waller, Ella Fitzgerald, and Jimmy Lunceford, whereas she was the "new-timer" who favored such R & B artists as Laverne Baker, the Clovers, Ruth Brown, and the Drifters. On the air, the regal Martha Jean exuded feminine savvy and sex appeal; her sultry voice was equally attractive to male and female listeners. Before long, she replaced Gerry Brown as the disc jockey on *Nite Spot,* then took over as the hostess of *Tan Town Homemaker* when ill health forced Willa Monroe to retire from radio. Steinberg also replaced Star McKinney as cohost of *Boy Meets Girl,* and she launched her own Saturday-afternoon show, *Premium Stuff,* which showcased the week's hottest R & B discs. By the end of the decade, Martha Jean truly was WDIA's queen of the airwaves. Her hard work and perseverance had won for her a privileged place in the station's male-dominated pantheon of radio personalities. As such, she was an important female broadcast pioneer, not just in Memphis but throughout the country.[35]

Paradoxical Profits

In 1954, WDIA made the transition from a 250-watt to a 50,000-watt outlet and began broadcasting twenty-four hours a day. In addition to the 150,000 African Americans living in Memphis, the station could now reach 350,000 African Americans living in the surrounding rural counties. Moreover, during the late-night hours, when WDIA's signal could be heard all over the mid-South, the potential black audience grew to 1.5 million, or 10 percent of the country's entire African American population. In conjunction with boosting the station's power and increasing its broadcast hours, WDIA launched a campaign promoting itself as the "Goodwill Station." A new daily segment, *Goodwill*, featured public-affairs announcements that covered everything from upcoming civic events to reports of lost mules and dentures.[36] A Goodwill Fund was set up to bankroll various WDIA-sponsored community projects, including Little League baseball teams, an orphanage, a bus for handicapped students, and college scholarships. The money came from a series of fund-raisers organized by the station's black disc jockeys. Two of these events, the "Goodwill Revue" and the "Starlight Revue," grew into large-scale annual extravaganzas that drew as many as twelve thousand people. These shows usually were organized around an R & B segment produced by Nat D. and A. C. Williams, as well as a gospel segment produced by Brother Wade, and were hosted by a parade of WDIA disc jockeys. Among the featured artists, who performed free of charge, were such local favorites as B. B. King, Bobby "Blue" Bland, the Spirit of Memphis, Elvis Presley, and Rufus Thomas (who also joined the WDIA air staff as a DJ during this period), as well as national attractions such as Sam Cooke and the Soul Stirrers, Ray Charles, Muddy Waters, and the Five Blind Boys of Alabama. By the end of the decade, the Goodwill Fund was pumping up to $100,000 a year into the local black community, with the bulk of the revenue coming from the two yearly revues.[37]

In contrast to WDIA's generosity toward the black community, the station's white owners were miserly, at best, when it came to compensating their African American employees. Nat D. Williams, who almost single-handedly created WDIA's format, was paid a paltry $15 a week when first hired by the station. At the height of his popularity and involvement in WDIA, he never made more than $200 a week—a great deal more than the other black DJs at the station. Predictably, all of the better-paying management, sales, and engineering jobs at WDIA went to whites. Meanwhile, the white owners' profits skyrocketed, from less than $2,000 in 1948 to clearing $100,000, after expenses and taxes, nine years later. In 1957, Pepper and Ferguson sold WDIA to Egmont Sounderling for $1 million—a twentyfold gain over their initial investment in the station. At the time of the sale, WDIA was the number one–ranked independent radio station in the country.[38]

During its heyday in the 1950s, WDIA was both a highly profitable media enterprise and a pioneering social experiment in race relations. The key to its unprecedented success was that both racial groups at the station, the white management team and the black air staff, benefited from their alliance, although in different ways. Pepper and Ferguson made a great deal of money on their investment, and they paid white employees better than their black coworkers, maintaining an occupational color line within the station. Yet, though white privilege was never totally abandoned at WDIA, especially in economic terms, the African Americans employed as air staff transformed the station into a vehicle for local black empowerment. They went along with the indignity of being underpaid because their motivation was more social than economic—as were their rewards. In the words of Martha Jean the Queen, their "mission" was "to serve, to sell, to inform, to entertain, and to educate our community."[39] The community orientation in their programming carried over into local cultural activities like the Goodwill Revue and the Starlight Revue. While WDIA's African American disc jockeys didn't become wealthy through their association with the station, they did become celebrities in their own community and role models for the younger generation. This trade-off enabled the station owners to prosper, while the air staff worked to serve the needs of the local African American population. In the process, WDIA became a model for other black appeal ventures around the country.

The Forgotten 15 Million

In the October 10, 1949, issue of *Sponsor,* a trade magazine for radio and television advertisers, an article appeared, titled "The Forgotten 15,000,000: Ten Billion a Year Negro Market Is Largely Ignored by National Advertisers." This article was an important breakthrough for the black appeal stations in their quest for inclusion and respectability in the radio industry. It was the first time a major trade publication on the business side of the industry had devoted attention to this new broadcast phonemenon, providing an in-depth look at black appeal radio in the context of the newly emerging, consumer-oriented "Negro market." The first installment of this historic two-part report profiled the postwar African American consumer, with information based, for the most part, on a national survey conducted in 1948 by the Research Company of America—the first survey of its kind ever commissioned by the advertising industry. The survey's authors estimated that the annual income of the nation's black population had reached $10 billion, a significant rise from pre–World War II levels. In addition, 60 percent of the African American populace now lived in metropolitan areas, where they tended to be better off economically than their rural counterparts. The data also indicated a dramatic increase in radio-set ownership among African Americans since the 1930s: over 90 percent of the black households in urban centers had at least one radio receiver, while in the rural areas, the figure was near 70 percent.[40]

The article pointed out that despite this new market's potential in terms of listeners and consumer dollars, national radio advertisers were still reluctant to invest in black appeal programs, mostly because of the "product-identification" stigma. In the words of the authors: "Advertisers who themselves may have no personal bias feel that if they beamed part of their radio budget directly to the Negro audience, they would lose among white buyers of their product what they might gain among the colored."[41] The first part of the feature concluded with the observation that while national advertisers held back from the African American radio market, local retailers were beginning to cash in on it.

A follow-up article published two weeks later examined the boom in black appeal radio ventures and their growing relationship to local retailers. Much of the material discussed three stations in the South with black

appeal programming: WUSN in Charleston, South Carolina; WEAS in Decatur, Georgia; and especially WDIA in Memphis, whose successful transition to a black appeal format was recounted in glowing terms. The article
praised WDIA owners John Pepper and Bert Ferguson for their forward-
looking business decision to take a chance on "Negro-beamed programs."
Profiles of Nat D. Williams, A. C. Williams, and Willa Monroe as the mid-
South's first black radio announcers accompanied photographs of Monroe
and Hot Rod Hulbert working behind the microphone. The piece concluded by suggesting that WDIA's unprecedented 69 percent ratings in the
fall of 1949 demonstrated that the station had actually gained, not lost,
white listeners during the changeover to black appeal programming.[42]

WUSN in Charleston was cited for the strength of its popular R & B
show *The A-Train,* which was broadcast in two segments every weekday
morning and late evening. The manager of the city's largest record store
drew up the program's playlists to reflect the best-selling R & B discs of the
day. Although the article did not mention the names and race of *The A-
Train* DJs, it pointed out that the show had evolved from a study of African
American radio listeners in Charleston. Conducted for WUSN by a local
advertising firm, the study found that 96 percent of the black households
in the city had at least one radio set, whereas only 33 percent owned tele-
phones. Moreover, African Americans in Charleston, who made up 48
percent of the city's total population, listened to the radio seven and a half
hours a day—three hours more than their white counterparts—and preferred to listen to popular black music, especially during the early morning and late evening hours. The article suggested that the disparity between radio and telephone ownership among urban African Americans
shown in the Charleston study might account for the relatively small black
listening audience in the national statistics, since most surveys were conducted by telephone.[43]

Lastly, the article highlighted the community-outreach shows developed by WEAS in Decatur, Georgia. The station's broadcast signal covered
nearby Atlanta, where close to two hundred thousand African Americans,
or 40 percent of the city's total population, resided. WEAS broadcast
sports events, such as the Atlanta Black Crackers baseball games and Morehouse College's football contests; live church services on Sunday mornings; and a weekly program on juvenile delinquency and black youth. In
addition to WEAS's programming, the article authors focused on the sta-

tion's advertising success stories, citing a number of local white-owned clothing, jewelry, and furniture retailers who had increased their sales by 50 percent or more after advertising on WEAS. Sixty-five local African American businesses were also advertising on the station, with good results.[44] The article did not mention that WEAS did not, as of October 1949, feature African Americans as announcers or DJs but maintained an all-white on-air staff. Readers were not likely, then, to note the irony of a photo of WEAS's top disc jockey, a bespectacled, sandy-haired young man known as "Jack the Bellboy." He was the only white DJ pictured in either installment of the article.

In the July 1952 issue, *Sponsor* revisited the phenomenon of "Negro appeal" radio. An updated, five-part study called "The Forgotten 15,000,000—Three Years Later" began with a section on the Negro market, then estimated to be worth $15 billion. In a question-and-answer format, the authors detailed the African American consumer market in terms of population, income, employment, education, migration, and home ownership. Statistics culled from the 1950 U.S. Census indicated that income, employment, education, and home ownership levels had risen considerably during the 1940s; the median income of the black workforce increased 192 percent in that decade, and home ownership was up 129 percent. These gains exceeded those recorded among the white population by about 50 percent. As the black population continued to grow at a faster rate than its white counterpart, unemployment among African Americans fell below the 10 percent mark for the first time since the end of World War II.[45]

The report's psychological profile of the black consumer revised standard portrayals of African Americans as too poor and too socially marginal to be considered a viable market, replacing these evaluations with curious new images. According to "many top psychologists and social researchers," black consumers in the United States now suffered from an "insecurity neurosis" that compelled them to buy well beyond their means; excessive consumption was their way of overcoming racial discrimination in the marketplace. This novel interpretation was expanded in the section "Selling to Negroes: Don't Talk Down," which quoted the white owner of WLIB, a black appeal outlet in New York City, as saying: "It is an accepted psychological fact that a minority people seek to attain more of the good things in life and articles of better quality than would ordinarily be expected of the general populace in comparable income levels. This understandable desire for recognition makes the Negro far more brand conscious than the average consumer." To bolster this argument, the authors quoted *Ebony* publisher John H. Johnson: "To the Negro, indulgence in luxury is a vindication of his belief in his ability to match the best of white men.[46] This notion of African Americans' propensity toward "conspicuous consumption" would permeate *Sponsor*'s reporting on the Negro market in the years ahead. Its underlying theme—that black people were an easy mark for national brand-name advertisers—would not go unnoticed by the trade publication's clientele.

The remaining segments in the article focused on the growing number of Negro appeal radio outlets springing up around the country, paying particular attention to their programming and advertising efforts. The authors estimated that the 200 to 250 stations that were devoting part or all of their broadcast hours to Negro appeal offerings reached 90 percent of the black population. The most popular programs among African Americans were disc-jockey shows, religious broadcasts, and community affairs programs—in that order. Advertising success stories on the black appeal stations were as plentiful as listeners. Anecdotes included the tales of Ben Reid, who sold three hundred barbecued-chicken dinners after just one advertisement on WERD in Atlanta, and J. Richard Trower, whose business developed into a chain of tailor shops as the result of sponsoring a five-minute daily community calendar show on WHOD in Pittsburgh. Boasting dramatic sales increases for their sponsors, the stations cited a wide range of consumer products and services: WDIA in Memphis—washing machines, patent medicines; WLIB in New York City—television sets, Safeway grocery stores; WLOU in Louisville, Kentucky—beer, men's clothing; WSOK in Nashville, Tennessee—refrigerators, cosmetics; and WEDR in Birmingham, Alabama—laundry starch, electrical appliances.[47] Conspicuously absent was any further discussion of the product-identification stigma that the 1949 articles had explored. Instead, the follow-up emphasized a mushrooming radio market that appeared to have no downside whatsoever.

The 1952 update is also interesting for its extensive use of photographs and the ads that appeared alongside of them. The photos presented a visual panorama of African Americans in radio—from DJs at work behind studio microphones, to remote broadcasts from community events, to station-sponsored advertising and merchandising campaigns involving local retailers. There were photos of young African Americans jitterbugging at a dance concert sponsored by WWCA in Gary, Indiana; of black radio reporters covering a story in a hospital emergency room in Harlem; of gospel singer Sister Rosetta Tharpe performing in the WDIA studios; and of black citizens participating in an on-air Red Cross blood drive in Chicago. In addition, there were numerous publicity shots of African American DJs, including Joe Adams (KOWL, Los Angeles); "Alley Pat" Patrick (WERD, Atlanta); "Okey Dokey" (WBOK, New Orleans); "Genial Gene" (WGIV, Charlotte, North Carolina); and "Louisville Lou" (WLOU, Louisville, Kentucky).[48] With this issue of *Sponsor,* black appeal stations moved from fad to fixture on the national radio scene.

Between 1953 and 1962, *Sponsor* published a yearly special section on "Negro Radio," usually in the fall. Each successive update charted information on the growth of black appeal stations and the Negro market. For example, the number of stations doing black appeal programming rose from 250 in 1953 to more than 800 by 1963; the Negro market went from $15 billion to $27 billion during the same period. Supplementing the figures on the growth of the black consumer market was a yearly statistical breakdown that highlighted African Americans' rising levels of employment, education, income, home ownership, and population—often showing whites gaining ground at a slower rate in these categories. In addition, the updates tracked the emergence of national advertising on black appeal stations from year to year. In the mid-1950s, the attraction of national advertisers was seen as the "last hurdle for Negro radio"; the country's leading brand-name products were still largely missing from the advertising mix on black appeal outlets. By the end of the decade, however, more than 350 brand-name sponsors were targeting the African American consumer on black appeal radio stations.[49] The Negro market was being assimilated into the mainstream of commercial broadcasting, at least with respect to radio advertising.

Resonating throughout this series of *Sponsor* articles were the recurring themes of advertising successes and the pivotal role of the disc jockeys in increasing audience and sales. One amusing incident involved a Ballantine beer promotion on WMBM in Miami, Florida. The station's program director and leading DJ, "Jockey" Jack Gibson, was given several cases of the brew as part of a Ballantine publicity campaign. Gibson decided to pass the beer on to his listeners. His initial announcement of the giveaway caused a huge traffic tie-up around the station in downtown Miami and got Gibson and the WMBM general manager arrested for disturbing the peace. The story made the front page in the local newspaper the next day, along with a photo of the culprits locked up in the city jail.[50]

Black appeal disc jockeys appeared in the limelight early and often in the *Sponsor* series. Heralded as "the heart of Negro Radio," they received the lion's share of the credit for the enterprise's ongoing vitality. In particular, they were lauded for the widespread appeal of their music shows in the local radio markets, their prodigious community-service endeavors on and off the air, and their spectacular successes as radio hucksters. Hardly anonymous "platter spinners," they were "Negro radio personalities with colorful names like Dogface, Gospel Boy, Sir Walter Raleigh and Lord Fauntleroy" and were touted as "community heroes" to the legions of fans who listened to them regularly. They were also in the forefront of the struggle for racial progress that was associated with the Negro appeal stations. The African American disc jockeys were characterized as "the greatest joiners in the world," belonging to "forty or fifty" religious, civic, and fraternal organizations in their hometowns; they were active at "the level of community affairs, public service and in some cases, civil rights." Their ubiquitous involvement and accessibility made them, in the words of one black listener, "one of us."[51]

The *Sponsor* series featured an ongoing barrage of reports on advertising bonanzas orchestrated by "fast-talking Negro disc jockeys" and attributed their triumphs to their ability to speak to the audience "in their own language." This grassroots rapport created listener trust, identification, and, ultimately, loyalty—which were then transferred to the products and services sold over the airwaves. The "Midas touch" of the DJ's made them indispensable to black appeal radio As the driving force behind the profits for the enterprise, the disc jockeys were constantly showcased in the "Negro Radio" updates, as well as in the accompanying publicity photos and in advertisements run by the black appeal stations.[52]

The "Negro Radio" series also extensively covered the launching of three black appeal commercial ventures on the national level: the National Negro Network (1954), the Keystone Broadcasting System's Negro Network (1957), and the Negro Radio Association (1960). The National Negro Network (NNN) was the brainchild of Leonard Evans, an African

American entrepreneur and publisher of a fledgling black appeal radio trade magazine called *Tuesday*. In the 1954 *Sponsor* segment on "Negro Radio," Evans was praised for his pioneering efforts to establish the country's first black appeal network. In its first year of operation, the NNN signed up thirty-five station affiliates and debuted its first nationally syndicated program, a soap opera called *Ruby Valentine*. The soap featured veteran black actress Juanita Hall and was sponsored by Pet Milk and Phillip Morris. The enthusiastic 1954 *Sponsor* report also mentioned several programs in the planning stages, including another soap opera, *The Life of Anna Lewis*, starring Hilda Simms; a variety show hosted by Ethel Waters; and a mystery series to feature Cab Calloway. But the NNN operated for only a year; a lack of capital forced Evans to suspend operations. The 1956 *Sponsor* update barely mentioned the causes of this failure, focusing instead on Evans's plans to revive his moribund network.[53]

The Keystone Negro Network was set up in 1955 as an outgrowth of the Keystone Broadcasting System (KBS), an association of independent, low-power radio stations linked together to provide group rates to national advertisers. When first highlighted in the 1957 "Negro Radio" update, KBS had 347 black appeal affiliates and the potential to reach almost 10 million African Americans; three years later, KBS had 463 black appeal affiliates and a potential audience of 12 million, or 72 percent of the total African American population. The 1960 *Sponsor* update cited the network as yet another example of the lucrative growth potential inherent in black appeal radio, especially with respect to attracting national advertising. The report also featured a photograph of KBS president Sidney J. Wolf chatting with his vice president, E. R. Patterson, and with Chicago-based DJ Sid McCoy; it was used to highlight the use of brand-name commercial spots, in this case produced by McCoy, by Keystone's black appeal affiliates.[54]

Finally, in 1960, a full decade after the birth of black appeal stations, "seven radio pioneers" founded the Negro Radio Association (NRA) and made up its original board of directors. Four of these men owned and operated groups of stations that catered to African American listeners: Egmont Sounderling, owner of the Sounderling Stations (KDIA, Oakland, California; WOPA, Chicago, Illinois; WDIA, Memphis, Tennessee); Joe Speidel, head of Speidel Broadcasting Corporation (WPAL, Charleston, South Carolina; WOIC, Columbia, South Carolina; WYNN, Florence, South Carolina); Robert W. Rounsaville, owner of the Rounsaville Radio Stations

(WMBM, Miami, Florida; WTMP, Tampa, Florida; WLOU, Louisville, Kentucky; WYLD, New Orleans, Louisiana; KPRS, Kansas City, Missouri; WCIN, Cincinnati, Ohio; WVOL, Nashville, Tennessee); and Stanley Ray Jr., head of the OK Group (WBOK, New Orleans, Louisiana; WXOK, Baton Rouge, Louisiana; KAOK, Lake Charles, Louisiana; WGOK, Mobile, Alabama; WLOK, Memphis, Tennessee; KYOK, Houston, Texas). The remaining board members were all single black appeal station owners: Harry Novick (WLIB, New York City), Norwood J. Patterson (KSAN, San Francisco), and F. M. Fitzgerald (WGIV, Charlotte, North Carolina) who was also the chairman of the NRA board. According to Fitzgerald: "The particular business and objective of the Association shall be to foster, study, develop and improve Negro radio programming; to study, foster and develop public service programming for the benefit of Negro groups, and to cooperate in the development of Negro talent and program product in the United States . . . and throughout the world."[55]

In spite of these lofty goals and optimistic predictions of rapid growth, the NRA failed to generate much enthusiasm for itself within the radio industry, where its biggest stumbling block appears to have been membership. During its first year, the association attracted only two new station members and lost four of the original thirty-seven charter stations that collectively bankrolled the operation. When interviewed for *Sponsor*'s 1961 "Negro Radio" update, F. M. Fitzgerald tried to put a positive spin on the organization's lackluster beginnings: "To gain a few and lose a few and still have an active association of members at the end of the hardest year, the first, is a tribute to the station owners who belong to the NRA. It shows that they are good operators who concern themselves with contributing something big and successful to the industry." Nevertheless, the only accomplishment that Fitzgerald could point to after a year at the helm of the NRA was the publication of an industry newsletter called the *Bronze Mike*. For reasons never revealed in the *Sponsor* series, the association floundered, and by the time of the 1962 update, it was moribund—a news item the "Negro Radio" report also failed to mention.[56]

The special treatment given to the short-lived Negro Radio Association in *Sponsor*'s "Negro Radio" reports illustrates the series' general avoidance of negative or controversial issues in favor of a tunnel-vision approach to the subject. In short, the series' authors saw only what they and the magazine wished to see, especially where race was concerned. For example, when it came to station ownership, color was suddenly an elusive subtext, to be found only in the accompanying photographs—if at all. All the black appeal radio station owners who were profiled in the series or appeared in the photos were white males, yet their race was rarely mentioned. Moreover, none of the handful of African American station owners in the country was ever pictured or profiled in the series, and the only one who was quoted, J. B. Blayton (WERD, Atlanta), was never acknowledged as the first African American in the country to own a radio station.[57] In effect, the authors of the "Negro Radio" reports were color-blind when writing about the owners of black appeal outlets.

In contrast, African American disc jockeys were highly visible in the gallery of photographs assembled for the series, and they were referred to constantly in the text of the reports. However, their efforts to organize black DJs into a professional trade organization, the National Association of Radio Announcers (NARA, 1954), were totally ignored by the series. (The role of white disc jockeys in black appeal radio was discussed at one point in the series, with Hunter Hancock of KFRC, Los Angeles, singled out as an example of a white DJ with a large black listening audience.)[58] Generally speaking, where on-air talent was concerned, the *Sponsor* series played up the race of the entertainers, but when the issue of ownership came up, color didn't enter the picture. This strategy helped conceal white ownership and control of the black appeal outlets; instead, the focus was on how these stations benefited the radio industry and the African American population. To be sure, this economic exploitation of black entertainment trends by white entrepreneurs was nothing new in American popular culture. From the postbellum rise of black minstrelsy in the 1870s, through the race-record business and the TOBA vaudeville circuit after World War I, to blackface radio entertainers during the 1930s and 1940s, the pattern was well established, only finding new forms in the black appeal radio industry.

7

Spin Doctors of the Postwar Era

ponsor's groundbreaking series on "Negro Radio" showcased African American disc jockeys, recognizing them as the driving force behind the emergence and profitability of the black appeal stations. Their pivotal position in the post–World War II radio industry enabled African American DJs to fill the coffers of their white employers even as they gave voice to the aspirations, concerns, and sensibilities of their own people. In the words of Martha Jean "the Queen" Steinberg, the mid-South's premier black female disc jockey in the the 1950s:

> We were the mayors back then. At that particular time, you have to understand that you didn't have any black politicians, no black judges, very few black lawyers . . . you didn't have any so-called black leaders. So we were the ones who spoke out. We were considered the mayors of the cities. . . . We were shaping the minds and hearts of the people, and we did a good job. We encouraged them to go to school, to get degrees, to be educated. Told them about racial pride. We talked to young girls about not having babies. We kept our communities intact.[1]

For the most part, the black disc jockeys who rose to prominence in the postwar years were inspired by the Al Benson, not the Jack Cooper, school of broadcasting. In their desire to celebrate and extend the black oral tradition, rather than emulate the white cultural mainstream, they relied on verbal strategies of African American folklore—especially rhyming and signifying. These traditional modes of expression were meant to be entertaining, but they also masked the messages going out over the air. Steinberg explains: "We were bright people—independent thinkers . . . even philosophers. But we had to act like clowns to get our point across and not upset anything, or let anyone know we were upsetting anything."[2] This "double-voiced" discourse, embedded in the DJs' speech and the musical messages, was the key to their appeal as African American broadcasters. Yet, ironically, it marked a return to the wellspring of the black oral tradition and an inversion of the blackface ventriloquy that had dominated the airwaves in the previous era.

The Travels of "Jack the Rapper": Jack Gibson

One of the most successful graduates of the Al Benson school of broadcasting was Jack Gibson, the man who would later be known as "Jack the Rapper" throughout the world of black entertainment. Gibson, a native of Chicago, was a graduate of Lincoln University, a black college located in Jefferson City, Missouri. In the early 1940s, he studied drama at Lincoln and led the student jazz orchestra. Degree in hand, he returned to his hometown seeking a job as a film actor; but after being rejected as "too light to play a Negro and too dark to pass for white," he ventured into radio. His first broadcasting job was in 1945 as a character actor in Richard Durham's pioneering black soap opera *Here Comes Tomorrow*. Within a year, he was also hosting a nightly thirty-minute music show on WJJD, the same station that sponsored the soap opera.[3]

In 1948, Al Benson took note of Gibson's music show and took the fledgling DJ under his wing, as an assistant on Benson's morning R & B show. According to Gibson:

I would go and pick him up every morning at his house. He always insisted that I stop at the local liquor store and get a bottle of Hennessy—quart bottles. I took that and the 78 records that we had with us in to the studio. I would set up his quart bottle of Hennessy with a glass and give his stack of 78s to the engineer. Al would sit there and take a sip, then signal his engineer to play a record or open the mike. I sat in the corner and watched, sometimes waiting for him to nod off so I could take over. But he never missed a cue. So I just watched him and answered the phones, which were always ringing off the hook.[4]

During his apprenticeship with Benson, Gibson heard and saw first-hand how his mentor was able to attract and hold such a huge audience: "He was very flamboyant and very outspoken and very earthy, and then I guess maybe the people at that time from Chicago—you know, they came from Louisiana and Mississippi—they were used to hearing people mess up the King's English. So Al was their man. And that taught me to break up a few verbs myself, and I found out that it worked!"[5] Having grown up in Chicago, Gibson was familiar with Jack Cooper's efforts on the local airwaves, as well as with the stylistic and language differences between the professional-sounding Cooper and Benson: "Jack Cooper, he was a straight announcer, so he'd say, 'Look here, I hope you all go to Aunt Mami's Beauty Saloon, because she has a new special.' Al Benson would probably say, 'Y'all need yo' hair fried? Better get on down to Auntie Mami's, she gotta thing goin' on. Tell her Ole Swingmaster send ya!' See, that was the difference, that was a personality against what we called a straight announcer."[6]

Jack Gibson worked for Al Benson until the fall of 1949, when an old college friend made a tempting offer. J. B. Blayton Jr.'s father had just purchased radio station WERD in Atlanta. Blayton was leaving Chicago for Atlanta to manage the outlet and wanted Gibson to come with him and be his program director. Gibson jumped at the chance to work for the first black-owned radio station in the country. As WERD's program director, charged with switching the station over to a black appeal format, he had a difficult first year; but with the support of the Blaytons, he changed the programming and replaced most of the all-white on-air personnel with African Americans. Gibson also worked as a regular disc jockey on WERD, putting to good use what he had learned from Al Benson. By 1951, WERD had become Atlanta's leading black appeal station, and Jack Gibson was the city's most popular DJ.[7]

Later in 1951, Gibson moved on to WLOU in Louisville, Kentucky, home of the Kentucky Derby, where he became known on the airwaves as "Jockey Jack." Resplendent in a silk jockey outfit and carrying a leather riding crop for publicity, he liked to open his show with the traditional Derby bugle call and the following incantation:

> My father wasn't a jockey, but he sure taught me to ride.
> He sat right in the middle, then rocked from side to side.
> Ride, Jockey Jack, Ride![8]

Two years later, Gibson was on the move again—this time to WMDM in Miami, where he hosted the station's afternoon R & B show and worked as program director. It was at WMBM that Jack Gibson made national headlines for his ill-fated Ballantine beer giveaway, when the police arrested him and his station manager for disturbing the peace. The Miami police assumed that Gibson, like the WMDM general manager, was white; both were held in a cell reserved for white lawbreakers, where the press photographed them peering out from behind bars. When Jockey Jack returned to his hotel in Miami's black business district, the manager, having seen the photo in the local press, concluded that Gibson was a white man trying to pass for black and demanded that he vacate his room. It took the bemused DJ a while to convince the manager otherwise.[9]

Late in 1954, Gibson returned to WERD in Atlanta, resuming his duties as program director and disc jockey and honing his skills as a broadcaster and community activist. In 1958, he accepted a similar position and the challenge of creating a black appeal format for WCIN in Cincinnati. Dudley Riley, a former DJ who grew up in Cincinnati, recalled the transition: "Well, CIN did not exist . . . as a black station in the city prior to Jack's coming. . . . I think Jack got to the people first, he related to the music they wanted to hear, and he himself was a dynamic type of individual. He brought that over onto the air, and then he got out and met the people. He brought the black businessmen into CIN for advertising and things of that nature, so then the blacks actually participated in CIN. Before it was practically all white."[10]

Early in 1962, the founder of Motown Records, Berry Gordy, lured Jockey Jack away from radio broadcasting and hired him as the fledgling labels' national director of Promotions and Public Relations. For the next five years, Gibson visited black appeal radio outlets around the country, promoting Motown's latest releases. He was also involved in producing the legendary Motown Revue concert tours, becoming a "big brother" figure to many of the label's young stars (like Diana Ross and Stevie Wonder).[11]

Although he left his disc-jockey career behind when he went to work for Motown, Jack Gibson never lost interest in black appeal radio. Over the years, as the industry changed, he became increasingly concerned with what he viewed as the decline of the community and personality style of broadcasting that he had helped pioneer in the 1950s. By 1976, this concern led to the founding of *Jack the Rapper,* a monthly trade publication that targeted black radio and music enterprises. Under Gibson's guidance, the magazine became an advocate for African American personality jocks and black appeal programming in an era of "urban contemporary" crossover formats. As an extension of his trade publication, he also launched the annual Jack the Rapper Black Family Affair Convention in 1977. Initially held in Atlanta, the three-day music and radio convention quickly grew into the largest regular gathering of African Americans working in these industries. Both endeavors catapulted Gibson back to the forefront of the black entertainment world, where he remains to this day.[12]

Journeyman Jock: "Joltin'" "Joe Howard

African American disc jockeys such as Gibson moved frequently from job to job because of low wages, lack of job security, and changing fortunes in the radio industry. As more black appeal stations went on the air, new and usually more lucrative employment opportunities opened up. "Joltin'" "Joe Howard was just such a journeyman in black appeal radio during the postwar years. A native of Galveston, Texas, his earliest broadcast influence was George Prater, a local product who hosted the city's first R & B show, *Harlem Echo,* on KGBC beginning in 1949. Prater, who had been paralyzed in an auto acident, broadcast out of a makeshift bedroom studio; his show was the most popular black appeal program in the market throughout the 1950s. Howard broke into broadcasting as a DJ in nearby Houston on KNUZ, the city's pioneering black appeal station. KNUZ's nightly R & B show, begun in the late 1940s, was called *The Beehive*. Howard got the job because of his excellent diction and his natural ability to read commercial copy.[13]

In 1952, Howard moved across town to a better-paying job with KYOK, a station that had just been taken over by the New Orleans-based OK Group. Once again, his ability to read copy was the deciding factor in his being hired. According to Howard: "It was a funny thing at KYOK. This was shortly after the OK chain had bought the station, and they brought in their format from New Orleans. All of their air personnel had names which made their identities unmistakable . . . or so the owners thought. Hotsy Totsy, Zing Zang, Dizzy Lizzy. So when I went over, they wanted to know what to name me . . . but I held out for my own name. The reason I held out and prevailed was because they really needed somebody who could read."[14] Like many other black DJs, male and female, on the airwaves during the postwar era, Howard resisted this type of stereotyping by white management.

In 1954, Joe Howard made a brief foray into mainstream white radio as an announcer and a DJ. He was hired, with a substantial salary increase, by WAKE in Atlanta to be the voice behind their commercial spots and to host an evening pop-music show. But the crossover venture was short-lived. When a major sponsor discovered that the voice in his radio ads belonged to a black man, he demanded that the station owners get rid of Howard. Ironically, the sponsor had initially sought Howard out to congratulate him on his job performance. As Howard recalled: "So I got fired. They called me in and told me as gingerly as they could. . . . I got fired because I sounded too much like a white man is the way they put it."[15] During this period, the black announcers who managed to cross over to mainstream white stations were hired because they *were* able to sound like the white announcers on the air; it was only when their racial ventriloquy was discovered, as in Howard's case, that problems arose.

WAKE's loss was WERD's gain. Howard was soon hired by J. B. Blayton Jr. to host the station's morning R & B show, even though Blayton was somewhat apprehensive about how Howard would get along with his "number-one cat," Jockey Jack Gibson. As it turned out, the two men became good friends; they often spent time together on Auburn Avenue, the hub of Atlanta's black community, and they sat in on each other's shows. Along with two of the station's other veteran disc jockeys, Roosevelt Johnson and Jimmy Winnington, they became known as the "four horsemen" of WERD. In the process, and under the tutelage of Jack Gibson, Joe Howard was finding his own voice and developing his own style as a personality jock.[16]

In 1956, both Howard and Gibson were offered disc-jockey positions at a new black-owned radio station in Inkster, Michigan, by Larry Dean Faulkner, the outlet's first program director. Faulkner, the son of a Chicago minister, had attended Fisk University in Nashville, where he helped launch that city's first black appeal station, WSOK; he was then hired by the owner of WCHB, Dr. Haley Bell, to do the same thing for Bell's Inkster operation. Faulkner's recruiting trip to Atlanta was only partially successful: Joe Howard accepted the offer, but Jack Gibson chose to stay with WERD for the time being. WCHB was located on the edge of the Detroit radio market, facing stiff competition from WJLB, the city's reigning black appeal outlet. At the time, WJLB featured an all-star lineup of black personality jocks: "Rockin'" Leroy White, "Frantic" Ernie Durham, "Senator" Bristow Bryant, and Miss Susie Strother—all of whom had large followings. Nevertheless, within a year of signing on the air, WCHB was challenging WJLB for the leadership position in the black appeal segment of the market, and "Joltin'" Joe Howard was the hottest new DJ on the Detroit airwaves.[17]

Faulkner borrowed Howard's nickname from "Joltin'" Joe DiMaggio, the baseball star; it fit nicely with Howard's animated, rapid-fire style of broadcasting. As Howard recalled:

What happened was when I went in, my style was new. The thing that was different about my style was that it was fast-paced. I talked faster than any other human being on radio, yet I was articulate and understandable. I used a lot of slang because that was the order of the day, but I used it in a cutesy way, rather than really getting down. Of course . . . I stole a lot of Jack's stuff. He was still in Atlanta. I stole a lot of it and went up to Detroit. I used the theme song he used to use by Big Jay McNeely called "The Goose." The record came on and was fast-paced with a break. When the break came, I would say something like—"It ain't the Lone Ranger and Tonto!" Every morning I would say something different. People around town got to betting on what I'd say. "I bet he says Little Red Riding Hood! No, I bet five dollars he says Dick Tracy!" Little gimmicks like that caught on."[18]

Over the next two decades, Joltin' Joe Howard was a popular fixture on black appeal radio in the Detroit market. He worked for WCHB until 1960, then switched over to WJLB for a seven-year run as their top DJ. In the late 1960s, Howard was involved in launching WGPR, Detroit's premicr progressive black FM station.

Space Commander: Douglas "Jocko" Henderson

Perhaps the most celebrated black disc jockey to emerge in the 1950s was Douglas "Jocko" Henderson, the space-age commander of the legendary *Rocket Ship* shows, broadcast in a number of key urban markets throughout the country:

> Once again it's rocket ship time.
> And those not on board must be outta their mind.
> The rocketeers are lined up side by side,
> ready to take their most exciting ride.
> From earth to the moon you gotta go,
> with your rocket ship commander—Jocko.
> We'll be on the moon if the fuel will last.
> So let's leave the earth with a big bad blast.
> [*Sound effect: rocket ship blasting off*]
> Way up here in the stratosphere,
> gonna holler mighty loud and clear.
>
> Eeeh, tiddley-tock,
> Yo! This is the Jock.
> Back on the scene,

with my record machine.
Saying oo-poppa-do,
How do you do?
Dy-no-mite!
Now on with the flight.[19]

Douglas Henderson grew up in segregated Baltimore, Maryland. His mother was a teacher, and his father, who had a doctorate in education, was the superintendent of the city's black schools. At the urging of his father, who had a strong desire that his son follow in his footsteps, Henderson attended the Tuskeegee Institute in Alabama from 1949 to 1952. But even while in college, his interests were gravitating toward radio; in particular, he was fascinated by the rhyming hipster Maurice "Hot Rod" Hulbert, who had reigned as the hottest black DJ in Baltimore since the debut of his *Rocket Ship* show on WITH late in 1950. While home on vacation in the summer of 1952, Henderson auditioned for a job as a DJ, and much to his father's dismay, he was hired. His original program, *The Doug Henderson Show,* debuted on WSID in June; it was a two-hour weekday afternoon time slot and paid him only $12 a week. Luckily, the novice disc jockey was able to supplement his meager radio salary by selling cars on the air until a better offer came along—which happened rather quickly.[20]

Late in 1952, WHAT in Philadelphia offered Henderson an afternoon show for $50 a week; he played hard to get until the offer reached $120 a week, then agreed to it. Henderson used the move to Philadelphia as an opportunity to create an new radio persona for himself—one that owed a great deal to his Baltimore idol, Hot Rod Hulbert. As he recalled:

Anyway, I began to stop using Doug Henderson and just picked up . . . formed the name Jocko because Jocko rhymed with Daddy-O and Mommy-O, and the hottest show on radio. And instead of just having a regular show, we had a rocket-ship show. . . . I borrowed the rocket-ship show from Hot Rod, who was in Baltimore during that time. That's what he called his show. And we began to rhyme up everything—"Yo tiddley yock, this is the Jock, back on the scene in my record machine, sing oop bop a-doo, how do you do." All kinds of rhyme. And the kids picked up on this.[21]

The practice of rhyming, part of the black oral tradition, was especially appealing to Henderson's African American audience.

"Jocko" Henderson reached overnight celebrity status in the Philadelphia radio market with his weekday afternoon *Rocket Ship* show. Within a matter of months, he was lured away from WHAT to rival WDAS for a $350 a week salary. Then, in 1954, he was hired by WLIB in New York City to host their morning show, and he began a daily commute between the two locations to do the broadcasts. In the mid-1950s, both WDAS and WLIB were highly rated black appeal outlets in their respective locales, and those two markets alone showcased many of the most popular and powerful R & B DJs in the country. In Philadelphia, the WDAS lineup included Jocko, the veteran Kai Williams, and the debonair John Bandy, known on the air as "Lord Fauntleroy." Bandy, whose family was from Jamaica, spoke with a British accent and wore an ascot as his trademark. Henderson was especially impressed with his demeanor on the air: "He used to rhyme up everything. . . . He was fantastic! Unbelievable!" (In the late 1950s, Lord Fauntleroy retired to a country estate outside Philadelphia, after a much-publicized interracial marriage to Gulf Oil heiress Roberta Pew.) WDAS's major competition came from WHAT, the station that initially brought Henderson to Philadelphia, whose lineup featured the city's original R & B DJ, Ramon Bruce (*Ravin' with Ramon*), as well as Larry Dixon and Georgie Woods—the "Man with the Goods." Woods would become the city's best-known African American disc jockey by the end of the decade, surpassing even Jocko in listenership and notoriety.[22]

Although Jocko Henderson continued to reside in Philadelphia, his broadcasting career was increasingly centered in New York City. At WLIB, he joined an impressive roster of personality jocks, including Washington, D.C., veteran Hal Jackson; Jack Walker, the "Pear-Shaped Talker"; Phil "Doctor Jive" Gordon; comic Nipsy Russell; and jazz pianist Billy Taylor. The other leading black appeal disc jockeys in the market during the mid-1950s were Willie Bryant, the "Mayor of Harlem," on WHOM; and Tommy Smalls, the city's second "Doctor Jive," who broadcast in the afternoons on WWRL. Smalls's career in radio scripted like a classic American tragedy. The young, bush-league DJ from Savannah, Georgia, became an overnight sensation in the New York market. At the height of his career on WWRL, he not only hosted the city's top-rated afternoon R & B show but promoted local R & B concerts that rivaled those of rock-and-roll kingpin Alan Freed. He was a talent scout for Ed Sullivan's famous *Toast of the Town* TV variety show and appeared in person on the nationally televised CBS program to introduce the R & B acts. He was also the co-owner of a popular Harlem nightclub, Smalls Paradise. Then, in 1960, the bottom fell out: Tommy Smalls became a target of a New York City "payola" investigation. At age thirty-four, he was indicted for accepting over $13,000 in bribes from eighteen different record companies and subsequently was banished from the radio industry. A decade later, he died in poverty, a forgotten man.[23]

Like Tommy Smalls, Jocko Henderson used his fame on the airwaves as a springboard to allied ventures in television and concert production. In the late 1950s, he launched *Jocko's Rocket Ship Show* on WNTA-TV, an independent Newark, New Jersey, television outlet. After hosting the live after-school dance party for black teenagers for about a year, Henderson abandoned the TV show. His inability to attract national sponsorship and network interest, despite excellent local ratings, left him angry and frustrated. As he later recalled: "The television industry, like radio before it, was very racist back then. Sponsors would not buy time, for example, on Nat King Cole's television show, even though he was popular among whites and blacks. If I had been a little further ahead in time, things might have been different for me. If I hadn't been black, *American Bandstand* [Dick Clark's popular ABC television show] might have been mine."[24]

Henderson's R & B concert productions fared much better than his short-lived TV show. When he began staging R & B revues at the Apollo Theater in the mid-1950s, he faced stiff competition from Tommy Smalls, who used the Apollo as a venue for his own concerts. But when Smalls's various enterprises were shut down after the payola investigations, the Apollo Theater became, in effect, the house that Jocko built. His much-ballyhooed concerts there showcased the latest R & B luminaries: Sam Cooke, the Coasters, Clyde McPhatter, Smokey Robinson, the Supremes, Marvin Gaye, and Stevie Wonder. Like Al Benson, Jocko Henderson was a star attraction himself, and his appearances at the Apollo concerts were as eagerly received as the R & B acts he introduced. In fact, his Apollo Theater entrances were legendary; in his own words: "The guys at the Apollo built a rocket . . . wired it up in the air . . . and when the show started, they would turn it loose and it would glide down with the smoke and the lights . . . rocket sounds . . . and everything. It would glide to the center of the stage and I'd get out in my space suit saying, 'Yo tiddley-yock, this the the Jock . . . your ace from outta space!' And this killed the people. They fell out . . . couldn't believe it!"[25] For these rocket-ship openings, Henderson wore an authentic U.S. Air Force space suit that had been donated to him as a publicity stunt by the Pentagon's space program.

During his Apollo Theater reign, the radio rocket man made international headlines for his most fabled space-age caper. In 1959, when Soviet cosmonaut Yuri Gagarin became the first man to orbit the Earth, one of Henderson's coworkers at WDAS in Philadelphia sent the Russian space pioneer the following telegram: "Congratulations! I'm really glad you made it. Now it's not so lonely up here" It was signed "Jocko Henderson, American Rocket Ship Commander." A few years later, a U.S. correspondent discovered that an enlarged copy of the telegram had been enshrined in a newly opened Moscow space museum. Apparently, the Russians thought Jocko was one of Yuri's American counterparts. Henderson was as surprised and bemused by the incident as everyone else: "Oh man, it was amazing. . . . You know, the Russians blew it up and encased it in plastic, first thing you see when you walk into the museum . . . and as far as I know, it's still there, even with the *New York Times* story saying, you know, Jocko ain't no rocket-ship man. He's a DJ. Yes, yes, yes, that's funny . . . that is really, really funny."[26]

At the height of his career on the airwaves, Jocko Henderson had a large and devoted following not only in New York and Philadelphia but also in Boston, Washington, D.C., Miami, Detroit, and St. Louis, where tailor-made tapes of his *Rocket Ship* show were broadcast regularly. His "Rocketeers" fan club at the time claimed to have fifty thousand members.[27] Henderson was so well known that when his idol and mentor, Hot Rod Hulbert, tried to break into the Philadelphia and New York radio markets in the late 1950s, he was invariably accused of imitating Jocko! Offended but undeterred, Hulbert tried in vain to set the record straight:

> All right Big Mommy-O and Big Daddy-O,
> keen teens in your blue jeans,

> ladies and Gentlemen everywhere:
> Commander Hot Rod is in place,
> the high priest of outer space.
> Not the imitator,
> I am the originator, the creator.
> Not the flower, not the root,
> but the seed, sometimes called the herb.[28]

In this instance, however, the teacher proved no match for the student; outside of Baltimore, Hot Rod was never able to overcome the stigma of being a Jocko imitator.

The 1950s were the glory days for the signifying spin doctors, who seemed to be on the air everywhere. There was Doctor Hep Cat in Austin, Texas; two Doctor Jives in New York City and another one in Durham, North Carolina; Doctor Daddy-O in New Orleans and Houston; Doctor Jazzmo in Shreveport, Louisiana; Doctor Bop in Columbus, Ohio; and Doctor Feelgood in Atlanta. In addition, the country's black appeal outlets were the launching pads for Jocko and Hot Rod, Jocky Jack and Joltin' Joe, Moohah and Gatemouth, Honeyboy and King Bee, Butterball and Spiderman, Sugar Daddy, Daddy Deep Throat, and Daddy Rabbit, Satellite Poppa and Poppa Stoppa, Ravin' Ramon and Rockin' Leroy, Alley Cat and King Kong, the Black Pope and Prince Omar, Lord Fauntleroy and Sir Walter Raleigh, Genial Gene and Frantic Ernie, Jive Master Kolb, and Jack Walker the Pear-Shaped Talker. Behind these radio pseudonyms were the voices of the country's premier "personality jocks," as they came to call themselves—African American DJs who used their wits, guile, and imagination to break down Jim Crow in the radio industry and reshape the soundscape of the nation's airwaves. In the words of historian Portia Maultsby: "We can best describe African American DJs as performers. They connected with the community. They shucked and jived with the community. In spite of the microphones, DJs were committed to having a personal conversation with their audiences . . . which they did. So the oral tradition of storytelling, speaking in rhythm and rhyme, speaking in an improvised style, as well as an animated delivery, is a cultural expression that was familiar to the masses. Which is why so many people enjoyed personality radio."[29]

Black Appeal Homemakers and
DJ Queens

African American women also made significant gains in the field of broadcasting during the rise of black appeal radio. Their roles, however, were initially much more restricted than those of their male coworkers, who were also much more numerous. The radio industry was still male dominated during this period. Women did not own any stations on the air, nor were they employed as managers, technicians, announcers, or even in sales. Aside from secretarial work, the only jobs open to them were as radio entertainers. Prior to 1950, white women had made some headway in the industry as on-air talent; such comedians as Gertrude Berg (*The Goldbergs*), Gracie Allen (*Burns and Allen*), Lucille Ball (*My Favorite Husband*), Eve Arden (*Our Miss Brooks*), and Marie Wilson (*My Friend Irma*) enjoyed long and prosperous careers on network radio, as did singers, for instance, Kate Smith and the Andrews Sisters. Moreover, numerous actresses were employed in leading and supporting roles for the networks' women-oriented daytime soap operas. These serials dramatized the daily lives of serious female characters such as Ma Perkins, Helen Trent, Stella Dallas, "Young Widder Brown," and "Our Gal Sunday."[30]

In contrast, portrayals of African American women on the airwaves before 1950 were dominated by network radio stereotypes—Aunt Jemima, Beulah, and Sapphire. The few exceptions to this trend, jazz vocalists Lena Horne, Ella Fitzgerald, and Billie Holiday, were occasionally heard nationwide on the networks' variety shows or late-night swing-band broadcasts. Vaudeville vocalist and Hollywood actress Ethel Waters briefly hosted an NBC variety show in the mid-1930s, and Marian Anderson's historic 1939 Lincoln Memorial concert, which drew seventy-five thousand people to the monument grounds, was broadcast nationally. (The world-renowned concert vocalist had been denied a permit to sing at Constitution Hall in the nation's capital by the Daughters of the American Revolution, due to her race.)[31] In general, however, blackface gender stereotypes were the order of the day on the nation's airwaves, and even when African American women managed to overcome the radio industry's racial and gender barriers, they did so solely as entertainers. Consequently, the voices of Mary McCleod Bethune, Mary Church Terrell, and Ida B. Wells, the era's most dynamic black female civic leaders, were never featured on the networks and rarely heard even on local outlets.

With the rise of black appeal radio, African American women were finally able to establish a foothold in broadcasting, but invariably, their early roles on these airwaves were as homemakers. Willa Monroe's *Tan Town Homemakers* on WDIA in Memphis was typical of the early radio shows hosted by black women. For the most part, the programs targeted middle-class housewives and offered a hodgepodge of cooking tips and recipes, housekeeping hints, child-rearing advice, and marital relationship counseling, as well as church and society news. In addition to Monroe, pioneering black appeal radio homemakers who emerged in the late 1940s and early 1950s included Louise Fletcher (*A Woman Speaks,* WSOK, Nashville); Alice Wyce (*Home Executive,* WERD, Atlanta); Robelia Polk (*Homemaker's Holiday,* WEDR, Birmingham, Alabama); Delores Estelle and Laura Lane on WMRY, New Orleans; Hilda Simms (*Ladies Day,* WOV, New York City); and Mary Dee (*Today's Calendar,* WHOD, Pittsburgh, Pennsylvania). By the late 1950s, many of the women who continued to broadcast as homemakers—Leola Dyson on WRAP, Norfolk, Virginia; Cathy Curry on WCIN, Cincinnati; and Sister Bessie Griffith on WMRY, New Orleans—were given new titles, such as "women's director" or "director of women's activities."[32]

For several African American women, homemaker shows became springboards to full-time jobs as disc jockeys. Mary Dee, a Pittsburgh native, began her association with WHOD in 1949 as the announcer of a weekday five-minute calendar of events for local black women. Her show quickly attracted a large audience and generated handsome profits for the sponsors. By the end of 1950, Dee's role at the station was expanded to include hosting two music shows, *Gospel Train* and *Movin' around with Mary Dee.* At the height of her career in radio in the 1950s, she not only was Pittsburgh's most popular black female DJ but was also doing a show on WSID in the Baltimore market. Carolyn Shaw on WOKJ, Jackson, Mississippi; Susie Strother on WJIB, Detroit; and Jackie Ford on KSAN, San Francisco, followed similar career paths. Shaw started by hosting a homemakers' program called *Kitchen Time.* Her job at the station eventually expanded to include deejaying the *Sepia Serenade* late-night show. Strother's first radio program was *Cradle Time,* an award-winning series on caring for newborns.

Its success paved the way for her to become the station's first female disc jockey. Ford also broke into radio as the hostess of a homemakers' show, built up an audience, and moved on to become the West Coast's first high-profile black female deejay.[33]

In spite of the prevailing gender bias in the broadcast industry, African American women emerged as featured DJs on many key black appeal stations around the country during the 1950s. In New York City, WLIB opted to hire two women of exceptional musical pedigree: Ruth Ellington, the sister of jazz titan Duke Ellington, and Nora Holt, the daughter of a distinguished Kansas City music professor. Ellington hosted a weekly program of recorded jazz standards and live interviews with prominent black musicians. Holt, a classically trained pianist and composer with a master's degree in music, had performed on the concert circuit in both Europe and the United States and had worked as a music critic for the *Chicago Defender* and then New York's *Amsterdam News* before venturing into radio. Her weekly *Concert Showcase* was the first program in the country regularly to feature the classical music of black composers. Evelyn Robinson, sister of boxing legend Sugar Ray Robinson, was the first female disc jockey on New York's WOV; she cohosted the nightly *Life Begins at Midnight* show from the Palm Café in Harlem during the 1950s. Lou Lutour, the first black female to broadcast regularly on WHOM, began as hostess of the youth forum *Teen Town*, then moved on to become a disc jockey and a commentator for the station. Lutour also worked as a dramatic actress; her *One-Woman Show,* which featured scenes from the lives of such famous African American women as Sojourner Truth, Harriet Tubman, and poet Phyllis Wheatley, was popular in Harlem during the 1950s.[34]

In Chicago, the pioneering female voice on the black appeal stations belonged to Gertrude Cooper, the wife of radio magnate Jack Cooper. As early as 1938, she launched the first in a series of homemaker shows with help from her husband, and over the next decade, she reigned as the city's premier black female broadcaster. At the start of the 1950s, however, Cooper's homemaker format was gradually eclipsed by the region's earliest African American women DJs. The first to emerge was Vivian Carter, the Chicago native who won Al Benson's female DJ contest in 1948 and soon became one of his "satellite jocks" on WGES. After establishing herself in the local radio market with Benson's help, Carter moved on to nearby Gary, Indiana, where she developed her own show on WGRY. In addition, Vivian and her new husband, Eddie Bracken, opened their own record store in Gary. In 1953, they launched an independent label, Vee-Jay Records, which was based in Chicago. VeeJay recorded many of the region's top R & B acts, including urban bluesmen such as Jimmy Reed and John Lee Hooker, as well as vocal groups such as the Spaniels, the Dells, and the Impressions. Vivian Carter continued her association with WGRY during the 1950s, but the lion's share of her time and energy was now devoted to the record business.[35]

Several other African American women emerged as popular DJs on Northern black appeal outlets during this period, including Dora Richardson on WUFO, Buffalo, New York; Marlene Moore on WAMO, Pittsburgh; Louise Johnson on WOPA, Oak Hill, Illinois; and Martha Jean the Queen Steinberg, who left WDIA and Memphis in the late 1950s for a job at black-owned WCHB in Inkster, Michigan. The Queen, by now a seasoned and polished broadcast veteran, was an instant sensation in the nearby Detroit market. She maximized her rapport with the city's large black working-class population by immediately developing a popular segment on her daily R & B show called "Toasting Time": "So I had a blue-collar salute . . . called it 'Toasting Time.' We played the blues and spoke to all of my blue-collar workers—'To all of you who earn your bread by the sweat of your brow, I want you to know that you are somebody. You are responsible for the wheels of this world going around. Don't ever forget it!' And then I'd say, 'For all my truck-driving friends and for my fellas at Ford and Dodge Main . . . and all of my gossiping barbers, and my beauticians. . . .' We would have that salute and it became very popular."[36] Here again, use of elements of black oral tradition—in this case, toasting—paid off in listener appeal.

The Queen's more controversial programming ploy was her regular advice to women on paydays. On that special day, she would repeatedly urge her female listeners to bank the money and pay the bills right away, even if they had to go to the factory gate to get the checks from their mates: "I told all my housewives that half of that paycheck was rightfully theirs. They had worked hard for it cooking and cleaning the house and looking after everybody. They had earned it!" Needless to say, many of her male listeners did not appreciate her advice; as she recalled: "They were angry with me, some of those men. They were threatening to bump me off!"[37]

In the South during the 1950s, two of the more successful female disc jockeys on black appeal outlets were Louise "Louisville Lou" Saxon on

WLOU, Louisville, Kentucky; and "Chattie" Hattie Leeper on WGIV, Charlotte, North Carolina. Saxon not only was one of WLOU's most recognized air personalities but also gave the station its nickname— "Louisville LOU." Her debut on WLOU was in 1952, when she teamed up with Jockey Jack Gibson to become the city's hottest DJ tandem. After Gibson's return to WERD in Atlanta, Louisville Lou became the station's leading disc jockey—and its official voice on the air. She remained a fixture in the Louisville radio market well into the 1960s.[38]

Like Nat D. Williams, Hattie Leeper pursued a dual career in broadcasting and education; but unlike the revered Memphis sage, her career in radio came first. By chance, she grew up just down the street from WBIV, the first black appeal outlet in Charlotte, and became involved in the station as a teen. She worked part time as a gofer for the staff, then as the host of a homemaker show, and finally as a disc jockey. The transformation took about seven years, during which the ambitious young woman also finished high school, earned a college degree, worked as a substitute teacher, and began taking graduate courses in administration. Her career on radio, launched in the mid-1950s, reached its zenith late in the decade. When she was hired as a regular disc jockey on WBIV, she was christened "Chattie" Hattie by Eugene Potts, the station's veteran black DJ, who was known on the air as "Genial" Gene. Potts was "a rhyming person—he rhymed everything," Leeper recalled; he also befriended the radio novice, becoming her mentor. By the late 1950s, Leeper had become a radio celebrity: "We were the superstars then. We were bigger than any of the big stars that came to town. I was emceeing all of the shows. . . . I got more rounds of applause, you know, when Chattie Hattie walked out there in all my fine glad rags I used to wear when I was young, beautiful and black. Honey, didn't nobody have nothing on me. . . . Because you were a legend in your own time and city. You were respected. Your fans loved you. Worshiped you!"[39]

Like many of the major black appeal DJs, Hattie Leeper used her radio career to branch out into other areas of the music business. She wrote some songs that became minor R & B hits, promoted many of Charlotte's biggest R & B concerts, and even managed a few local black acts. At the same time, she continued to pursue an academic career, which ultimately led to her becoming the professor in charge of the communications program at Gaston College in Dallas, North Carolina. This lifelong devotion to educational uplift no doubt influenced her strictly professional approach to broadcasting: "Many people thought I was a white announcer, until they saw me in person, because I had good diction. I didn't crack slang. And I didn't show thirty-two teeth. . . . I wasn't on there just being a monkey, you know. I wasn't an Uncle Tommy on radio. I was never that type of an individual. I mean, it was always a profession that I felt dignified to be in, and I manifested that in everything I did on the air—and off."[40]

Hattie Leeper's revulsion toward African American disc jockeys being cast, sometimes willingly, in stereotyped roles on the airwaves was not unwarranted. In the 1950s, a number of the white-owned black appeal stations created "franchise names" for their black DJs that were, at best, shallow parodies of the era's more prominent signifying spin doctors. One of the most visible culprits was the OK Group, which ran black appeal outlets in Mobile, Alabama (WGOK); New Orleans (WAOK); Baton Rouge (WXOK); Lake Charles, Louisiana (KZOK); and Houston (KYOK). Franchise names for the African American men they hired as DJs included "Okey Dokey" in New Orleans, "Diggie Doo" in Baton Rouge, and "Hotsy Totsy" in Houston; for the women they came up with "Miss Mandy" in Mobile and both "Dizzy Lizzy" and "Zing Zang" in Houston. These names offended a number of black men and women who worked for the OK stations, and more often than not, DJs found ways to subvert the caricatures and assert their own identities. Novela Smith, who replaced blues singer Gladys Hall as Dizzy Lizzy on KYOK in the late 1950s, used the newsbreak to let people know who she really was: "Being a maverick . . . I thought do something for yourself, Novella. Identify yourself because you're not Dizzy Lizzy material! So after the news, I said—'This is Novella Doe Smith, reporting KYOK Instant Jet News.' I always identified myself. So every thirty minutes it was Novella Doe Smith. And then after the news I'd go into the Jive, Jam and Gumbo Show."[41]

Veteran broadcaster Irene Johnson, a popular gospel disc jockey on WGOK for many years, experienced similar difficulties in establishing her own identity on the airwaves: "I came into radio during the time they used the names, and nobody knew I was Irene Weaver Johnson . . . because they had a name for me—Miss Mandy. I think the whole concept was to use the names, and everybody who went into that format basically sounds the same.

So it didn't sound like they were making changes."[42] After a protracted struggle, Johnson was also able to assert her true identity on WGOK's airwaves.

Obstacles such as being saddled with a franchise name or being pigeonholed in a homemaker's role were part of a larger pattern of discrimination that African American women encountered on black appeal radio. They had to contend not only with the race and gender biases of their white male employers but also with a certain amount of resistance from their black male coworkers. Hattie Leeper's experience, in this respect, was typical: "There were mixed emotions there, me being the only female. There were some die-hard men there that thought, you know, females should be home having babies, in the kitchen cooking. This is not an industry for females. And they tried to do little things to discourage me, you know, at least some of them."[43] These difficulties, however, seem only to have stiffened the resolve of the African American women who chose careers in radio broadcasting. Martha Jean the Queen seemed to be speaking on behalf of all of the black women who gained a foothold in the industry during the 1950s, when she proclaimed: "In this business, you have to think like a man, act like a woman, and work like a dog!"[44]

PART IV

"Rockin' the Pot": Black Counterfeit Radio

Ah ya wid me out deah in raydeeoland? Ah ya readeh ta pardee? We gonna blow ya mihn tanite, bay-beeh. Put some soul in ya eaar-hole. Aaaaaaaaahhhh-Woooooooooo-Whaaaaaaaa! Dis heah de Wolfman comin' atcha on de Big X. Down heh wid de donkeys an' Ah needja soul, bay-beeh, needja soul. Aaaaaaaaaahhhh-Wooooooooooo! Whereva ya ah, whadeva ya doin', de Wolfman wancha ta lay ya hands on de raydeeoo an' squeeze ma knobs. Have moicy! We gonna feeeeeeel hit tanite, baybeeh. We gonna get nakid an' blow de evil weed. . . . Rock 'n' roll wid de Wolfman. Dis heh foist pladdah gonna knock ya out. Gonna give de fellahs some zing fo' de ling nuts. Have Moicy! Ah haftah change ma undies everytime Ah heah hit ya know. Hit git de Wolfman soooooooo excited. Aaaaaaaaaahhh-Wooooooooooooo!

—Robert Smith (Wolfman Jack),
aircheck, XERB, Tijuana, Mexico

8

The White DJ
Crossover Crusade

acial ventriloquy, first heard on network radio in the 1930s, resurfaced after World War II, but in a radically changed commercial and cultural context. Radio shifted from being a major conduit for national advertising to being a major conduit for local advertising with the rise of network television; this changeover resulted in the industry's discovery of a "Negro market." On the cultural level, radio programming made a similar shift from a national to a local focus. The disc jockey became the centerpiece of radio broadcasting, and "Negro appeal" program formats sprang up on stations located in African American population centers throughout the country. But these changes also set a new cycle of racial masquerading in motion on the airwaves. This time around, white DJs hosted black music shows and imitated the speech of their African American counterparts.

Prewar racial ventriloquy had been dominated by white comics like Gosden and Correll (*Amos 'n' Andy*), who adapted blackface minstrelsy to radio. The networks had also featured a considerable number of white dance bands and vocalists who "covered" the popular blues and jazz of the day—a practice teeming with racial mimicry. The disc jockeys who first appeared on local stations during the 1930s were predominantly white males; Jack Cooper and a few other African Americans were the rare exceptions. This initial wave of white DJs played the records of the era's popular white singers and swing bands for white listeners, largely ignoring the race-record releases by the most renowned jazz and blues artists. The best known among these DJs were Al Jarvis (KFWB, Los Angeles); Arthur "Red" Godfrey (WJSV, Washington, D.C.); Martin Block (WNEW, New York City); Freddie Robbins (WOV, New York City); Dave Garroway (WMAQ, Chicago); Peter Potter (KLAC, Los Angeles); and Gene Norman (KLAC, Los Angeles).[1]

Starting in the late 1930s and continuing through the 1940s, a growing number of white DJs who were jazz oriented began featuring a mix of white and black artists; some even played race records exclusively. In the forefront of this "crossover" trend was a Jewish trumpet player with a raspy voice, known to his many listeners as "Symphony Sid." Sid Torin, born and raised in New York City, had been fascinated with jazz as a teenager. He launched his own radio show on WBNX in 1937, at first brokering the time himself through the sale of advertising spots. Symphony Sid built up a large following in Harlem by featuring the most popular race records of the day. In 1940, Torin switched over to a late-night shift on New York's WHOM, and for the next decade, he ruled the local airwaves as the city's most celebrated jazz disc jockey and spokesman. Most notably, he championed the bebop jazz innovations of Charlie Parker and Dizzy Gillespie at a time when very few other DJs would play their music on the air. His career reached its zenith in the postwar years, when Symphony Sid hosted live late-night broadcasts from Birdland, a nightclub that was the mecca of the bebop movement. These broadcasts, heard in thirty-eight states on the fledgling ABC radio network, made Symphony Sid a household name among jazz aficionados nationwide.[2]

Another white disc jockey who became something of a cult figure in New York jazz circles was Al "Jazzbo" Collins, also a native of the city. Collins broke into radio at the University of Miami, where he attended college and worked part time as an announcer and DJ on the campus station. After a decade of experience as a footloose jazz DJ, which took him from Miami to Pittsburgh to Salt Lake City and then to Chicago, he finally returned to New York in the early 1950s, where he launched his fabled late-night show *The Purple Grotto* on WNEW. The imaginary locale of the show was inspired by the cavelike basement radio studio that was the station's home. Collins embellished his *Purple Grotto* fantasy with a collage of nighttime sound effects, including the hooting of a "Tasmanian owl" named Harrison. In addition, he hosted the show by candlelight in order to "get away from mechanical contrivances," and he never mentioned the actual time or the station's call letters: "I just wanted people to relax and forget the time of day—or where they were."[3]

Jazzbo Collins perfected a mellow yet eccentric on-air delivery, often associated with the urban hipsters of the postwar era. His laid-back manner of speech, coupled with his frequent use of the latest jazz slang, stood out on the airwaves—especially with the surrealistic *Purple Grotto* soundscape in the background. A final touch was added when Collins began to concoct a series of hip fairy tales for his audience. They were inspired by the outrageous comedy routines of Lord Buckley, the "most immaculately hip aristocrat" of avant-garde humor, who was also a cult figure in New York's bohemian subculture during the 1950s. As for his musical selections, Jazzbo played a mix of black and white jazz artists, preferably those with a pleasant sound and a relaxed vocal or playing style. His playlists regularly included Billie Holiday, Ella Fitzgerald, Nat King Cole, Duke Ellington, and the Modern Jazz Quartet, as well as Frank Sinatra, George Shearing, Dave Brubeck, and Les Brown. Collins has maintained that his choice of records was strictly a matter of musical taste: "There was no separation as far as color was concerned. . . . It was the music that I was interested in, whether it was Hampton Hawes or George Shearing. I would play it for whatever the musical sound was, the contrasts and harmonies, and so forth."[4]

One of the first white disc jockeys to cross the musical color line in the segregated South was "Jitterbug" Johnny Poorhall, who hosted a late-night show on WHBQ in Memphis, Tennessee, during the late 1930s and early 1940s. His preference for such African American swing bands as the hometown Jimmie Lunceford Orchestra or Chick Webb's popular Harlem-based ensemble, as well as vocalists such as Jimmy Rushing and Fats Waller, attracted a sizable black listening audience before the advent of WDIA. Drafted during World War II, Poorhall never returned to the airwaves after serving in the armed forces.[5]

During the major postwar shift in black popular music, rhythm and blues eclipsed the swing-band craze, changing the musical profile of the nation's airwaves. In the South, the region's musical formats changed dramatically without moving the color line. Racial ventriloquy helped maintain segregation as it had in the past, but the key players now were white DJs and their employers, rather than network blackface comics.

Crossover Colossus: WLAC

During the postwar boom in black appeal radio, numerous stations in the South initially tried to capture the newly discovered Negro market without desegregating their on-air staffs. Among them, WEAS in Decatur, Georgia; WJIV in Savannah, Georgia; WPAL in Charleston, South Carolina; and WJMR in New Orleans, Louisiana; featured R & B music shows hosted by white DJs. Their success varied. By far the most successful of the crossover stations was WLAC in Nashville, Tennessee. Originally affiliated with the CBS network and owned by local business interests, WLAC was unique in two respects: (1) as a clear-channel station, it did not have to share its spot on the AM dial (1510) with competing signals during the evening hours; (2) WLAC's fifty-thousand-watt output blanketed a large region of the country—especially after dark, when atmospheric conditions were more favorable for broadcasting. On a normal night, the elasticity of the ionosphere enabled the station's radio waves to ricochet over most of the United States east of the Rocky Mountains. Consequently, WLAC could cultivate a huge audience, particularly in rural areas not reached by local broadcasters or serviced only by low-power outlets that signed off at sundown.[6]

WLAC's crossover to black appeal music programming in the late-night hours happened almost accidentally. After the war, CBS began to cut back on its nighttime broadcast schedule, leaving the affiliate stations to fend for themselves. Like many such affiliates, WLAC resorted to the cost-effective DJ format to fill the void. One of the station's veteran announcers, Gene Nobles, was given the late-night time slot and generally played his favorite white swing artists. One fall night in 1946, Nobles was doing his regular show when a group of black ex-servicemen who were in Nashville attending college on the GI Bill sneaked into the segregated office building to talk him into playing some of their favorite race records on the air. The bemused disc jockey complied, substituting the likes of Roy Milton, Pete Johnson, and Louis Jordan for his regular lineup of Glenn Miller, Frank Sinatra, and Jo Stafford. To the astonishment of Nobles and his employers, the race-record experiment provoked a flood of fan mail (mostly from out of state) pleading for more. Within a year, WLAC was devoting its entire late-night schedule to black appeal music shows.[7]

Gene Nobles was a folksy flimflam man whose greatest love in life was playing the ponies—not platters. Born and raised in Hot Springs, Arkansas, he worked as a carnival and bingo barker in between tours of the South's major racetracks during the Great Depression. In the late 1930s, his skills as a glib-talking barker landed him his first job as a radio pitchman. He worked at a succession of stations in Arkansas, Alabama, and Georgia, before arriving at WLAC in 1943. Hired as a staff announcer, Nobles soon took over the *Midnight Special,* from 10 P.M. to 1 A.M. At first, his show featured white swing-band recordings and mail-order commercials (his pitch for live baby chicks—a hundred for only $1.99—became a broadcast legend), but in time, Nobles became more experimental. Fortified with a nightly bottle of Seagram's V.O., he began to articulate a style of risqué racetrack lingo that he called "slamgage." According to Nobles, it was his way of speaking "from the heart of my bottom."[8]

Late in 1946, after the visit from the black GIs, Nobles persuaded the station manager to allow him to play more race records on his show; the manager agreed, on the condition that Nobles find his own sponsors. Nobles made a pitch to Randy Woods, the owner of a local record store, and got a few ads for Woods's fledgling mail-order record operation on the show. The ads were so successful that, before long, Woods was sponsoring the entire show, now called *Randy's Record Shop.* Over the next few years, the partnership between Nobles and Woods flourished.[9]

Woods used the profits from his now-thriving mail-order record business to bankroll Dot Records, a label that specialized in cover versions of rhythm-and-blues hits in the 1950s. Dot's brightest star, teenage idol Pat Boone, recorded sanitized reissues of Ivory Joe Hunter's "I Almost Lost My Mind," Little Richard's "Tutti Frutti," and Fats Domino's "Ain't That a Shame"—all million-sellers for the label. Dot's other teen-oriented artists included Gale Storm, a television comedy star who made the top-ten chartbusting cover of Smiley Lewis's "I Hear You Knocking," and Hollywood heartthrob Tab Hunter, who flopped as a rock-and-roll crooner. The independent label prospered; by 1955, it accounted for 15 percent of the discs on the top-forty charts. Randy Woods was well on his way to becoming a multimillionaire. Gene Nobles, in contrast, plowed the profits from his percentage of the mail-order take into his lifelong obsession: betting on the horses. Over time, his racetrack "sabbaticals" from WLAC's airwaves grew in frequency, duration, and extravagance.[10]

Whether Nobles won or lost at the track, his frequent absences from the station were a lucky break for William "Hoss" Allen, who broke into radio as a substitute DJ on *Randy's Record Shop*. Allen, from nearby Gallatin, Tennessee, had grown up in close proximity to the local black community; his nanny and many of his playmates had been African American. He had served in the armed forces during the war and attended Vanderbilt University in Nashville on the GI Bill, before becoming a WLAC salesman in the late 1940s. While working at the station, the "Hossman," as his classmates had called him, became Nobles's drinking buddy and understudy, eventually taking over as the regular disc jockey on *Randy's Record Shop*.[11]

Once on the air, Allen's familiarity with African American music and culture became his biggest asset. He prided himself on discovering new R & B hits and sounding black. At the height of his career on WLAC in the late 1950s, the Hossman typified the rebellious lifestyle and mind-set associated with many of the white disc jockeys who crossed over to an R & B musical format. He used the latest African American street slang on and off the air; he was in awe of the leading rhythm-and-blues artists, disdainful of the white rock and rollers; he hung out in the music clubs on the black side of town; and he lived the hedonistic high life of a celebrity DJ to the hilt. The nonstop drinking and carousing finally caught up with him in the late 1960s. In a midlife crisis of sorts, he swore off alcohol and even quit deejaying for a while. When he returned to WLAC's airwaves a few years later, Hoss Allen was as sober as the proverbial judge and played only gospel music.[12]

During WLAC's halcyon days, its the most popular disc jockey was John Richbourg. His deep, soulful Southern drawl made him one of the station's most recognized voices in the postwar era. Richbourg, known on the airwaves as "John R," had grown up in rural South Carolina in the 1910s and 1920s. As a child, he accompanied his cotton-broker father to the plantations, where his lifelong fascination with black music began: "I used to listen to the farmhands as they would come in at the end of the day singing . . . this particular plantation worked about 200 people. And to hear that many people singing spirituals, songs of faith, was something that was always exciting."[13]

Returning to the South after an unsuccessful stint as an actor in New York City, Richbourg found a job as a radio announcer in Charleston, South Carolina, and then moved on to WLAC in the early 1940s. He served briefly in the navy toward the end of war and returned to announcing for the Nashville station late in 1945. WLAC's switch to a nighttime R & B format gave Richbourg the chance to immerse himself in rhythm and blues. Before long, he was indisputably the station's most knowledgeable and ardent spokesman for black music, and his popularity skyrocketed.[14]

At the height of his career as a DJ in the 1950s and 1960s, John R's late-night broadcasts reached an estimated 14 million people in thirty-eight states. Although the majority of his listeners were black, his white listeners also numbered in the millions. This vast and diverse audience empowered Richbourg as a R & B hit maker; he could "break" a record— transform it into a major hit—simply by highlighting it on his show. John R introduced his listeners to many artists who would rise to the top of black popular music during this period, including James Brown, Charles Brown, Ray Charles, the Coasters, the Dixie Hummingbirds, Aretha Franklin, B. B. King, Jimmy Reed, and Otis Redding. Many of them became Richbourg's friends. They regularly listened to his show and often called in or stopped by the station to chat with him on the air. Phil Walden, Otis Redding's manager, recalled that "Otis always listened to John R on the road. He also called him pretty often and they would talk on the air." Fellow DJs from all over the eastern United States also tuned in, especially for his early-morning segment (1 to 3 A.M.) showcasing new R & B releases. As Hoss Allen recalled: "All the jocks around the country would stay up and listen to him just to hear what the hell he was goin' to play."[15]

Most listeners took in John R's distinctive Southern drawl, black vernacular speech, familiarity with African American music, and friendly rapport with the R & B artists who appeared on his shows and concluded that he was a black man. R & B pioneer James Brown recalled: "He had so much soul that people in the black community thought he was black!" When they met him in public, Richbourg's African American fans invariably were shocked. One devout listener, the Reverend F. M. Beavers, who later became a good friend, reminisced: "I was in heaven 'cause I was finally gonna see this black man I'd listened to since childhood. Then I saw he was a white man—I almost fainted!"[16]

Artifice accounts to some degree for Richbourg's African American sound. His drawl and his appreciation for the music came from his deep Southern roots, but, according to Hoss Allen, John R also relied on his acting skills to perfect a black accent for his shows, and he took great care to lace African American street slang into his radio discourse. Still, it would be a mistake to see Richbourg as simply exploiting African American culture; he also worked behind the scenes to desegregate Nashville radio. He and Hoss Allen taught radio courses at the Nashville School of Broadcasting, which, like WLAC, was a segregated operation; but on the side, they also surreptitiously used the school's and the station's facilities to train black students. Yet John R did use his fame as one of the country's most influential R & B DJs to feather his own nest with payola bribes from the record companies, and he was in the habit of taking a percentage of the artists' royalties in return for playing their new releases on the air. However, his financial gains from these endeavors were modest in comparison to Randy Woods's cover-version enterprise. Richbourg did not get wealthy as a result of these fairly common DJ practices, and later in his life, when he was battling cancer and couldn't pay his medical bills, many of the successful African American artists he had featured on his shows came to his financial aid. Their voluntary support in his hour of need testifies to John R's unique status as a popular friend of black music—and of the artists that made it.[17]

A Knack for Sounding Black

Throughout the 1950s and well into the 1960s, WLAC maintained its position as the most listened-to nighttime R & B outlet in the country. A clear majority of its 15 million listeners during this period were African Americans living in the South; yet WLAC strictly maintained the color line with on-air staff. Only in 1968 did the station employ its first African American announcer, as a news reporter—not as a disc jockey.[18] Like John R and Hoss Allen, the DJs who achieved celebrity status on WLAC were Southern white males whose success owed a lot to their talent for sounding

Jack L. Cooper, Chicago's black radio pioneer.

Detail from the photograph files of the Archives of African American Music and Culture at Indiana University, Bloomington. Courtesy of the Chicago Historical Society.

Bluesman Sonny Boy Williamson, star of KFFA's (Helena, Ark.) *King Biscuit Time.* Courtesy of BMI Archives Photo Collection.

Al Benson, Chicago's premier black disc jockey in the postwar era.

Detail from the photograph files of the Archives of African American Music and Culture at Indiana University, Bloomington.

"Jocky Jack" Gibson riding the turntable at WJJD (Chicago, 1947).

From the photograph files of the Archives of African American Music and Culture at Indiana University, Bloomington.

WERD's four horsemen (Atlanta)–from left, Roosevelt Johnson,
"Joltin' Joe" Howard, Jimmy Winnington, and "Jocky Jack" Gibson.

Detail from the photograph files of the Archives of African American Music and Culture at
Indiana University, Bloomington.

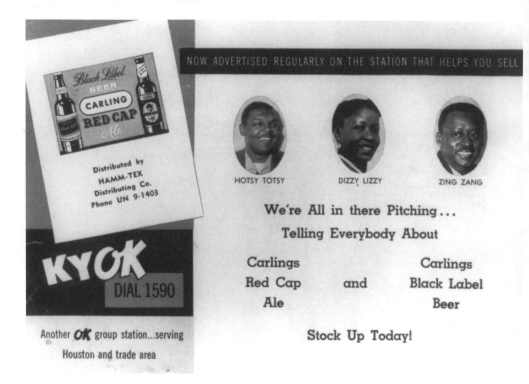

KYOK (Houston) advertisement.

Detail from the photograph files of the Archives of African American Music and Culture at Indiana University, Bloomington.

WWRL (New York City) disc jockey
Tommy "Dr. Jive" Smalls.

Detail from the photograph files of the Archives of African American
Music and Culture at Indiana University, Bloomington.

Entertainer and WDIA (Memphis) disc jockey
Rufus Thomas.

Courtesy of BMI Archives Photo Collection.

Crossover DJ John Richbourg on WLAC (Nashville).

Detail from the photograph files of the Archives of African American Music and Culture at Indiana University, Bloomington.

Rock-and-roll disc jockey Alan Freed.

Courtesy of BMI Archives Photo Collection.

Philadelphia DJ and host of ABC's *American Bandstand,* Dick Clark.

Courtesy of BMI Archives Photo Collection.

Border radio legend Wolfman Jack.

Courtesy of BMI Archives Photo Collection.

The legendary James Brown, owner of three black radio stations in the 1970s.

Courtesy of BMI Archives Photo Collection.

Soul vocalist Sam Cooke.

Courtesy of BMI Archives Photo Collection.

Soul tunesmith Curtis Mayfield.

Courtesy of BMI Archives Photo Collection.

Superstar Stevie Wonder, owner of
KJLH FM (Los Angeles).

Courtesy of BMI Archives Photo Collection.

J. B. Blanton, owner of WERD
(Atlanta).

Detail from the photograph files of the
Archives of African American Music and Culture at Indiana University, Bloomington.

Berry Gordy, founder of
Motown Records.

Courtesy of BMI Archives Photo Collection.

Peggy Mitchell, WEDR's (Birmingham, Ala.) first black female disc jockey.

From the photograph files of the Archives of African American Music and Culture at Indiana University, Bloomington.

NARTA activist Clarence Avant (center), receiving an award from BMI executives Dexter Moore (left) and Rick Riccobono.

Courtesy of BMI Archives Photo Collection.

Dr. Martin Luther King Jr. and DJ Georgie Woods at 22nd Street and
Columbia Avenue, Philadelphia, 1965.

Photo by Jack T. Franklin. The African American Museum in Philadelphia,
Jack T. Franklin Collection.

black. But the phenomenon was not limited to WLAC. Once again, racial ventriloquy was in vogue on the nation's airwaves.

Vernon Winslow and "Poppa Stoppa"

One of the most bizarre examples of postwar racial ventriloquy was the rise of "Poppa Stoppa" as the premier disc jockey in New Orleans. Vernon Winslow, an art professor who taught in the city at Dillard University, adopted Poppa Stoppa (a local black vernacular term for a condom) as the name for a fictitious African American radio personality. Winslow, who was born and raised in Chicago, had attended college at Morehouse in Atlanta and at the University of Chicago. After earning his advanced degree in art at the Art Institute of Chicago and taking the position at Dillard, he began writing a column for a local black newspaper, the *Louisiana Weekly*, on New Orleans nightlife. When he realized that, unlike Chicago, his new hometown had no black appeal radio programs on the air, he wrote to some of the local stations proposing a weekly broadcast that would highlight the city's African American musical talent and the burgeoning local music scene. Poppa Stoppa, a mysterious black trickster, would host the show. Winslow chose a name with strong cultural connections: "Poppa Stoppa was the name I came up with. It came from the rhyme and rap that folks in the streets were using in New Orleans. Poppa Stoppa language was for insiders, most white folks couldn't understand it—so it became a unique identity, and black people were proud of it as a way to show solidarity and brotherhood. I wrote my radio scripts in that language and Poppa Stoppa was my mouthpiece, so to speak."[19]

One station, WJMR, responded to Winslow's proposal, asking for both a sample script and a personal interview. Having lost its network affiliation, the station was groping for an entrée into the city's sizable African American radio market. Once the light-skinned Winslow had explained his plan for the show at the interview, the station owner asked him suspiciously: "By the way, are you a nigger?" When Winslow replied that he was indeed a "Negro," the owner exclaimed: "Well I'll be damned! Don't get me wrong, you got a good idea here, but white folks would tear my station down if I put you behind the microphone."[20] Their conversation ended in a compromise: the owner hired Vernon Winslow to write the scripts, select the records, and teach a white understudy how to talk like Poppa Stoppa.

Late in 1947, *Jam, Jive and Gumbo,* hosted by Poppa Stoppa, debuted on WJMR. Within a year, it was the top-rated radio show in town. Predictably, almost everyone in New Orleans thought Poppa Stoppa was black. But according to Clarence Harmon, one of a succession of white DJs employed as Poppa Stoppa: "The people didn't know because they hadn't heard anything like that before. They couldn't tell whether. . . . Well, they didn't even know if I was white or black."[21] When R & B vocalist Irma Thomas got to the station for an appearance on the show in the early 1960s, she thought she knew whom she'd find behind the mike: "I had to do an interview for one of the records that I had released . . . and when I got there, I'm looking for this black jock—and here's this little white man sitting there talking with this big voice that sounded black. And I was really taken aback. And he laughed, 'cause he saw the expression on my face, and he knew what it was, why I looked that way."[22]

For over two decades, various students played Winslow's character, and Poppa Stoppa remained one of New Orleans' most celebrated disc jockeys. WJMR even franchised the name and peddled the show to other stations in the region. In an absurd turn of events, Vernon Winslow was fired by WJMR's white manager for going on the air as Poppa Stoppa when one of his pupils failed to show up for work. When the undeterred Winslow resurfaced on rival station WEZZ as "Doctor Daddy-O" in the early 1950s, he wrote the scripts *and* supplied the voice for his fictitious host.[23]

A Cascade of Crossovers

Elsewhere in the South, with black appeal radio gaining momentum, more and more white disc jockeys joined the crossover trend. In the beginning, stations like WJMR and WLAC hired white crossover DJs to maintain a segregated workforce while they cashed in on the black radio market. Ed "Jack the Bellboy" McKenzie got his start as an R & B deejay in the late 1940s on WEAS, an all-white operation in Decatur, Georgia (just outside Atlanta). In the mid-1950s, he became the featured crossover jock on WJIV, another segregated black appeal outlet in nearby Savannah. During this period, the leading R & B disc jockey on WJAZ in Albany, Georgia, was a clean-cut, white youngster who called himself "Doctor Blues." In Macon,

Georgia, the first disc jockey to play R & B on the airways was a white new-comer known as "Honeyboy."[24]

In Shreveport, Louisiana, record-store entrepreneur Stanley Lewis, following in Randy Woods's footsteps, sponsored the city's top R & B show on KWKH in 1950, which until then had been a country music outlet. Lewis bought a block of time from the station (4 to 8 P.M.) and then hired a white DJ, Ray Bartlett, to host the show and hawk Stan's Record Shop's mail-order bargains. Bartlett—"Groovy Boy" on the air—was a ranter and raver with a "colored accent." He established himself as Shreveport's most popular disc jockey before moving on in the early 1950s. Groovy Boy was replaced by another white DJ, Frank Page—"Gatemouth Page, the Mouth of the South"—a jive-talking rhymer as well as an accomplished pitchman. Page's show was broadcast on KWKH and on sister station KJHS, a fifty-thousand-watt powerhouse in Little Rock, Arkansas. During the evening hours, when Brother Gatemouth was on the air, KJHS's signal blanketed the Midwest all the way to the Canadian border; his *No Name Jive* program could be heard in the heartland and the hinterlands. One avid listener and frequent mail-order customer at Stan's Record Shop was Robert Zimmerman, a northern Minnesota teenager who would later be known to the pop-music world as Bob Dylan. According to Dylan's biographer, the rhythm-and-blues discs he first heard on Gatemouth Page's late-night broadcasts were an important influence on his music.[25]

Some Southern stations with black appeal formats eventually integrated their air staffs. For example, Ken "Jack the Cat" Elliott, working in tandem with Vernon "Doctor Daddy-O" Winslow, turned WEZZ into the highest-rated black appeal outlet in New Orleans during the late 1950s. Art Neville, a veteran rhythm-and-blues musician in the city, describes Elliott as a "white guy from Kenner who sounded just like us—if you go by voice. . . . Called himself Jack the Cat. So, like, to me Jack the Cat got to be the hippest dude around. And everybody come home from school and we got Jack the Cat on the radio."[26] The first black appeal outlet in Houston, KNUZ, employed a white DJ named "Spinner Joe" to host its afternoon R & B show. Joe Howard, who also worked for the station in the early 1950s, remembered Spinner Joe as a "white guy who tried to sound black." On WBIV, Charlotte, North Carolina's first integrated radio station, Chattie Hattie Leeper and Genial Gene Potts shared the airwaves with "Hot Scott." As Leeper recalled: "We had a blond-headed DJ, we called him Hot

Scott. And he sounded exactly like a soul brother. I mean, he talked that talk just like a brother—and he would go out to make public appearances with me and the other DJs, and folks would ask me—'When you gonna bring Hot Scott out and let us meet him?' And I'd say—'This is Hot Scott right here.' And they'd say—'No it can't be. We're talking about the black Hot Scott!'"[27]

The sudden proliferation of white crossover disc jockeys on the airwaves in the South during the postwar era was symptomatic of the far-reaching social changes beginning to take place in the region, especially with regard to race relations. Racial segregation was coming under attack on many fronts: in the courts, in the schools, in public accommodations and transportation, in the job market, in the voting booth, in the music business—and on the airwaves. This broad-based civil rights struggle intensified during the rise of rhythm and blues, thus opening a role for music to play in the assault on the color line. Unexpectedly, that assault came from both sides: for numerous white DJs who championed the music, R & B became a vehicle for rebelling against the white cultural mainstream or for subverting the racial status quo. To be sure, many white DJs who crossed over did so for the money, but some also had a cultural agenda that was at least equally important to them as the money. One DJ with cultural priorities was Zenas "Daddy" Sears, Atlanta's most accomplished and controversial crossover jock during the postwar years.

Zenas "Daddy" Sears

Zenas Sears was a progressive thinker and activist who found his niche in the civil rights movement on the radio in Atlanta, his adopted hometown. He grew up in a prosperous and refined household in Baltimore; his parents, both Southerners, were well educated and socially conscious—traits he would emulate in his later years. After college, Sears started out as an actor, but moving to Atlanta in the late 1930s, he found better employment opportunities in radio. In his first broadcasting job as a disc jockey on WATL, the restrictive format required him to play one Bing Crosby vocal in every three records. During the war, Sears was drafted into the military and assigned to an AFRS FM radio station in India. Most of the troops in this region were African American units moving supplies along the Burma Road. As the host of an evening music show, Sears was flooded with requests for race records. The station had none, so he asked his audience for help. Within a few weeks, he had a sizable collection of discs by black artists—and the first race-record show on the Burma Road.[28]

After the war, Sears returned to Atlanta a changed man. His close contact with black troops overseas had given him a new passion in life—black music—and a new cause—racial justice for African Americans. He initially went back on the air on WATL; but when his employers heard him featuring black artists on his revamped show, they fired him. He resurfaced on WGST in 1948. It was an unusual choice: the station was owned by the Georgia Institute of Technology (Georgia Tech), a state-supported college. Sears succeeded in convincing both the university's academic hierarchy and the segregationist governor of Georgia, Herman Talmadge, of the benefits his show had to offer, particularly with respect to race relations. Talmadge gave the final go-ahead only after Sears agreed to stay away from political issues on the air—an agreement Sears had no intention of honoring, as he later recalled: "We did all the get-out-the-vote stuff anyway. Nobody white listened to the radio after the news at ten o'clock. We'd start off at ten fifteen P.M., and would run as long as we could sell it, which was usually to about two A.M."[29]

A few months after his debut on WGST, some of his black listeners gave Sears his radio moniker. One night, Sears was on the air when a local hospital called to tell him his wife had gone into labor. Sears rushed off to the hospital, leaving a record playing on the turntable. After it finished, the audience heard the repetitive sounds of a scratching needle in an empty record groove for the rest of the night. When word got out that Zenas Sears had abandoned the show to witness the birth of his twin boys, his audience began to call him "Big Daddy"—which was later shortened to "Daddy."[30]

Zenas "Daddy" Sears used his late-night show on WGST to promote both race music (soon to be known as rhythm and blues) and civil rights. His pioneering efforts to broaden the appeal of black music and improve race relations in Atlanta won him the respect of the local African American community, where he soon became a familiar figure in the record stores and nightclubs, seeking out the latest R & B hits or new talent. Before long, he was using black street slang and promoting local R & B artists on the airwaves. Within a few years of his debut on WGST, Sears was not only the city's leading late-night rhythm-and-blues disc jockey but also a major regional R & B talent scout, record producer, and concert promoter. When he realized that no recording studios in Atlanta were open to African Americans, he began to produce his own sessions with local black artists in the WGST studios after broadcast hours. Three of his initial clients, Little Richard, Ray Charles, and Chuck Willis, went on to rhythm-and-blues stardom in the 1950s. Little Richard's regional hit "Every Hour" and Ray Charles's breakthrough national hit "I Got a Woman" were both recorded by Daddy Sears in the WGST studios. His close working relationship with these and many other R & B luminaries inevitably led to large concert productions, not only in Atlanta, at venues like Georgia Tech's Herndon Stadium, but also at the Apollo Theater in New York. Sticking to his cultural agenda, Sears became one of the South's most important rhythm-and-blues impresarios in the 1950s.[31]

Sears was equally active in the civil rights struggles of the day—especially in Atlanta, which was a hotbed of protests and organizing efforts during this period. As an outspoken and articulate champion of racial equality, both on the airwaves and at public forums, Sears was applauded by African Americans, courted by the city's politicians, and vilified by the Ku Klux Klan (KKK). His nightly show on WGST became a valuable source of news and information on local civil rights activities, in part through his close friendships with the movement's Atlanta-based leadership, including Dr. Martin Luther King Jr. and his colleagues in the Southern Christian Leadership Conference (SCLC). Because of his stature as a spokesman for racial tolerance and his close bonds to the black community, Sears was often called on by city officials such as the mayor and the chief of police to mediate racial conflicts. Such earnest efforts to improve race relations made him a controversial public figure. He was highly praised by his civil rights allies, both black and white, but branded a "nigger lover" by his racist adversaries. The KKK repeatedly threatened him with hate calls and a cross burning in front of the station.[32]

Pressure from his detractors eventually led to Daddy Sears's departure from WGST in 1954, but by then, he had become a major figure in Atlanta's growing black appeal radio market. He found a new time slot for his R & B show on another local outlet, WAOK, and soon was able to buy the station, with help from a like-minded business partner. By the time the purchase was finalized in 1956, Sears had switched the station over to a black appeal format and hired an integrated staff. Among those who joined him on WAOK's airwaves were "Alley Pat" Patrick, one of the city's most popular African American DJs, and the veteran white crossover jock Ed "Jack the Bellboy" McKenzie. For the next two decades, with Daddy Sears at the helm, the station maintained a steady commitment to black appeal music and public-affairs programming.[33]

Zenas "Daddy" Sears stood out among his peers because he was a hip-talking intellectual with strong moral convictions when it came to race relations and social justice. These convictions often put him at odds not only with the white power structure but also with many of the commercial practices common in the radio industry at the time. For example, he refused to accept payola for playing specific discs on the air, and on one occasion, he even sided with WAOK staff members who were trying to organize a union at the station. As his business partner wryly observed: "He was more community minded than business minded."[34] But Sears's passion for black music and his proclivity toward sounding like a streetwise African American on the airwaves were traits he shared with most of the other white R & B DJs. His crossover saga was somewhat unique in that he combined civil rights activism with racial voyeurism.

The West Coast Trio: Hancock, Otis, and Oxford

The South was by no means the only region in the country where white R & B disc jockeys flourished. Out on the West Coast, the two crossover jocks who pioneered rhythm-and-blues programming during the postwar era were Hunter Hancock (KFVD, KGFJ) in Los Angeles and "Jumping" George Oxford (KWBR, KSAN) in the San Franscisco Bay Area. Hancock was a shrill-sounding, fast-talking Texan who broke into radio in Los Angeles on KFVD in 1943. At first, he hosted a conventional white pop show on Sunday afternoons, but the music would soon change. As Hancock recalled: "About six weeks after I started at the station . . . there was a clothing store— Todd's—in downtown L.A. that wanted a program to appeal to the Negro market. They bought an hour show on Sunday afternoon, and it happened to be on my shift. Well, they wanted jazz like Count Basie and Duke Ellington and Lionel Hampton . . . we played that, and it was popular."[35]

Hancock called his revamped show *Harlem Matinee*. In 1948, just after *Harlem Matinee* moved to a weekday afternoon time slot, he again switched musical formats. On this occasion, the catalyst for the change was a local record company promo man: "His name was Jack Foston, and he was with Modern Records. He was the one who came up and said—'Hey, you're playing the wrong records.' He showed me some charts indicating that the vast majority in the Negro market would like what was then called race music—not jazz. So I started playing it, and he was right."[36]

During the 1950s, Hunter Hancock was Los Angeles' most influential R & B disc jockey. He was especially popular with local black and Latino teenagers, which inspired him to stage "record hops" in their neighborhoods. In 1953, he launched an additional R & B show, this time on KGFJ, called *Hunting with Hunter*. For almost a decade, it was cohosted by a black woman known only as "Margie." Her sultry contralto voice was in stark contrast to Hancock's high-pitched histrionics, making them one of the oddest interracial couples on the airwaves. Hunter Hancock never consciously tried to sound like an African American, but during his early years as an R & B DJ, his listeners assumed him to be black. "Well, not for a long time did most of them know I was white. . . . For a long time I was the only one in L.A. doing what they call a race music program. So it didn't matter that I was white. I was playing their music and that's what they wanted."[37]

As for his musical selections, Hunter Hancock admitted that he knew very little about R & B. "I really didn't pick the records myself so much to play on the air, because I wasn't born to it, so to speak. So I depended on other people to let me know what to play. . . . I checked with several of the record stores in black neighborhoods, and with some of the local distributors of black records, find out what was good, what was selling—and I played those."[38] Hancock remained on the air in Los Angeles until the mid-1960s, when he retired from radio rather than adapting to his employers' new top-forty rock-and-roll formats.

Another white disc jockey who championed R & B in the Los Angeles market during the 1950s was Johnny Otis, whose career on the airwaves was an outgrowth of his work on the black side of the music industry. The son of Greek immigrants, Otis grew up in a black neighborhood in Berkeley, California, where he immersed himself in the local music and culture at an early age. As a result, his crossover odyssey began in his childhood, and it went much further than those of his peers: "I did not become black because I was attracted to Negro music. My attitude was formed long before I moved into the music field. Nor did I become a member of the Negro community because I married a Negro girl. I became what I am because as a child, I reacted to a way of life, the special vitality, the atmosphere of the black community. I cannot think of myself as white."[39]

Johnny Otis began his musical career as a teenage drummer for the West Oakland Rockers, a local blues band. During the early 1940s, he went on the road with a series of black swing bands, including Harlen Leonard and the Kansas City Rockets. By the end of World War II, he was based in Los Angeles, where he formed his own big band and made his first recordings. From this vantage point, Otis witnessed the rise of the region's pioneering R & B bands and revised his strategy accordingly; he downsized his swing band, sought out new vocal talent, and scouted around for an independent record label. By the end of the decade, Johnny Otis was a key figure in Los Angeles' burgeoning R & B scene. Besides being a bandleader, the multitalented impresario was active as a songwriter, record producer, talent scout, and nightclub operator. These efforts paid off handsomely in 1950, when two of his songs—"Double Crossin' Blues" and "Mistreatin' Blues"—which he recorded with his band and vocalist Little Esther Phillips for the Savoy label, rocketed to the top of the R & B charts.[40]

During the 1950s, the "Johnny Otis Show," an R & B revue, was a headline attraction on the "chitlin circuit" nationwide. At the same same, Otis continued to write and produce a string of R & B hits, from "All Night Long" in 1951 to "Willie and the Hand Jive" in 1958. But toward the end of the decade, his music and career were eclipsed by the rise of rock and roll. He dropped out of the national spotlight and returned to working almost exclusively in the Los Angeles area. Hired by KFOX, he launched his long-running R & B show in 1957. As a disc jockey, Otis continued to be fiercely loyal to black music and openly critical of rock and roll, which he saw as a crude caricature of rhythm and blues for the benefit of white teenagers. His career as an R & B DJ in the Los Angeles market has spanned five decades and continues on KPFK-FM today.[41]

Up the coast, in the San Francisco Bay Area, the first DJ to host an R & B radio show was "Jumping" George Oxford, who debuted on Oakland's KMBR in the early 1950s. According to one characterization, he was "a hambone jock who broadcast high on the frenzy scale while plugging E-Z credit furniture stores and dropping veiled innuendos about his lust for his female listeners."[42] Oxford moved across the bay to KSAN in San Francisco in 1954, where he hosted the region's most highly touted R & B show for the rest of the decade. He was replaced on KMBR by Phil Mc-Kernan, a white R & B devotee who was also the father of the Grateful Dead's original drummer and cofounder, Rod "Pigpen" McKernan. The Grateful Dead began their long, strange musical career as a crossover band in the mid-1960s, playing rhythm-and-blues standards.

Northern Crossovers

During the postwar years, white R & B disc jockeys also became a fixture in Northern urban markets with a sizable African American audience. Danny Stiles, typical of this group, began his radio career as a jazz DJ on WHBI in Newark, New Jersey, in 1946, playing black artists such as Billie Holiday and Billy Eckstine. In the early 1950s, Stiles switched over to an R & B format: "You could see by 1952 that this was where the music was going. You could tell black and white kids were all crazy for rhythm and blues. We got 5,500 people at a dance in Newark. As a disc jockey, it seemed clear to me this was the place to be. I just went along for the ride."[43] Danny Stiles's ride as an R & B DJ became a lifelong enterprise; he was still on the air in the New York market in the 1990s.

In Philadelphia, Joe Niagara—"You hear the word from this rockin' bird!"—on WBIG was the first crossover jock in the city, starting in 1947. A native of South Philadelphia's Italian enclave, Niagara was a hip-talking homeboy who had one of the top-rated R & B shows in the market for almost a decade. His success opened up WBIG's airwaves to Tom "Big Daddy" Donahue, who migrated to the station in 1950, a year after launching his career as an R & B disc jockey on WINX in his native Washington, D.C. Porky Chedwick, Pittsburgh's best-known white crossover jock, was featured on WAMO in the 1950s, where he referred to himself on the air as a "Porkulatin' Platter Pushin' Poppa." Detroit's WXYZ imported Ed "Jack the Bellboy" McKenzie from Atlanta to host an R & B show in the late 1950s. Tom Clay, Don McLeod, and Dale Young were the other white DJs in the Motor City who made names for themselves playing R & B during this period.[44]

In Milwaukee, the white enfant terrible of R & B was Chuck Dunaway, who, at age twenty, became the city's top-rated disc jockey and its most important R & B promoter. With financial backing from a local record distributor, Dunaway was able to produce his own radio show and stage local

R & B concerts. In his own words: "We got 10% of everything we sold on our three hours on WMIL. We were raking money in. I mean we had shows coming in, we were hiring acts, we tied up with the Fox theater chain and just really had a good time promoting shows in the movie houses." Dunaway's choice of music and his flashy lifestyle were influenced by the "Magnificent" Montague, the legendary black DJ who was based in Chicago at the time. As Dunaway recalled: "I'd go to Chicago once every two–three weeks to visit. And I'd run into people like Montague and he would distort my mind a little bit. I went back and got me a convertible and a driver and a bodyguard . . . and wore these crazy suits and just had a good time—and it was that flamboyant attitude I guess I got from Montague, who gave me some direction on how to dress and how to act to look successful."[45]

White male crossover jocks proliferated on the airwaves after the second world war, modeling their shows, their personas, sometimes even their lifestyles on those of the era's most renowned black appeal disc jockeys. They borrowed not only the race of music they played but the black vernacular as well. While a growing number of radio race rebels helped popularize jazz, R & B, and then rock and roll among a new generation of listeners, they also tended to perpetuate the legacy of blackface stereotypes on the nation's airwaves. In effect, the white crossover DJs were responsible for the second major wave of racial ventriloquy in the history of U.S. radio broadcasting. Their counterfeit rendering of black vernacular speech renewed its currency, especially for the white audience, even as it recycled age-old African American verbal caricatures rooted in the popular culture.

9

The Rock-and-Roll Rebels

isc jockeys like Chuck Dunaway in Milwaukee and Dewey Phillips in Memphis were part of a generation of white cultural rebels, many from working-class backgrounds, who came of age during the 1950s. One aspect of their rebellion, the championing of rhythm and blues, had racial implications; but the class and generational dimensions often tended to overshadow race. Crossover jock Dewey Phillips, for instance, breached the color line not only because he enjoyed black music and culture but also because immersing himself in R & B amounted to thumbing his nose at the bourgeois conventions of his white elders. This shallow, adolescent rebelliousness, without moral or political conviction, prompted no social or political action. Phillips was nothing like Zenas Sears; he never publicly spoke out on race relations, marched on a picket line, or voted in an election. His impact as a DJ was limited to the popular music wars of the era, and it was in this context that he stood out as one of radio's more outrageous pioneers of rock and roll—R & B's racially mixed teenage offspring.

"Daddy-O" Dewey Phillips

Dewey Phillips grew up poor during the Great Depression in rural western Tennessee, where his parents worked as tenant farmers. By the time he reached his teens, he was working in the fields alongside his family. He didn't stay in school long, joining the army as soon as he came of age. After a tour of duty during the final years of World War II, Phillips returned to civilian life in Memphis; there, he hoped to make it as a blues singer, an ambition he had harbored since childhood. Frequenting the black nightclubs along Beale Street, listening to R & B groups, and singing in after-hours jam sessions whenever possible, he got to know some of the local musicians, but his vocal aspirations went nowhere. While waiting for a break in his singing career, he held a variety of jobs—one of which was selling records in a downtown department store. Dewey hit on the idea of hawking the store's records as a sidewalk DJ. He set up some loud speakers, with a connecting microphone and turntable, in front of the department store and blasted out his favorite R & B hits in between motormouth spiels to potential customers. And so began a Memphis radio legend.[1]

Phillips's instant notoriety as the city's first sidewalk DJ coincided with the unprecedented popularity of WDIA's pioneering black appeal format, leading to Dewey's debut in radio. Hoping to take advantage of WDIA's celebrated breakthrough, a rival Memphis station, WHBQ, switched over to an R & B evening format in 1949. The station owner's search for a white host who knew something about black music ended with Phillips's audition later that year. His nightly show, *Red, Hot and Blue,* was a huge success in the local market during the 1950s, in spite of—or perhaps, because of—the fact that he habitually violated the basic rules of broadcast decorum. "Daddy-O" Dewey, as he called himself, talked to, whistled at, and sang along with the discs he played on the airwaves; listeners rarely knew which was which. He spoke an atrocious mix of redneck and black street slang and so often mispronounced names and misread commercial spots that WHBQ eventually allowed him to improvise advertising pitches. Alcohol and drugs contributed to his erratic on-air performances, and he sometimes flaunted his excesses during his nightly broadcasts. He was fond of telling his listeners about periodic drinking binges (two of which resulted in hospital stays after car wrecks), and he often alluded to the bottle of "Carnation Milk" he consumed each night during his show.[2]

In the beginning, *Red, Hot and Blue* was strictly an R & B show. Phillips's familiarity with the latest national trends, which he gained in his work as a record salesman, was reflected in his nightly playlists. His close association with Beale Street musicians made him inclined to feature discs by such Memphis talents as B. B. King, Howling Wolf, Junior Parker, and

Bobby Blue Bland. It was also through these contacts that Dewey got to know Sam Phillips, a like-minded white R & B fanatic who in the early 1950s was just launching Sun Records. Sam and Dewey, although not related, came from similarly impoverished rural Southern backgrounds. They were also about the same age, and both were heavy drinkers. The two hillbilly hepcats struck up a close friendship, and before long, *Red, Hot and Blue* became the principal test market for new releases on the Sun label. In return, Sam Phillips was the catalyst for Dewey Phillips's ascendancy as the region's premier rock-and-roll DJ.[3]

Until the mid-1950s, Sun Records specialized in recording African American blues musicians from the Memphis region, but Sam Phillips was on the lookout for a crossover act. In private, he often said to his secretary: "If I could find a white man who had a Negro sound and a Negro feel, I could make a million dollars." On a humid July day in 1954, Elvis Presley walked into the Sun studios and made his first record. After the historic session, Sam rushed a demo over to Dewey at WHBQ. Dewey played Presley's cover version of Arthur "Big Boy" Crudup's "That's All Right Mama" on his show that evening; the feedback was so positive that he replayed it, over and over. In a matter of days, the record's sales skyrocketed in Memphis, then all over the South. Shortly after the breakthrough, Dewey became the young singer's sidekick and confidant. He was the first person to interview Elvis on the airwaves, he bought Elvis his first touring car, and he used his radio and music contacts to spread the word about the rising star. The association with Elvis boosted Dewey's public visibility, increased his radio audience, and eventually led to a high-profile job as the host of a locally televised teenage dance show, *Dewey Phillips' Pop Shop*.[4]

At the height of his media career in the mid-1950s, Dewey Phillips was a local legend, idolized by Memphis teens as the harbinger of rock and roll. As his radio and television audience grew, it also became younger and more integrated—which, in turn, was reflected in his changing musical format. In addition to his blues and R & B regulars, Phillips began to feature rock-and-roll newcomers, black and white; he mixed in some Chuck Berry, Little Richard, Fats Domino, and Bo Diddley along with Bill Haley, the Big Bopper, Jerry Lee Lewis, and Elvis Presley. The revised playlists staked out a new middle ground between rhythm-and-blues and country-and-western musical formats, blurring the color line in the process. This innovation, coupled with his well-known involvement with the artists he featured on the air, enhanced Phillips's celebrity status as the city's Pied Piper of rock and roll.[5]

But Phillips's good fortune and fame could not survive his reckless lifestyle. In addition to alcohol, he became dependent on painkillers—especially morphine—as a result of the injuries he sustained in the auto accidents. On the air, his behavior became more erratic. Finally, one night on WHBQ, Daddy-O Dewey totally lost his composure and blurted out over the air: "Now right, now wait a minute Phillips, you got the wrongest request. Flat messin' up here, I got a morphine shot in me and I can't see very good here." The station fired him; an earlier indiscretion had already cost him his television job. His career gone and his life out of control, Dewey Phillips died in poverty a few years later, at the age of forty-two.[6]

George "Hound Dog" Lorenz and Alan "Moon Dog" Freed

The two most influential white R & B jocks in the North to become identified with the rise of rock and roll were George "Hound Dog" Lorenz and Alan "Moon Dog" Freed. Lorenz, a native of upstate New York, was drawn to black music as a teenager in the 1940s. He dropped out of high school to work as a musician in a local band, then drifted into radio later in the decade. After a short-lived stint as a DJ on WXRA in Buffalo, where he was fired for playing R & B discs, Lorenz moved on to WJJL in Niagara, New York. There, he established himself as the major crossover jock in the region and was given the honorary nickname "Hound Dog" by his black listeners.[7]

In 1954, Lorenz returned to Buffalo to host his own nightly R & B program on WBBW, a fifty-thousand-watt clear-channel outlet that could be heard throughout the Northeast after dark. The show, *On the Avenue*, was broadcast live from the Club Zanzibar in downtown Buffalo. Lorenz was the featured Master of Ceremonies, who introduced the guests to the audience; the featured pitchman, who ad-libbed the commercials over instrumental selections; and the featured DJ, who played the hottest R & B hits. Moreover, it was in this setting that Hound Dog first popularized the technique that would make him famous. "Rocking the pot," the practice of abruptly turning up the volume (pot) to coincide with the basic beat of a disc, then quickly turning it back to its original level. This technique was initially developed by black disc jockeys during the late 1940s in cities like Chicago, where it was referred to as "riding the gain."[8]

Within a year of his debut on WBBW, Hound Dog Lorenz was a household name among the growing legions of teens who tuned in on a nightly basis to hear him rocking the pot. By 1956, his teenage devotees had established a national fan club, which claimed to have seventy thousand members. At the height of his career on WBBW in the late 1950s, Lorenz was a major force in the region's music industry. In addition to his prowess as a rock-and-roll hit maker, he produced Buffalo's first interracial rock-and-roll shows. Some of the best-known acts he showcased during this period were James Brown, Elvis Presley, Chuck Berry, Bill Haley and the Comets, Fats Domino, Jerry Lee Lewis, and Little Richard.[9]

One of George Lorenz's collaborators in the interracial concert enterprise was Alan Freed, who also got into the concert-production end of the music business through his work as a crossover jock. In the typical Midwestern household where Freed grew up, his father worked as a clothing salesman, and his mother stayed home to raise her three sons. Young Alan, a devotee of swing music, played trombone in his Salem, Ohio, high school band and led his own group, the "Sultans of Swing"—named after a famous Harlem-based jazz band. Freed spent a year at Ohio State University in 1940, then joined the army when the war broke out. He started in radio as the host of a classical music program on WKST in New Castle, Pennsylvania, and moved on to a series of jobs on stations in western Pennsylvania and Ohio. In his first R & B venture, he took over a youth-oriented pop show in Akron, Ohio, in 1950; within a year, he had built up a large following among local teenagers. By this time, Freed was already a heavy drinker, on and off the air, and a nearly fatal auto accident had left him even more dependent on booze. Alcohol would plague him for the rest of his life.[10]

It was not in Akron but in nearby Cleveland where the "Moon Dog" first came to life on the airwaves. Freed moved to Cleveland early in 1951 to host a classical music show on WJW, fifty-thousand-watt clear-channel outlet (like WBBW in Buffalo and WLAC in Nashville). The program's sponsor, Leo Mintz, an entrepreneur who owned the city's largest record store, was also on the lookout for a DJ to host a late-night R & B show on WJW. Mintz had noticed the growing demand for rhythm-and-blues discs in his store, among not only black customers but also white teens. He thought that promoting the new trend would boost his record sales. In Alan Freed, Leo Mintz found an ideal pitchman for the music, and Freed was a willing accomplice. He had already witnessed the appeal of R & B to white teenagers, and he was by now regularly listening to John R (John Richbourg) late at night on WLAC. John R became his role model—but Freed's "Moon Dog" fantasy was of his own making. On his first late-night R & B program on WJW in July 1951, he opened the show with saxophonist Todd Rhodes's instrumental "Blues for Moon Dog"; in the middle of the record, as Rhodes launched into a honking sax solo, Alan Freed opened the mike and began to howl over the music.[11]

In the beginning, the *Moon Dog Show* on WJW was a full-fledged exercise in racial ventriloquy. Freed affected a black accent to go along with his raspy voice (due to polyps on the vocal chords). He also mixed the latest street slang into his on-air diatribes, featured only black music on his show, and tried to keep his listening audience guessing about his skin color. Consequently, most of his listeners at first though he was black. One of those he fooled was "Screaming" Jay Hawkins, who was an aspiring R & B vocalist when he first heard Freed on WJW in 1952: "That cat was stone wild. I went to find out who we had in Cleveland that would dare—I mean how could a black cat get away with such shit?" When Hawkins finally met the Moon Dog in person, he was shocked: "I says, oh no, you're the one playing black music on a white station? And he says—'that's me'—So I shook his hand and I said—'Well then you. . . . You're doing us good!'"[12] Freed would later become instrumental in launching Screaming Jay Hawkins's career, breaking his first national hit: "I Put a Spell on You."

The *Moon Dog Show* on WJW quickly attracted a large following among black and white teenagers; before long, it was this segment of his audience that Freed courted. He continued to play rhythm and blues but now called it "rock and roll"—a new label for the music favored by local teens. Then, late in 1952, he changed the name of his program to *The Moon Dog House Rock and Roll Party*. It was on this show that Alan Freed evolved into Cleveland's Mad Hatter of rock and roll, as his demeanor and antics on the air became more outlandish. Fortified with a nightly bottle of J & B scotch whiskey, he howled and yelled encouragement over the music, pounded out the "big beat" on a studio telephone book, and adopted the urban teen parlance of his faithful listeners. The effect was electrifying.[13]

Always the opportunist, Freed astutely used this new surge of radio fanfare to corner the local market on youth-oriented R & B concerts. His first venture, "Moon Dog's Coronation Ball," was held in the Cleveland Armory in 1952; Leo Mintz bankrolled it, and the headliners included the Dominos ("Sixty Minute Man"), saxophonist Paul Williams ("The Hucklebuck"), and female vocalist Varetta Dillard. The Coronation Ball turned into the nation's first rock-and-roll riot when twenty thousand teens, mostly black, packed the Armory. Seeing twice as many people as the Armory could hold, the fire marshal canceled the show, and the police were summoned to subdue the angry teenage crowd. The incident received widespread and sensationalist coverage in the mainstream press, which, predictably, seized on it as an ominous sign of rising teenage delinquency. Almost overnight, Freed was catapulted into the national limelight as the instigator of the riot. The unrepentant prophet of rock and roll vowed to do it again.[14]

True to his word, Freed continued to stage R & B dance concerts in the region, but on a smaller scale. In addition, he hosted the shows in person, in effect owning up to his true racial identity. The revelation, however, didn't seem to bother his young black listeners, and it dramatically increased his white teenage audience. Within a matter of months, Alan "Moon Dog" Freed was the hottest DJ in the Northeast and a new force in the burgeoning rhythm-and-blues market. He could make or break a new release in the region simply by choosing to give it airplay or not. With his star on the rise in the radio industry, Freed signed a high-paying contract with WINS in New York City. Moving there in 1954, he quickly established himself as the top DJ in the number-one radio market in the country. For the rest of the decade, Alan Freed reigned as the airwaves' undisputed king of rock-and-roll broadcasting.[15]

Robert "Wolfman Jack" Smith

By far the most madcap crossover odyssey of the rock-and-roll era belongs to Wolfman Jack, the legendary border radio DJ who captivated an entire generation of youthful listeners from Texas to California with his raucous outlaw broadcasts from northern Mexico. Born Robert Smith in Brooklyn, New York, he grew up in a ethnically mixed working-class neighborhood.

As a Brooklyn teenager in the early 1950s, young "Smitty" was the proud owner of a high-powered ham radio receiver, a gift from his father, who hoped it would keep the rambunctious youth off the streets at night. The teen radio enthusiast tuned in to not only local evening DJs, such as Tommy "Doctor Jive" Smalls on WWRL and, later, Alan "Moon Dog" Freed on WINS, but also such late-night broadcasters as Jocko Henderson on WDAS in Philadelphia, Hound Dog Lorenz on WBBW in Buffalo, John R on WLAC in Nashville, and even Paul Kallinger, a renegade country-and-western DJ who broadcast on XERF, located in Mexico.[16]

Later in the 1950s, after deciding to follow in the footsteps of his radio heroes, Robert Smith made a pilgrimage to Nashville to meet John R. The two struck up a close student–teacher relationship, which continued well into the 1960s. According to Smith: "John R was real nice, we kept in touch. He had a little deejay school over the years. When you met him, he would start teaching you. I was his star pupil for awhile. It blew my mind. I'd call him and ask questions about warming my voice with exercises before the show, he taught me basic things like that."[17]

Robert Smith's first job as a disc jockey was also his first venture into racial ventriloquy. Hired as a DJ in 1959 by WYOU in Newport News, Virginia, a low-power daytime outlet with an R & B format, he developed his earliest black radio persona: "I met this guy by the name of Tex Cathings . . . and he was the only disc jockey on the station then. Anyway, I created this character called Daddy Jules, a great character—'All right, baby, this is Daddy Jules!'—Anyway, he taught me the finer techniques. He said, 'If you're gonna talk like a black man, you better learn to use the slang and the language properly, so you don't sound like a white guy putting on black folks.'" Smith took Cathings's advice to heart: "I was attracted to black music, and I tried to be somebody black people approved of. That's why I kept my identity a secret for a long time as a DJ. There is nothing worse than a square white person playing black music!"[18]

Robert Smith lost his job as Daddy Jules on WYOU when the format changed, and he headed further south, to Shreveport, Louisiana. There he was reborn on KCIF as Big Smith, a deep-voiced country-and-western jock with a Texas drawl. The new venue paid the bills, but he missed his R & B show and remained on the lookout for a chance to get back to his radio roots. The opportunity soon came from an unlikely source. Smith had long been fascinated by the high-power border radio stations, broadcasting out of Mexico—especially XERF, which he listened to as a youth. Since the 1930s, these renegade broadcast outlets had used powerful transmitters, ranging from 250,000 to 1 million watts, to beam unauthorized and un-regulated English-language programming into the North American heart-land. Much to the chagrin of the FCC, they were out of the reach of the federal government, because their studios and transmitters were located just south of the border in Mexico. After paying off the appropriate Mexi-can authorities, these stations operated with impunity; they were unre-stricted with respect to wattage, broadcast hours, language, or format. This situation, brought on by the lack of a broadcast treaty between the two na-tions, attracted an odd assortment of crackpot radio pitchmen, preachers, and prophets—from the controversial goat-gland mountebank Doc Brink-ley in the 1930s, to the flamboyant Reverend Ike in the 1950s, to Wolfman Jack.[19]

The birth of Wolfman Jack in the border radio badlands happened ac-cidentally. In 1960, Smith paid a visit to XERF, located just across the bor-der from Del Rio, Texas, only to discover a moribund operation ripe for a Yankee takeover. After bailing the station out of debt and paying off cer-tain well-connected Mexican officials, he found himself in control of a 250,000-watt transmitter aimed at the heart of the colossus to the north. It was a boyhood dream come true, and the beginning of his grandest radio caper. Smith immediately hired a number of local Mexicans to renovate the station's physical facilities and protect him from retaliation by the for-mer XERF regime, which was not happy with the takeover. He relished his new role as "El Jefe" of the outlaw station, in spite of the dangers: "I used to look like Viva Zapata! I had a forty-five strapped to one hip and a Smith and Wesson strapped to the other—and what do you call them?—ban-doleras strung across my chest. I had bodyguards. I got ambushed goin' through the pass one night. I know what it feels like to have bullets goin' by my head!"[20]

After renovating and securing XERF's facilities, Robert Smith re-vamped the broadcast format. The station now signed on the air in the early evening with Big Smith's country-and-western show for the American farmer, followed by a Spanish-language segment for the benefit of the Mex-ican authorities; then came the cash-for-salvation preachers, long a staple of border radio; and finally, at the midnight hour, Wolfman Jack took to the airwaves, breaking the sound barrier with his howling hilarity. Smith's new audio caricature owed something to Lon Chaney's famous Hollywood werewolf, Alan Freed's "Moon Dog," and the jive-talking Daddy Jules. The gravelly voice sounded black, and most of the music was rhythm and blues. But Wolfman Jack also sought to downplay race by lapsing into adolescent fantasy and high jinks. The lupine prankster promised his youthful listeners a radio roller-coaster ride they would never forget: "Ah ya readeh, baybee? De Wolfman gonna blow ya mihnd tanight!" He routinely exhorted them: "Get naked!" "Squeeze my knobs!"—all the while punctuating his discourse and the music with grunts, growls, hoots, and howls. In between these teenage tantrums and his favorite R & B discs, the Wolfman hawked an outrageous assortment of mail-order bargains—everything from bogus sexual-potency pills (Mr. Satisfy), to bushels of live baby chicks, to his own brand-name roach clips: "You get dese little roach clips heah and ya can catch de little roaches by deah hin' legs and throw them dem right out de winda!"[21]

For close to four years, Robert Smith was El Jefe at XERF, supporting a commune of up to fifty Mexican families, who worked and lived in the station compound, and paying the necessary bribes to keep the operation afloat. Simultaneously, Wolfman Jack built up a huge teenage following in the United States, where his late-night broadcasts became legendary—and his identity remained a mystery. But as XERF's popularity and profits increased, so did Mexican interest in the station; and in 1964, Smith was forced to cash in his chips and move on. Wolfman Jack then vanished from the airwaves for almost a year, only to reappear on another border radio powerhouse, XERB, located near Tijuana on the Pacific Coast. This station blanketed most of the Southwest, but its signal was especially loud and distinct in southern California, which quickly became a Wolfman Jack stronghold. In addition, Smith cut a deal with a number of the other border radio outlets, including XERF, which allowed him to broadcast tapes of his XERB show on their airwaves. From these strategic locations along the Mexican border, Wolfman Jack could once again be heard long into the night throughout most of the United States and even in Canada. As for his true identity, it came to light only when he appeared as himself in the George Lucas motion picture *American Graffiti,* which was released in 1973. The film became a youth cult classic and transformed the border radio renegade into an American cultural icon.[22]

As rock and roll grew in popularity, the fame and influence of disc jockeys skyrocketed, with crossover white DJs in the forefront of the new musical craze. Many DJs had maintained close ties with record outlets through the earlier R & B years. Now, as the market for rock and roll broadened through radio's influence, the relationship between record labels and on-air jocks saw unprecedented growth in the music-industry practice of "payola."

Payola and the Power of the Playlist

The rise of rock and roll in American popular culture not only scrambled racial identities along the color line; it also uncovered a lucrative youth market, which quickly caught the attention of both the record and the radio industries. In the record business, it was the smaller independent labels that initially took advantage of this newly emerging consumer bloc; consequently, their profits and numbers increased, as did their share of the hit records on the pop charts. Many of these upstart companies—Atlantic in New York City, Chess in Chicago, and Sun in Memphis—started out as R & B standard-bearers, then moved into rock and roll as the youth market gained momentum. Others, such as the Dot label in Nashville, were created specifically to exploit the rock-and-roll bonanza, which, by the end of the 1950s, was attracting even major record corporations such as RCA Victor. On the radio side of the enterprise, it was the R & B DJs who first promoted rock and roll on the nation's airwaves. By the end of the decade, their popularity was exploding, and their ranks were multiplying as more and more mainstream DJs switched over to a rock format. These new growth sectors in the two media industries were, from the outset, linked in a mutually beneficial way. The disc jockeys introduced the record labels' latest rock-and-roll releases to their teenage listeners and, in return for this service, usually received some form of payola—expensive gifts, junkets, vacations, and, most often, hard cash—from the record promoters, who were the middlemen in the transactions.

Payola existed in the music industry long before the advent of rock and roll and, in fact, even predated commercial radio. The practice of paying someone to plug a song became prevalent after the passage of the 1909 copyright laws, which established a royalty structure for the infant record industry. At first, it was the Tin Pan Alley singers of the era who were awarded payola for plugging a new song during public appearances—which, by the 1920s, included radio venues. During the 1930s, the popular swing DJs became the major beneficiaries of these financial favors in return for playing certain records on their shows. Payola became pervasive and was even expected among both white and black R & B disc jockeys in the postwar era.[23]

Payola itself was not illegal, but the transactions had to be reported to the Internal Revenue Service (IRS). A problem arose because the record labels were routinely writing it off as a business expense, but many of the disc jockeys failed to list their payola on their individual income tax returns. Because the widespread practice was conducted in secret, it seemed tainted. With the triumph of rock and roll in the late 1950s, payola suddenly became a national issue. The ensuing controversy focused on the DJs who accepted the payments, rather than on the record companies that made them.

In May 1959, nearly fifty record labels bankrolled a lavish and lascivious four-day bacchanal in Miami, where the promoters plied some two thousand white disc jockeys with "Booze, Broads and Bribes," as the banner headlines in the *Miami Herald* proclaimed. Besides the around-the-clock receptions, parties, concerts, and gambling junkets to nearby Havana, the convention featured one of the largest contingents of hookers ever assembled in a Miami Beach hotel. (The prostitutes were recruited from as far away as New York City.) Although the record companies spent an estimated $250,000 on this spectacle and their top executives were in attendance, it was the DJs who were pilloried in the press. Articles in the major newspapers and magazines around the country not only documented their Miami Beach debauchery but also exposed their role in payola transactions and charged them with being a corrupting influence on the nation's youth.[24]

The media frenzy that followed the convention—which *Time* magazine called "The Big Payola" and other publications characterized as a full-fledged "orgy"—caught the attention of the Legislative Oversight Subcommittee of the U.S. House of Representatives' Commerce Committee. Fresh from its sensational exposé of the networks' rigged television quiz shows, the subcommittee wasted little time in scheduling a public probe into music industry payola. Most of the witnesses summoned to the hot seat in the spring of 1960 were rock-and-roll DJs, among them Alan Freed and Dick Clark, the two most famous of the era. Both men had used their fame as broadcasters to launch a variety of lucrative business ventures in the music industry. Their divergent career paths after testifying at the hearings climaxed a compelling cautionary tale for disc jockeys on both sides of the color line.[25]

The Demise of Alan Freed

Alan Freed had championed the black roots of rock and roll, both as a DJ and as a music industry entrepreneur. It was this racial disposition that helped bring about his early rise to fame; ironically, it would also lead to his downfall. After moving to WINS in New York City in the mid-1950s, Freed continued to attract a huge teenage audience on the airwaves and to produce large rock-and-roll dance concerts throughout the Northeast. Most of these concerts were highly successful, in terms of both attendance and revenues, and they enhanced Freed's status as a music-industry power broker. But as the region's first large, racially mixed teenage gatherings, they were also controversial. To many white parents and media pundits, the dance concerts were a troublesome sign of the cultural race mixing that was undermining the moral values of America's youth—and Alan Freed was the Pied Piper from hell.

The backlash against Freed began to gain momentum in the wake of a rock-and-roll show he staged in Boston on May 3, 1959. The event was marred by a confrontation between Freed and the local police, who wanted to keep the arena's lights on during the show. Freed resisted their demands and reputedly told the audience: "I guess the police in Boston don't want you kids to have a good time." After the concert, roving bands of young people—perhaps three hundred out of a crowd of six thousand—went on a rampage; they attacked innocent bystanders, vandalized property outside the arena, and skirmished with the police who were called in to restore order. There were no arrests, but fifteen casualties were reported, including a nineteen-year-old sailor who was hospitalized with knife wounds to the chest. The local press blamed Freed for the outbreak, and in a matter of days, he was charged with "inciting a riot" by the city authorities.[26]

The Boston indictment made the national news headlines, forcing Freed to cancel the remainder of his rock-and-roll concert tour; his financial losses were considerable. Then, when he returned to New York City, he was fired by WINS. Management claimed that the controversy over his concerts was driving away advertisers. Not only were the criminal charges at issue, but rumors were also rampant that Freed's concert ventures were bankrolled by local mobsters. If that weren't enough, he was also under attack in Harlem, where black DJs, led by Willie Bryant, had organized public meetings to protest what they viewed as his self-serving appropriation of their music, language, and livelihood. In spite of these mounting problems, Freed managed to get another job in the New York market on WABC, in part because its parent company was already backing his live rock-and-roll dance party on a local TV station. But that show was abruptly canceled after black teenage heartthrob Frankie Lymon did the "bump and grind" with a white female fan in front of the cameras, outraging the city's elders. When the payola hearings commenced, Freed tried to keep a low profile; he chose to testify in private, was a cooperative witness, and ducked the press going in and out. After the testimony, he returned to his job in New York relatively unscathed—or so it seemed at the time.[27]

Not long after his testimony, WABC asked Alan Freed to sign a statement that he had never taken payola in the past and would never do so in the future. Not wishing to perjure himself, he refused to sign the document. Subsequently, his radio show was terminated, and he was out of work again. In 1962 a New York grand jury indicted him, along with seven other local DJs, on charges of accepting "commercial bribery"—a violation of an old and obscure state law. In Freed's case, he was charged with pocketing $30,000 of payola. At first, he disputed the indictment, telling the local press: "What they call payola in the disc jockey business, they call lobbying in Washington!" Eventually, however, he would make a guilty plea in return for a fine and a suspended sentence, then move west to Los Angeles, where he vainly tried to resurrect his career. But Freed had become a pariah in the music industry, and by the early 1960s his health was deteriorating from years of heavy drinking. When the IRS laid claim to the few remaining assets left in his name, it landed the knockout punch. He died broke and disillusioned in 1964 at age forty-two from alcohol-related liver damage.[28]

Dick Clark: White Boy Makes Good

In contrast to Alan Freed's unruly public image, Dick Clark was middle-class America's shining white prince of rock and roll. Presiding over the nationally televised *American Bandstand,* he almost single-handedly reinvented teenage dance music in the eyes and ears of his estimated 20 million viewers. Clark's bleached and sanitized version of rock and roll was palatable to the cultural mainstream in part because he purged the music of its black sounds, styles, and images. His boy-next-door persona and the "Pepsodent pop" or "Philadelphia shlock" version of rock music he promoted were seen as reassuring signs that the younger generation was finally returning to its musical senses. Rock and roll, severed from its black roots, was becoming just another harmless teen music fad, and Dick Clark was leading the way.[29]

Clark began his career in the entertainment business as a disc jockey on WFIL in Philadelphia during the mid-1950s. He was a protégé of Bob Horn, a local crossover jock who hosted *Bob Horn's Bandstand* on WFIL and also pioneered the city's first teenage dance show on television. In 1956, Horn was fired from his TV job after a drunk-driving arrest, and Dick Clark stepped in as his replacement. Within a year, the young impresario had signed a deal with ABC, and the program, now called *American Bandstand,* went national. It quickly became the most popular rock-and-roll dance show on television, and in the process, Clark emerged as both a highly visible teenage role model and a major player in the music industry.[30]

At first, *American Bandstand* was strictly a Jim Crow operation. The teen audience, made up of well-groomed dance couples from various local high schools, was all white—as were Clark's guest artists. It was only after a few years of good ratings and press that Dick Clark began to integrate his popular TV program, and even then, he did so with great caution. In the interim, he was content to showcase a new line of youthful white rockers, many of them, like Paul Anka, Fabian, Frankie Avalon, and Bobby Rydell, hometown products in whom Clark had a financial stake. The first black rock-and-roll act given top billing on *American Bandstand* was Chubby Checker, whose 1960 cover version of Hank Ballad and the Midnighters' 1958 R & B hit "The Twist" climbed to the top of the pop charts and set off a nationwide dance craze. Checker (born Ernest Evans) had worked in a local poultry plant before signing with Cameo/Parkway Records, the same Philadelphia label that made Bobby Rydell into an overnight teenage sensation. His one-hit career in rock and roll was orchestrated, in part, by Clark, who also owned stock in Cameo/Parkway. Clark paved the way for the crossover triumph of "The Twist" by making it a regular attraction on *American Bandstand.* In addition, Clark's wife,

Bobbie, came up with the "Chubby Checker" nickname, which was inspired by the sobriquet of another portly black rock and roller—Fats Domino.[31]

By the start of the payola hearings in 1960, Dick Clark was a multimillionaire with a maze of investments in thirty-three different Philadelphia-based entertainment enterprises, including record companies, music publishing firms, radio stations, talent agencies, and even a record-pressing plant. His public disclosure of this formidable business empire at the hearings led the *Washington Post* to suggest that payola be renamed "Clarkola." But beyond the raised eyebrows, Clark emerged from the congressional hearings with his reputation and fortune still intact. New federal legislation to curb payola would force him to divest some of his holdings, but his overall wealth continued to multiply; by 1980, his estimated worth had reached $180 million.[32]

Dick Clark's good fortune despite the payola revelations was something of an anomaly. Many of the other DJs who were put in the spotlight suffered as a result of the exposure. In addition to New York City's indictments, the IRS began a widespread audit of high-profile disc jockeys, culminating in a series of federal indictments that ensnared not only Alan Freed but also other prominent rock-and-roll broadcast personalities, including Bob Horn—Clark's mentor. Moreover, station owners throughout the country used the uproar over payola as a pretext for purging the airwaves of DJs who were even suspected of any wrongdoing. Toward that end, many owners demanded that their employees sign sworn statements dissociating themselves from payola. Those who refused were fired. Consequently, a number of well-known rock-and-roll DJs, including Joe Niagara and Tom "Big Daddy" Donahue in Philadelphia, Joe Smith in Boston, Joe Finan in Cleveland, and Don McLeod in Detroit, lost their jobs. But the worst was yet to come.[33]

The Impact of Top Forty

The disc jockeys' position of power and influence in the music industry of the 1950s stemmed from their popularity on the airwaves and their control of their own playlists. This situation created a dilemma for radio station owners. On the one hand, they were dependent on the DJs for their audience, ratings, and advertisers. On the other hand, they chafed at the record companies' penchant for funneling payola directly to their jocks. They weren't so much against payola per se as angry at being left out of the loop. Once the national payola scandal subsided, station owners found a way to reroute the flow of payola while appearing to eliminate it from radio. The vehicle for this maneuver was "Top Forty."

"Top Forty" was a radio music format ostensibly focused on *Billboard*'s routine listing of the country's best-selling pop records. Its centerpiece was a rotating playlist that featured these pop hits on an ascending scale; the higher the ranking, the more airplay a song was awarded. In theory, this new "scientific" method of determining a station's musical selections was a foolproof means of ensuring that the most popular records of the day got the most airplay. In practice, Top Forty transferred the control over the playlist from the DJ to management. General managers and program directors were now responsible for compiling the playlists, with help from the latest *Billboard* pop charts. Disc jockeys were relegated to following a script with respect to what they played and when they played it.

Top Forty's architect, Todd Storz, had pioneered the format on KOWH in Omaha during the mid-1950s. The owner of Storz Broadcasting, a radio chain with outlets in Omaha (KOWH), New Orleans (WTIX), Kansas City (WHB), Minneapolis (WGDY),(WGDY), and Miami (WQAM), Storz also experimented with cash giveaways as a means of increasing listenership. The official story of the Top Forty innovation is that he got the idea after spending the afternoon in an Omaha bar with a friend, listening to the customers play the latest hit discs over and over on the jukebox. Many of the DJs who were disenfranchised by the change, however, believe Storz and his fellow radio station owners were more interested in payola than in popularity. According to one of Storz's former employees: "Todd used to sit and scheme for hours about how he could tap into this cash flow. It drove him crazy, and a lot of other station owners too, to know that all of these payoffs were flowing right by them into the hands of the deejays. He kept looking for a way to get a share, to get the record companies to channel money to the station owner."[34]

Ironically, Todd Storz was courting the nation's rock-and-roll disc jockeys during the same period that his Top Forty format was gaining a foothold in the radio industry. In fact, Storz was the man behind the infamous Miami Beach DJ convention that ignited the payola scandal. He organized the first of these conventions in Kansas City in 1958, and he was the major sponsor of the Miami Beach fiasco a year later. It is not clear what Storz wished to accomplish by organizing these disc jockey conventions, but he quickly dissociated himself from the second one after it got such bad press, and he never sponsored another. Whatever his intentions, Storz's Top Forty format took the country by storm. Station owners adopted it en masse, proclaiming that Top Forty's scientific approach to compiling the playlist would both attract a larger audience and cleanse the radio industry of payola once and for all.[35]

The fallout from the payola scandal and the rise of Top Forty radio had the unintended effect of curtailing the postwar wave of racial ventriloquy on the nation's airwaves. By the mid-1960s, Top Forty was commercial radio's format of choice, and most of the previous decade's most popular crossover jocks, including Alan Freed, George Lorenz, Hunter Hancock, and Dewey Phillips, were no longer on the air. Their departure ended the final cycle of racial masquerading in the radio industry. The halcyon days of postwar crossover occurred during a period when AM radio was experimenting with diversity at the local level; stations were searching for new audiences and open to new formats. But when conformity returned to the airwaves through Top Forty, much of the racial ventriloquy fell by the wayside, a casualty of both the format change and the changing times. What was a novelty on the airwaves in the placid 1950s became an affront to black listeners in the turbulent 1960s.

The white crossover jocks left behind an ambiguous cultural legacy. They helped usher in a new era of black appeal radio, even as they parodied black DJs—their speech and their playlists—on the airwaves for fun and profit. They helped popularize rhythm and blues, then most of them abandoned it for rock and roll. And finally, they rebelled against the color line—but their rebellion was as backward-looking as it was forward-looking. To be sure, a number of the crossover jocks, such as John R and George Lorenz, supported racial equality and justice, and a few, like Zenas Sears, even joined the civil rights struggle. But in their efforts to breach the racial divide, they also became involved in recycling blackface audio stereotypes from the *Amos 'n' Andy* era, which once again caricatured African Americans for the amusement of a white audience.

PART V

"Burn Baby Burn": Black Power Radio

The masses of African Americans who have been deprived of educational and economic opportunity are almost totally dependent on radio as their means of relating to the society at large. They do not read the newspapers, though they may occasionally thumb through *Jet*. Television speaks not to their needs, but to upper middle class America. One need only recall the Watts tragedy and the quick adaptation of the "Burn Baby Burn" slogan to illustrate the pervasive influence of the radio announcer on the community. But while the establishment was quick to blame the tragedy of Watts most unjustly on the slogan of Magnificent Montague, it has not acknowledged all the positive features which have grown out of your contributions to the community. No one knows the importance of Tall Paul White to the massive nonviolent demonstrations of the youth of Birmingham in 1963; or the funds raised by Purvis Spann for the Mississippi Freedom Summer Project of 1964; or the consistent fundraising and voter education done for the Southern Christian Leadership Conference and the Civil Rights Movement by Georgie Woods, my good friend in Philadelphia. . . . In a real sense, you have paved the way for social and political change by creating a ͺ powerful cultural bridge between black and white. . . . I salute you.

—Martin Luther King Jr., keynote
address, NARTA Convention,
Atlanta, September 28, 1967

10

"A Change Is Gonna Come"

During the early 1960s, the growth of the civil rights movement transformed the nation's political landscape. A series of sit-ins staged by black college students in protest against the South's segregated public accommodations—hotels, restaurants, libraries, and so forth—prompted similar actions across the country and drew so much attention from the press that race became a key public issue for the first time in decades. The first sit-in occurred in Greensboro, North Carolina, on February 1, 1960, when four students refused to leave an F. W. Woolworth Company lunch counter after being denied service; they were eventually arrested. The news media coverage of the incident caught the attention of other black college students in the region and inspired similar sit-ins in other localities. Whereas protests in the past, such as the Montgomery, Alabama, bus boycott, had galvanized only local communities, these sit-ins suggested that concerted action could achieve significant change by drawing the nation's—and the world's—attention to the abuses of segregation. Idealistic, brave, not quite prepared for the danger they would face, a group of young protesters formed the Student Nonviolent Coordinating Committee (SNCC) in 1960. These black students were determined to change the balance of political and social power in the South through direct action, even if it required putting themselves in mortal danger. It was a landmark moment in itself, but it also foreshadowed and inspired a variety of youth rebellions in the 1960s.[1] The Southern Christian Leadership Conference (SCLC), whose leader, the Reverend Martin Luther King Jr., was a veteran of the Montgomery bus boycott and an advocate of nonviolent protest, joined the students' direct action crusade by staging a sit-in of their own in an Atlanta department store in the fall of 1960. Fifty-five of the protesters were arrested, but only Dr. King was sentenced to four months hard labor on a Georgia prison farm. His sentence was commuted after a huge public outcry and a good deal of political arm-twisting by the Democrats' presidential candidate, John F. Kennedy, and his brother, Robert Kennedy.[2]

As the struggle intensified over the next few years, the civil rights movement broadened its scope of activities, spreading beyond the South. In 1961, the Chicago-based Congress of Racial Equality (CORE) sponsored a series of "Freedom Rides" to desegregate public transportation facilities in the South. Interracial groups of students and clergy—Freedom Riders—recruited by CORE in the North headed south on Greyhound buses to target bastions of segregation, where they were usually met and arrested by local police or attacked by angry white mobs. The protests continued despite the violent responses; by 1963, both sides were determined to prevail. That May, Birmingham, Alabama, police chief Theophilus Eugene "Bull" Connor used police dogs and high-powered water hoses to break up large demonstrations against segregation and job discrimination that were led by King and the SCLC. A horrified nation of television viewers saw scores of protesters beaten and otherwise injured on the evening news. Injured or not, twenty-five hundred protesters were arrested. Shortly after the Birmingham protest, NAACP leader Medgar Evers was murdered in front of his home in Jackson, Mississippi—shot in the back by an unknown assassin. The reaction of the civil rights forces to these violent transgressions was swift and massive. Three months after Evers was gunned down, 250,000 people gathered in Washington, D.C., and marched to the foot of the Lincoln Memorial to hear Martin Luther King Jr. speak. His historic "I Have a Dream" speech captured the righteousness of their cause and the power of their nonviolent crusade.[3]

Soul Music's Social Message

As the civil rights campaign gained momentum, visibility, and adherents during the early 1960s, black popular music was once again undergoing a major transformation. Rhythm and blues, the dominant African American musical genre in the postwar era, was giving way to "soul" music. The sound was not new in the sense that one tradition was replacing another. Rather, R & B's standard twelve-bar blues musical paradigm gave way to one based on gospel song structures, chord progressions, harmonies, and vocal styling. Soul also continued the gospel tradition of delivering "good news," positive lyrical messages in the music. Many of these messages now had a social rather than a religious nature. Ray Charles is credited with pioneering this new genre in the mid-1950s, when he jettisoned his Nat King Cole–inspired blues combo and vocal styling for a secularized gospel sound. Charles transformed the religious standard "My Jesus Is All the World to Me" into his first national hit "I Got a Woman." This paradigm shift soon caught on with other R & B singers and vocal groups, as well as with a number of gospel artists, who switched genres in order to develop careers as secular entertainers.[4]

Contrasting Styles

During the political ferment of the 1960s, soul music spread like wildfire, lighting up the pop charts, the "chitlin circuit," and the airwaves. Production centers flourished in New York City (Atlantic), Detroit (Motown), Memphis (Stax), and Chicago. Atlantic Records' stable of soul artists included Ray Charles, Solomon Burke, Wilson Pickett, Aretha Franklin, and the Drifters. Ahmet Ertegun, who founded Atlantic in 1947, took on Jerry Wexler as a new partner in 1953. The son of European immigrants and a native of New York City, Wexler had covered popular black music as a *Billboard* reporter before joining the Atlantic team. By watching the veteran arranger Jesse Stone in action, Wexler was able to learn studio production from the ground up; before long, Wexler was producing records on his own. In the 1960s, Jerry Wexler produced the hit recordings of both Wilson Pickett and Aretha Franklin.[5]

Wexler was not the only white member of the Atlantic production team. Most of the hit songs recorded by the Drifters and the Coasters were composed by Jerry Leiber and Mike Stoller, both of whom grew up in close proximity to African Americans and, like Johnny Otis, developed an early affinity for black music and culture—one that eventually led to their career as songwriters. Leiber and Stoller first started working together in the early 1950s in Los Angeles, where they wrote such R & B hits as "Hound Dog" and "Kansas City." They joined the Atlantic operation in New York later in the decade, teaming up with the Coasters and then the Drifters to produce a string of hit records for the label. Their songs for the Coasters, renowned for their witty portrayals of teenage angst and high jinks, included "Young Blood," "Yakety Yak," and "Charlie Brown." In their collaboration with the Drifters, Leiber and Stoller pioneered the use of lush string arrangements behind the group's sweet gospel harmonies. This "uptown" black pop innovation would soon become the centerpiece of Motown's highly successful soul formula.[6]

According to music critic and historian Nelson George, Motown in Detroit and Stax in Memphis were the "twin towers" of the soul sound in the 1960s. But they had little in common as record companies, especially with respect to their makeup and musical orientation. Motown's owner, staff, and musicians were all African Americans, and it was located in the heart of the Detroit ghetto. Yet its lavish uptown musical productions—the fabled "Motown sound"—were designed appeal to a crossover teenage audience. The label even promoted itself as the "Sounds of Young America." In contrast, Stax was initially white owned, and its workforce—including the talented studio band—was integrated; but the down-home gospel-tinged music that became the "Memphis sound" or "Southern soul" was created for a black adult audience. Furthermore, Stax's unsophisticated production techniques hardly compared to Motown's hallmark instrumental and vocal overdubbing.[7]

To a large degree, the original Motown sound was shaped by owner Berry Gordy's strategy of making records that would sell in the black market but, more important would cross over onto the white pop charts. Gordy estimated that 70 percent of the sales of a Motown release needed to be in the white market for the record to become a national hit. Gordy also realized that to achieve maximum crossover, the songs he recorded had to be compatible with AM radio; more specifically, they needed to be tailored to the omnipresent Top Forty format. Based on these considerations, Motown's formula for its tunesmiths emerged: short pop songs with a simple hook and a danceable beat. Motown's master craftsman, Smokey Robinson, saw the logic: "I've just geared myself to radio time. The shorter a record is nowadays, the more it's gonna be played. This is the key thing in radio time, you dig? If you have a record that's 2:15 long its definitely gonna get more play than one that's 3:15 at first, which is very important."[8]

Motown producers also perfected an instrumental framework that exploited the higher treble frequency ranges so prominent in AM broadcasting; hence their penchant for string arrangements. Motown constantly showcased young singers—from Little Stevie Wonder to Diana Ross to Michael Jackson—whose high-pitched voices stood out on AM radio. This early crossover formula for hit making was the key element in Motown's corporate strategy of capturing the teen market over the airwaves. It worked to perfection, turning Gordy's Motown into a multimillion dollar enterprise.

In contrast to Motown's top-down strategic planning, Stax's distinctive Southern soul sound was built from the bottom up during the creative interplay between musicians and producers in the studio. Management provided little input and seems to have thought about exploiting radio only after the recordings were completed. So, for example, after Carla Thomas recorded "'Cause I Love You" for the label in the early 1960s, Stax owner Jim Stewart gave WLAC's John R a percentage of the song's publishing rights in return for airplay. In addition, WDIA disc jockey Rufus Thomas, who wrote the tune, featured it regularly on his show. Between the two of them, they were able to break "'Cause I Love You" in the South, where it eventually became a regional hit. John R was also instrumental in launching the career of Stax soul star Otis Redding. The DJ showcased Redding's first hit for the label, "These Arms of Mine," on WLAC—again in return for a percentage of the publishing. Generally speaking, Stax relied on an informal network of R & B disc jockeys, black and white, to introduce the company's records to the public, and pretty much ignored Top Forty radio. Hence the Memphis record label was not as prosperous as Motown.[9]

The Chicago Sound: Sam Cooke and Curtis Mayfield

Unlike the other cities, Chicago didn't have one specific record company that defined its soul music sound. As a consequence, the evolution of Chicago soul depenced on two key local artists: Sam Cooke and Curtis Mayfield. Cooke pioneered the soul genre in Chicago, where he grew up singing in his father's Baptist church. While still in his teens, he replaced R. H. Harris as the lead singer in the nationally renowned Soul Stirrers. Once in the gospel group, the young crooner became a sensation—especially among young female admirers. Cooke's sexual charisma and innovative vocal style were molded in his years with the Soul Stirrers, well before he crossed over to soul music in the late 1950s. Unlike most of the leading male vocalists in gospel music, Cooke perfected a silky-smooth midrange vibrato. He abandoned the harsh and repetitive exhortations of his rivals for a more subdued vocal timbre and the use of melodic melisma. His was a voice enriched with black pop sensibilities and well suited for AM radio.

Sam Cooke was not only an exceptional vocalist but also a talented tunesmith—and an independent-minded entrepreneur. During his early years as a gospel artist, he wrote a number of sacred songs, including his signature piece, "Touch the Hem of His Garment." When he moved on to the pop-music arena and recorded his first national hit, "You Send Me" (1957), he set up his own publishing firm to handle the royalties his songs generated. Simultaneously, Cooke signed a lucrative contract with a major record label, RCA Victor, which agreed to promote him as a crossover act in the teen market. It was during this period that he wrote and recorded a string of soul classics, including "Chain Gang," "Only Sixteen," "Twisting the Night Away," "Having a Party," "Wonderful World," and "Bring It on Home to Me." Every one of these releases crossed over to the pop charts.[10]

In 1959, Cooke cofounded, along with black music entrepreneur J. W. Alexander, SAR Records. Bankrolled with Cooke's royalties, SAR was an experimental soul label that set out to mine the wealth of musical talent coming out of the black church, especially in Chicago. Among the newly converted soul artists who first recorded for SAR were Lou Rawls, Bobby Womack, and Johnny Taylor. Just as the business was building and his recording career soared, Sam Cooke was shot dead at a Los Angeles motel; he was twenty-nine years old. Memorial services in Los Angeles and then Chicago drew two hundred thousand mourners. Jesse Jackson eulogized Cooke at the funeral in Chicago, and Ray Charles sang his favorite gospel hymn. Two months later, "A Change Is Gonna Come" was released as a single. It rose to the top of the pop charts and quickly became an anthem of the civil rights movement. The song proved to be Cooke's most enduring composition.[11]

Curtis Mayfield, a youthful admirer of Sam Cooke, became his most important disciple. Like Cooke, Mayfield grew up in Chicago singing gospel in the local churches, then moved on to a career in soul music. Mayfield first achieved prominence as a songwriter, composing dance songs, such as "Monkey Time" for Major Lance, and romantic ballads, such as "For Your Precious Love" and "He Will Break Your Heart" for Jerry Butler. In the late 1950s, he joined Butler's group, the Impressions; a bit later, when Butler left the group to pursue a solo career, Curtis Mayfield became its lead vocalist. He immediately signed a contract with a major label, ABC Paramount. The deal allowed him and his group to continue to produce their own records in Chicago, in conjunction with a local team of musicians and arrangers. It was with the Impressions that Mayfield's vocal talents first became noticeable. His high and poignant tenor voice, cradled in the group's soft gospel harmonies, was ideal for such lyrical love ballads as "Gypsy Woman" and "I'm So Proud." Moreover, his sweet-sounding falsetto was in sharp contrast to the deep and brooding vocal styles of Muddy Waters and Howling Wolf, which had dominated Chicago's music scene since World War II. Like his idol Sam Cooke, Curtis Mayfield broke with the prevailing vocal traditions in both gospel and urban blues to establish his own version of Chicago soul. Both men, in this respect, were part of a generation of African American musicians who became trendsetters in the 1960s.

In the wake of the 1963 March on Washington, Mayfield began to record a series of "sermon songs," as he called them, in support of the ongoing civil rights struggle. He transformed the traditional spiritual "Amen" into a movement marching song and turned another gospel standard into the inspirational "Keep on Pushing." Then, in 1965, he penned his most famous civil rights anthem, "People Get Ready," a song that captured the movement's early religious fervor and political optimism. Along with soul diva Nina Simone ("Mississippi God Damn") and the gospel-based Staple Singers ("Freedom's Highway"), Curtis Mayfield helped pioneer the trend toward social consciousness in soul music. It was a trend that he would continue to champion during the 1970s.[12]

The message songs of Curtis Mayfield, Sam Cooke, Nina Simone, James Brown, and other soul luminaries were put to good use on the airwaves by African American DJs, who began to mix the music with their on-air social commentary in order to heighten the appeal of the discourse.

Chuck Scruggs, a black DJ on KSOL in San Francisco during this period, described how this new programming strategy evolved:

> There were a lot of message songs during the 1960s. . . . As a jock during that time I would take those message songs and add a line or two of editorial . . . something that would fit the title or the theme of the song, or would fit a current event. For flow, for content and flow. So for example when George Wallace was in the news, I'd play "Hit the Road Jack" right after mentioning him. I didn't play a message song in isolation, and then go from that to something else that had no connection. I tried to make a transition. I'd go from a message song like "Keep On Pushing" to, say, "Stand By Me." You see what I mean? And I'd make the transition with words of hope for my listeners. You know—"Stand by me people 'cause we gotta keep on pushing for our freedom."[13]

Dumping Jim Crow on Black Radio

Throughout the country, African American DJs were instrumental in popularizing the new soul music genre, and they were responsible for setting up the radio "grapevine" on which civil rights information circulated in the black community. As a result, soul music became a race-coded soundtrack for the assault on Jim Crow, and black appeal radio became an important means of spreading the civil rights message. Numerous African American DJs gained stature as political activists and race leaders in their respective communities; they marched on the picket lines, spoke at protest rallies, helped raise money for the cause, and served as officers in local civil rights organizations. These activities kept them closely attuned to the grassroots struggle, which was reflected in what they said and played on the air.

Georgie Woods

The civil rights saga of Philadelphia DJ Georgie Woods illustrates the extent to which black DJs came to the forefront of the struggle for racial equality. Woods was born in Burnett, Georgia, in 1927. His father was a firebrand preacher whose outspoken opinions on race made him a target for the KKK. After the Klan burned a cross in their front yard in 1936, Georgie's mother moved the children north to Harlem, but his father remained in Georgia. Five years later, Mrs. Woods died suddenly, leaving fourteen-year-old Georgie in charge of his younger brothers and sisters; he quit school and went to work as an unskilled laborer. Woods joined the navy toward the end of World War II and served a tour of duty in the Pacific. When he returned to Harlem at the end of the war, he took advantage of the GI Bill to enroll in a broadcasting school. Yet, even with a degree in radio announcing, Woods found it difficult to break into the field. Then in the early 1950s, he was hired as a DJ by WWRL. A few months later, however, the station manager fired him for playing the Clovers' "One Mint Julep" because the record "promoted alcohol consumption."[14]

In 1953, Woods was lured to Philadelphia by a job offer from WHAT, where he joined a team of DJs that included Jocko Henderson and Larry Dixon. At first, he hosted a morning wake-up show. Then, with his popularity on the rise, Georgie Woods—the "Guy with the Goods"—was also given an afternoon time slot. It was on his afternoon show, called *The Snap Club* on WHAT and, later, *The House of Jive* on rival WDAS, that he became a local teen idol, rivaling Dick Clark as the city's "king of rock and roll." His on-air demeanor, geared to his teenage audience, was anything but subtle: "I had a cowbell. I used to beat on the phone to the rhythm of the music. I had a whistle and when things got hot, I would blow the whistle and ring the bell."[15] To supplement his meager DJ salary ($25 a week on WHAT), Woods began to stage record hops and then rock-and-roll concerts in the Philadelphia area. By the end of the decade, he was the city's most important black concert promoter.

In the early 1960s, Woods formed a close working relationship with Cecil Moore, a prominent black lawyer who was the driving force behind the local NAACP chapter. In association with Moore, Woods staged a series of benefit concerts, called "Freedom Shows," for the NAACP at the Uptown Theater. Late in 1962, Cecil Moore and Georgie Woods were elected as the president and vice president of the Philadelphia NAACP; early the next year, they organized and led large demonstrations at city construction sites where job discrimination was at issue. Simultaneously, the duo launched a recruitment campaign that pushed local NAACP membership over the thirty thousand mark, making it the largest chapter in the country. Woods's activities on the airwaves were crucial to the success of these endeavors. He constantly urged his listeners to join him on the picket lines, and he recruited many of them into the NAACP. As Woods recalled:

> I got into civil rights because there was discrimination against black people everywhere, and I felt it personally. Then I met Cecil Moore and he asked me to join in some pickets and demonstrations and things like that, and I'd go on the air and tell people where I was going to be demonstrating, and a mob of people would show up and I had a microphone and I was directing people. When school let out I had all the kids in town listening to me. When school got out all the teenagers came and got into the picket line because I was there demonstrating for our rights.[16]

In addition to these local efforts, Woods was active in the civil rights struggle at a national level. He and Cecil Moore were the first civil rights activists in Philadelphia to bring Martin Luther King Jr. to town, for a series of rallies and speaking engagements early in 1963. During his visit, Dr. King befriended Woods, and the two remained in close contact over the next few years. Martin Luther King Jr. was heard regularly on Georgie Woods's radio show. If King was in town, he appeared in person; otherwise, he would call in from civil rights hot spots around the country. Just before the historic 1964 voting rights march in Selma, Alabama, Dr. King telephoned Woods on the air and urged him and his listeners to come down and participate in the demonstrations. Woods left for Selma the next day. On the march with King, Woods was among the demonstrators who were attacked by Alabama state police on the bridge leading into Selma. The attack sparked an escalation of the protest as the nation watched the unfolding racial drama on network television. When he returned from Alabama, Georgie Woods was the featured speaker at a Philadelphia rally in support of the Selma demonstrators, which drew twenty thousand people. It was during this period that Woods also became a fund-raiser for Dr. King's crusade: "We'd meet with Berry Gordy and tell him we needed a show for the civil rights movement, and I put Berry together with Dr. King, and Berry Gordy never said no, whatever he could do to help the movement, he was there for us."[17]

Mobilizing the Troops

Georgie Woods was by no means the only black DJ on the front lines of the civil rights struggle in the early 1960s. Numerous African American broadcasters participated in the movement in one way or another. Some even put themselves in life-threatening situations as the result of their actions. This was the case with Peggy Mitchell, a native of New York City, who moved to Birmingham, Alabama, in the mid-1950s after marrying a prominent black doctor who lived there. Mitchell was hired by WEDR, the local black appeal outlet, to host a half-hour daily "platter and chatter" show; it featured the latest R & B hits, as well as interviews with such R & B luminaries as B. B. King, Ruth Brown, and James Brown. In addition, Mitchell and her husband were active in the Alabama NAACP, and they were personal friends of King, who often stayed at their house when he was in Birmingham on civil rights business. This close association with Dr. King, coupled with her work for the NAACP and her high visibility as the city's only black female DJ, eventually put Peggy Mitchell's life in jeopardy. She was regularly followed to and from civil rights meetings and demonstrations. On one occasion, stalkers tried to run her off the road. On another occasion, her car was shot full of holes, as was the front picture window in her house. The day after the shooting, she was fired by WEDR's station manager because "he didn't want any further trouble with the Klan." A few days later, a traumatized Mitchell returned to New York City; she never went back to Birmingham or to her career in radio.[18]

The Reverend Erskine Fausch, who hosted a morning gospel show on Birmingham's WENN, was also subjected to KKK intimidation. Because of his civil rights activities, Fausch routinely received hate mail and even threatening phone calls while on the air. The station was bombed more than once in the early 1960s, and its antenna tower was cut down with help from WENN's own engineer, who was a Klan member. During the 1963 Birmingham civil rights demonstrations, Fausch and his associates ingeniously outmaneuvered Bull Connor's police force over the local airwaves.

It was at a time when there was great police resistance, when certain barriers were placed, physical barriers to close off certain streets to keep the demonstrators from going in certain directions, and where Bull Connor's police tanks and fire hoses and other things would be there to turn back the crowds. Plans were made to disperse certain people, not on one side of town, but on several sides of town so that the police could not be in all of those places at the same time and hold back the crowds. And the young people would have their portable radios, and the signal for them to come out of the basements en masse was "All Men Are Made by God." When I played that song, that would be the signal for them to come out, which they did. And it sort of put things in a tizzy, because when the police would gather on Fifth Avenue to stop the marchers from going that way, they'd get a call that a bunch were coming out from Sixth Avenue, and another was gathering on Nineteenth Avenue. So it worked very well, and they never knew how we pulled it off.[19]

The strategic role that African American DJs played in the rise of the civil rights movement was recognized early on by black leaders, especially Martin Luther King Jr. Even before the upheavals in the 1960s, King began to cultivate friendships with an informal network of black radio broadcasters around the country. These contacts gave him access to the local airwaves wherever he and his associates traveled to further the cause, and they became a key means of mobilizing people at the grass roots. Dr. King had first used radio in Atlanta. Arriving there from Montgomery, Alabama, in the mid-1950s, he developed a close working relationship with Zenas "Daddy" Sears at WAOK and "Jockey" Jack Gibson at WERD, both of whom regularly gave him airtime. At WERD, he had access at a moment's notice. Jack Gibson recalled:

Back then, the SCLC had their offices right below our studios. If Dr. King wanted to make an announcement, he'd take a broomstick and hit on the ceiling. That was the signal that somebody downstairs wanted to make an announcement, and we knew by the taps which party it was. So when I'd hear his tap, if I was on the air, I'd say—"We interrupt this program for another message from the president of the SCLC, Martin Luther King Jr. And now, here is Dr. King!" But while I was saying it, I'd let a microphone out the window, and it would come down to him, and he'd pull the microphone in from his window, and he'd make his announcement. And then I'd say, as I was pulling the microphone back up—"We've just heard another message from Dr. Martin Luther King Jr., and now, on with the programming!"[20]

Jack Gibson also describes how black DJs customized the civil rights messages to enhance their impact on the listeners:

> You have to understand that we were the voice that the people listened to and if you gave us a message to say, "There will be a meeting tonight of the SCLC at the First Baptist Church" . . . we would go ahead and elaborate all around it and do our own thing by saying—"Now look . . . we are going to have a meeting tonight at the First Baptist Church over there on Hunter Road, and Dr. King says to be there at seven sharp, no CP [colored people] time, and you know what I mean, don't be showing up at no seven-thirty or eight. Come on out at seven and be there 'cause this is important for me and you and for our children—ya understand me?" That would be one of the ways we were able to personalize a message for our audience, and it worked. People came out on time.[21]

At the height of the civil rights struggle in the 1960s, King's network of black radio contacts extended far beyond Atlanta. He was now connected to a large number of African American broadcasters, located in key urban markets throughout the country. Among the most prominent were Nat D. Williams (WDIA) in Memphis; Louise Fletcher (WSOK) in Nashville; Paul White (WEDR) in Birmingham; Hot Rod Hulbert (WITH) in Baltimore; Georgie Woods and Mary Mason (WHAT) in Philadelphia; Hal Jackson and Jocko Henderson (WLIB) in New York City; Larry Dean Faulkner and Martha Jean the Queen Steinberg (WHBC) in Detroit; and Purvis Spann, Herb Kent, and Wesley South (WVON) in Chicago. All these individuals had impressive credentials not only as black broadcasters but also as civil rights activists and leaders. Nat D. Williams, the most vocal black spokesman on the airwaves in Memphis, was an early supporter of Dr. King, who on more than one occasion was the featured guest on Williams's award-winning public-affairs show *Brown America Speaks*. Louise Fletcher was active in Nashville's NAACP chapter, and she often interviewed Dr. King on her program *A Woman Speaks*. Tall Paul White played a role similar to Rev. Fausch's in the 1963 Birmingham protests. White did the afternoon show on WEDR and used soul hits such as "Keep on Pushing" to get his signal out to the decentralized army of youthful demonstrators, while Fausch used coded gospel songs over his morning show on WENN to mobolize the troops in the field.[22]

Farther north, in Baltimore, Maurice "Hot Rod" Hulbert championed the civil rights cause on WITH. His involvement in the struggle dates back to the mid-1950s, when he teamed up with a young activist named Parren Mitchell to lead a series of protests against a Baltimore real estate company that would not sell property to African Americans. Mitchell would later become the first black congressman from Baltimore. Hulbert remained active in the 1960s; he was present at the 1963 March on Washington, and he participated in civil rights protests in Baltimore and Philadelphia. Likewise, Jocko Henderson marched in demonstrations in Philadelphia and New York City, and he often talked to civil rights leaders on his shows: "Yeah, like whenever Martin Luther King was in town, many times I interviewed him on my show . . . same thing with Jesse Jackson, he used to come by the house all the time."[23]

In Detroit during the 1960s, Larry Dean Faulkner and Martha Jean "the Queen" Steinberg gave voice to the civil rights movement on black-owned WCHB, the "Voice of Freedom." Steinberg was not shy about taking credit for these endeavors:

> If it hadn't been for black radio, Martin Luther King would not have gotten off the ground in my estimation because we were the first to talk about it. . . . It was new, it was exciting. Everybody became curious. We talked like the African drummers used to talk years ago. We talked in a code—"Yes Mammy o Daddy, get on down!" We talked about what to do, but some people didn't know what we were talking about. . . . We were the cause of the civil rights movement . . . after it started moving about the nation we let everybody know what was going on, because no one would interview Martin Luther King. No one knew Jesse Jackson. Nobody interviewed these preachers, so we did that ourselves, on a low-key basis, but we did.[24]

The Chicago soul music station on the cutting edge of the civil rights struggle was WVON, the home base for such activists as Purvis Spann and

Herb Kent. Spann, who grew up in the Mississippi Delta, was involved in raising money and recruiting volunteers for the 1964 "Mississippi Freedom Summer" project. When three young civil rights workers involved in the project were murdered that summer, Spann led the delegation of Chicago mourners in attendance at their funerals. Herb Kent was also a WVON civil rights activist and participated in a number of the station's political ventures; as he recalled: "WVON played a big part in the civil rights era, both with the music being played—like homeboy Curtis Mayfield . . . and because we talked about it on the air. We did many things. We campaigned for money. We did a sit-in in this trailer. People would come out and look at us in there fasting. . . . We were certainly right there in the middle of the civil rights movement, and we delivered the messages. We let people know and talk about what was going down. And of course, we had the first black talk show in the world, and that's Wesley South."[25]

Wesley South, more than anyone, was responsible for giving Martin Luther King Jr. a platform on WVON. South's pioneering late-night talk show *Hot Line* focused almost exclusively on local and national civil rights issues. King, future mayor Harold Washington, and Jesse Jackson were among the civil rights leaders who were frequent guests on the program. Beginning in 1964, Jesse Jackson hosted his own show on WVON, a live Saturday-morning broadcast from a local church. WVON was also the home station for Roy Woods, a pioneer in black radio journalism, who covered the civil rights struggles around the country for the station and acted as news director. One of Woods's most famous exposés was an award-winning audio documentary on the Alabama KKK, which included tape recordings of their secret rallies and cross burnings.[26]

From announcements of rallies, to interviews with African American leaders, to reporting on threats to the black community and the civil rights movement's response, the disc jockeys were essential to the progress of the struggle for equality. In effect, black disc jockeys were the media nerve centers of the civil rights movement. They created a communications network that facilitated the flow of information among the faithful and mobilized public opinion in support of the crusade.

11

Microphones in the Riot Zones

During the mid-1960s, the struggle for racial equality achieved significant political gains, but racial tension and inner-city violence spread across the nation. Massive pressure from below finally compelled the U.S. Congress to pass the Civil Rights Act and the Voting Rights Act in 1964. But in the same year, the civil rights movement–backed Mississippi Freedom Party was denied recognition at the Democratic National Convention. It was also in 1964 that a long, hot summer of violence erupted in New York, Chicago, and Philadelphia. In each instance, spontaneous protests against "police brutality" in African American neighborhoods rapidly degenerated into a frenzy of looting and burning. A year later, in the summer of 1965, the Watts ghetto in Los Angeles exploded after an altercation between the police and black citizens, who were outraged by the white officers' treatment of a reckless-driving suspect. Over the next few days the rioting raged out of control, and order was restored only when the California National Guard moved in to occupy the riot zone. The toll of the Watts uprising was staggering: thirty-four dead, over one thousand injured, close to four thousand arrested, and property damage estimated at $40 million.[1]

It was also in 1965 that Martin Luther King Jr. was awarded the Nobel Peace Prize. But there was no peace. Violence flared in the cities over the next two summers, with major eruptions in San Francisco (1966) and Newark, New Jersey, and Detroit (1967). Dr. King's assassination on April 4, 1968, unleased another wave of destruction across the country. Over that tragic Easter weekend, as the nation watched the television coverage in shock and horror, rioters looted stores, fought with the police, and burned down inner-city business districts with Molotov cocktails. Smoke and flames from Washington, D.C.'s famous "Black Broadway," the U Street corridor, could be seen from the White House a few miles away.[2]

Peacemakers in the Neighborhoods

African American disc jockeys were literally on alert during the urban race riots of the 1960s. They worked around the clock to save lives and minimize destruction in the black community. Over the airwaves, they urged restraint and caution, implored people to stay off the streets, and gave out information on the location and extent of each disturbance, as well as any reports of casualties. The DJs also stayed in touch with local police, politicians, and civil rights leaders, giving them access to the audience as part of an effort to quell the burning, looting, and killing. When not on the air, some of the black DJs even took to the streets, visiting the riot zones to urge calm or mediate confrontations between police and angry mobs of African Americans. In some instances, their presence at potential flash points in black neighborhoods helped defuse tense situations that could have led to more bloodshed. They were the peacekeepers, as well as the eyes and the ears, of their audience at a time of crisis.

During the summer of 1964, Jocko Henderson found himself on the air in two major markets where racial disturbances broke out: "I was there . . . in New York when they had the riots, and in Philadelphia when they had the riots. I was on the scene with my quiet machine tryin' to keep 'em quiet."[3] Georgie Woods was also caught up in the Philadelphia disturbances, but not on the airwaves: "No I wasn't on the air, I was out in the streets for three days, telling people to stop rioting. . . . We finally got the riot under control, Cecil [Moore] and I teamed up together, we got the woman who was supposedly shot by police who was supposed to be pregnant—and that sparked the riots. We got her and put her in an open convertible and drove her around the neighborhood to quiet things down."[4]

Woods was initially summoned to the scene of the riots by Howard Leary, the Philadelphia police commissioner at the time. According to Sid Booker, a friend and business associate of Woods who witnessed the outbreak of hostilities:

> George came on the scene, the police were standing there, and they were throwing things at the police. . . . The cops were getting ready to move on 'em, and George walked up from behind the police, they saw George and said—"Hey Georgie! Hey Georgie!" George said—"Come on man, let's cool this out." He walked over there and they said—"OK Georgie, OK!" The whole crowd turned around and went home. And the police, they were getting ready to crash. But they all listened to him, 'cause he had gained their respect. As soon as they saw him that was it. It was over with.[5]

Georgie Woods never received a word of thanks from the city for his peacekeeping efforts: "So we were able to stop the riots and save the city an awful lot of money. Did they give me a commendation? No. Did they say thank you? Nope, never, but that's OK, we did our job anyway." This snub may have been connected to an event on the final day of the trouble. On that Sunday, with the lawlessness waning, Commissioner Leary ordered Woods to close down a scheduled R & B show at the Uptown Theater. According to Woods: "We had a full house with twenty-two hundred people inside and a line of five hundred people outside. The police commissioner called me and said he was gonna close me down, and I wanted to know why; there had been no trouble at the Uptown, no disturbances whatsoever around that area. I said—'No way, you want to see a riot, close me down and we're gonna take all these people in the Uptown and march straight down to the First Philadelphia Bank, and we'll show you what a riot really is!' They panicked, and the Uptown didn't close."[6]

Georgie Woods's heroics in Philadelphia went unnoticed by the mainstream media, but the "Magnificent" Montague was not so lucky. The Los Angeles press demonized him for allegedly inciting the Watts rebellion. At the time of the 1965 uprising, the mercurial Nathanial Montague was the top-rated black disc jockey in the local market; 75 percent of the city's African American listeners regularly tuned in to his nightly show on KGFJ. Before moving to Los Angeles, the Texas-born spin doctor had perfected his unorthodox style of broadcasting in San Antonio, Chicago, New York City, and Tijuana, Mexico. By the time he was hired by KGFJ early in 1965, the Magnificent Montague was known for his honey-coated baritone voice, keen wit, and chameleon-like radio persona. When in a romantic mood, he would recite love poems to his female listeners over the soul ballads of Sam Cooke and Otis Redding. When playing the hottest dance tracks of the day, he would punctuate them with wild exhortations, such as his trademark "Burn, baby, burn." Moreover, Montague was an avid collector of books on African American history and culture, a streetwise philosopher who peppered his radio discourses with historical anecdotes and cautionary tales about the black experience in America. This innovative style made him an overnight sensation on KGFJ. One of his fans was fellow Los Angeles DJ Larry McCormick: "I have a lot of admiration for Montague. He had a dynamite style—it was a fiery style that got people excited . . . he was a pioneer in L.A., he was the earliest to pot down a record and talk over it—talk with it. He played himself with the record and people loved that. That was something nobody out here did in those days, so it was kind of daring."[7]

The Magnificent Montague was riding a wave of popularity in August 1965 when the Watts rebellion erupted. The mobs of black rioters who took to the streets spontaneously adopted "Burn, baby, burn" as their battle cry— many of them using it interchangeably with "Burn, Whitey, burn"— while Montague, on the air, was urging them to go home. Nevertheless, the mainstream Los Angeles media blamed him for the mayhem, and the police chief and the mayor demanded that Montague be taken off the air. KGFJ's white owners, however, were reluctant to fire him outright— perhaps fearing they would spark another uprising. Instead, they reduced his airtime and barred him from saying "Burn, baby, burn" over mike. Unrepentant, Montague started to use "Have mercy, baby" or "Keep the faith, baby" as his audio signature piece. But his days on KGFJ were numbered. According to Larry McCormick: "After the Watts riots, some people in official positions accused him of instigating the riots by doing what he had always done, and the radio station, they didn't back him up . . . they cut him slowly, cut him away and eventually cut him loose."[8]

The Magnificent Montague's fall from grace was startling and unusual. Few black DJs were scapegoated during the urban riots in the mid-1960s, if for no other reason than that they were actively involved in efforts, both on and off the air, to restore the peace. While these peacemaking efforts were unknown to most of the outside world, they were much appreciated by the black residents of the riot zones. DJs Georgie Woods and Martha Jean Steinberg were among those who repeatedly defused volatile situations. At the height of the 1967 race riot in Detroit, for example, Steinberg mediated a tense standoff between the local police and a group of Black Panthers:

> I remember that the Black Panthers were in a house and they wouldn't come out. And they [the police] had tanks all ready to blow up the house. And I'll never forget, they called me and asked me to try to talk to the leaders . . . and the white police chief. So I begged him—all his lieutenants wanted to blow up the house— they were mad. But I asked the man please don't blow that place up. I said just give us a few more minutes. We had several leaders go in and talk to those young people. They finally came out, the Black Panthers finally came out, and we did not have blood on our hands.[9]

Helping a Nation in Mourning

It was during the bleakest hours of the civil rights struggle, just after the assassination of Martin Luther King Jr., that African American DJs rose to an enormous challenge as communicators. All over the country, black disc jockeys suspended regular programming and gathered people around the microphone to ponder and probe the unfolding American tragedy with the listeners. Throughout the Easter weekend, they continued their on-air vigils for Dr. King, as well as their appeals for calm and restraint. While it is difficult to gauge their effectiveness, most of the DJs who experienced that ordeal believed they played a decisive role in containing the destruction and bloodshed. In the words of New York City DJ Del Shields: "On the night that Dr. King was killed . . . on that night, all across the country, the black disc jockey went on the microphone and talked to the people. It was black radio that doused the incendiary flames burning all across America."[10]

Del Shields's assertion has been confirmed by some unlikely sources on the other side of the color line. In Denver, Colorado, police chief

George L. Station publicly praised KDKO, the city's premier black appeal station, for its actions in the aftermath of the King assassination: "The sound judgement and counseling that was broadcast by your staff is to be commended. I am sure that it was only by the tremendous cooperative efforts of each and every person on the air that Denver remained peaceful." In Memphis, both the police chief and the mayor paid tribute to WDIA for its role in helping the city through its most tragic ordeal in decades. And in Los Angeles, the city leaders this time around passed a resolution praising KGFJ (now without the Magnificent Montague) for having been "instrumental in keeping racial trouble from developing, and maintaining a helpful, informative approach to assist in easing tensions when any trouble did have an opportunity to blossom."[11]

On the evening that Dr. King was murdered, African American disc jockeys on the air responded to the crisis immediately. In New York City, Del Shields was hosting *The Total Black Experience in Sound* on WLIB-FM. As he recalled: "Somebody came running down the hall and said Dr. King was shot. I said—'Get out of here!' He said—'No man, it's on the AP'— and he brought me the [Associated Press] wire. I said—'Oh my God!'— and I made the announcement." Shields also turned on WLIB-AM, which was required to go off the air at sunset, and broadcast over both stations simultaneously. When the news reached the streets, trouble broke out: "Within an hour . . . the word came back that people were rioting in Harlem." Shields played excerpts from Dr. King's recorded speeches until the rest of the staff could get to the station; they, in turn, expanded the coverage: "We put community leaders and reporters on the air to talk and relate and try and keep the people abreast of what was going on." In addition, Shields and the WLIB staff contacted other black stations around the country, to exchange news and information: "We discovered all across the country everybody was doing the same thing. Some of the disc jockeys were going into the community and talking to the people. And the people were listening in to us to find out what was going on. They weren't tuned into NBC or CBS—no way. . . . Had we not been on, telling the people—'Don't burn, baby'—and all of that, it would have been worse."[12]

Georgie Woods again went into the streets of his community: "I was on WHAT at the time that he died and that was devastating, and again I had to take to the streets, and we were able to get a handle on it before anything got started here. I left the air immediately and went to the streets of the city and said—'Hey, cool it, chill out'—and the people listened."[13] In Chicago, WVON DJ Purvis Spann also hit the streets, but after the rioting had erupted: "The city was burning away. West Side looked like a war zone. Buildings burning. Sirens, gunshots . . . the National Guard. Just like a war zone. I would go in and talk with folks, saying that violence was not the way."[14] As the most listened-to black radio station in Chicago, WVON played a pivotal role in containing the riot. According to WVON's Lucky Cordell: "Our guys came into the station, everybody. All of them came in and stayed there, must have been twenty-four hours, imploring the people not to do this, and the basic theme was, this is disrespectful to Dr. King. . . . Don't do this and call yourself a follower of King."[15]

Baltimore and Washington, D.C., were also involved in racial conflagrations during the aftermath of the King assassination. In Baltimore, the National Guard was called in to restore order. Federal troops patrolled the riot zones in the nation's capital. Maurice "Hot Rod" Hulbert was on the air in Baltimore when the trouble broke out:

> They had riots all over the country, and Baltimore, we had our share too—burnings and whatnot. Gus Harris was a major in the state militia, and they told me on the air to talk to our people and quiet them. So I said something to the effect—"OK everybody, go home. Let's get off the streets. We cannot solve the problem by burning down our businesses. Let's get off the streets and do it now!" So we were trying to get everybody off the streets, because as long as they were out there, the more problems we were going to have. And problems were jumping up all over—down off Gay Street, on North Avenue, in different sections of the city . . . and the state militia came out and quelled it.[16]

Washington, D.C's top black disc jockey in the mid-1960s was the outspoken Bob "Nighthawk" Terry, who was heard nightly on the city's leading soul station, WOL. On the night that Dr. King was killed, Terry was openly outraged—not only by the assassination but also at the "brothers on the block," whom he challenged: "Why ya burnin' down your own communities, brothers? Don't see no riotin' down at the White House and the Congress, no siree, everybody up on U Street lootin' and shootin' your own!" In addition, Nighthawk had some harsh words for white listeners who "run back to Maryland and Virginia suburbs every evening and leave the problems back here in the city."[17] Terry's outburst is understandable, given the dire circumstances, but most black DJs refrained from voicing their anger and frustration on the air during the crisis. Instead, they urged their listeners to honor Dr. King's commitment to nonviolence. The loss of King, however, marked a critical turning point in the civil rights struggle. In particular, it fueled the rise of a militant Black Power movement, which attracted a growing number of adherents among the younger African American disc jockeys. This change becomes especially clear when one examines the fortunes of the NARA—the National Association of Radio Announcers.

The Rise and Fall of the NARA

During the civil rights era, although the cultural and political influence of black disc jockeys was rising, their economic situation hardly changed at all. For the most part, African American DJs remained ghettoized in black appeal stations, where their salaries were, at best, about half of what their white counterparts were making in the same market. Nearly all black appeal outlets were white owned and managed; African Americans rarely filled the better-paying staff positions in management and advertising. While payola was still legal, it was common knowledge in the radio business that the record companies paid white DJs a lot more to promote new releases, including R & B discs, than they paid black DJs. These conditions had existed since the inception of black appeal formats in the late 1940s, and they led to the formation of the first trade association for African American DJs in the mid-1950s.

Originally called the National Jazz, Rhythm & Blues Disc Jockey Association, the organization was founded in the basement of a Harlem cabaret, Tommy Smalls's Paradise Club, in 1955 by the "Original Thirteen." The group, which included Jack Gibson, Maurice Hulbert, Hal Jackson, Jack Walker, and Tommy Smalls, discussed their common grievances—from low salaries, to lack of employment opportunities in mainstream radio, to the uneven distribution of payola along racial lines. At a national convention in New York City a year later, with about one hundred black disc jockeys in attendance, the organization renamed itself the

National Association of Radio Announcers (NARA) in order to be more inclusive of black radio broadcasters, whatever their on-air staff positions, as well as to attract financial support from the record companies and the radio station owners.[18]

Disinclined to support a national trade organization of black DJs, most white owners of black appeal stations saw NARA as a potential threat to their power. However, the record companies that recorded African American artists recognized black DJs' pivotal role in popularizing their new releases and proved eager to bankroll NARA's annual conventions. Beginning in 1957, the record industry became the major patron of the NARA's annual gathering, giving record companies an ideal opportunity to promote their new records and artists, as well as to cultivate contacts among the black jocks. All the key labels producing black popular music set up lavish hospitality suites at the convention; they sponsored the official luncheons and dinners, provided free entertainment showcases, and even paid hotel and travel expenses for many DJs. This infusion of music industry cash and talent transformed the annual NARA convention into a weekend of around-the-clock revelry and high jinks. Gala receptions, concerts, cocktail and dinner parties, as well as nightclub and gambling excursions, were so plentiful that the delegates were hard pressed to find the time for the annual business meeting, much less any organized discussion of the grievances that brought them together in the first place. As Jack Gibson put it: "We partied until it was time to go to church."[19]

By the 1960s, the NARA had developed a reputation in the entertainment world as a "payola-prone group of party boys." But the situation was about to change. For openers, the congressional hearings and subsequent legislation outlawing payola had a sobering effect on the organization. Like the infamous 1959 Miami Beach convention for white DJs, the NARA gatherings had become conduits for payola—which was, actually, the hidden agenda of the early gatherings. But in view of the public uproar, the NARA was forced to renounce the practice, in statement if not in deed, to protect itself from the payola fallout. At the same time, the prominence of the civil rights movement in the early 1960s politicized many African American DJs around the country, especially the younger ones, who began to demand that the NARA become actively involved in the struggle for racial equality within the radio industry.

By the 1964 convention, the NARA was developing a new sense of purpose and mission. Held in Chicago, the annual gathering was attended by more than 250 disc jockeys and record company representatives. While the record labels continued to foot the bill, they no longer set the agenda—at least, not during daylight hours. Morning and afternoon strategy sessions were now scheduled to discuss the association's new political agenda, and the record companies were asked to close down their hospitality suites during the sessions. In addition, one of the evenings was devoted to a benefit concert at the Chicago Coliseum, which was open to the public; it proved to be the NARA's first major fund-raising effort.[20]

One of the highlights of the 1964 convention's business sessions was the report given by Charles Johnson, the young president of the association's Los Angeles chapter and chairman of a year-old legislative committee. The committee's investigation of employment practices in the radio industry had uncovered widespread racial discrimination. Of the sixty thousand people employed in radio broadcasting, fewer than six hundred were African Americans. The ownership ratio was even more lopsided: only five of the nation's fifty-five hundred commercial stations were black owned. Johnson had met with FCC and NAB officials to discuss these committee findings. Expressing "surprise" at the figures, the officials of both organizations had promised to support any NARA initiatives to close the gaps in employment and ownership. The FCC officials even suggested that the NARA bring specific incidents of discrimination to their attention, so that they could form a test case. Johnson also reported on his chapter's successful campaign to integrate KFWB, the top station in the Los Angeles market. Noting that Larry McCormick, the station's first African American DJ, had been hired earlier in the year as a result of picketing at KFWB by supporters from local NAACP and CORE chapters, Johnson argued that any station which violated the fair-employment provisions of the 1964 Civil Rights Act should be subject to such actions.[21]

While discussion of tactics and strategies to combat job discrimination tended to dominate the work sessions at the Chicago convention, the NARA also took action on other fronts. Since 1964 was an election year, the association decided to conduct a vigorous voter registration campaign over the airwaves, in conjunction with civil rights organizations working to get out the black vote. In addition, the delegates approved a reorganization plan that set up five regional divisions with their own elected officers and volunteer staff. The intent was both to decentralize national decision making and to facilitate more activism at the grass roots.[22]

There was also a good deal of internal criticism among the disc jockeys at the 1964 convention. In their ongoing efforts to clean up their tarnished public image, the delegates revisited the payola issue, not only reaffirming the 1960 policy prohibiting NARA members from accepting payola but also chastising those DJs who still allowed the record labels to pay their hotel and travel expenses. Del Shields, a leading spokesman for the newly emerging activist wing of the association, delivered a fiery speech at the convention that cataloged the deficiencies of his more complacent colleagues: their lack of "professionalism," their "playboy" mentality, their lack of racial pride, and their habit of "Uncle Tomming" for white employers. He also lambasted the white owners of black appeal stations, who "got into the business by default," knew nothing about "what the black man needs," and refused to "share the profits with us." Shields concluded by reminding the delegates: "You are important. I don't think you realize your worth. Look at all the record people here . . . look at all the money they're spending. They came because you are important."[23]

After the 1964 Chicago convention, some NARA dissidents who felt the organization was not doing enough began to organize an insurgency among the rank and file. Most of the leaders of this group, such as Georgie Woods and Del Shields in Philadelphia (WDAS), Al Bell in Washington, D.C. (WUST), Ed Wright in Cleveland (WACQ), and Charles Johnson in Los Angeles (KAPP), were DJs with ties to the civil rights movement. Al Bell, for example, had been a disc jockey on KOKY in Little Rock, Arkansas, during the 1957 integration crisis at Central High School. The experience radicalized him, and for a period of time in the late 1950s, he was an organizer for the SCLC, attending training workshops led by Dr. King in Georgia and helping mobilize people for local demonstrations. The NARA dissident group's most influential adviser was Clarence Avant, a savvy entertainment industry insider who managed jazz organist Jimmy Smith and film-score composer Lalo Shiffren. Avant urged the group to come up with a new plan of action for the NARA—one that included expanding the association to include television broadcasters and establishing a professional broadcasting school for African Americans. In addition, he suggested that they field a slate of candidates in the upcoming NARA election, in order to wrest control of the organization away from the old guard.[24]

At the 1965 NARA convention in Houston, Texas, the insurgents' slate of candidates, headed by Ed Wright and Del Shields and calling themselves the "New Breed" (a name they borrowed from a line in the James Brown hit "Papa's Got a Brand New Bag"), scored an upset victory over the incumbents. The next year, in New York City, the association officially changed its name to the National Association of Radio and Television Announcers (NARTA) and endorsed the New Breed's ambitious agenda for change. Among other things, that agenda called for increasing black ownership of broadcast outlets, formation of a black radio news service, increasing black employment in the broadcast industry (especially at the management level), and establishing a professional college of broadcasting to train African Americans for jobs in the industry.[25]

The more-politicized thrust of the organization was evident at the historic 1967 NARTA convention in Atlanta, where delegates heard not only Dr. King praising their efforts on behalf of the civil rights cause but also SNCC firebrand H. Rap Brown. Voting overwhelmingly for two more years of New Breed leadership, delegates elected Del Shields as the executive director of the association and again supported plans to found a black college of broadcasting. Shields—now based in New York at WLIB-FM—and Clarence Avant began making the rounds of the record companies and television networks, seeking funds and broadcast equipment for the college. Shields also organized a meeting between a group of white black appeal station owners and a delegation of New Breed DJs to discuss job discrimination and to solicit financial and technical support for the school. Within a year, Shields and Avant had lined up pledges from ten record companies for $50,000 each, to be used as the down payment on a school site in northern Delaware. The formal announcement was put on the agenda for the upcoming NARTA convention.[26]

Then the sky fell on the New Breed, wiping out four years of hard work and damaging beyond repair their leadership position within the NARTA. First came the murder of Dr. King and its bitter aftermath as the mood of the country turned ugly and racial divisions deepened. Then, in the summer of 1968, when word of the impending deal with the record labels hit the black radio grapevine, Shields and Avant's lives were threatened by anonymous callers, who had their own agenda for the record industry's "reparations." Shields was even beaten up in Harlem by thugs whom he felt were agents of the "Black Mafia." To be sure, a black criminal element had long been associated with the music industry, mainly through their control of nightclubs; hence it is certainly possible that some in their ranks sought to muscle in on NARTA's good fortune. But the rhetoric of those making the threats was laced with militant Black Power slogans, which suggests that the culprits were rogue political opportunists—or even agent provocateurs.[27]

Whatever their source, the provocations came to a head at the 1968 NARTA convention, held in Miami, and the thugs targeted both the New Breed leadership and white record industry executives in attendance. On the first day, a bomb threat at the convention hotel and rumors of a "contract" out on Del Shields's life persuaded Shields to return to New York. White record executives, such as Atlantic's Jerry Wexler, and Phil Walden, Otis Redding's manager, were threatened with violence by roving bands of unidentified "militants" unless they paid "reparations" on the spot. New Orleans record producer Marshall Sehorn and others were actually beaten up when they refused to pay. As word got out, the record industry representatives left—taking their half-million dollars in pledges with them. As a result of all this, dissension split the ranks of the black disc jockeys who remained at the convention. Many blamed the debacle on the New Breed's attempts to radicalize the association.[28]

The New Breed led the NARTA for another year, but with their ambitious plans for the association now in shambles, they piloted a sinking ship. With help from Georgie Woods, Del Shields persuaded Motown's Berry Gordy to donate $25,000 to the NARTA, which, in turn, announced the pledge at the 1969 convention in Washington, D.C., and honored Gordy as the organization's man of the year.[29] But the good news was not enough to offset financial wrongdoing charges against Shields, or the delegates' rage when they learned he had spent $10,000 on security for the convention. The association elected new leadership, a Southern faction that vowed to put their financial house in order. Although Georgie Woods was elected to the executive director post two years later, much of the New Breed leadership, including Del Shields, Clarence Avant, and Al Bell, had withdrawn from the association by the 1970s. The New Breed had disintegrated. The association also floundered; the schisms between the old guard, the moderate Southern faction, and the black power advocates only widened. The record industry withdrew its financial support and no longer sent its executives to the conventions.

With the quiet death of the NARTA in the mid-1970s, African American broadcasters lost the little political clout they had in the radio industry. With no power base, they could do little to address economic and other forms of discrimination in the workplace. In the coming years, the organizational sites of struggle would shift to the realm of ownership, and black entrepreneurs would supplant the disc jockeys as the activists and power brokers in broadcast circles.

12

The FM Frontier

W hen inventor Edwin Armstrong developed frequency modulation (FM) in the mid-1930s, it should have undermined the
dominance of AM. In spite of its superior, relatively static-free
sound quality, however, some three decades passed before FM secured a
foothold in the radio industry. Armstrong's tireless efforts to promote FM
were constantly blocked by NBC kingpin David Sarnoff. Committed to
television as the broadcast medium with a big future, Sarnoff bank-rolled
its development with profits from NBC's two AM radio networks; an
industry-wide shift to FM broadcasting and consequent revenue reductions did not at all fit with his agenda. Ultimately, David Sarnoff prevailed,
keeping FM radio dormant well into the postwar era and television's boom
days.[1] During the 1960s, however, economic, social, and technical changes
combined to make FM broadcasting look more attractive, especially to
would-be innovators and mavericks. For nearly a decade, FM seemed to offer an unprecedented opportunity to radicalize black radio.

The record industry delivered the technical innovation for the shift to
FM. In the 1950s, the 45 rpm disc ruled the pop charts and the AM airwaves; Top Forty AM radio formats were, in fact, organized to take advantage of the 45's three-minute time limit and mono-track fidelity. The high
fidelity 33⅓ rpm long-playing (LP) disc remained a distant second in sales

and radio airplay. But when the record industry began to produce and then privilege multitrack stereo recordings in early 1960s, AM radio seemed outmoded, because it could not duplicate stereo in its narrow frequency band. FM, however, not only could broadcast in stereo but also had an economic advantage. In the major broadcast markets, all the AM frequencies had long been in use, and their value had skyrocketed. WDIA's price escalation was typical: its owners sold the Memphis station for $1 million in 1958, a decade after they had launched it for $50,000. In contrast, FM stations could be purchased at bargain-basement prices—even in major urban markets.

Progressive FM

The two most controversial social movements of the 1960s, the counter-culture/antiwar movement and the Black Power movement, also contributed to FM's rise to prominence. The first FM stations to identify with those movements did so by experimenting with "underground radio" formats, as they were initially called by their listeners. The counterculture outlets were located in urban centers with large college-student populations, for instance, Boston (WBCN-FM); New York City (WOR-FM, WNEW-FM); Washington, D.C. (WHFS-FM); Los Angeles (KPPC-FM); and San Francisco (KMPX-FM, KSAN-FM). Soon after their appearance, the music and broadcasting trade magazines began to call them "progressive FM" stations. Several characteristics set them apart from AM Top Forty. The progressive FM outlets played albums instead of 45s and broadcast in stereo; they supported their local counterculture, especially its music scene; and they returned control over the playlist to the disc jockey.[2]

A boom-and-bust cycle plagued most of the progressive FM operations and eventually wiped them out. The brief and tumultuous heyday of underground radio in San Francisco was fairly typical. Its architect, Tom "Big Daddy" Donahue, a renegade rock-and-roll jock from Philadelphia, had migrated to California after losing his job during the payola purges. Working as a producer and promoter in the Bay Area's burgeoning rock-music scene during the mid-1960s, Donahue was caught up in the counterculture centered in San Francisco's Haight-Ashbury district. Sporting long hair and a beard, indulging in LSD and pot, he ended his fifteen-year marriage and formed a relationship with a woman half his age. His weight ballooned to four hundred pounds—a "big daddy" indeed. Donahue had been and continued to be an outspoken critic of the Top Forty format. Although out of radio, he still harbored a desire to return to the airwaves—but only on his own terms.[3]

In the spring of 1967, Big Daddy was offered the 8 P.M. to midnight time slot on KMPX, a nearly bankrupt FM outlet that, at the time, was specializing in foreign-language broadcasts. The owner, Leon Crosby, signed off on a contract that was similar to the old brokerage deals on AM ethnic stations. Donahue was given complete control over his music selections, and he was also responsible for soliciting the ads for the program. His playlists showcased the cutting-edge rock and soul albums of the era, with a special emphasis on giving airplay to up-and-coming local bands such as Santana, the Grateful Dead, Sly and the Family Stone, and Jefferson Airplane. In contrast to the frantic and mindless chatter of Top Forty DJs, Big Daddy used the jargon of the counterculture to perfect a mellow, laid-back, and musically hip on-air delivery. Rather than talking over and between selections, he constructed "sets" of rock and soul songs from various albums. These musical sets, which were from fifteen to thirty minutes long, were unified in theme; they would tell a story, convey a social message, evoke a mood, or highlight a certain artist. The DJ's commentary was limited to the breaks between the sets. This novel approach to music programming would soon be referred to as "free-form" deejaying by its FM practitioners and aficionados. More important, it marked a shift toward racial hybridity—both in the selection of songs and the choice of words—and, conversely, the demise of racial ventriloquy on the airwaves.[4]

Tom Donahue's groundbreaking nightly show on KMPX was a Bay Area sensation. Leon Crosby was so impressed that he promoted Donahue to program director and put him in charge of reorganizing the whole KMPX format along the lines of his own show. Big Daddy hired a talented and diverse staff from the ranks of the local counterculture—among them AM disc jockeys who had "dropped out" of the mainstream media, female ("chick") engineers, and a sales force of "hippie" dope dealers—who transformed the station into the voice of the Haight-Ashbury cultural revolution. By the time of the much-publicized 1967 "Summer of Love," KMPX was the top-rated FM outlet in the market. But Crosby constantly pressured Donahue to rein in his rebellious DJs, avoid politics on the air, and play more corporate advertising spots. The power struggle climaxed in the spring of 1968: Crosby fired Donahue, and the entire KMPX staff went out on strike.[5]

The KMPX strike lasted two months—until Donahue negotiated a deal to move his entire operation over to KSAN, a rival FM outlet. The station was owned by Metromedia, a broadcast company that controlled a dozen radio stations, including the highly successful New York City progressive FM outlet WNEW. As program director, Donahue could select his own staff. In addition to the KMPX strikers, he hired Stefan Ponek as the station's first news director. At the time, the Bay Area was embroiled in several radical, and sometimes violent, political struggles: antiwar protests, the six-month-long San Francisco State College student and faculty strike, Berkeley's "People's Park" uprising, and the spectacular rise of the Oakland-based Black Panther party. Ponek formed a team of radical journalists led by Wes "Scoop" Nisker and Larry Bensky, whose local news coverage gave KSAN a distinctively dissident political voice that was not present on any other commercial station in the region.[6]

Donahue's most controversial political move, however, was to hire Roland Young as KSAN's first black DJ. Young, a gifted jazz musician and a visionary music programmer, was also an outspoken Black Power militant with close ties to the Black Panther party. His late-night shows on KSAN were legendary for their jazz-based excursions into "world music," with a special emphasis on folk and popular genres from the African diaspora. His lengthy and carefully constructed sets of album selections drew his listeners into these multicultural explorations, exposing them to rare musical voices, instruments, styles, rhythms, and textures. Young also voiced his radical political views on the air, which inevitably created friction with the station owners.[7]

That friction peaked in less than a year. At a December 1969 antiwar rally in Golden Gate Park, Black Panther spokesman David Hilliard told a crowd of 150,000 that he would "kill" anyone, including Richard Nixon, who "stands in the way of our freedom." Hilliard was arrested by federal agents for threatening the life of the president. That night on the air, Young dedicated his show to Hilliard and urged his listeners to send the White House telegrams that repeated Hilliard's threat—word for word. The next day, federal agents visited the station and consulted with management; Roland Young was fired. Over the next few months, most of the remaining political activists on the KSAN staff, including Scoop Nisker and Larry Bensky, lost their jobs. Before long, KSAN had totally abandoned its radical counterculture orientation for a commercially driven, album-oriented rock (AOR) format.[8]

Black Power and Black Appeal on FM

Roland Young was one of a number of African American DJs with ties to the Black Power movement who began to migrate into FM radio in the late 1960s. Most did so to create their own shows and express their political views on the air—freedoms rarely enjoyed in the AM broadcast spectrum. In 1967, Del Shields migrated from WDAS-AM in Philadelphia to WLIB-FM in New York City to host his own nightly show. At the time, WLIB was an AM/FM combo owned by Harry Novick, a white entrepreneur who had been involved in black appeal radio since the 1950s. The daytime AM operation's well-established R & B format still showcased such DJs as Jocko Henderson and Hal Jackson. The new nighttime FM operation had an experimental jazz format, and Harlem-born Shields was one of the first DJs hired to host a regular evening show.[9]

Shields called his WLIB-FM show *The Total Black Experience in Sound;* it was a bold programming concept, calculated to expand the frontiers of the existing black radio formats. His unique soundscape included not only the avant-garde jazz of John Coltrane and Miles Davis but also the message songs of soul artists like Curtis Mayfield and Nina Simone. He mixed in the recorded poetry of Nikki Giovanni and the Last Poets, as well as excerpts from the speeches of Martin Luther King Jr. and Malcolm X. Shields's own social commentary further enhanced this free-form collage of black music and oratory: "Each time I did an editorial comment, I had extracted from the Temptations a little piece that said—'Think about it, think about it, think about it'—so you know, I'd play it to make my point." Shields also used his show to reach out to the black prison population in the region: "I had like an underground network in the jails of New York. Prisoners would call me, and tell me what was going on, or they'd write me anonymous letters, so we had contact, and I got the word out for them."[10]

Del Shields's pioneering nightly show on WLIB-FM coincided with his troubled leadership role in the NARTA. The NARTA experience radicalized his outlook on black radio, especially with respect to ownership. Like many of his fellow activists in the industry, Shields quickly concluded that African American ownership of stations was essential to an independent political destiny, both in broadcasting and in the country as a whole. While still at the helm of the NARTA, he had pressured both the FCC and the NAB to increase the number of black-owned stations nationwide. After being forced from office, he continued to explore the ownership route with a small group of friends.

In 1970, with financial backing from his friend Clarence Avant and Shield's cousin, comic Bill Cosby, Del Shields purchased an FM frequency in Los Angeles and launched KAGB-FM, with staff recruited from the ranks of the New Breed faithful and a format that was an expanded version of *The Total Black Experience in Sound*. The station struggled to gain a foothold in the local radio market. Shields's air staff were unknown to L.A.'s African American listeners, and they were political outsiders. In Los Angeles, the radical Black Power movement had recently degenerated into fratricidal warfare, pitting local Black Panther party members against their counterparts in Ron Karenga's US (United Slaves) organization. The conflict was, in part, orchestrated by FBI informers and agent provocateurs, who infiltrated both groups. In the context of this bloody confrontation, projects affiliated with the Black Power insurgency, such as KAGB-FM, could not establish much local credibility. At best, the station's radical new format met with bemused indifference; at worst, it was viewed with suspicion and mistrust. Shields would later claim that KAGB was "ahead of its time," though his critics maintained that the station was "out of tune" with L.A.'s black population. Whatever the reason, *The Total Black Experience in Sound* failed to attract listeners or advertisers in the Los Angeles market. Less than two years after signing on the air, Shields filed for bankruptcy; a few months later, he sold the station and then used the proceeds to repay the original investors.[11]

KAGB-FM's failure underscored the difficulty of mixing commerce with radical politics on the airwaves. Veteran AM disc jockey Joe Howard developed a more commercially successful FM format at WGPR in Detroit, where he became program director in 1969 after the station was purchased by a local African American businessman. Howard resurrected the original black appeal format, organized around a team of personality jocks who controlled their own playlists, and spent a lot of time doing on-location broadcasts in the community. The two most popular weekday programs were an upbeat R & B morning drive-time show hosted by Lee Garrett ("Rockin' Mr. G") and a sultry nighttime soul ballads show hosted by "T and Sherry," two novice female DJs recruited from the local Motown talent pool. (Garrett, a blind musician and songwriter, was also associated with Motown and from time to time worked for Stevie Wonder.) In addition to these offerings, the weekday schedule included an early-morning gospel program, a midday jazz strip, an R & B afternoon drive-time show, and a late-night jazz strip. On the weekends, the Saturday schedule featured a mix of blues, jazz, and call-in shows; the Sunday lineup was devoted to church broadcasts and gospel music.[12]

Joe Howard had initially envisioned a much larger role for news and public-affairs programming on WGPR-FM, but the start-up budget limited him to music shows. When the station began to prosper, the owner was reluctant to reinvest the profits in the operation, especially for news and public-affairs staff. Howard, eager to become a co-owner of the station, believed he could use his share of the profits to buy a percentage of WGPR. But in the station owner's understanding of their agreement, Howard was to get a bonus for turning WGPR into a moneymaker—and no more. This misunderstanding led to Howard's departure late in 1970, but most of the air staff he had put in place remained with the station, and the format continued to prosper in the Detroit market.[13]

WGPR was by no means the first FM station to return to a DJ-driven, black appeal format in the late 1960s. That distinction belonged to WBLK-FM in Buffalo, which made the transition in 1966. In this case, there was no inherent conflict between the owner and program director—because the man who purchased the station and changed the format was George "Hound Dog" Lorenz, the legendary R & B crossover jock. In the early 1960s, Lorenz had terminated his popular nightly show on Buffalo's WKBS-AM in protest against the station's new Top Forty format. A few years later, he took over WBLK-FM and converted the failing classical music outlet into a black appeal operation. Lorenz's musical format showcased both vintage and contemporary R & B around the clock; and with the exception of himself, all the DJs on the air were African Americans. In addition, WBLK's format featured a number of public-affairs offerings that targeted various constituencies in Buffalo's black community; there were programs that focused on church and women's concerns, as well as a weekly show produced by the local NAACP chapter and a *Black Muslim Hour*. In 1966, FM was still a newcomer in the Buffalo radio market, and it took WBLK a few years to develop a loyal audience and an advertising base. But by 1970, the station was the top-rated FM outlet in the region, and it was finally making a modest profit. When Hound Dog Lorenz died early in 1972, however, WBLK-FM was sold to a corporate media conglomerate.[14]

In terms of ratings and advertising revenue, undoubtedly the most successful FM station with a progressive black format was WBLS in New York City. Its rise to prominence in the country's largest radio market during the early 1970s received national attention and set the trend for black FM radio over the next decade. As half of the WLIB AM/FM combo owned by Harry Novick, the station had been on the air as WLIB-FM since 1967, with a free-form jazz format that included Del Shields's *The Total Black Experience in Sound*. As the white owner of the city's oldest and most prosperous black radio enterprise, Novick was a controversial figure both at the stations and in Harlem. Black staff members applauded his liberal political and cultural policies, but they also chafed under his one-man rule. Likewise, local African American leaders supported the slant of the programming, but they also felt that the combo should be black owned. These simmering tensions boiled over in 1970, when Novick arbitrarily fired a female talk-show host on WLIB-AM; the staff at both stations walked out in protest, and they were off the air for two weeks before the dispute was resolved. The incident was seized on by a group of local black media entrepreneurs as an opportunity to force the beleaguered owner to sell. They formed a corporation called Inner City Broadcasting under the leadership of Percy Sutton, Harlem's most powerful politician, and veteran WLIB disc jockey Hal Jackson. The group launched a public campaign to take over the WLIB enterprise and pressured Novick into meeting with them to discuss the proposition. After lengthy and often acrimonious negotiations, Harry Novick reluctantly capitulated.[15]

Once in control of the WLIB combo, Inner City Broadcasting reformatted both stations. WLIB-AM became "Your Total Black News and Information Station," offering more news and public-affairs programming than any other black radio outlet in the country. The task of fine-tuning the format for the FM station, now called WBLS, was given to Frankie Crocker, who became its program director in 1972. Crocker was a savvy—some would say "slick"—young disc jockey with a proven track record in the highly competitive New York radio market. Not only had he been a leading DJ on WWRL, a local black appeal outlet, in the mid-1960s, but later in the decade, he was the first African American to cross over and host a show on the Top Forty powerhouse WMCA. Taking its title from Del Shields's former program, WBLS-FM's format was called "The Total Black Experience in Sound," but Crocker's version lacked the radical Black Power political message. As Shields recalled: "When he came to WBLS . . . he continued without the talk and the political activism that I had. . . . Frankie did it with just the music, and when they were all black, WBLS tore the city up."[16]

Frankie Crocker's own afternoon drive-time music show on WBLS established the station's new format in terms of both content and style. His playlists featured the best-selling jazz artists of the day, such as Grover Washington Jr. and Weather Report. Conspicuously absent were the avant-garde jazz releases favored by his predecessor. In addition, Crocker showcased the music of such high-profile R & B artists as Aretha Franklin, Stevie Wonder, Marvin Gaye, and Isaac Hayes, and he blended into this mix the latest disco dance tracks, popular in local nightclubs. As for his style, Crocker perfected an on-air delivery that came to epitomize black, upwardly mobile New York City hipness; it was mellow, suave, and seductive all at once. He went by the radio name "Hollywood," coined the phrase "Sock it to me, Mama!" to introduce his favorite selections, and promised to "put the dip in your hip and the glide in your slide." This mix of personal charm and popular music genres caught on in the local FM market, catapulting Crocker and WBLS into the broadcast spotlight.[17]

Inner City Broadcasting's decision to group all the news, talk, and public-affairs programming in the WLIB-AM format enabled Crocker to devote the entire WBLS-FM format to black music. The only exception to the all-music lineup was *Black View of the Arts,* a weekday-evening cultural feature produced and hosted by David Lampell, who was also a newscaster on WLIB. To round out his air staff, Crocker handpicked a crew of young, hip, and ambitious DJs whose air sound was similar to his own. Among the program director's new recruits were two classy women, Vi Higginson and La Mar Rene, who hosted weekday music shows immediately before and after Crocker's slot. This particular rotation of hosts caught on with listeners, perhaps because black women DJs were still a novelty on the local FM airwaves. Within months, the reconditioned "Total Black Experience in Sound" was the talk of New York radio, and WBLS was ranked among the top three in the FM market.[18]

Success in the market brought in advertising billings, but it also spawned imitators. Before long, WBLS's format was being cloned by WKTU-FM and WKSS-FM. In effect, all three stations were now competing for the same audience. To maintain WBLS's momentum and ratings, Crocker began to add to the playlist white artists who ranked high on the pop charts and whose sound was compatible with the current black popular music: Elton John, Bette Midler, Boz Scaggs, Hall and Oates. By the mid-1970s, "The Total Black Experience in Sound" had become "The Total Experience in Sound." According to Frankie Crocker, the format was changed to "increase the percentage of white artists played, and in turn, the number of white listeners, and ultimately, white advertising dollars."[19] This new crossover format would soon become known as "urban contemporary" in the radio industry.

Aside from being a shrewd marketing strategy, the urban contemporary format was also a move toward racial hybridity on the airwaves. In this respect, it was similar to the "underground" FM format that Tom Donahue developed in San Francisco. But where Donahue's hybrid format innovation was applauded by the white counterculture, Crocker's crossovers created a storm of controversy in black radio circles. Seen as a retreat from black empowerment formats and a return to an assimilationist approach to radio programming, urban contemporary was widely criticized by African Americans employed in the industry, especially veteran and New Breed DJs such as Jack Gibson, Georgie Woods, and Del Shields, who blasted it as a "sellout" and an insult. Woods's objections were typical: "It doesn't sound black to me. They call it urban contemporary so they don't have to call it black. Don't you know what they're doing to us? They change the name from black radio to urban contemporary so that it will attract a lot of white people, so that it can make a lot of money. Once again, profit before principle. Urban contemporary? It's either black or white, there's no urban contemporary!"[20] Yet, in spite of the uproar, the instant success of the urban contemporary format in key urban markets tended to steamroll over the opposition. It would prove too profitable to ignore.

WHUR-FM: Meltdown in Chocolate City

Perhaps the most progressive format experiment on black FM radio in the early 1970s occurred at WHUR in the nation's capital. Formerly known as WTOP-FM, the *Washington Post*–owned station was donated to Howard University in 1971. Although a commercial outlet, it was given an educational mission: to serve as a "training laboratory" for students enrolled in the university's new School of Communications. On the recommendation of the faculty in the Radio Department, Howard renamed the station WHUR (Howard University Radio) and hired Phil Watson as the first general manager. Watson was a black media activist who had worked for the left-wing Pacifica radio network in the 1960s, which owned and operated community-oriented, noncommercial FM stations in the San Francisco Bay Area (KPFA), Los Angeles (KPFK), New York City (WBAI), and Houston (KPFT). Pacifica's public affairs–heavy formats gave voice to the antiwar movement and, to a lesser extent, the Black Power movement. Watson's tenure had been as development director at KPFK in Los Angeles and as a member of the Pacifica news team that covered the turbulent 1968 Democratic National Convention in Chicago.[21]

Phil Watson called WHUR's original format "360 Degrees: The Black Experience in Sound." It was an eclectic mix of Pacifica-inspired grassroots news and public-affairs programs, black personality jocks hosting free-form music shows, and two blocs of cultural programming produced by and for the city's Latin and Caribbean populations. WHUR's news department had ten paid staff members, unprecedented in black radio. Each weekday, they produced a series of five-minute hourly news updates, a fifteen-minute noontime news show, and an hour-long evening news roundup called *The Daily Drum*. With a symbolic switch of sound metaphors, the news staff adopted the rhythms of a conga drum, rather than those of a Teletype, as the signature piece of their newscasts. The coverage focused on subjects of special interest to the city's majority African American population but was by no means confined to local issues. WHUR news reporters were sent out to cover events as far-flung as the Symbionese Liberation Army's kidnapping of newspaper heiress Patty Hearst in California and the sixth Pan African Congress in Tanzania. To afford such a large news staff, Watson set up a salary scale comparable to those paid at public radio stations—well below the wage standards in commercial radio. Nevertheless, WHUR's news operation attracted a talented array of young and dedicated black reporters, the most notable being Jean Wiley, Ivy Young, and Kojo Nambe.[22]

WHUR's public-affairs department had five full-time employees, who supervised a large staff of work/study students and community volunteers. Its diverse lineup of programming included political discussion shows, such as *The People's Platform* and *Dialogue; Black World—Third World,* an examination of the cultures, ideologies, and social movements prominent in the African diaspora; *Inside/Outside,* a prison reform program produced by a collective of ex-cons; two weekly shows devoted to black literature and poetry, *Word Soldiers* and *Interpreters; Lifeline,* a medical program hosted by a doctor from the Howard University Hospital; and *How to Eat to Live,* a health and diet show hosted by a panel of Black Muslims. In addition, the station broadcast a special series of Congressional Black Caucus hearings on Africa, the military, and the media, as well as the on-campus speeches of such controversial African American leaders as Angela Davis, Muhammad Ali, Stokely Carmichael, Amiri Baraka, Fannie Lou Hamer, and Dick Gregory. Muhammad Ali also recorded an unusually transgressive promo for WHUR. He begins by lauding the station for its lofty educational and racial goals; then, at the end of the spot, when some voices in the background start to rib him, he blurts out: "And there's some crazy niggers down here, too!"[23]

The musical side of WHUR's format showcased "360 Degrees" of black music: jazz, blues, R & B, gospel, soul, and reggae were all regularly featured—and often mixed together. The DJs, who initially controlled their own playlists, gravitated toward the new free-form style of programming popular in progressive FM circles. They combined the avant-garde jazz of John Coltrane and Sun Ra with the deep blues of Muddy Waters and Howling Wolf; the politically charged reggae of Bob Marley and Jimmy Cliff with the urban soul of Marvin Gaye and Curtis Mayfield; and the civil rights songs of the SNCC Freedom Singers and the Staple Singers with the militant street poetry of the Last Poets and Gil Scott Heron. A local artist, Heron's premiere jazz and poetry album *Pieces of a Man* was given extensive airplay on WHUR; in particular, his angry Black Power manifesto "The Revolution Will Not Be Televised" was played so often that it became the station's unofficial theme song during its first year on the air.[24]

WHUR's original lineup of DJs included two young black women: Charlene Watts hosted the weekday-morning drive-time show, and Dyanna Williams did a late-night program called *Ebony Moonbeams*. Both women were hip, socially aware, and self-consciously female on the air, and they quickly developed a loyal audience. But by far the most well known disc jockey on WHUR in the early days was Robert "Nighthawk" Terry, the legendary "Big Bird" of the airwaves in the town he called "Chocolate City." During the 1960s, Terry was a fixture on WOL-AM, the city's top-rated black appeal station; his unmistakable talk and irreverent attitude won him a huge following among African Americans. Then, in 1970, WOL switched over to a Top Forty pop format. Nighthawk reluctantly went along with the change, but he also expressed his displeasure with it on the air. Once, he introduced an obligatory Frank Sinatra ballad as follows: "All right out there in Soul Land, this is the Nighthawk speakin'. Italian Americans of America unite. Pick up your pizza pies, grease your heads with olive oil, place your machine guns over your hearts. Here comes your leader, little Frankie Sinatra, blue-eyed and pale, but he sure can wail." A number of similar incidents eventually got Terry fired. But Watson hired the Nighthawk to host an evening music show, and once back on the air, he soon became the station's most popular DJ.[25]

During its first year on the air, WHUR's groundbreaking format won enthusiastic support from faculty, students, and members of the black community. Radio Department faculty also worked at WHUR; Andre Perry, who taught radio programming courses, served as the station's original program director, and Russ Johnson, who taught radio production, hosted a music and talk show. Up to twenty students worked for WHUR part time in work/study positions, and and a planned internship program would have increased student participation. The Reverend Cecil Moore, head of the city's United Black Front, had initially opposed Howard's ownership of the station because he felt the university did not represent the local black population, but he was now one of WHUR's biggest fans. He told a reporter: "WHUR is the best thing that ever happened to radio in this city." School Board president Marion Barry, City Council chairman Sterling Tucker, and even FCC commissioner Ben Hooks spoke about the station in glowing terms in a January 1973 *Washington Post* article titled "WHUR: A Refreshing Voice in the Vanguard of Black Media."[26]

All the praise and high hopes, however, obscured the tensions developing between Phil Watson and James Cheek, Howard's president. When Cheek was appointed in 1969, he set out to establish a professional school of communications to train black students, much like the institution New Breed activists Del Shields and Clarence Avant had envisioned. WHUR was a key part of an ambitious plan that also included a doctoral program in communications; undergraduate programs in radio, television, film, and journalism; a community newspaper; and eventually, a public TV station and a master's program in film. During Watson's first year as general manager, WHUR ran up a large debt; incoming revenue could not offset the costs of building a state-of-the-art radio broadcast facility, boosting the station's signal to fifty thousand watts, and paying the large number of staff members. The station's relatively low local ratings made advertisers skittish. President Cheek began to pressure Watson to rein in spending and increase revenues.[27]

The tension between the two men also had a political dimension. The left-leaning Phil Watson and moderate Republican James Cheek were not likely to agree about much politically. Moreover, Cheek was trying to cultivate close ties with the Nixon administration—both to protect Howard's generous yearly federal subsidy and to further his own career in the Republican Party. Predictably, Cheek objected to the station's radical political agenda and began to intervene in programming and personnel matters. For example, he ordered Watson to discontinue the campus speaker series after the station aired a fiery speech in which former Howard student Stokely Carmichael criticized the university's educational policies. Cheek also forced Watson to fire a programmer who aired a recording of black Vietnam veterans that contained profanity. (Ironically, the record, *Guess Who's Coming Home*, was produced by Wallace Terry, an award-winning black journalist who later became a member of Howard's journalism faculty.) Phil Watson was fired early in 1973, after only a year and a half on the job.[28]

One of Cheek's aides, John Paul Simpkins, replaced Watson and followed the president's orders to make WHUR more profitable and tone down its radical politics. New program director Tom Jones and Simpkins implemented broad changes at the station. In the news department, they eliminated the travel budget and scrutinized assignments more closely. Censorship became an issue when Simpkins and Jones killed a news report on a strike by medical students, ignoring protests from the news director and staff. The two newcomers made other decisions that worsened the relationship between the news department and management; many of the station's best reporters, including Jean Wiley and Ivy Young, found work elsewhere. The public-affairs programming fared no better: management stripped funds earmarked for the campus and Black Caucus remote broadcasts from the budget and eliminated the student work/study stipends, as well as the volunteer community programmers—thereby cutting out the two groups that had produced the bulk of the public-affairs offerings.[29]

Similar cutbacks and restrictions affected the music and cultural programming. The bilingual shows were among the first axed. The Puerto Rican host of *Latin Flavor,* Hector Corporan, recalls being told that he "no long fit the station profile" because he "sounded too foreign." The new playlist policy required DJs to select their music from the albums chosen by the program director and kept on reserve in the air studio. When Nighthawk Terry violated this policy by featuring his own records on his show, Tom Jones took him off the air but stopped short of firing him; instead, he gave Terry the job of operations director. To protest his demotion and the new playlist policy, Nighthawk went back on the air as a guest DJ on Russ Johnson's show. Furious, Jones called the station and ordered the two off the air; when they refused, he showed up at the station with the university police and had them removed. The next day, Simpkins fired both men.[30]

Outrage spread across the Howard campus. In the School of Communications, faculty were furious that a colleague had been fired without due process and banned from radio studios where he taught production classes. They demanded that Simpkins be removed as WHUR's general manager. Howard students, who had been turned out of the station when the work/study positions were eliminated, fired off a letter to the FCC, charging that WHUR had violated its educational mission, as stated in the license application, to provide a "training laboratory" for students. Then, they set up a picket line in front of the station, held a news conference, and went public with the FCC letter. President Cheek was able to defuse the situation by removing Simpkins and enabling his successor, Tom

Jones, to institute a student intern program at the station. But management's chief goal was still to pursue an upscale commercial niche in the FM market. Jones changed the format name tag in 1974 from "360 Degrees: The Black Experience in Sound" to "Ebony Lifestyle." By the end of the year, WHUR began to see higher ratings and, more important, billed over $1 million in advertising for the first time in its history.[31]

Virtually all the progressive black FM radio ventures in the late 1960s and early 1970s faced the same conflict. In almost every instance, the original Black Power political agenda, characterized as "nation building" by Phil Watson, yielded to the station's profit-making mission. Some stations, like WHUR, abandoned their political agendas only after considerable internal strife and struggle. Other outlets, like WBLS in New York City, avoided political controversy by privileging a cultural approach to programming; but in the end, even their all-black music formats were subject to ratings and market pressures. The few exceptions to this trend toward commercial accommodation, such as KAGB in Los Angeles, remained true to their black empowerment mission—but folded in the process. By the mid-1970s, the movement to radicalize black FM radio had failed, its leaders silenced. The movement's significant legacy to black radio took the form of programming innovations, such as the free-form deejaying style and call-in shows, and putting the radio ownership issue at the top of the political agenda—where it would remain for the next two decades.

PART VI

"Payin' the Cost to Be the Boss": Black-Owned Radio

In today's society most forces seem to pull people apart, marginalizing them and isolating them. Average citizens seem to have little real opportunity to speak directly to the officials who daily make critical decisions which affect thousands of people. This is the arena where "Community Focused Talk Radio" can play a major role. Community-focused talk radio can build a sense of family between individuals, thus enabling them to solve their own problems . . . provide valuable solace for the lonely and elderly, marshal resources to solve community problems, provide priceless business and entrepreneurial information . . . provide guidance in handling a difficult situation, alert the community as to how and when their active participation may be required, and become an electronic university to educate across the lines of age and class. Community-focused talk radio provides the necessary link between the public servant and those who are served. . . . [It] gives a voice, provides a platform and creates the marketplace where constructive community interchange can take place.

—Cathy Hughes, founder of Radio One

Bridging the
Ownership Gap

lthough industry insiders were well aware of the racial balance of power in radio station ownership, public discussion of the situation did not get underway until the 1970s. The first two black-owned stations in the country were established in 1949, but the number did not grow decisively or steadily over the next two decades. As we have seen in preceding chapters, African Americans in the radio industry were largely relegated to jobs as entertainers and then disc jockeys—and even those positions were not secure.

In a provocative essay, "The White Captivity of Black Radio," Fred Ferretti, who covered the radio industry for the *New York Times,* reported on the glaring disparities. One of the first mainstream media reporters to address these issues, Ferretti revealed that in 1970 only sixteen of the country's eight thousand radio outlets were black owned—.002 percent of the national total. Of that total, 310 stations targeted black listeners on a full-time basis. White ownership dominated the black appeal operations and garnered most of their advertising billings, which in 1969 amounted to $35 million overall. White control over management and programming policies invariably meant that white owners hired white managers to run their operations. Ferretti could locate only one black station manager in a white-owned station. Moreover, the white-owned and -managed stations that catered to

African Americans eagerly adopted the new Top Forty soul music format in the 1960s, effectively ending the black disc jockeys' control over the musical content of their own shows. Top Forty formats also marginalized—and in many cases, eliminated—the local news and public-affairs programming that had been a hallmark of black appeal radio in earlier years.[1]

Ferretti was especially critical of the five major white-owned soul radio chains that dominated the black appeal market: Rollins, Inc.; Rounsaville Radio Stations; Sounderling Broadcasting Corporation; Speidel Broadcasters, Inc.; and United Broadcasting Company. These radio chains all featured the Top Forty soul format, and Ferretti discovered that many of them were also "cooking" their personnel numbers to make it appear that their stations had black news and public-affairs staffs. One case that stood out was that of Charles Anthony, who hosted an afternoon drive-time show on Speidel's WSOK in Savannah, Georgia. In addition to his disc jockey position, Anthony was listed as being the station's program director, news director, and public-affairs director. Commenting on this arrangement, he told the reporter: "I wish I had the money to go with all my titles."[2] If Anthony was performing all those duties, he obviously wasn't being paid for it.

Ferretti also surveyed the nation's sixteen black-owned stations, finding that only nine of these outlets were wholly black owned; the other seven were controlled by African Americans but had some white investors. The ten AM stations were all located in the South (six) and the Midwest (four), and soul music superstar James Brown owned three of them. One AM/FM combo was owned by the Bell Broadcasting Company in Inkster, Michigan. Two of the FM stations were noncommercial outlets owned by black colleges: Hampton University's WHOU-FM in Hampton, Virginia, and Shaw University's WSHA-FM in Raleigh, North Carolina. Although Ferretti failed to include two other noncommercial FM outlets owned by black colleges, their inclusion would not have changed his bleak assessment of black-owned radio. The numbers spoke for themselves.[3]

The Ownership Issue up to 1970

In 1949, two African American entrepreneurs purchased radio stations. In the spring, businessman Andrew "Skip" Carter bought KPRS-AM in Olatha, Kansas; that fall, he moved the station to Kansas City, Missouri.

The one-hundred-watt daytime operation had been off the air for two years before Carter revived it as a black appeal station. Almost overnight, KPRS became the most listened-to African American outlet in the Kansas City market. That fall, in Atlanta, accountant J. B. Blayton purchased one thousand-watt WERD-AM for $50,000 and made his son, J. B. Blayton Jr., the station manager. Young Blayton hired radio veteran Jack Gibson as his program director; together, they turned WERD into a black appeal outlet. Like KPRS, it was an instant hit with African American listeners, and both stations became important and profitable radio outlets in their respective locales. Yet seven years passed before another black-owned station signed on the air.[4]

When WCHB-AM was launched in 1956 in Inkster, Michigan, a black suburb of Detroit, it was the first African American–owned station built from the ground up. Dr. Haley Bell, a wealthy black dentist, founded the station as a family enterprise; he and his two sons-in-law co-owned the station's parent company, Bell Broadcasting, and one of them, Dr. Wendell Cox, also served as WCHB's first general manager. The black appeal AM operation was successful enough to bankroll an FM sister station, WCHD-FM, which went on the air in the early 1960s. But generally speaking, black ownership gains were minimal during this period, and the ratio of white to black owners was growing larger. Restaurateur Charles J. Pickard's acquisition of WMPP in Chicago in 1963 created the fifth African American–owned radio outlet in the country—out of approximately seven thousand stations overall.[5]

When "The White Captivity of Black Radio" was published in 1970, the storm brewing in the African American community over black radio was largely focused on employment and programming issues, rather than on ownership. The soul radio chains' marriage to the Top Forty format generated the most protest, and even some organized opposition. In Columbia, South Carolina, black citizen groups formally complained to the FCC about the employment practices of WOIC, owned by the Speidel group. Their major grievance was that African American DJs were given titles like public-affairs director, news director, and program director but not the appropriate duties, pay, or authority to make decisions. In Nashville, WVOL, a Rounsaville outlet, was involved in a long labor dispute with its black air staff; at issue were wages, playlist restrictions, and the station's refusal to hire African Americans in management positions.[6]

In Washington, D.C., United Broadcasting's WOOK was the target of local protests over hiring practices. When United ignored the protests, the SCLC launched a nationwide boycott of the company's radio stations—none of which had African Americans in management positions. About the same time, the Atlanta NAACP, allied with local black broadcasters, spearheaded efforts to open up employment opportunities for African Americans at the city's radio stations, all of which were under the control of white business interests after the Blaytons resold WERD in 1969.[7]

In addition to protests over employment practices were some grass-roots outbursts against the lack of meaningful programming in the Top Forty soul formats. An ad hoc group in Kansas City, Kansas, picketed the local soul station in the summer of 1970, demanding that it upgrade its informational programming and become more responsive to the social needs of the local black community. The next year, in Newark, New Jersey, Black Power activists protested against WNJR, part of the Rollins chain, for doing away with its community affairs shows. Their criticism of the station, published in a local newspaper, read in part:

> Stations like this feed our communities and our children monotonous music, skimpy news, and very little relevant programming. The only thing our children can aspire to are songs about drugs, getting high, and abnormal love affairs, with nothing about what's going on and what needs to be done to better our community. We are protesting . . . against the pattern of paternalistic, mediocre broadcasting that has set in at the so-called soul stations around the country. Are the Black and Puerto Rican communities to be continually insulted by programming that imagines all we can do is wiggle our backsides and chug-a-lug brew?[8]

Within the broadcast industry, the NARTA was the first organization to raise the ownership issue on a national level. As early as 1964, the association's Legislative Committee began compiling figures on black-owned stations and passing them on to the NAB and the FCC. In 1967, the demand for more black ownership became a plank in the official NARTA agenda, and under the leadership of the New Breed, the organization began to seek ways to encourage the sale of radio stations to African Americans. A year later, the ownership question became even more relevant to

New Breed leaders after they participated in a retreat at the Center for the Study of Democracy, a liberal think tank located in Santa Barbara, California. Del Shields and his fellow NARTA activists spent a weekend there with a number of prominent media experts and scholars, discussing the plight of black radio. At the end of the retreat, the think-tank specialists recommended the obvious; as Shields recalled: "They sat there and they said—'The problem is that you don't own anything. So unless you own something, you can't change it . . . rather than you talking about conditions for the disc jockeys and for radio announcers, own the station.' "[9]

Among those in attendance at the Santa Barbara retreat was Nicholas Johnson, the maverick FCC commissioner who, in 1968, was one of the country's most outspoken advocates of broadcast reform. He volunteered to work with the New Breed on a campaign to increase black ownership in broadcasting. After returning to the nation's capital, Johnson began to raise the issue in government and industry policy-making circles; in addition, he helped coordinate NARTA's lobbying efforts at the FCC and the NAB. Del Shields and his associates, with aid from Nick Johnson, facilitated the sale of two AM radio stations to entertainer James Brown. But the discord and factional strife that eventually destroyed NARTA also undermined its push for black-owned broadcast outlets. Then Richard Nixon's election to the presidency in 1968 made Johnson a political outcast, and he soon left the FCC. With its leadership in disarray, the campaign for minority ownership stalled.[10]

The Decade of NABOB and NBMC

The 1970s would see the number of African American–owned stations soar, from 20 to 140 within ten years—an increase of over 700 percent. However, black-owned outlets still made up less than 2 percent of the nation's total. During this period, an informal network of new African American media advocacy groups, including the National Association of Black Owned Broadcasters (NABOB), the National Black Media Coalition (NBMC), and the Communications Brain Trust, which had been formed by the Congressional Black Caucus, was engaged in developing specific economic and political strategies to bolster African American ownership in the broadcast industry. Moreover, these groups were in the forefront of the lobbying efforts to implement these new "affirmative action" proposals.

NABOB can be traced back to the first conference on minority ownership in broadcasting in 1973. Sponsored by the NAB and the brainchild of Pattie Grace (its community affairs director) and a handful of black station owners, the conference committed the NAB to a policy of doubling the number of black-owned stations over the next three years. That goal, however, was never reached, and after three years of trying to implement it from within the association, a renegade group of black owners moved on to form NABOB in 1976. Among its founders were Skip Carter, longtime owner of KPRS in Kansas City, and Percy Sutton's son, Pierre Sutton, a vice president at Inner City Broadcasting. The first president of the association was Elliott Franks, the new owner of WOIC in Columbia, South Carolina. He characterized the NABOB mission as follows: "The black broadcaster faces some very real problems that are not addressed within the context of the National Association of Broadcasters (NAB). We look to NABOB to impact upon the solutions to the problems which restrict black entry into broadcast ownership and constrain financial growth once the property has been established."[11]

The NBMC was an outgrowth of Black Efforts for Soul Television (BEST), a media pressure group founded in the nation's capital in 1969. The organization's founder and first coordinator, Bill Wright, was a strong advocate of using broadcast license challenges as a tactic to increase African Americans' access to the airwaves. Toward that end, he and his staff conducted a series of workshops for black media activists around the country, designed to show the participants how to file a "Petition of Denial" with the FCC during the obligatory license renewal of the targeted station. The petitions were based on racial discrimination in the workplace and in the programming. One of the workshops was held in Houston, and among those in attendance was Pluria Marshall, who at the time was the director of the city's Operation Bread Basket. Marshall, a native of Houston, was a former DJ with a history of media activism. In the mid-1960s, he helped organize a successful DJ strike for higher wages a KYOK, a local soul station; in addition, he was active in NARTA for a few years and was a former chairman of Houston's Black Broadcasters' Coalition.[12]

Bill Wright's workshop had a profound effect on Pluria Marshall. It renewed his interest in grassroots broadcast reform, and he quickly became one of Wright's most promising disciples. In 1971, Marshall organized Black Citizens for Media Access, for the purpose of challenging the licenses of Houston's two soul radio outlets: KYOK and KCOH. Under threat of these challenges, both stations signed agreements with the citizens' group, specifying that they would hire more African Americans, especially in management positions, and improve the quality of programming. Then, in 1972, Wright fell gravely ill, and in a matter of months BEST ceased to exist. Determined to carry on his mentor's work, Marshall moved up to Washington, D.C., and, with help from a network of former BEST supporters, founded the NBMC in the fall of 1973.[13]

Under Pluria Marshall's leadership, the NBMC quickly emerged as a formidable broadcast pressure group. It took over BEST's role as the key facilitator of license challenges by black media activists, lobbied the FCC for policy changes that would improve the lot of minority broadcasters, and worked to uncover and expose racial discrimination in the broadcast industry. Marshall was blunt about the NBMC's mission: "We got into the broadcast game to kick ass and take names. We're here to hold their feet to the fire." One of the fronts where the NBMC made some headway was at the FCC. With help from Ben Hooks, the first African American to serve as an FCC commissioner, the NBMC was able to arrange a meeting with FCC chairman Richard Wiley. At that meeting, Marshall made the case for increased minority ownership in broadcasting; in response, Wiley offered to arrange for an FCC-sponsored conference on the subject. But before the plans for the gathering could be finalized, there was a change in political administrations, and Wiley stepped down as the head of the FCC.[14]

With the Democrats in power, the political climate became more favorable for movement on the minority ownership issue. The Carter White House sent its own set of proposals for increasing the number of minority-owned broadcast outlets to the FCC for consideration. In response to the White House initiative, as well as to mounting pressure from the NBMC, NABOB, and the Congressional Black Caucus, the FCC held its long-awaited conference late in 1977. Tax certificates, distress sales, and new frequency allocations were proposed as a means of increasing opportunities for minorities.[15]

Of the three proposals, only the tax certificate plan, under which the FCC would issue tax credits to station owners who sold their stations to minorities, gained widespread support in the broadcast industry, including a strong endorsement by the NAB. Moreover, White House policy supported the strategy. According to NABOB's executive director, James Winston: "It was viewed throughout the industry as a win-win proposition," benefiting "minorities and sellers."[16]

The distress-sale proposal allowed station owners whose licenses were in jeopardy of not being renewed to sell to minority buyers at a price somewhat below market value. Otherwise, the owners would lose everything. Initiated by the Congressional Black Caucus and endorsed by the White House, the distress sale was opposed by the NAB, which feared that "unscrupulous minority groups" would use the policy to "blackmail" white station owners into selling with threats of costly license challenges.[17]

The plan to open up new radio frequencies for minority broadcasters divided the participants. While it was favored by the NBMC, NABOB, and the Congressional Black Caucus, it was not on the White House wish list, and it was strongly opposed by the NAB. The white station owners would support new frequency allocations only if they could also get a piece of the action, but minority broadcast advocates objected that the competition would undermine the purpose of the policy. The conference ended with a standoff on this issue.[18]

"Capital formation" emerged as a major concern during the conference deliberations. How could minority entrepreneurs get their hands on enough money to buy a station? In 1978, radio stations in the major urban markets, where most African Americans lived, were selling for big bucks; the market value of KDAY in Los Angeles was $9 million, that of WVON in Chicago was $10 million, and that of WBLS in New York City was $17 million. Few black entrepreneurs could raise that amount of money, and minority entrepreneurs had nowhere to turn for financial backing. The private sector's minority lending record was abysmal, and the federal government had no record at all. At the time, the Small Business Administration (SBA) did not make loans to minority broadcasters. Black radio station owner Ragan Henry told the conference participants: "If you don't deal with the dollars, then there's no need to talk about policy."[19]

The FCC conference seems to have given the Carter administration the push to end the policy log jam. In February 1978, the White House reversed SBA policy, authorizing it to make loans to minority broadcasters who wished to purchase stations. Two months later, the FCC endorsed tax certificates and distress sales, but it tabled new frequency allocations for minority broadcasters, rendering the option dead in the water. For the first time in its forty-five-year history, the FCC had adopted a policy to increase minority ownership in the broadcast industry. Over the next three years, close to one hundred new black-owned radio stations went on the air. A new era seemed to be at hand.[20]

Networking Black Radio

Another major breakthrough in the ownership struggle during the 1970s was the launch of two black-owned radio networks: the National Black Network (NBN) in New York City and the Pittsburgh-based Sheridan Broadcasting Network (SBN). Their only predecessor, a black-owned and -operated network, had failed. Leonard Evans, an African American entrepreneur who published a black radio trade magazine called *Tuesday,* founded the National Negro Network in 1954, with syndicated program offerings including a newscast, two black soap operas (*The Story of Ruby Valentine* and *The Life of Anna Lewis*), and two variety shows, hosted by Cab Calloway and Ethel Waters, respectively. Evans's network attracted clientele by offering its program fare at bargain-basement prices to black appeal outlets around the country. Although Evans had about fifty regular subscribers, he lacked capital and operated in the red from day one; he had to fold about a year after he began.[21]

NBN: The Trailblazer

The country's first successful black-owned radio network, NBN, was launched in July 1973 by Eugene Jackson, Sidney Small, and Del Rayee, the owners of Unity Broadcasting Corporation. Small and Rayee were veterans of mainstream network radio, but Jackson was a newcomer to the industry. A native of Kansas City and a college graduate, Jackson had worked as an engineer for Colgate-Palmolive. After the King assassination, however, he turned to venture capitalism: "I felt the solution to black problems was not social, but economic." He moved to New York City, earned a master's degree in business from Columbia University, and worked as a fund-raiser for minority economic development ventures. One of the projects, a plan to start a black radio network, was being developed by a small group of broadcasters that included Sid Small and Del Rayee. Jackson raised an unprecedented $1 million to bankroll the operation; then, together with Small and Rayee, he founded the Unity Broadcasting Corporation, the network's parent company, in 1973. Jackson was the driving force behind the new network and would be its first president.[22]

NBN started primarily as a black news service, producing five-minute newscasts on an hourly basis, a nightly sports report, a nightly business report, and a news commentary show. From the outset, NBN had an impressive roster. Radio journalist Roy Wood, who hosted the commentary show (*One Man's Opinion*), was famous for his award-winning coverage of the civil rights movement during the 1960s while working for WVON in Chicago. He taught for a year in Howard University's new journalism program before becoming a leading figure at NBN. Sportscaster Frank Bannister, who held a doctorate in sports education and had played major-league baseball for the New York Mets, was well known and respected in black sports circles. Mal Goode, who was the first African American to work as a reporter on network television when he joined the ABC news team in 1962, had won numerous honors as a broadcast journalist. Goode was considered an expert on international affairs; his distinguished service as the president of the United Nations Correspondents Association gave him a unique edge in covering the United Nations for the network.[23]

The NBN struggled for its first two years of operation. Although it quickly signed up affiliates, national advertisers were slow to come on board. By 1976, after having run up a deficit of $2 million, Jackson and his associates managed to reverse their fortunes: NBN brought in $2.5 million that year, and revenues exceeded expenditures. NBN's success seemed assured. With eighty-two affiliates, it reached an estimated 17 million listeners. The network had about fifty full-time employees, two-thirds of whom worked in the news operation, and close to two hundred black reporters, or "stringers," in the field on a part-time basis. The number and scope of its program offerings had expanded in impressive ways. The new public-affairs shows included *Black Issues and the Black Press,* a weekly half-hour review of the major stories featured in African American newspapers, and *Yesterday, Today, Tomorrow,* an educational series designed to highlight the relationship between black Americans and black Africans. On a weekly cultural program, *The Ossie Davis and Ruby Dee Story Hour,* the famous theatrical couple used folktales, poetry, music, and drama to tell stories by and for African Americans.[24]

The NBN's growth and prosperity continued throughout the 1980s; by the end of the decade, the network had ninety-four affiliates, 20 million potential black listeners, and was grossing over $10 million a year. Program additions included new consumer-oriented shows such as *Energy Insight* and *Short Cuts,* a women's series produced by Marie Haylock and titled *The Action Woman,* a feature on black entertainers called *Stage Door,* and a late-night call-in show, *Night Talk,* hosted by Bob Law from WWRL in New York City. Law's pioneering show quickly became the most popular black radio talk program in the country. In the meantime, the parent company, Unity Broadcasting, was working to diversify its holdings in the broadcast industry. As early as 1980, the company purchased its first two radio stations, the WDAS AM/FM combo in Philadelphia; a few years later, it bought into a cable franchise in New York City. By the 1990s, the Unity Broadcasting Corporation seemed to be positioning itself to become the nation's first major black media conglomerate.[25]

SBN: The Powerhouse

The other African American network, the Sheridan Broadcasting Network (SBN), enjoyed an even more rapid rise. SBN was an outgrowth of the Sheridan Broadcasting Corporation (SBC) and the Mutual Black Network (MBN), both founded in 1972. The SBC was the brainchild of Ronald Davenport, dean of the law school at Duquesne University in Pittsburgh. A native of Philadelphia, Davenport attended law school at Temple University in his hometown and went on to earn an advanced law degree from Yale. In the mid-1960s, he was involved in the civil rights struggle in the South, defending jailed activists in Mississippi during the 1964 Freedom Summer project and in Alabama during the volatile Selma marches. Later in the decade, Davenport was hired as a law professor at Duquesne and settled in Pittsburgh with his wife. Although successful in his new career, he had come to the conclusion that the gains of the civil rights movement could be enjoyed and sustained only if African Americans made economic progress, in particular, ownership and control of businesses and cultural institutions. On the lookout for a promising business venture even while serving as dean of the law school, Davenport recognized an opportunity late in 1971: when a local soul radio chain, the Dynamic Broadcasting Corporation, put four of its stations up for sale (WAMO AM/FM in Pittsburgh, WUFO-AM in Buffalo, and WILD-AM in Boston), Davenport and his wife set up Sheridan Broadcasting, named after the street they lived on, and began to recruit black investors. Within a year, they raised the necessary capital and purchased the four stations for $2 million.[26]

The Mutual Broadcasting System (MBS), a low-budget and loose-knit radio network with some five hundred affiliates, set up the Mutual Black Network (MBN) in the spring of 1972—a few months before the NBN made its debut. Initially a black news service, with teams of journalists based in New York City and Washington, D.C., MBN produced a series of daily five-minute newscasts and sportscasts for distribution to Mutual's soul radio affiliates. Its news director in New York was Sheldon Lewis, a broadcast journalist from Charleston, South Carolina, where he had worked as a reporter for WPAL-AM and WUSN-TV. The Washington, D.C., office was headed by Ed Castleberry, a veteran newscaster from WEDR-AM in Birmingham, Alabama. Ron Davenport had become aware of MBN's news service in the course of overseeing the operation of WAMO-AM, a Mutual affiliate, and immediately saw its potential to reach and service a national black audience. Over the next few years, as the understaffed and underfinanced news network struggled to stay afloat, Davenport entered into negotiations to purchase MBN. Finally a deal was cut, and the buyout proceeded in two stages. In 1976, SBC purchased 49 percent of NBN and took over the management of the news service; less than two years later, it bought the remaining 51 percent, moved the network headquarters to Pittsburgh, and renamed it the Sheridan Broadcasting Network (SBN). The total cost of the buyout came to about $5 million.[27]

Even before the final transaction, Ron Davenport and his associates at Sheridan Broadcasting were broadening the scope and increasing the number of the syndicated programs produced by MBN. To produce and host *Straight Up*, its first daily news commentary show, the network hired Bev Smith, who would gain prominence for her outspoken editorials on race relations and her undercover reporting on prostitution, homelessness, and drug trafficking in the inner-city ghettos. Other new public-affairs offerings included a weekly update of business developments relevant to the black community, *Minority Business Report;* a daily health feature, *To Your Health;* and a weekly spotlight on environmental news. Expanded sports coverage featured regular broadcasts of black college football games and the network's first weekly sports show, *The Black College Sports Review.*[28]

When Sheridan Broadcasting gained complete control over MBN in 1978, the network had ninety-one affiliates and was bringing in about $3 million a year in revenues, giving SBN a slight lead over its principal rival, NBN, which that year had eighty affiliates and grossed $2.5 million. Over the next decade, the Sheridan radio network continued to expand its reach and beef up the syndicated program offerings. Journalist Bob Ellison was hired as SBN's first White House correspondent; in addition to his stories for the daily newscasts, he produced a thirty-minute public-affairs show called *White House Report.* The network also launched a series of short features, such as the ninety-second daily financial report *Money Smarts,* and a sixty-second movie review, *Coming Soon.* Three new sports shows—*Major League Baseball Notebook, NFL Playbook,* and *NBA Report*—were created to provide in-depth coverage of the nation's most popular professional athletes and teams. In addition, Sheridan continued to broaden its commitment to black college sports. It established a national poll for black college football teams and an annual awards banquet for black college athletes. The Sheridan network's support of black colleges reached well beyond its sports department. In 1985, SBN began to simulcast Lou Rawls's yearly *Parade of Stars* telethon, which raised money for the United Negro College Fund (UNCF). The simulcast turned the Rawls extravaganza into the most lucrative telethon fund-raiser in the country. In addition, Sheridan donated over $1 million to UNCF in the 1980s and gave black college radio stations free use of its syndicated programming. By the end of the decade, the Sheridan radio network had over 150 affiliates and close to $15 million in yearly revenues.[29]

AURN: The Crowning Achievement

Late in 1991, the Sheridan Broadcasting Corporation consummated the biggest deal in the history of black radio, purchasing NBN from Eugene Jackson and merging it with SBN to create American Urban Radio Networks (AURN). Headquartered in Pittsburgh, the new network has signed up over 250 affiliate stations, with the potential of reaching 90 percent of the nation's African American population. It is the only black radio network on the airwaves in the 1990s and the third largest network in the radio industry. Its five divisions—news, public affairs, sports, entertainment, promotion and marketing—offer affiliates a variety of programs and services.[30]

The news division offers affiliate stations a choice between two separate newscast services: the 3.5-minute newscast on the hour (from 6 A.M. to 10 P.M. on a daily basis) or the 5-minute newscast at half past the hour. The news operation has bureaus in New York City, Chicago, Los Angeles, and Atlanta, and in Washington, D.C. Its syndicated satellite newscasts reach an estimated 8 million listeners on a weekly basis. AURN's public-affairs division produces both regular and special-information programs. Many of its regular public-affairs shows are popular holdovers from the 1980s, including Bob Law's *Night Talk* and Bev Smith's *Straight Up*. The special programs focus on yearly events, such as Black History Month (*A Salute to Great Black Americans*), Mother's Day (*In Celebration of Black Mothers*), Father's Day (*Strong Men Getting Stronger*), Dr. Martin Luther King's Birthday (*King: A Man and His Dream*), and the national elections (*Election Day: Urban America*). The network also offers affiliates syndicated short features on health, money, consumer affairs, and minority business ventures.[31]

AURN's sports division features the same lineup of syndicated programming that the old Sheridan network had in place in the 1980s. In contrast, the entertainment division has created an entirely new line of syndicated cultural shows highlighting black music (*USA Music Magazine*), film (*Coming Soon*), media (*Inside Scoop*), comedy (*STRZ Funline*), and women (*Cameos of Black Women*). Also new, the promoting and marketing division provides AURN's affiliates and advertisers with a wide range of services—everything from sweepstake promotions to market research to direct mail campaigns.[32]

Ron Davenport's American Urban Radio Networks is one of black radio's most important success stories of the 1990s, and his crowning achievement as a pioneering African American media entrepreneur. Over the past decade, AURN has been a major source of black radio's syndicated programming—in the process, becoming indispensable to its growth and prosperity. But perhaps even more impressive, Davenport's new radio network conglomerate is competitive with its white corporate counterparts on a national level. This radio industry breakthrough culminates four decades of network-building ventures by black entrepreneurs.

The Tom Joyner Morning Show

Another significant breakthrough for black radio networking in the 1990s has been the emergence of *The Tom Joyner Morning Show* as a popular fixture in urban radio markets nationwide. Joyner's weekday broadcast is the most prominent black radio program in years to be syndicated nationally by a mainstream media corporation, ABC. It is currently heard on ninety-three stations by nearly 1.4 million daily listeners. The show is an outgrowth of the recently established "Urban Adult" format, which targets African American adults with a musical mix of classic soul and R & B hits from the 1960s, 1970s, and 1980s. But the show is far more than a disc-jockey driven operation. Tom Joyner has assembled a team of four comedians—J. Anthony Brown, Miss Dupree, George Wallace, and Myra J.—along with newscaster Sybil Wilkes and commentator Tavis Smiley; they produce an upbeat and fast-paced series of comedy routines, impersonations, satirical skits, news updates, interviews, and listener call-ins to blend with Joyner's musical selections. The more notable segments include a daily soap opera spoof titled "It's Your World"; a "Player Hall of Fame," which lampoons public figures involved in sex scandals; and Smiley's hard-hitting commentaries challenging a wide spectrum of racial injustices, from the auction of slave memorabilia at Christie's in New York City to discriminatory advertising policies in the radio industry. In addition to this full lineup, Joyner takes his show on the road, doing special broadcasts before large and enthusiastic audiences at host stations around the country.[33]

Tom Joyner was born and raised in Tuskegee, Alabama, where he eventually graduated from Tuskegee Institute with a degree in sociology. He broke into radio in 1970 when a college friend offered him a job as a DJ on an AM station in nearby Montgomery. Over the next two decades, Joyner honed his skills as an "old-school" personality jock on a series of stations in Montgomery, Memphis, St. Louis, Chicago, and Dallas (which eventually became his home). In the late 1980s, he began to host both a morning drive-time show in Dallas and an evening drive-time show in Chicago; he accomplished this feat by commuting between the two locations on a commercial jet each weekday. The novelty attracted national media attention, and Joyner became known as the "Fly Jock." In 1994, the ABC Radio network offered to fund and syndicate a beefed-up version of his Dallas-based program. A few months later, *The Tom Joyner Morning Show* debuted nationally.[34]

Since 1994, Joyner's show has been successful on several fronts: it has built up a large and influential audience among African American baby boomers throughout the country; it has helped rejuvenate the careers of such R & B acts as Kool and the Gang, the Manhattans, and Jerry "Iceman" Butler; and it has paved the way for other black radio syndication ventures by proving they can be profitable and competitive in urban markets. Yet the raucous style of comedy that Joyner and his cohorts perform has generated some controversy in black media circles. Critics charge that some of the material is offensive to African Americans; in particular, they cite the show's fake black history segments, which satirize the notion of a Black History Month. Some of the harshest critics even contend that the program is a throwback to the days of *Amos 'n' Andy*. Joyner concedes that some material may offend certain listeners, but he defends the concept of the show: "The formula is, if you can make people laugh, then you can get them to listen. And if you can get people to listen, you might be able to get them to make a difference."[35] Given the size and loyalty of the audience, Tom Joyner's old-school formula seems to be working.

Deregulation and the Downsizing of Diversity

During the 1990s, large media corporations with deep pockets have aggressively taken advantage of the FCC's deregulation of radio ownership, which took place in two stages between 1992 and 1996. In previous decades, a company could own only two stations (one AM, one FM) in a market and no more than seven nationwide. The rationale for this policy was that it would ensure diversity in radio ownership and programming. During the Reagan era, however, deregulation became the FCC's major preoccupation, superceding the goal of diversity. Stations were no longer required to meet public-interest standards in programming; license renewals were simplified, while renewal periods were lengthened; and the door was left open for the rapid resale of licenses when the three-year minimum holding period for station ownership was eliminated.

The rising price tag for stations, coupled with the 1990 economic recession, created radio industry pressure for ownership consolidation in order to minimize losses. Such mergers would cut administrative costs and give owners more leverage with advertisers. The FCC caved in to industry pressure in 1992, adopting a new "duopoly" rule, which allowed broadcasters to own a combination of two AM and two FM stations in a market. Over the next four years, more than 50 percent of the country's ten thousand commercial stations were involved in duopoly mergers.[36]

The landmark 1996 Telecommunications Act gave more momentum to radio ownership concentration. The new law allows a company to own up to eight stations (five FM, three AM) in a single market, and the national limit has been eliminated. These changes set off another frenzy of mergers and buyouts among radio group owners, leading to the rise of "superduopolies"—larger and larger radio groups with significant ownership blocs in local and regional markets. The two big winners to date are Westinghouse/CBS, with 175 stations and $1.5 billion in yearly revenues, and Hicks, Muse, Tate and Furst Holdings, which owns 395 radio stations with $1.46 billion in revenues.[37]

Ownership consolidation is having an adverse effect on the prosperity and proliferation of black-owned stations. The decline in revenue and numbers is taking place because a majority of these stations are individually owned and operated, putting them at a big disadvantage when competing with the new duopolies and superduopolies for advertising dollars. Advertisers are much more likely to buy spots on a cluster of stations than on a single station in the same market, since the cluster gives them access to a larger pool of consumers. Recently, NABOB executive director James Winston warned his members: "The industry is consolidating rapidly. Small owners—particularly ours—are being squeezed out of the business by duopolies and superduopolies. The radio business is all about advertising. If you can't compete because you can't deliver the audience for the price that a group of stations can, you are going to get squeezed out of the business because the advertisers are going to stop coming to you. And that's what the new rules mean. And that's a major threat to African American ownership."[38]

Ownership deregulation and consolidation, however, are not the only reasons for the current plight of black-owned radio. The two FCC policies (distress sales and tax certificates) that facilitated the sale of stations to minority broadcasters in the 1970s and 1980s are no longer operational. The FCC's deregulation of public-service requirements in the 1980s virtually eliminated the need for distress sales; the last one took place in 1986. From 1978 to 1986, thirty-eight radio stations were sold to minority owners under the agency's distress sale program. The FCC's tax certificate policy was invoked in the sale of nearly 250 radio stations between 1978 and 1994. But a series of high-profile "fronting" scandals—white investors using minority figureheads to secure tax write-offs in station buyouts—gave the Republican-controlled Congress a reason to demand that the policy be rescinded, which in turn caused the FCC to terminate the tax certificate program in 1995. According to media activist Pluria Marshall: "Killing the tax certificate—it was just pure, unadulterated racism. And along with the elimination of the ownership caps on radio and television, you will probably see the demise of minority ownership, period. I'd say within the next ten years—we could lose eighty stations."[39]

The recent decline in the number of black-owned stations lends credence to Marshall's gloomy forecast. African American ownership peaked in 1991 at 110 AM and seventy-one FM stations. The next year, with the duopoly policy in effect, there was an unprecedented loss of one AM and seven FM outlets. The FCC's 1996 superduopoly policy sparked another round of losses; that same year, five black-owned FM stations were sold to corporate radio groups. The lone African American FCC commissioner during this period, Andrew Barrett, who cast the only vote against doing away with station ownership limits, warned that "consolidation makes small independent black owned stations a harder sell to advertisers. It is used to establish local and regional pockets of concentration, thus having a negative impact on black radio stations." Echoing Barrett's concerns is Cathy Hughes, founder of Radio One and one of the few African American owners to take advantage of deregulation: "The allowing of multiple station ownerships in the same market pits the big guys against the little guys. In the world of broadcasting, all African American broadcasters are the little guys. So it's the big fish gobbling up the little fish, and over the past few years, the number of stations that we own has been declining. You either have to buy or you have to sell."[40]

Current ownership trends in the radio industry have put African American broadcasters on the defensive for the first time in decades. The gains made over the past twenty years are being rolled back. The situation may be grave at present, but that should not detract from the accomplishments of the many black radio entrepreneurs who have successfully bridged the ownership gap since the civil rights era. Their stories mark a major turning point in the history of black radio.

14

Entrepreneurs with Attitude

Before the civil rights era, the first black radio station owners, such as J. B Blayton in Atlanta and Haley Bell in Detroit, were college-educated professionals from outside the broadcast industry whose approach to the business centered on local markets, and whose political agendas were modest, at best. As described in earlier chapters, the civil rights struggle demonstrated black radio's unrivaled potential to engage and mobilize African Americans for a common cause, and it inspired the black political uprisings within the broadcast industry that eventually brought the ownership issue to a head. The next wave of black radio entrepreneurs showed more political motivation than the pioneers had. Although radio still attracted black professionals—for instance, law professor Ron Davenport, venture capitalist Eugene Jackson, and *Ebony* publisher Robert Johnson—the majority of the new entrepreneurs came from other sectors of the black community. Along with celebrated black entertainers like James Brown and Stevie Wonder and powerful black politicians like Percy Sutton and Willie Brown were people who had come up through the ranks of black radio—Cathy Hughes, Purvis Spann, and Roy Woods, among others. What distinguished them from their predecessors was the desire to advance an African American social agenda.

"The Hardest-Working Man in Show Business"

James Brown's brief career as a black radio entrepreneur in the late 1960s and early 1970s launched subsequent African American ventures into station ownership. Brown was not an exemplary businessman, but he brought public attention to black-owned stations. An unlikely candidate for stardom, he grew up in abject poverty, left school in the seventh grade, spent four years in prison for petty theft, and failed to catch on as a boxer or minor-league baseball player before finally embarking on a career as a performer in 1953. Over the next decade, James Brown built up a huge following on the "chitlin circuit," playing uniquely propelling, nonstop polyrhythmic R & B dance music and calling himself the "Hardest-Working Man in Show Business." In tune with the civil rights struggle, James Brown and his music came to represent black pride and empowerment in an era of social turmoil. His first top-ten hit, "Papa's Got a Brand New Bag" (1965), announced the arrival of a "New Breed" of African Americans:

> Come here Sister, Papa's in the swing,
> Ain't you hip about what that New Breed bring?
> He ain't no drag, Papa's got a brand new bag.

He made racial themes even more explicit in "Say It Loud, I'm Black and I'm Proud" (1968), which was adopted as an anthem by the Black Power movement. That year, his fans proclaimed Brown "Soul Brother #1" after he changed his hairstyle from a "process" to a "natural," completing his transformation from social misfit to militant black cultural icon.[1]

James Brown purchased his first radio outlet, WRDW in Augusta, Georgia, largely to dramatize his rags-to-riches success story for the hometown folks—especially those who had doubted his talent and tenacity. Located in his hometown, the station had been his boyhood haunt; in the 1940s, he had shined shoes on its front steps and run errands for the staff. When he brought WRDW in 1967, it was already the top-rated black appeal station in the Augusta market. The only major change Brown made was to hire a black management team to run the outlet. A year later, Del Shields approached Brown's accountant, Greg Moses, who also worked with NARTA, about buying another black appeal station—WJBE in Knoxville, Tennessee. Brown liked the idea, so Moses and the singer's business manager, Ben Burt, set up a company, James Brown Broadcasting, and purchased the Knoxville station. A few months later, the new company acquired WEBB in Baltimore and became the first black-owned radio chain in the country.[2]

During the late 1960s, James Brown's celebrity status among African Americans was comparable to Muhammad Ali's or even Martin Luther King Jr.'s. He was by now a wealthy man and an influential figure on the national political scene. In addition to the three radio stations and a music publishing firm, Brown owned a fleet of cars, a Lear jet, and two multimillion-dollar homes. Moreover, he was being courted by the Washington political elite, especially in crisis situations. In the aftermath of Dr. King's assassination, Brown's scheduled concert in Boston was broadcast live on local television so that he could make an appeal for calm. Afterward, he was flown to the nation's capital, where a riot was in progress, and repeated his calls for restraint and nonviolence on a number of local black radio outlets. During the 1968 presidential campaign, both major party candidates—Hubert Humphrey and Richard Nixon—sought out James Brown for an endorsement. Brown, an early supporter of the slain Bobby Kennedy, was initially contemptuous of Nixon's solicitation: "I don't want to be his bullet proof vest. I didn't want to protect him from my people— deceive them."[3] His endorsement belatedly went to Humphrey.

Four years later, James Brown endorsed President Nixon for a second term. By then, he was also an honorary spokesman for "Black Capitalism," a Nixon administration program to revive the inner-city ghettos through private enterprise. Ironically, this new role as a model black capitalist came at a time when Brown's economic empire was starting to crumble. In the early 1970s, after his longtime manager Ben Burt died, Brown was unable to find someone he trusted enough to manage his various business interests. The radio stations faltered, and Brown's career as an entertainer slumped in the mid-1970s, causing a decline in profits from his live appearances and record sales. To avoid bankruptcy, he sold many of his prized possessions, including the Lear jet and two of the radio stations. He tried to hold onto WRDW in Augusta, but in 1980 the station was sold at a public auction, after Brown defaulted on a $268,000 loan. By then, the James Brown Broadcasting enterprise was already out of business.[4]

While Brown seemed to recognize the critical role that black radio played in the day-to-day lives of African Americans, he proved to be ill equipped to manage his chain of stations—or even to hire a manager with appropriate experience. All three stations did well enough to generate profits for the parent company; but little of that money was reinvested in the radio chain. The profits supported Brown's lavish lifestyle, and when he ran out of money, he sold the stations to salvage his floundering career. In effect, Brown's radio stations were the accoutrements of his success as a showman, and ultimately expendable.

Percy Sutton Takes on the Inner City

Most of James Brown's successors assumed hands-on control of the day-to-day operation of their stations. Some, like Percy Sutton, had long dreamed of running their own radio station. Sutton was born and raised on a family farm just outside San Antonio, Texas; both his parents were college educated, and along with running the family farm, they worked for the local black school system—his father as a principal and his mother as a teacher. In his youth, Percy aspired to be a broadcast announcer, but segregation prevented him from even entering the city's only radio station. This experience sparked his early interest in owning a station. "I never wanted the mechanical side of radio, I wanted the ownership side. I wanted to talk on the radio about all the discriminatory things—about the injustices I saw all around me."[5]

As a high school graduate, Percy Sutton enlisted in the armed forces in 1941 and remained on active duty until the end of the war. Then he settled in Harlem and took advantage of the GI Bill to earn a bachelor of arts degree from Columbia University and a law degree from the Brooklyn Law School. In the late 1950s, Sutton set up a law practice in Harlem. Among his early clients was Malcolm X, whom he represented until the militant leader's assassination in 1965. (Sutton represents Malcolm's family today.) During this period, the young lawyer was also active in the NAACP. Moving up through the ranks to become the spokesman for the Harlem chapter in the early 1960s, he used this leadership position as a springboard to a career in politics. In 1965, Percy Sutton was elected to the New York State

Assembly from the Harlem district; two years later, he became the first African American to be elected president of the Borough of Manhattan, making him the most powerful black politician in New York City.[6]

During his years in Harlem, Sutton was so preoccupied with his law practice and political career that he neglected his search for a station to buy. By 1965, however, he had entered into informal discussions with Harry Novick, owner of WLIB-AM, about purchasing Novick's Harlem-based outlet. But seven years and "seventy-three visits to financial institutions" passed before Sutton secured the $2.5 million loan he needed. During that time, Novick added an FM station, WLIB-FM, to his operation and became somewhat reluctant to sell. Sutton formed the Inner City Broadcasting Corporation and negotiated the purchase of WLIB-AM in 1972 for $2.5 million. A few months later, Inner City brought WLIB-FM for an additional $600,000. Sutton's forty-year-old dream had come true.[7]

Not surprising, Sutton had a political agenda for Inner City's radio operations. In a 1972 interview he stated: "Communication will form the substance of politics from now on. What we can bring to black people in America in terms of information will determine what black politics will be in the future. Image is part of it, but communicating facts to the electorate may soon be all of it. When you think of how differently the informed person will respond, the potential for change in this country becomes fascinating."[8]

Inner City immediately expanded the news and public-affairs offerings on WLIB-AM, which became "Your Total Black News and Information Station," offering more public-service programming than any other black appeal outlet in the country. Its informational shows focused on local, national, and international issues of concern to New York's black population—everything from housing in Harlem to Shirley Chisholm's presidential campaign to the freedom struggles in Zimbabwe, Angola, and South Africa. There were also special bilingual programs in Spanish and French for the city's Latino and Haitian populations. WLIB's four-hour weekday-morning talk show, hosted by Judy Simmons, was the highest-rated black program of its kind in the country.[9]

By the end of the 1970s, Inner City Broadcasting was the largest black business enterprise in Harlem, with a net worth of $15 million. With radio stations in New York thriving, the company now also owned San Francisco outlet KBLX-FM and had national ambitions. As Pierre Sutton, Percy's son and the new president of the company, explained in 1978: "We want to get into the top ten markets in the country. If we can do that, we would be talking to half the black folks in the United States." During the 1980s, Inner City Broadcasting made some progress toward this goal, purchasing stations in Miami, Detroit, and San Antonio. In the 1980s, it also purchased a local cable TV franchise and the dilapidated Apollo Theater, which was transfomed into a state-of-the-art television soundstage and performance center. In less than two decades, the company evolved from a single-station operation, into a national radio chain, and then into the country's most prosperous black-owned media conglomerate. Inner City would continue to be a major player in the broadcast industry well into the 1990s.[10]

Stevie Wonder's Pride and Passion

Inner City Broadcasting's first attempt to buy a station outside the New York market targeted KJLH-FM in Los Angeles, a three thousand-watt outlet owned by black funeral-home magnate John Lamar Hill since 1970. In its earlier days, KJLH broadcast out of a storefront on Crenshaw Avenue, in the heart of L.A.'s inner city; in spite of its limited wattage, the station could be heard throughout Watts and Compton, the city's African American population centers. Its progressive FM music format showcased a lineup of renegade AM jocks, who controlled their own playlists. They mixed together contemporary jazz fusion, sophisticated soul balladry, and classic West Coast R & B from the 1950s and 1960s. The popular format had made KJLH the top-rated black FM station in the Los Angeles market by the time Hill decided to sell it in the late 1970s—but only to a black buyer. At first, Inner City had the inside track. But while the New York–based company was trying to raise the funds, Stevie Wonder entered the picture, checkbook in hand, and bought the station for $2.2 million. Wonder lived in Los Angeles at the time, knew KJLH, and had a communitarian vision for the station. According to his manager, Edward Abner: "Stevie is a communicator, a fantastic communicator, and he understood that radio could be used to serve the community. He thought that it had a larger duty to the community than playing records. He thought that it owed the community something; it should be speaking to the issues, it should be informing and educating its listeners. So he thought that if he owned the station, in addition to the music that he would play, that he would be able to inform, communicate, enlighten, and participate with the community, and that's what he's done with KJLH."[11]

By the time he purchased KJLH-FM in 1979, Stevie Wonder was an established star in the music industry and well known for his racial consciousness and activism. He was an early proponent of establishing Martin Luther King's birthday as a national holiday and an outspoken opponent of apartheid in South Africa, where his music was banned. These social concerns, as well as his commitment to the local black populace, became the centerpiece of the station's new format. Wonder's KJLH management team first expanded and upgraded the news and public-affairs programming; they added new informational and call-in shows, hired a team of reporters to cover local news events, and opened up their airwaves to black community groups. In addition, KJLH developed an innovative community outreach program, called "Survival in the Eighties," which provided a number of services such as helping to pay electric and utility bills for destitute families. The station also adopted a new motto: "We Are You." As KJLH's general manager Karen Slade explained: "'We Are You' holds true for all of our talk shows and public-affairs shows. So if you feel it, if it affects you, it affects us. And that's our bond with the community."[12]

KJLH-FM's pivotal role in the Los Angeles inner-city ghetto became apparent to the whole country in the early 1990s after a white jury acquitted four white police officers of violating black motorist Rodney King's civil rights, in spite of viewing a videotape that had been nationally televised and clearly showed the officers beating King. Four days of violence plunged the city into turmoil. KJLH switched to an all-talk and information format, turning its microphones over to African American political leaders, celebrities, community activists, and reporters and providing on-the-scenes news updates from the riot zones, dialogue with listeners who called in to voice their concerns, and warnings that people should stay off the streets. Throughout the ordeal, the station served as the nerve center of the black community; and in the aftermath, it was widely praised, even in the mainstream media, for being an island of sanity.[13]

In addition to being the sole owner, Stevie Wonder is also an avid fan of KJLH and a high-profile promoter of the station's accomplishments. According to Karen Slade: "Stevie, being the creative artist that he is, the station tapped into his creative sense—and he loved it. He fell in love with KJLH, and everywhere he went in the world, he would talk about his radio station."[14] In many instances, this special passion for radio also has been a trademark of the African American station owners who came up through the ranks of the industry.

Dues for Cathy Hughes

One of the most successful and controversial black entrepreneurial trail-blazers to come up through the ranks of the radio industry in the post–civil rights era is Cathy Liggins Hughes. During her remarkable career in radio broadcasting, she has managed to build, from the ground up, the largest African American–owned and –operated radio chain in the country. Hughes is a tenacious businesswoman, but she has also worked, at one time or another, as a media activist, a college instructor, and an outspoken radio talk-show host—all an outgrowth of her unwavering commitment to fostering racial progress in the broadcast industry.

Hughes's passion for radio began in her youth in Omaha, Nebraska: "I was a radio fanatic from a very early age . . . from the day my mother broke down and brought me a transistor radio. I took it everywhere. I even made a carrying case for it." Because Omaha lacked a black appeal outlet, Hughes listened to country music stations during the day: "I grew up with Conway Twitty and Willie Nelson." But late at night, she was able to pick up two legendary R & B shows: "I used to listen to Wolfman Jack and *Randy's Record Shack* . . . and it was just wonderful to hear Lloyd Price, the Coasters, and the Drifters. That was heaven. I would get up the next morning after only a couple hours of sleep because I had stayed up all night listening to the radio . . . pretty soon I got in trouble with my radio because at night my mother would come in and make certain I wasn't listening to my radio. I would hide it under my pillow."[15]

Hughes's middle-class family valued education and personal achievement. Her mother, a college-educated nurse and a professional musician, had played trombone for the popular all-female swing band the International Sweethearts of Rhythm. Her father was Omaha's most prominent black certified public accountant (CPA) and the first African American to earn an accounting degree at Creighton University. Hughes's parents sent her to an elite Catholic girls' school, hoping to prepare her for college, but she was a rebellious teenager: "I was fast at sixteen. I was having sex in the back of cars and all of that." She became pregnant, married, and gave birth to her son at the age of seventeen; her marriage to the boy's father, Alfred Liggins, lasted less than three years.[16]

Cathy Liggins completed high school as a single mother. As a student enrolled at the University of Nebraska, she attended classes at the Omaha campus and volunteered at the city's first black appeal radio station, where she learned the advertising and sales side of the business. In 1969, Liggins left college to go to work full time for her father, who was expanding his accounting business. When he suddenly died a year later, she went to Washington, D.C., to close down his business office there. She liked the vitality of the large black community in the nation's capital and soon decided to stay.[17]

Late in 1971, Liggins was offered a job teaching radio advertising and sales in Howard University's newly opened School of Communications, whose founder and first dean was television journalist Tony Brown. Liggins had known Brown from Omaha, where she had helped set up a series of speaking engagements for him at the university. Nevertheless, she was surprised when he offered her the position, especially since she had no college degree.

Later, she learned about Brown's unique vision for the school:

He believed that to teach students communications you needed people who were communications practitioners—not a whole bunch of academic types . . . so Tony assembled a distinguished group. Quincy Jones was a visiting lecturer, Melvin Van Peebles, Stan Lathums, Ed Bradley—the list read like a Who's Who. We had a very exciting, although very nontraditional and unorthodox faculty. Howard University almost hyperventilated and keeled over sideways. There most have been at least eighteen of us, none of whom had degrees, but all actively involved in our professions.[18]

After a year in the classroom, Cathy Liggins became the sales manager at WHUR-FM. She recalled the period as one of difficult transition for the station: "The general manager and sales manager had revolving doors at WHUR. They were going through management and staff fast—it was like every other week there was somebody new. Tony Brown knew that I knew sales . . . he made me sales manager of the radio station. We were billing only $30,000 a year then." Once on the job, Liggins quickly discovered that WHUR's lackluster sales figures were partly due to the university's myopic billing system: "I never will forget, I was pitching the McDonald's account, and having the head buyer say to me—'Well Cathy, I really loved your presentation, you really worked hard at it, but the last time we did business at WHUR, Howard sent us bills for tuition.' " Liggins managed to streamline WHUR's billing procedure for the university's accounting office, even as she was creating a whole new series of sales packages for the station. As a result, sales gained momentum, and during 1974, her first full year on the job, the station grossed over $1 million.[19]

Liggins's record as WHUR's sales manager impressed Howard University president James Cheek, and he promoted her to station manager late in 1975. (Liggins learned of her promotion in the *Washington Post;* apparently, the notification letter from President Cheek disappeared in the campus mail.) Liggins replaced Tom Jones at a time when the station was experiencing a good deal of internal strife. Students were still angry about their lack of access to the station's airwaves and cynical about the new internship program, which lacked hands-on studio experience. The staff had just organized a union, in part to resist the changeover from the original "360 Degrees: The Black Experience in Sound" format to the "Ebony Lifestyle" concept that Jones had initiated. And the faculty in the School of Communications who were still associated with WHUR resented President Cheek's dictatorial powers over the station. Liggins recalls that her promotion caused some animosity: "Here I am general manager, so I go to my office and the first thing I'm greeted with from some of the students and faculty and staff . . . instead of them sharing my joy, they were like—'You're not qualified to be general manager. You've never been a general manager before . . . you're an Uncle Tom.' "[20]

Liggins embarked on an ambitious agenda as station manager. To bolster her management skills, she attended an intensive six-week broadcast management seminar at Harvard University in Massachusetts. Back at WHUR, she upgraded the internship program by paying the interns a stipend for their services and reserving the Sunday-evening time bloc for student programming. Her greatest challenge—and triumph—at WHUR, however, was the creation of the station's first commercially successful format, which achieved a major breakthrough in the ratings. When Cathy Liggins became WHUR's general manager, the recently created "Ebony

Lifestyle" format existed, for the most part, in name only. Staff cutbacks and defections had decimated the news and public-affairs operations; few of the station's programs that focused on local issues and concerns survived. The "jazz purists," as Liggins called them, now had a stronger presence and controlled most of the major airshifts: "I had no ratings because we were playing twenty-seven minutes of Pharoah Sanders holding a note!" she would later complain.[21]

The first new public-affairs program that Cathy Liggins put on the air at WHUR was *The Morning Sound,* a daily audio magazine featuring local news, weather, sports, and traffic updates, along with interviews and call-in segments. It was produced and hosted by an up-and-coming media activist named Jerry Phillips, whom Liggins had hired along with four staff members to work on the show. Over the next decade, *The Morning Sound* developed a loyal following among local black listeners, due to its community focus and accessibility. Liggins also extended the *Daily Drum* evening news show from thirty minutes to an hour and hired more reporters in order to get the news staff to cover a wider range of national and local news of interest to African Americans. These efforts to bolster the public-affairs and news offerings were generally supported by WHUR's staff, although they were leery of her motives.[22]

Changing WHUR's music format, however, proved to be much more of a struggle. The station's entrenched jazz DJs were contemptuous of the newer trends in popular black music, especially in jazz, and they were unconcerned about their low ratings in the market. Initially, Liggins had no ideas for revamping the music format. Only after attending a seminar on "Psychographic Programming" at the University of Chicago in the summer of 1977 did she began to develop the concept that evolved into the celebrated "Quiet Storm" format. Psychographic radio formats were, at the time, the latest programming trend in the industry; they were designed to blend into the lifestyles of a specific demographic target. Liggins took the idea and applied it to a group of her female friends—mostly single, black, upwardly mobile career women—and decided there was a need for an evening radio show in the local market that appealed to the musical sensibilities of professional black women.[23]

Moving from theory to practice, Liggins developed a playlist of LPs that appealed to her female focus group and then talked one of her student interns into trying out the new musical format on the Sunday-evening airshift. The intern, Melvin Lindsey, at the time was already hosting the Sunday-night student time slot. Liggins convinced him to drop his "Mister Magic" moniker and call the new show *The Quiet Storm*, in honor of the Smokey Robinson song: "I told Melvin, a good title would be *Quiet Storm*. It has subliminal seduction in it. Smokey's line—'Blow Baby Blow'—has all types of sex appeal." The premiere broadcast, which featured a playlist of romantic ballads and sensual love songs by contemporary R & B vocalists—especially black women—was an overnight sensation on the local airwaves: "The switchboard lit up that night and the next two days with calls from listeners asking about 'that different show.' They all wanted more." By the end of 1977, *The Quiet Storm* was the top-rated weekend music show in the Washington, D.C., market.[24]

The surprising strength of *The Quiet Storm*'s Sunday-night ratings gave Cathy Liggins the leverage to move the show into the the the 7 to 11 P.M. weeknight time bloc, replacing the evening jazz programming. Within a year, this format change transformed WHUR into the number two–rated FM outlet in the nation's capital; and the station was now billing over $2 million in sales. But even as she was succeeding as station manager, Liggins was becoming disillusioned with Howard. By then, Tony Brown and most of his handpicked communications faculty had moved on, and the School of Communications was settling into a more conventional mode of instruction. Liggins's proposals for upgraded facilities and an expanded student internship program routinely fell on deaf ears in the president's office, where the major decisions about the station still were made. One of her pet projects, to franchise the *Quiet Storm* show, even got her in hot water: "I got Smokey Robinson to sign off on it. All the documentation was done. I applied for the papers—and I almost lost my job. I was told that the legal department at Howard handled that, I had stepped outside my bounds."[25]

In the fall of 1978, Cathy Liggins resigned as WHUR's general manager in order to accept a similar position at double the salary with WYBC-AM, a new local gospel station. She also married television producer Dewey Hughes during this period, and together, they began to explore the possibility of buying a radio station in the area. An opportunity arose almost immediately, when WOL-AM, a former soul radio powerhouse that was the target of a federal payola probe, was put on the market as a distress sale. Cathy Hughes developed a business plan for the buyout and began meeting with prospective lending institutions. After being turned down thirty-two times, she found a bank in New York City willing to fund the purchase. In 1980, Cathy and Dewey Hughes became the new owners of WOL.[26]

Having worked as a general manager at both FM and AM stations, Cathy Hughes recognized FM radio's advantage in technology and ratings for music formats. Her solution was to abandon WOL's traditional soul music soundscape for a talk-radio format—a bold move at the time. There were numerous talk shows on the air but no black-owned stations with an all-talk format. Hughes's model for a community-based talk-show approach to programming was Philadelphia activist DJ Georgie Woods: "We studied Georgie Woods because Georgie Woods did a more talk-oriented format for his show. Everybody else was doing music. But we liked Georgie Woods's approach to the community." Hughes recruited a talented crew of broadcasters to host the talk-show strips and went on the air with great expectations: "We had Rudolf Brewington. We had a star-studded lineup. We had Bernie McCain, Dr. Charles Spellman. We had everything except the two critical Rs. R & R. We had no ratings and no revenue."[27]

Within a year of going on the air with a talk-show format, the Hugheses were given an ultimatum by their New York bank; either go back to WOL's old soul music format, which was more cost-effective than the talk-show lineup, or lose the funding. Dewey Hughes was unwilling to go along with the bank's demands; he was quickly growing weary of the radio venture and anxious to get back into television production. Cathy Hughes, determined to stay the course, worked out a compromise with the bank: she could keep one daily talk show, but only if she hosted it herself. Dewey Hughes then gave her full control of the station and moved to Los Angeles to pursue a career in television. (A year later, the couple ended their marriage amicably.) Cathy Hughes remained in Washington, D.C., to launch her new careers as WOL's sole owner, general manager, and daily talk-show host.[28]

Cathy Hughes's first order of business was to relocate WOL from the upscale white Georgetown section to the heart of the local black community. She bought an abandoned storefront residence on the H Street corridor, a moribund black business district that had been devastated in the 1968 riots, to house the station. As she recalled: "This building had been a shooting gallery for heroin addicts, and the community helped me build it back up. That first year at Fourth and H, we didn't have much of a profit because most of what we made we used up renovating the facilities . . . and in the end, it was absolutely glorious." The relocated station became a hub of activity and the voice of local community concerns. Before long, the outlet was also attracting commercial sponsors from local African American businesses, and it was developing a sizable audience of loyal listeners, whom Hughes called the "WOL family."[29]

Much of WOL's success in the 1980s can be attributed to Cathy Hughes's rise to prominence as a radio talk-show host. On her morning show, she developed and maintained a strong rapport with her listeners, even as she took on the most controversial issues of the day. First and foremost an outspoken crusader for her race, Hughes used her talk show to promote everything from the anti-apartheid protests at the South African Embassy to the maverick presidential campaigns of Jesse Jackson. When Washington, D.C., mayor Marion Barry was videotaped smoking crack cocaine in a downtown hotel during an FBI sting, Hughes called the incident a setup to embarrass the local black community and raised enough money over the airwaves to pay Barry's legal expenses. But after the born-again mayor returned from prison and won back his old job, the two had a falling out, and Hughes became one of Barry's most vocal critics.[30]

Cathy Hughes's most celebrated radio campaign targeted the *Washington Post*. In 1986, the newspaper announced that it was launching a new Sunday magazine, and that the cover story in the first edition would profile an African American. Expectations were high in the WOL family; as Hughes recalled: "We got to speculating. John Thompson and the Georgetown Hoyas were hotter than a firecracker then. Everybody loves John Thompson, he's an incredible example of black manhood. He's helped so many young people. We speculated Colin Powell. We speculated a whole host of African and American dignitaries." As it turned out, the story was on a teenage hoodlum from New York who was accused of murdering a local Howard University student. Hughes mobilized her equally irate listeners for a "recall" campaign, aimed at returning copies of all subsequent issues of the *Post* magazine to the publisher. On the next thirteen Sundays, WOL supporters dumped close to a half-million copies of the publication on the front steps of the *Washington Post* headquarters. The widely covered recall campaign ended only when both the editor and the publisher of the newspaper agreed to appear on the WOL morning show, where they apologized for their indiscretion. "For six months after the protest," quipped Hughes, "that magazine looked like *Ebony*."[31]

By 1987, WOL was back with the original all-talk format, and it was finally making a healthy profit. Hughes used this turnaround as leverage to purchase another station in the market, WMMJ-FM. But once again, the bank rejected her plan to change the format—in this case, from a satellite-fed easy-listening service called "Evergreen" to an urban contemporary approach. "Asking me to do Evergreen was like asking Angela Davis to sell memberships in the Klan," recalled an irate Hughes. Nevertheless, she swallowed her pride and went along with the bankers, but only until she could dissuade them. It took eighteen months to do so. Under Hughes's direction, WMMJ finally switched over to an Urban Adult format in 1989, now calling itself "Magic 102.3." Within a year, the station was rated among the top ten in the market, and it was no longer losing money. Once again, Cathy Hughes had proved her bankers wrong when it came to format decisions.[32]

During the early 1990s, Hughes founded her own company, Radio One, to oversee her broadcast properties, and she brought her son, Alfred Liggins Jr., into the business as her partner. In addition, she teamed her new company with a highly successful black investment firm, Syndicated Communication. Their first joint venture was to purchase the Baltimore AM/FM combo WWIN for $7 million in 1991. Two years later, they bought another AM/FM combo in Baltimore, WERQ, for $9 million, giving Radio One control over 10 percent of the commercial stations operating in the city. Next came the Washington, D.C., FM powerhouse WKYS, purchased for a staggering $35 million in 1995, and then both WHTA-FM in Atlanta ($18 million) and WDRE-FM in Philadelphia ($20 million) in 1996. At present, Radio One owns nine radio stations, making it the largest and most prosperous black-owned radio chain in the country.[33]

Blackgrounding
Public Radio

The post–civil rights era witnessed a growing African American presence in the public sector of the radio industry, but black colleges, rather than entrepreneurs, were the major owners and operators of the new stations. The FCC established this sector in 1946, when, during a reorganization of the FM spectrum, 20 percent of the new FM radio channels (88 to 92 MHz) were set aside for noncommercial broadcasters. Colleges and universities were virtually the only institutions in the country to show an interest in developing the new noncommercial radio channels. Between 1948 and 1966, the number of "educational" stations, as they were commonly referred to on the air, climbed from 46 to 292. Because these college stations had low power (ten watts) and low yearly budgets (under $10,000) and preferred formats based on the instructional missions of the host institutions, their listenership was very limited, especially when compared to the popularity of the commercial stations.[1]

This marginalization was reduced with the passage of the Public Broadcasting Act in 1967. Shifting the emphasis from educational to "public" radio, the legislation created the Corporation for Public Broadcasting (CPB) to disburse federal funds for upgrading noncommercial radio and television. Only "CPB-qualified" stations—those having at least five paid staff members, broadcasting at least eight hours a day all year, and programming for the "general public"—could receive federal funds. During the first round of funding, only seventy-three stations, or 17 percent of the noncommercial outlets, qualified; in effect, CPB subsidized the wealthiest stations, while neglecting the smaller ones. These subsidized stations were further enhanced when National Public Radio (NPR) was established in 1970 to provide network programming for its FM affiliates.[2] Black college radio also benefited from this legislation, some stations becoming potent rivals of other public outlets and the dominant black commercial stations in their localities.

Black College Radio

Prior to the 1967 Public Broadcasting Act, only two black college stations were on the air: WESU-FM at Central State University in Wilberforce, Ohio (1962), and KUCA-FM at the University of Central Arkansas (1966). Both were low-budget ten-watters and unqualified for CPB funding. However, the availability of funds sparked an upsurge in the number of black colleges applying for noncommercial licenses. In 1969, both WSHA-FM at Shaw University in Raleigh, North Carolina, and WHOV-FM at Hampton University in Virginia signed on the air. They were joined in the 1970s by eighteen new black college outlets, including WCLK-FM at Clark College in Atlanta, KGRM-FM at Grambling College in Louisiana, WHCJ-FM at Savannah State College in Georgia, WEAA-FM at Morgan State University in Baltimore, and WAMF-FM at Florida A & M University in Tallahassee. As this list indicates, most of these stations were located in the southeastern part of the country, where the historically black colleges (HBCs) were concentrated.[3]

Most of the black college stations, however, were low-budget and low-power operations that did not initially qualify for CPB's radio grants and were funded by the colleges' academic budgets. As each station was under the stewardship of the academic program at its institution specializing in broadcast communications, organizational structures and program formats varied widely. Generally, the academic program hired the paid staff and shaped the operation as a training laboratory for students. With no shared model or mission among the HBC stations during this period, and often with continually shifting management strategies at individual stations, they evolved in quite dissimilar ways.

WSHA-FM in Raleigh exemplifies a fairly typical search for a mission and an audience beyond academia's walls. The Shaw University station was launched in 1969 as a ten-watt outlet with one paid staff member—the general manager. Most of the on-air staff were drawn from the ranks of student volunteers, who modeled their programming on the top-rated black commercial stations in the market. Predictably, they created a music format that targeted their peers by featuring the popular soul music and dance tracks of the day. The student DJs also tended to emulate the mannerisms of the market's top black personality jocks. In these early days of its development, little news or public affairs aired on WSHA. With minimal faculty involvement, it was largely a student-oriented and -operated station.[1]

Boosting its power to twelve thousand watts in the mid-1970s, and to twenty-five thousand watts in the early 1980s, WSHA implemented a series of upgrades to make the station CPB qualified. By hiring additional staff and setting up a more structured, faculty-supervised student internship program, the station was in a position to revamp the format. At this point, WHSA expanded the news and public-affairs offerings; everything from local talk shows to SBN's syndicated newscasts was added to the information mix. Then, as jazz was belatedly enshrined as the new centerpiece of music programming, student DJs were relegated to the late-night and weekend airshifts, and experienced jazz programmers were recruited to host the drive time shows. These changes not only secured CPB funding for the station but also greatly increased its listening audience. In less than a decade, WSHA evolved from a low-power student-oriented outlet into the top-rated black public station in the market.[5]

The HBCs characteristically adopted a jazz and information format as an alternative to the classical music and information format favored by NPR's flagship stations. Clark College's WCLK-FM in Atlanta pioneered the use of this noncommercial format in the late 1970s. Under the direction of the Department of Mass Communication, the fledgling twenty-five-hundred-watt station was given a mandate to create a format that was "distinctly different from other stations in the market . . . to duplicate other stations' programming is to waste scarce radio spectrum and misuse public money provided to non-commercial stations." WCLK's musical philosophy was "based on a bedrock of commitment to America's premier contribution to world culture: Jazz." Hence the station would pursue a "proactive role with respect to the nurturing, promotion and development of jazz as a vital and authentic American classical music," a policy that led to a music format that devoted 90 percent of its schedule to jazz programming.[6]

WCLK's news and public-affairs mission was to "promote cultural, artistic, educational and economic linkages" with the city's African American population. The director of news operations was responsible primarily for the production of a series of daily five-minute local news updates. In addition, the station broadcast regular national and international news updates, provided by NBN in the 1980s and, more recently, by AURN. The public-affairs department also had a paid director, who coordinated the production of a series of weekly programs on health (*Health Break*), travel (*Travel Line*), the arts (*Friday File*), and the city's black colleges (*Atlanta University Center Forum*). WCLK also broadcast Bob Law's syndicated *Night Talk* show on a regular basis and employed a gospel coordinator to produce a strip of Sunday-morning programs devoted to gospel music and local church news. In addition to the paid staff, student interns, faculty supervisors, and community volunteers worked in the news and public-affairs department on a part-time basis.[7]

By the 1980s, many of the more powerful HBC stations located in the larger urban markets had adopted a jazz and information format: Morgan State University's WEAA-FM (fifty thousand watts) in Baltimore, the University of the District of Columbia's WDCU-FM (twenty-five thousand watts) in Washington, D.C.; Norfolk State University's WNVB-FM (twelve thousand watts) in Norfolk, Virginia; and Alabama State University's WVAS-FM (twenty-five thousand watts) in Montgomery. With a mission and orientation typical of these black public outlets, WVAS signed on the air in 1984 with five paid staff members and a broadcast signal that covered eleven counties in central Alabama, including the city of Montgomery. The station's musical format was jazz, and it had an active news and public-affairs department, which was also used as a radio journalism lab by students majoring in the field. Faculty from the School of Journalism supervised the local news and public-affairs programs produced by ASU students. The audience was made up mostly of well-educated, middle-class African American professionals from twenty-five to fifty-four years old. After only a year on the air, WVAS was ranked seventh in the Montgomery market in competition with the commercial outlets and second among noncommercial stations. Since the mid-1980s, WVAS-FM has maintained its position as the premier black public radio station in central Alabama.[8]

In contrast to this elite group of HBC stations with public radio credentials are the more common student-oriented outlets. These low-budget operations still make up a majority of the black college stations on the air; they include twenty low-power FM stations, five low-power AM stations, and twelve cable radio outlets. Most of these stations are staffed and managed by students whose programming targets the black youth market (sixteen to twenty-five years old). Over the past decade, they have become the underground radio voice of the hip-hop generation. In these student-run stations, hip-hop DJs who control their playlists and promote their youth culture over the airwaves showcase "fresh" rap, alternative R & B, house, and dancehall releases. They also "flava" (flavor) their on-air announcing with hip-hop vernacular and adopt such hip-hop monikers as "Lady Lush," "X-Man," "Johnny B Badd," "Buck Wild," "DJ Terminator," "MC Erotic," "Tiger Shark," and "Ayatollah Slim." In addition, they "chill" with the audience by opening up the phone lines so listeners can "rap the mike" or give "shoutouts" to a local "posse" or "crew." This grassroots approach to deejaying, grounded in the emerging hip-hop subculture, recalls the free-form DJ formats on progressive black FM stations in the 1970s.[9]

KPVU-FM at Prairie View A & M University in Texas typifies the student-run station. Located in Prairie View, a small, rural town about sixty miles northwest of Houston, the university is the oldest HBC in the state; its approximately three thousand students largely come from Houston. All of the station's staff positions, from general manager down, are held by students, who receive internship credits or work/study stipends for their work at the station. The format includes a brief daily newscast, produced by broadcast journalism students, and occasional sports specials, but most of the programming is music driven. As many as fifty student DJs host weekly shows of two to four hours in length, and while there are a few gospel and reggae programs on the weekends, the vast majority of the shows are hip-hop oriented—both musically and culturally.[10]

A similar hip-hop format is in place at WHBC-AM, the cable radio outlet at Howard University in the nation's capital. The station broadcasts fourteen hours a day and can be heard in the campus dorms and the

Blackburn Cultural Center. (About one-third of Howard's eleven thousand students live on campus.) WHBC has been a student-run operation for the past twenty years; at present, about eighty student volunteers work at the station. A news staff produces a daily five-minute newscast, and a sports staff broadcasts the Howard Bisons' athletic events. But the large majority of the student volunteers are DJs who host their own two-hour shows once a week. They go by names like "Q45," "DJ Xclusive," "B-Boy J," "DJ Deuce," "AK Schmoove," "DJ Maad Nice," "T-Dub," and "DJ Vengeance," and they call their shows *Planet Black, B-Boyz in a Cipher, Radioactive, Girlfriend, Sonar Eclipse, Mo' Butta fo' Yo' Biscuit, The Queen's Throne, Hip Hop Happy Hour, The Joint II, Southern Fried Flava, Straight Up Philly, Keepin' It Real, 2 Dope Boyz in a Cadillac,* and so forth. WHBC's lineup of hip-hop DJs and shows is the trademark format of the student-oriented black college stations, which collectively play an important role in the reproduction of hip-hop culture within their respective student communities. It is interesting to note that in the past decade, hip-hop formats have sprung up on commercial FM radio in key markets around the country. These new formats are commonly referred to as "Urban Hits" or "Urban Rap."[11]

Since 1979, a yearly Black College Radio Convention (BCRC), held in Atlanta, has been a student-oriented gathering, funded for the most part by donations from the record industry. Founded by educator Lo Jelks, who continues to be the driving force behind the convention, the two-day conference features panels and workshops on such subjects as fundraising for noncommercial stations, careers in radio broadcasting, audience research, station relations with record companies, public radio grants, FCC policies, and the future of HBC radio. A prominent African American from the radio industry is always the keynote speaker. The major social events are an awards banquet and a series of parties sponsored by the record labels. On average, some 150 to 200 people, mostly students from the participating stations, attend the annual BCRC. Some faculty attend as chaperons or panelists, but they are rarely involved in the planning of the convention; they have no influence over its agenda. Conspicuously absent from these conferences are the paid staff members from the larger black college stations with jazz and information formats, who tend to identify with the public radio sector and attend public radio conventions. The BCRC has not managed to bridge the chasm between the student-run outlets and their professionally operated counterparts. Hence it falls short of being a cohesive national organization that represents the interests of HBC stations.[12]

African Americans in NPR

In the public radio sector as in commercial radio, African Americans slowly gained access to employment opportunities, but it was an uphill struggle. NPR's operations began in 1971, with the organization professing lofty goals that implicitly spoke to the special informational needs of minorities. The mission statement promised to "promote personal growth rather than corporate gain" and to "not only call attention to the problems, but be an active agent in seeking solutions." Yet, in its first two decades of spectacular growth—from a marginal, college-based educational radio network with ninety affiliates in thirty-two states and a weekly audience of just over 1 million listeners, to a national public radio network with 438 outlets in all the major urban markets and a listening audience of 7.3 million—NPR failed to incorporate African Americans into its master plan. NPR's own research indicated that the network's listeners were white, college-educated professionals and white-collar workers between the ages of thirty-five and fifty-six. Only seven of forty HBC stations were CPB qualified and NPR affiliated by the end of the 1980s. According to NPR's first black news director, Adam Clayton Powell III: "When I walked in here in July 1987, NPR had no—zero—minority hosts, correspondents, newscasters, directors, executive producers or senior editors."[13]

From the late 1980s through the 1990s, NPR's record has improved significantly, beginning with Powell initiating the network's first affirmative action program in the late 1980s. More recently, NPR's first black chief executive, Delano Lewis, has been the driving force behind increasing the number of minority employees to 30 percent of the network's total workforce. Lewis has also launched a new program called the "Initiative on Audience Development," which targets minorities and college students, and he has urged the CPB to channel more funds into noncommercial minority stations. But these initiatives come at a time when a hostile Congress is deeply cutting public broadcasting funds, reducing them from $312 million in 1995 to $260 million in 1997. Such major reductions may doom Lewis's new agenda for minorities in public radio.[14]

Black Community Radio

In addition to the forty-odd noncommercial HBC outlets in the public radio sector, a handful of nonprofit "community" radio stations on the air are run by and for African Americans. These mostly low-power and low-budget operations emerged as part of an alternative radio movement pioneered by the Pacifica network in the 1950s and institutionalized with the formation of the National Federation of Community Broadcasters (NFCB) in 1974. Community radio stations are owned and operated by nonprofit foundations, which, in turn, are controlled by a local board of directors. These outlets rely almost exclusively on listener donations for their economic livelihood and have tailored their organizational structures and program formats to meet the particular social and cultural needs of their communities. In spite of their structural differences, all NFCB stations are unified in striving to provide a vital alternative to commercial radio through encouraging innovative programming and grassroots community participation in their day-to-day operations. By the 1990s, 125 stations were affiliated with the NFCB; of that number, ten were controlled by African Americans.[15]

The first noncommercial black station to use a community radio model was WAFR-FM, a three thousand-watt outlet in Durham, North Carolina, that signed on the air in the summer of 1971. Its founders, an enterprising group of students from North Carolina Central University (NCCU) who had no previous experience in radio broadcasting, set up a nonprofit corporation—the Community Radio Workshop, Inc.—to apply for the broadcast license and solicit federal funds for the operation. WAFR, standing for "Wave AFRica," took an Afrocentric stance long before the concept became popular. The NCCU student founders, who also formed the core of the original staff, assumed African names for their airshifts as DJs: "Shango" (Donald Baker), "Brother Hussan" (Robert Spruill), "Baba" (Adewela Babafine), "Oba" (Obataiye Adinwole). The programming they created foregrounded the cultural and historical connections between African Americans and "the mother continent" by creating a progressive, free-form FM format that mixed the avant-garde jazz of John Coltrane, Miles Davis, Albert Ayler, and Sun Ra with the African sounds of Miriam Makeba, Olatunji, Fela Ransome Kuti, and Hugh

Masakela. Also in the mix was the militant jazz poetry of the Last Poets and short, drop-in "messages" from Malcolm X, Martin Luther King Jr., and Dick Gregory, as well as Frantz Fanon, Leopold Senghor, and Kwame Nkrumah. Nothing else sounded remotely like WAFR on the airwaves in the Durham radio market.[16]

In its first year, WAFR broadcast only twelve hours a day, with volunteer DJs hosting all of the station's airshifts. There was no news or public-affairs programming, but the DJs frequently varied their music shows with interviews of local black newsmakers and call-in listener commentary on current events. By 1973, the station's cadre of youthful leaders made some headway in recruiting local black activists and educators to help produce public-affairs shows. One new program, *Children's Radio Workshop,* which featured a group of youngsters and their instructors from a local black day-care center, was produced by childhood education specialist Mary McDonald and won a CPB award for innovative children's programming in 1974. A weekly roundup of African news called *Wave Africa* and a new series on African American history, *To Build a Nation,* hosted by NCCU history professor Earl Thorpe, expanded the public-affairs programming.[17]

A fall 1973 *Ebony* article praised WAFR-FM as a pioneering black community radio venture and spotlighted the young activists who had created it. The national publicity brought into the station a flood of inquiries and even visitors—some of whom, like soul superstar Stevie Wonder, jazz saxophonist Julian "Cannonball" Adderley, and DJ Frankie Crocker, were well-known celebrities. Stevie Wonder was so impressed by what he heard on WAFR that he agreed to do a benefit for the station. However, a car accident on the way prevented Wonder from appearing at the benefit, and the cancellation dashed the station's hopes for developing a major fundraising drive among its listeners. From the day that it signed on the air, WAFR had been dependent on CPB for a special yearly grant covering operating expenses. By 1974, CPB was becoming impatient with WAFR's failure to establish financial accountability or a local funding base. When CPB decided against renewing the public grant earmarked for WAFR for the 1975–76 fiscal year, the station could not survive. It went off the air in June 1975.[18]

The West Coast's first black-controlled community radio station, KPOO-FM, a ten-watt outlet in San Francisco, came to be known as "Poor People's Radio." White media activist Lorenzo Milam—the legendary

"Johnny Appleseed" of the community radio movement—and a small group of like-minded associates had launched several community-based public radio stations, mostly on the West Coast. They founded KPOO in 1972 to serve San Francisco's inner-city black population in the Fillmore District, but the station started out with a staff of white community radio activists allied with Milam. The conflicts that arose between the white staff and black volunteers came to a head in the mid-1970s. Protests by African American volunteers and listeners forced Milam and his allies to turn the station over to a board of directors controlled by the local black community. During the transition, most of the white staff was replaced. In the 1980s, KPOO broadened its target audience to include San Francisco's Latino, Asian, and Native American populations, in effect becoming the country's first multicultural public radio station. In the late 1990s, KPOO features music, news, public affairs, and cultural programs for the ethnic groups involved in the station, some of them in foreign languages. This diversity in the programming and workforce has created a broader base of community support for KPOO, which manages to survive on funds donated to the station by local listeners and benefactors.[19]

WRFG-FM, "Radio Free Georgia," a low-power and shoestring-budget operation, began broadcasting in Atlanta in the summer of 1973. Its evolution from a biracial community station to a black-controlled station was much like that of KPOO. The station was initially staffed by black and white activists who, as students, had been affiliated with SNCC and SDS (Students for a Democratic Society). Its location in the integrated low-income neighborhood of Little Five Points was well suited to its original format, which was created to appeal to a mixed local audience. The music shows featured jazz, blues, country, bluegrass, and both black and white gospel. The news and public-affairs programs emphasized issues of concern to Little Five Points residents. Having worked for the *Great Speckled Bird,* Atlanta's radical "underground" newspaper in the late 1960s and early 1970s, the core of the volunteer news staff were seasoned reporters, whose coverage of local politics and the city's police force translated into insightful investigative reporting. But WRFG's foothold in Little Five Points was still tenuous when the station's internal racial divisions, exacerbated by an undercover agent provocateur, drove it from the airwaves for a short period of time in the mid-1970s. When the station resumed its broadcasts, its programming was entirely oriented toward Atlanta's black community. Although the new focus pitted the station against the more powerful and better-endowed Clark College station, WCLK-FM, WRFG has survived as a listener-supported black community station with a progressive political and cultural format.[20]

In one of the rare instances of a rural black community radio venture, in Warren County, North Carolina, a nonprofit organization called Sound and Print United put WVSP-FM on the air in 1977, after four years of planning and fundraising. Broadcasting from the hamlet of Warrenton, with six paid staff members, the station used a format that emphasized jazz, blues, local news, and public affairs to target the county's large African American population, the most poverty-stricken group in the state. By 1982, crucial aid from the federal government enabled WVSP to expand its paid staff to sixteen. By this time, it had also developed a cadre of nearly fifty volunteers and had a sizable rural black audience. The audience and the volunteers were especially attracted to the station's cultural orientation and its active involvement in community issues, such as a grassroots campaign to prevent the dumping of toxic waste in the county. When the Reagan administration cut back funding, WVSP sharply reduced its paid staff; its survival now depended on the community. But the low income levels among African Americans in Warren County and the novelty of a rural black station trying to operate noncommercially were obstacles to building a listener funding base. As a result, in 1984, WVSP moved to the more populous city of Rocky Mount in adjacent Nash County, desperately hoping to attract new listeners and financial support from the middle-class African Americans living in that locale while retaining its Warren County audience. Factions developed among the staff, and several leadership changes failed to improve the management of the station's finances. Within two years of the move, WVSP went off the air permanently.[21]

The demise of stations like WVSP and WAFR largely resulted from the structural limitations of black-controlled community radio ventures in the public sector. Community stations rely not only on local volunteer programmers but also on local funding, usually listener donations. Black community stations that target low-income African American populations like the rural poor or inner-city youth enter a no-win situation. Because they seek to engage and empower an audience that lacks the means to offer them financial support, their livelihood must come from other sources. The CPB had provided both WVSP and WAFR with seed money and annual funds to help with operating expenses, but when the grants dried up, neither station could develop alternative sources of funding. Since the 1970s, black community stations generally have found themselves in the same financial cul de sac, with no visible route to increasing their numbers or individual strength.

The country's largest black community radio station is WPFW-FM, a fifty thousand-watt outlet launched in the nation's capital in 1977 by the Pacifica network after a ten-year legal battle for the market's last noncommercial frequency. Pacifica pioneered the community radio movement with the founding of KPFA-FM in Berkeley, California, in 1949. The nonprofit foundation gradually broadened its reach, establishing stations in Los Angeles (KPFK-FM, 1959), New York City (WBAI-FM, 1960), and Houston (KPFT-FM, 1970). While Pacifica has always sought to involve African Americans and other minorities in its programming and operations, WPFW was the first station in the nonprofit radio network to be built and controlled from the ground up by African Americans. The station's mandate to serve the majority (70 percent) black population in Washington, D.C., focused its recruitment of leadership and on-air talent on the local citizenry. WPFW's board of directors also drew on African American community and media activists living in the area.[22]

WPFW signed on the air with hometown composer Duke Ellington's classic "Take the A Train," performed live from a downtown jazz club. Its music format, "Jazz and Jazz Extensions," filled the void created in the mid-1970s when WHUR-FM abandoned its jazz format in pursuit of higher ratings. In addition to in-depth excursions into jazz history and promotion of the local jazz scene, the station also featured regular blues, oldies, salsa, Caribbean, Brazilian, and African musical shows. WPFW's news and public-affairs format stressed local, national, and international issues of concern to the black community. Weekly programs with a political focus on the criminal justice system, the city government, the local labor movement, the Congressional Black Caucus, Africa, Latin America, and the Caribbean combined with cultural shows for children, teens, women, and senior citizens, as well as a poetry and a comedy program. Moreover, in the station's broad selection of offerings, WPFW devoted special days of programming to in-depth explorations of the music of such jazz greats as Duke Ellington, Louis Armstrong, Billie Holiday, and Charlie Parker or to the significance of such black leaders as Martin Luther King Jr. and Malcolm X. The same day-long, in-depth approach was used to explore social issues ranging from local drug abuse to apartheid in South Africa.[23]

During the 1980s, WPFW's innovative format attracted the largest black public radio audience in the country, but listener financial support developed only slowly. The station, being CPB qualified, received about 20 percent of its $400,000 annual budget from the federal government; the rest came from listener donations and the Pacifica network, which kept WPFW out of debt with a critical yearly infusion of money. Organizational instability was an ongoing problem. In the 1980s, WPFW weathered five leadership changes, three changes of address, and a license challenge by a right-wing media watchdog group. It also managed to survive the competition from a new jazz-formatted noncommercial FM station, the University of the District of Columbia's WDCU-FM, which signed on the air in 1983. The cadre of one hundred volunteers, who have remained fairly stable over the years, has given WPFW and its sound a measure of continuity that, more than anything else, has enabled it to endure.[24]

WPFW has gone through four more leadership changes and another change of address during the late 1980s and early 1990s. At one point, it was about to shut down because of its mounting debts. Currently, however, the station seems to be on the rise again; its streamlined format and fundraising drives have boosted listener ratings and contributions to the station. After two decades of struggle, WPFW has entered a period of financial and organizational equilibrium.[25] As we have seen, however, the environment for such stations is unstable, and none can become complacent about its long-term survival.

Sold to the Highest Bidder

From the 1970s through the 1990s, African Americans have made noticeable gains in the public radio sector of the broadcast industry. In 1967, only two small black-owned noncommercial stations existed. Both were located outside the major urban markets, and their audience was minuscule. By the mid-1990s, more than fifty noncommercial black college and community stations (about 2.5 percent of the total number of noncommercial outlets on the air) are reaching millions of listeners in numerous urban markets, especially in the South. In addition, from the late 1980s into the 1990s, the number of African Americans employed by NPR has grown significantly, as have the number of NPR-funded programs and series devoted to black subjects; and NPR has recently hired Delano Lewis as its first black chief executive officer.

Nevertheless, the outlook for African Americans in public radio is far from rosy. Recent federal cuts in public radio's annual funding levels have reduced its ability to meet commitments to minority broadcasters and audiences. If the federal cutbacks continue, CPB-qualified stations could lose their annual government subsidies. This would be particularly difficult for the black-owned stations receiving CPB grants, given their history of financial struggles. Moreover, the fallout from the FCC's deregulation of commercial radio ownership is beginning to have an impact on the sale of noncommercial stations. This troublesome new development recently came to light in the furor surrounding the sale of WDCU-FM in the nation's capital.

The station was put up for sale in 1997 because its owner, the University of the District of Columbia (UDC)—a predominantly black public college, governed by Washington's recently appointed financial control board—was ordered to close a $10.1 million budget deficit. At the time, WDCU-FM's jazz format was attracting the fourth-largest black audience in public radio, and the station was close to being financially self-sufficient; it was put on the market only when its value was found to be much higher than expected. There were seven first-round bids for the station, beginning at $1 million. Among those bidding were religious broadcasters, public interest groups, C-SPAN (the cable TV public-affairs service), and a coalition of local public stations (WETA-FM, WAMU-FM) and NPR. A second and final round of bidding began at $10 million. The winning bid of $13 million was made by Salem Communications, a religious broadcasting corporation.[26]

Salem Communications is a relatively new enterprise that owns a chain of forty-two (mostly commercial) stations nationwide. Its assets also include a syndicated news service, Salem Radio News (SRN), and *The Oliver North Show,* hosted by the former marine colonel of Iran-Contra notoriety. Salem's corporate format mixes evangelical preachers, who pay for their airtime, with conservative talk-show hosts like North and SRN's decidedly right-wing Christian slant on the news. This format is used on its commercial and noncommercial outlets; the only difference between them is that the commercial outlets also run advertising spots. Salem's nonprofit arm, the Community Resource Education Association, was set up to run its noncommercial stations. It was to become the legal owner of WDCU's license once the sale was approved by the FCC.[27]

WDCU-FM's $13 million price tag sent shock waves throughout the public radio sector. In an urgent memo to public radio executives, WETA-FM program director Craig Curtis predicted: "This sale dramatically changes life below 92 FM [the noncommercial frequency band]. It represents the loss of a major public radio frequency in a large and important market, allows a commercial business to operate de facto in the noncommercial band, and it establishes a benchmark price that may tempt other non-commercial license holders, especially in times of financial crisis." Public broadcasting leaders loudly protested the sale. Robert Conrad, CPB's chief operating officer, made public a letter to the city's financial control board, condemning the transaction and demanding that CPB be reimbursed the $1 million it had invested in WDCU. NPR president Delano Lewis urged the control board to reconsider selling the station and filed a petition with the FCC to block the approval of the license transfer, as did a listener support group called "Save Jazz 90."[28]

The public outcry, the local press coverage, and the public radio establishment's threat to hold up the purchase of the station at the FCC ultimately forced Salem Communications to back out of the deal. At the last minute, Salem turned the contract over to C-SPAN, which then proceeded to purchase WDCU-FM for the agreed-upon $13 million. The sale was approved by the FCC in September; there was much gloom but little opposition to the takeover by this more "neutral" public broadcasting entity. "Jazz 90" signed off the air at midnight on September 26, 1997. Two weeks later, WCSP-FM signed on in its place, with a public-affairs format based on C-SPAN's congressional coverage.[29]

Afterword:
Talking Drums

> The Ashanti okyerema (court drummer) is the actual symbol
> of knowledge and wisdom. During court cases he drums out
> counsel and recommendations.[1]
>
> —John Collins

For the last half century, black radio outlets throughout the United States have been the "talking drums" of their respective communities. This traditional West African means of communication, which uses "tonal" drums to reproduce the region's "tonal" languages, has always played a pivotal role in sustaining the oral traditions and expressive cultures thriving in the area. Historically, West African talking drums have been used to interpret the law, pay tribute to the deities, venerate the ancestors, praise royalty, promote kinship, pass on social customs, celebrate cultural events, comment on current events, document the past, and regulate the tribal cycle of life. The drummers who mastered this difficult art form were not only superior musicians but also accomplished storytellers, historians, poets, and sages. They were, in effect, the living repositories of West African history, thought, and culture.[2]

Centuries later, in urban America, black radio resonates as an electronic reconfiguration of the talking drum tradition. For most African Americans, it is their primary source of music, news, information, and commentary on a daily basis. At the hub of this cultural enterprise are the black radio broadcasters who assemble and send the messages—much like their ancestral precursors, the master drummers. Certainly the times, technology, and locales are vastly different, suggesting at first glance that such linkages are suspect. But a closer look reveals some noteworthy threads of cultural continuity between talking drums and black radio. These are especially evident in the similar communication strategies they employ to privilege oral traditions.

One of the major similarities coalesces around an emphasis on locality. Tradition and technology limited the talking drums to a village or a court of royalty and their respective inhabitants. Likewise, black radio outlets tend to target a specific locale and constituency, and for the most part, they are based in that community. This convergence of culture and communications medium at the local level was no doubt the norm in traditional West African societies, but it is rather novel in contemporary America, where the dominant corporate media and entertainment industries promote mass consumption, not grassroots communication. Yet, over the years, black radio has continued to maintain a local identity and orientation, even if profit margins suffered as a result. To be sure, the balancing of market and community concerns sometimes favored profitability, but in general, black radio has always been rooted in locality—a predisposition that does not correspond with the prevailing trends toward ownership consolidation and program syndication in the radio industry. This disparity suggests that the cultural traditions associated with black radio are at least as influential as market forces in determining its local character.

Another affinity between these two modes of communication is their ubiquity. Like the talking drums in West African social life, black radio is present everywhere in the lives of most African Americans. Whether in the home, workplace, or car, it provides the soundtrack for their daily routines and rituals. While radio technology creates the potential for this sort of media saturation, cultural practices determine how the technology is put to use. Studies as far back as the late 1940s have shown that African Americans tend to listen to more radio than their white counterparts, and they tune in to black-identified outlets almost exclusively.[3] The persistence of these listening patterns underscores black radio's importance as a constant source of information and entertainment for African Americans.

The final thread of cultural continuity between talking drums and black radio can be found in the multidimensionality of their communication efforts. Just as the drumming speaks to all aspects of West African life, black radio broadcasts foreground a broad range of African American interests and concerns; they are a montage of many black voices. As the launching pad for a host of styles of music, language, identity, gossip, fashion, personality, business, politics, and religion, black radio plays a key role in meeting a wide variety of social needs. Over the past fifty years, it has been instrumental in creating and sustaining a black public sphere, where these self-expressions are constructed and challenged. From WDIA's pioneering "Negro appeal" broadcasts in the late 1940s to KJLH's around-the-clock coverage of the Los Angeles riots in the early 1990s, black radio has been a critical sounding board for African Americans, especially in times of crisis.

The assertion that black radio is an integral part of an evolving African American public sphere is based on the historical trends and conflicts chronicled in this book. Black music's growth in popularity since World War II, for example, has been greatly enhanced by black radio's promotion and exposure of African American recordings. From rhythm and blues to rap, it has been responsible for breaking hit records and showcasing new talent throughout the country. Throughout its history, as it developed, black radio disc jockeys emerged as local celebrities and trendsetters, bringing their distinctive personality traits and vernacular styles to the forefront of the debates over black identity taking place in the popular culture. Like many African American musicians, black DJs had a cultural impact that went well beyond the color line—as is evident in the host of imitators they spawned. But more important, they were public figures and opinion makers in their respective communities. As such, African American disc jockeys not only fostered new musical trends but also used their access to the airwaves to shape the course of black civil society at the grass roots.

Since the civil rights era, black radio has been a major site for political dialogue and debate. It has also been used to mobilize African Americans for political action. This dual function has served to create an African American political "grapevine" that is capable of linking local constituencies to a local station, which itself is connected to an informal network of black radio outlets around the country. The original black radio grapevine was organized by African American DJs for the civil rights movement; at the time, they were responsible for most of what went out over the air as news and public affairs. In the 1980s and 1990s especially, black DJs have lost much of their political autonomy, but the vacuum has been filled by the increasing number of African American newscasters and talk-show hosts. These radio broadcasters continue to debate the current political issues and mobilize African Americans around specific concerns or projects. From the Million Man March to the CIA/crack cocaine controversy, they have been instrumental in sustaining black radio's presence in the political discourse on race.

Efforts of this nature did not go uncontested; they clashed with the racial orthodoxy of the dominant white media, and they were constrained by black radio's marginal status in the broadcast industry. Lacking a strong ownership base and a fair share of the advertising revenue, African American radio broadcasters have always faced an uphill economic struggle. This has impeded their efforts to grow as an enterprise, and it has compelled them to organize in order to defend and further their own interests. Toward that end, black radio entrepreneurs and activists have formed their own corporations, networks, trade associations, unions, and advocacy groups, in an ongoing effort to overcome racial barriers and maintain a foothold in the industry. But because of these obstacles, African American gains in ownership, market shares, and employment opportunities have been slow in coming. Resistance to change has been commonplace on all of these fronts.

As the new millennium approaches, black radio continues to face a number of formidable challenges that threaten its livelihood. The industry's recent move toward digital technology works in the favor of the larger, white-owned media conglomerates. They are in a much better position to pay the cost of conversion to the new technology than are the smaller, black-owned enterprises. This could prove a serious disadvantage. The FCC's deregulation of the radio industry is beginning to have a negative impact on African American ownership. For the first time ever, black-owned stations are declining numerically. Furthermore, ownership consolidation in the industry is undermining the commercial potential of independently owned black outlets; when it comes to attracting advertisers, they are finding it hard to compete with the new radio "superduopolies" springing up in urban markets. Advertising concerns also sparked the "urban contemporary" crossover trend in black radio formatting, which is still a bone of contention among African American broadcasters and listeners. On the one hand, market forces encourage the continuation of this profitable crossover strategy. On the other hand, the defenders of black-identified radio and personality jocks resist such format changes.

These struggles over the future of black radio are further complicated by the recent demographic shifts in the African American population.

Afterword: Talking Drums

Over the past three decades, the rise of a relatively prosperous black middle class has coincided, for the most part, with their flight to the suburbs. Simultaneously, the African American majority still living in the inner-city ghettos has experienced economic and social decline. This fracturing of the black community along class lines is compounded by a growing generation gap brought on by the rise of hip-hop culture among African American youth. In response to these internal divisions, black radio has pursued a strategy of format segmentation, based on age and income levels. The all-purpose, community-oriented station is fast becoming a relic.

From digital technology to demographic fragmentation, new developments are constantly reconfiguring the playing field for African Americans involved in the radio industry. They will need expertise, savvy, and an innovative game plan to take advantage of these changes while maintaining their current base of operations. The task is large and the stakes are high. But to their credit, black radio broadcasters have weathered many crises in their long struggle for racial equality, freedom of expression, and self-sufficiency. Against great odds, they have made radio a centerpiece of African American life. This resilience in the face of adversity offers some hope that black radio will remain an independent and progressive voice in the local community, the industry, and the society as a whole.

Notes

Notes to the Preface

1. William Barlow, *Looking Up at Down: The Emergence of Blues Culture* (Philadelphia: Temple University Press, 1989).
2. Jannett Dates and William Barlow, eds., *Split Image: African Americans in the Mass Media*, 2d ed. (Washington, D.C.: Howard University Press, 1993).
3. See Erik Barnouw, *A Tower in Babel: A History of Broadcasting in the United States*, vol. 1: *To 1933* (New York: Oxford University Press, 1966), and *The Golden Web: A History of Broadcasting in the United States*, vol. 2: *1933–1953* (New York: Oxford University Press, 1968).

Notes to the Introduction

1. As quoted in Henry Louis Gates, *The Signifying Monkey: A Theory of Afro-American Literary Criticism* (New York: Oxford University Press, 1988), 1.
2. Mel Watkins, *On the Real Side* (New York: Simon & Schuster, 1994), 271.
3. Susan Gubar, *Racechanges: White Skin, Black Face in American Culture* (New York: Oxford University Press, 1997), 5.
4. Gilbert Osofsky, ed., *Puttin' on Ole Massa* (New York: Harper & Row, 1967), 21–24. Also see Lawrence Levine, *Black Culture and Black Consciousness* (New York: Oxford University Press, 1977); B. A. Botkin, ed., *Lay My Burden Down: A Folk History* (Chicago: University of Chicago Press, 1945); Henning Cohen, "A Negro 'Folk Game' in Colonial South Carolina," *Southern Folklore Quarterly* 16 (1952): 183–84.
5. Joseph Boskin, *Sambo: The Rise and Demise of an American Jester* (New York: Oxford University Press, 1984), 36, 72.
6. Eric Lott, "Blackface and Blackness: The Minstrel Show in American Culture," in A. Bean, J. Hatch, and B. McNamara, eds., *Inside the Minstrel Mask: Readings in Nineteenth Century Blackface Minstrelsy* (Hanover, N.H.: Wesleyan University Press, 1996), 11.

7. Barbara Lewis, "Daddy Blue: The Evolution of a Dark Dandy," in Bean, Hatch, and McNamara, eds., *Inside the Minstrel Mask,* 268.
8. Alexander Saxon, "Blackface Minstrelsy," in Bean, Hatch, and McNamara, eds., *Inside the Minstrel Mask,* 72.
9. Hans Nathan, "The Performance of the Virginia Minstrels," in Bean, Hatch, and McNamara, eds., *Inside the Minstrel Mask,* 40. See also Sterling Brown, Arthur Davis, and Ulysses Lee, eds., *The Negro Caravan* (New York: Dryden Press, 1941), 574.
10. Boskin, *Sambo,* 80.
11. Ibid., 14.
12. Mark Twain, *The Autobiography of Mark Twain* (New York: Harper & Brothers, 1959), 59–61; Frederick Douglass, *North Star,* Oct. 27, 1848.
13. Eric Lott, *Love and Theft: Blackface Minstrelsy and the American Working Class* (New York: Oxford University Press, 1993), 18.
14. Robert Toll, *Blacking Up: The Minstrel Show in Nineteenth Century America* (New York: Oxford University Press, 1974), 92, 134–54.
15. Gaines M. Foster, *Ghosts of the Confederacy: Defeat, the Lost Cause and the Emergence of the New South* (New York: Oxford University Press, 1987), 110–19, 140, 194.
16. Toll, *Blacking Up,* 195–210.
17. Ibid., 215–29. Also see Ann Charters, *Nobody: The Story of Bert Williams* (New York: Macmillan, 1970); Lewis Bland, "James Bland, Negro Composer: A Study of His Life and Work" (M. A. thesis, Howard University, 1958).

Notes to Chapter 1

1. See Florette Henri, *Black Migration: Movement North 1900–1920* (Garden City, N.Y.: Anchor Books, 1976), 25–160, 269–321; Charles Johnson, "The Negro Migration: An Economic Interpretation," *Modern Quarterly* 14 (1934): 314–25; John Hope Franklin, *From Slavery to Freedom: A History of Negro Americans* (New York: Vintage Books, 1969), 399–487; Allan Spear, *Black Chicago: The Making of a Negro Ghetto, 1890–1920* (Chicago: University of Chicago Press, 1967), 81–82, 114–15, 225–28.
2. See Langston Hughes and Milton Meltzer, *Black Magic: A Pictorial History of Black Entertainers in America* (Englewood Cliffs, N.J.: Prentice-Hall, 1967), 66–70; Daphne Duval Harrison, *Black Pearls: Blues Queens of the 1920s* (New Brunswick, N.J.: Rutgers University Press, 1988), 17–41.
3. David Ewen, *All the Years of American Popular Music* (Englewood Cliffs, N.J.: Prentice-Hall, 1977), 186–87.
4. Ronald G. Foreman Jr., "Jazz and Race Records, 1920–1932: Their Origins and Their Significance for the Record Industry" (Ph.D. diss., University of Illinois, Chicago, 1972), 92–97.
5. Jeff Titon, *Early Downhome Blues* (Urbana: University of Illinois Press, 1977), 205; Robert Dixon and John Godrich, *Recording the Blues* (New York: Stein & Day, 1980), 19–23.
6. Census figures on radio cited in *The Chicago Daily News Almanac and Yearbook* (Chicago, 1934), 306.
7. Erik Barnouw, *A Tower in Babel: A History of Broadcasting in the United States,* vol. 1: *To 1933* (New York: Oxford University Press, 1966), 119–21.
8. Ibid. 126–28. Also see Gunnar Myrdal, *An American Dilemma* (New York: Harper & Brothers, 1944), 330.
9. Barnouw, *Tower in Babel,* 87, 90, 131, 190.
10. Stanley Dance, *The World of Earl Hines* (New York: Charles Scribner's Sons, 1977), 134.

11. *Chicago Defender,* 16 Sept. 1922, 8; Chris Albertson, *Bessie* (New York: Stein & Day, 1972), 69.

12. William Randell Jr., "Black Entertainers on Radio, 1920–1930," *Black Perspective in Music* (Spring 1977): 67–74.

13. James Lincoln Collier, *Duke Ellington* (New York: Oxford University Press, 1987), 193–94.

14. "Social Progress Column," *Opportunity,* no. 6 (July 1928): 218; *New York Herald Tribune,* 10 Sept. 1930, 8.

15. Randel, "Black Entertainers on Radio," 70–73; Norman Spaulding, "History of Black Oriented Radio in Chicago, 1929–1963" (Ph.D. diss., University of Illinois, Urbana, 1981), 32–33.

16. Spaulding, "History of Black Oriented Radio," 24, 33–34, 71–78.

17. Randel, "Black Entertainers on Radio," 71.

18. Barnouw, *Tower in Babel,* 276–84; Robert McChesney, *Telecommunications, Mass Media and Democracy: The Battle for Control of U.S. Broadcasting, 1928–1935* (New York: Oxford University Press, 1994), 29.

19. McChesney, *Telecommunications,* 30–31.

20. Estelle Edmerson, "A Descriptive Study of the American Negro in U.S. Professional Radio, 1922–1955" (M.A. thesis, University of California, Los Angeles, 1954), 122–23, 125, 133, 206.

21. Ibid., 354.

22. J. Fred MacDonald, *Don't Touch That Dial: Radio Programming in American Life from 1920 to 1960* (Chicago: Nelson Hall, 1970), 344–45; Joseph Boskin, *Sambo: The Rise and Demise of an American Jester* (New York: Oxford University Press, 1984), 139–140.

23. Boskin, *Sambo,* 201; MacDonald, *Don't Touch That Dial,* 350. Hattie McDaniel quote in the film documentary *Black Shadows on a Silver Screen* (New York: Post-Newsweek Productions Inc., 1975)

24. Cab Calloway, *Of Minnie the Moocher and Me* (New York: Thomas Crowell, 1976); 180. MacDonald, *Don't Touch That Dial,* 330, 335. Also see James Lincoln Collier, *Louis Armstrong: An American Genius* (New York: Oxford University Press, 1983).

25. Edmerson, "Descriptive Study of the American Negro," 28, 30, 39, 42, 67.

26. Boskin, *Sambo,* 179.

27. Edmerson, "Descriptive Study of the American Negro," 76–77.

28. MacDonald, *Don't Touch That Dial,* 288–89.

29. The Scottsboro Boys were nine young African American males who were tried and convicted of raping two white women in Scottsboro, Alabama, in 1934, and then sentenced to death. Kaltenborn provoked a public outcry from state officials when he asserted in a CBS commentary that the defendants could not get a fair trial in Alabama, and that therefore the trial should be moved elsewhere. See MacDonald, *Don't Touch That Dial,* 293.

30. *Chicago Defender,* 16 Feb. 1938, 15.

31. MacDonald, *Don't Touch That Dial,* 337. Also see George G. Daniels, ed., *The Swing Era: The Golden Age of Network Radio* (New York Time-Life, 1971).

Notes to Chapter 2

1. Melvin Patrick Ely, *The Adventures of Amos 'n' Andy: A Social History of an American Phenomenon* (New York: Free Press, 1991), 14–17.

2. Ibid., 23–31.

3. Ibid., 36–38.

4. Ibid., 11–14, 31–32, 36–38.

5. Ibid., 54.

6. Ibid., 95. Also see Al Rose, *Eubie Blake* (New York: Macmillan, 1979), 107.
7. Mel Watkins, *On the Real Side* (New York: Simon & Schuster, 1994), 221–23.
8. Ibid., 273.
9. Ely, *Adventures of Amos 'n' Andy,* 55–60.
10. See Freeman Gosden and Charles Correll, *All about Amos 'n' Andy and Their Creators Gosden and Correll* (New York: Rand McNally, 1929).
11. Erik Barnouw, *A Tower in Babel: A History of Broadcasting in The United States,* vol. 1: *To 1933* (New York: Oxford University Press, 1966), 229–31; J. Fred MacDonald, *Don't Touch That Dial: Radio Programming in American Life from 1920 to 1960* (Chicago: Nelson Hall, 1970), 113, 342.
12. MacDonald, *Don't Touch That Dial,* 344; Ely, *Adventures of Amos 'n' Andy,* 131; Joseph Boskin, *Sambo: The Rise and Demise of an American Jester* (New York: Oxford University Press, 1984), 165–67.
13. Ely, *Adventures of Amos 'n' Andy,* 163, 173. Also see Arnold Shankman, "Black Pride and Protest: The Amos 'n' Andy Crusade," *Journal of Popular Culture* 12, 2 (fall 1979): 245.
14. Ely, *Adventures of Amos 'n' Andy,* 171–73. Pittsburgh *Courier*'s *Amos 'n' Andy* petition, press clippings file, Schomberg Center for Research in Black Culture, New York City.
15. Shankman, "Black Pride and Protest," 246–47; Ely, *Adventures of Amos 'n' Andy,* 174.
16. Shankman, "Black Pride and Protest," 241.
17. Ely, *Adventures of Amos 'n' Andy,* 163, 167–68, 175, 177.
18. Watkins, *On the Real Side,* 277–78.
19. Ibid., 279.
20. Ibid., 280.
21. Al Raglin, quote from interview by Sonja Williams, for *Black Radio: Telling It Like It Was* (Washington, D.C.: Smithsonian Institution, 1996).
22. James Fly, quoted in Erik Barnouw, *The Golden Web: A History of Broadcasting in the United States,* vol. 2: *1933 to 1953* (New York: Oxford University Press, 1968), 173.
23. Woodrow Wilson, quoted in Watkins, *On the Real Side,* 190.

Notes to Chapter 3

1. Mark Newman, *Entrepreneurs of Profit and Pride: From Black Appeal to Radio Soul* (New York: Praeger, 1988), 57–58.
2. Ibid., 58–59; Norman Spaulding, "History of Black Oriented Radio in Chicago, 1929–1963" (Ph.D. diss., University of Illinois, Urbana, 1981), 71.
3. Newman, *Entrepreneurs of Profit and Pride,* 59.
4. Ibid., 64.
5. Ibid., 62, 67. Also see Arnold Passman, "Introductory Draft of the Life of the First Black DJ"(unpublished manuscript, Berkeley, California, 1986).
6. Newman, *Entrepreneurs of Profit and Pride,* 62–64.
7. Ibid., 65.
8. Ibid., 66–67. Passman, "Life of the First Black DJ."
9. Newman, *Entrepreneurs of Profit and Pride,* 60, 69–73.
10. Ibid., 67.
11. Spaulding, "History of Black Oriented Radio," 72.
12. Ibid., 72; Newman, *Entrepreneurs of Profit and Pride,* 67–68.
13. Newman, *Entrepreneurs of Profit and Pride,* 75; Spaulding, "History of Black Oriented Radio," 74–75.
14. Spaulding, "History of Black Oriented Radio," 72; Newman, *Entrepreneurs of Profit and Pride,* 68.
15. Newman, *Entrepreneurs of Profit and Pride,* 68–69; Spaulding, "History of Black Oriented Radio," 72.

16. "Negro Disc Jockeys," *Ebony*, Chicago, ed. (December 1947): 44–49.
17. John Latouche and Earl Robinson, "Ballad for Americans" (New York: Robbins Music Corporation, 1939). Used by permission.
18. Martin Duberman, *Paul Robeson: A Biography* (New York: Alfred A. Knopf, 1989), 236–37.
19. J. Fred MacDonald, *Don't Touch That Dial: Radio Programming in American Life from 1920 to 1960* (Chicago: Nelson Hall, 1970), 328.
20. Duberman, *Paul Robeson*, 240, 243; MacDonald, *Don't Touch That Dial*, 347.
21. Duberman, *Paul Robeson*, 255.
22. *Saturday Night Bondwagon*, January 29, 1944 (Mutual Broadcasting System network origination); Duberman, *Paul Robeson*, 254; MacDonald, *Don't Touch That Dial*, 348.
23. *Word from the People*, April 24, 1945 (CBS network origination). A year later, Robeson was on hand to pay tribute to his collaborator on the occasion of Corwin receiving the prestigious Wendell Wilkie One World Award. In his speech to the gathering, which was carried live on CBS, Robeson praised the radio producer's work on behalf of the United Nations and world peace. See *One World Award Programs*, March 31, 1945 (CBS Pacific network origination).
24. Duberman, *Paul Robeson*, 324–34.
25. Ibid., 341–62.
26. Ibid., 364–73, 403.
27. Ibid., 384–85.

Notes to Chapter 4

1. John Hope Franklin, *From Slavery to Freedom: A History of Negro Americans* (New York: Vintage Books, 1969), 578–79.
2. Erik Barnouw, *The Golden Web: A History of Broadcasting in the United States,* vol. 2: *1933–1953* (New York: Oxford University Press, 1968), 7–9, 53–54, 143–45; Giuliana Muscio, *Hollywood's New Deal* (Philadelphia: Temple University Press, 1997), 30–33.
3. Barnouw, *Golden Web*, 159–60, 190–92.
4. Ibid., 196; J. Fred MacDonald, *Don't Touch That Dial: Radio Programming in American Life from 1920 to 1960* (Chicago: Nelson Hall, 1970), 348.
5. Estelle Edmerson, "A Descriptive Study of the American Negro in U.S. Professional Radio, 1922–1955" (M. A. Thesis, University of California, Los Angeles, 1954), 174; *Freedom's People,* December 17, 1941 (Federal Radio Education Committee syndication, NBC network origination); press release, U.S. Office of Education, Washington, D.C., December 17, 1941.
6. Barnouw, *Golden Web*, 180, 192.
7. Franklin, *From Slavery to Freedom*, 597–98.
8. William Robson, interviewed by John Hickman on *Recollections*, WMCA (New York City), August 13, 1945.
9. William Robson, *Open Letter on Race Hatred*, in *Radio Drama in Action*, ed. Erik Barnouw (New York: Farrar, Straus & Co., 1945), 70.
10. Ibid., 76–77.
11. Barnouw, *Golden Web*, 181.
12. MacDonald, *Don't Touch That Dial*, 353–54.
13. Ibid., 349, 353; Barnouw, *Golden Web*, 162–63, 296.
14. Barnouw, *Golden Web*, 160.
15. Ibid., 195.
16. *The Mildred Bailey Show*, 1943 (AFRS origination); 1944–1945 (CBS network origination).

17. *Jubilee,* 1942–1948 (AFRS origination).

18. *Jubilee,* August 7, 1943, program #59 (AFRS origination).

19. MacDonald, *Don't Touch That Dial,* 349, 352.

20. Barnouw, *Golden Web,* 196–97.

21. *Chicago Defender,* 15 Sept. 1948, 14; MacDonald, *Don't Touch That Dial,* 357, 359–60; *Variety* (19 June 1946): 23.

22. *Chicago Defender,* 13 May 1946, 13.

23. Barnouw, *Golden Web,* 269–71, 280–81.

24. Ibid., 266.

25. *Daily Worker,* 29 June 1949, 9.

26. *Variety* (13 July 1949): 13; *Afro-American,* 16 July 1949, 7.

27. *New World a-Coming,* 1944–1957 (WMCA [New York City] origination).

28. Roi Ottley, "The Story of Negro Music," on *New World a-Coming,* WMCA (New York City), October 14, 1946.

29. Roi Ottley, "The Story of the Vermont Experiment," on *New World a-Coming,* WMCA (New York City), November 16, 1946.

30. Roi Ottley, "Negroes in the Entertainment Industry," on *New World a-Coming,* WMCA (New York City), February 25, 1947.

31. Dorothy Parker, "Arrangements in Black and White," adapted for radio by Roi Ottley, on *New World a-Coming,* WMCA (New York City), May 8, 1946.

32. Roi Ottley, "The Mammy Legend," on *New World a-Coming,* WMCA (New York City), March 12, 1947.

33. "Tribute to Canada Lee," on *New World a-Coming,* WMCA (New York City), February 10, 1945.

34. Ibid.

35. Richard Durham, interview by the author, October 1981. Also see J. Fred MacDonald, "Radio's Black Heritage: *Destination Freedom,* 1948–1950," *Phylon* 39, 1 (March 1987): 66–73.

36. MacDonald, "Radio's Black Heritage," 70, 72.

37. Ibid., 69.

38. Richard Durham, "The Story of Denmark Vesey," on *Destination Freedom,* WMAQ (Chicago), July 18, 1948.

39. Richard Durham, "Truth Goes to Washington," on *Destination Freedom,* WMAQ (Chicago), August 15, 1948.

40. Richard Durham, "The Long Road," on *Destination Freedom,* WMAQ (Chicago), August 7, 1949.

41. Hugh Cordier, "A History and Analysis of *Destination Freedom*" (M. A. thesis, Northwestern University, 1950), 25.

42. Ibid., 5

43. Ibid., 27.

44. Ibid., 28–30.

Notes to Chapter 5

1. Norman Spaulding, "History of Black Oriented Radio in Chicago, 1929–1963." (Ph.D. diss., University of Illinois, Urbana, 1981), 76–77.

2. "Negro Disc Jockeys," *Ebony* (December 1947): 44–49.

3. *Broadcast Magazine,* July 1, 1937, 18. Also see J. Fred MacDonald, *Don't Touch That Dial: Radio Programming in American Life from 1920 to 1960* (Chicago: Nelson Hall, 1970), 365–66.

4. Hal Jackson, interview by Sonja Williams, April 11, 1995, New York City, for *Black Radio: Telling It like It Was* (Washington, D.C.: Smithsonian Institution, 1996), 5–6.

5. Ibid., 6–7, 11–12.

6. Robert Palmer, *Deep Blues* (New York: Viking Press, 1981), 173–98. Also see William Barlow, *Looking Up at Down* (Philadelphia: Temple University Press, 1989), 330–31.

7. Palmer, *Deep Blues*, 94–97.

8. U.S. Bureau of Census, *The Statistical Abstract of the United States* (Washington, D.C.: Government Printing Office, 1969), 21–24; John Hope Franklin, *From Slavery to Freedom: A History of Negro Americans* (New York: Vintage Books, 1969), 597; "Negro Disc Jockeys," 44; "The Forgotten 15,000,000," *Sponsor* (10 October 1949): 55.

9. Mark Newman, *Entrepreneurs of Profit and Pride: From Black Appeal to Radio Soul* (New York: Praeger, 1988), 82–83; Spaulding, "History of Black Oriented Radio," 78–79.

10. Spaulding, "History of Black Oriented Radio," 79–80, 127.

11. Ibid., 79; Newman, *Entrepreneurs of Profit and Pride*, 83; Sid McCoy, interview by Sonja Williams, November 1995, Chicago, for *Black Radio: Telling It like It Was*, 7.

12. Spaulding, "History of Black Oriented Radio," 82.

13. Newman, *Entrepreneurs of Profit and Pride*, 83–84; Lucky Cordell, interview by Lex Gillespie, September 1995, Chicago, for *Black Radio: Telling It like It Was*, 33.

14. Spaulding, "History of Black Oriented Radio," 118.

15. Newman, *Entrepreneurs of Profit and Pride*, 84.

16. Spaulding, "History of Black Oriented Radio," 80, 127.

17. Ibid., 81. Also see "Rites Set for Al Benson, Black Broadcasting Pioneer," *Chicago Tribune*, 8 Sept. 1978, C5.

18. Spaulding, "History of Black Oriented Radio," 83–99.

19. "Negro Disc Jockeys," 44; "Forgotten 15,000,000," 25, 54; "The Bluest Voice on the Delta," *Washington Post*, 19 Aug. 1988, C1, C4–5.

20. Cited in Mel Watkins, *On the Real Side* (New York: Simon & Schuster, 1994), 64.

21. Sid McCoy interview, 8.

22. Spaulding, "History of Black Oriented Radio," 96–97.

23. Ibid., 97. Also see Dizzy Gillespie and Al Fraser, *To Be or Not to Bop: Memoirs—Dizzy Gillespie* (Garden City, N.Y.: Doubleday & Co., 1979), 281–82, 339–41.

24. Lavada Durst, interview by the author, 28 April 1995, Austin, Texas. Also see Billy Porterfield, "Dr. Hep Cat's Redemption," *Austin American Statesman*, 5 Jan. 1990, B1, B5; Lavada Durst (Doctor Hep Cat) aircheck, KVET, Austin, Texas.

25. Lavada Durst interview. Also see *The Jives of Dr. Hep Cat* (Austin: Lavada Durst, 1953).

Notes to Chapter 6

1. See William D. Miller, *Mister Crump of Memphis* (Baton Rouge: Louisiana State University Press, 1964), 21–28; William D. Miller, *Memphis during the Progressive Era* (Memphis: Memphis State University Press, 1957), 6–34; Robert Lanier, *Memphis in the Twenties* (Memphis: Zenda Press, 1979), 2, 18, 21–26, 33–34.

2. Louis Cantor, *Wheelin' on Beale* (New York: Pharos Books, 1992), 7, 13–17. Also see Mark Newman, *Entrepreneurs of Profit and Pride: From Black Appeal to Radio Soul* (New York: Praeger, 1988), 109–12.

3. Cantor, *Wheelin' on Beale*, 23–24.

4. Ibid., 22.

5. Margaret McKee and Fred Chisenhall, *Beale Street Black and Blue* (Baton Rouge: Louisiana State University Press, 1981), 92.

6. Cantor, *Wheelin' on Beale*, 25–40. Also see A. C. Williams, *The Role of Nat D. Williams and WDIA in Blues Promotion 1940–1960* (Washington, D.C.: Smithsonian Institution, 1983), 1–4.

7. Nat D. Williams, "Down on Beale Street," *Memphis World*, 16 Aug. 1946, 4.

8. Nat D. Williams, "Down on Beale Street," *Memphis World*, 6 April 1946, 4.

9. Cantor, *Wheelin' on Beale*, 37–39.

10. Newman, *Entrepreneurs of Profit and Pride*, 113.

11. Cantor, *Wheelin' on Beale*, 127–29.

12. McKee and Chisenhall, *Beale Street Black and Blue*, 94.

13. Cantor, *Wheelin' on Beale*, 48.

14. Nat D. Williams, "Down on Beale Street," *Memphis World*, 23 Nov. 1948, 4.

15. Cantor, *Wheelin' on Beale*, 47.

16. Ibid., 85–86.

17. Ibid., 58–62.

18. Ibid., 62–64.

19. Maurice Hulbert, interview by Jacqui Gales Webb, May 1995, Baltimore, for *Black Radio: Telling It like It Was* (Washington, D.C.: Smithsonian Institution, 1996), 9–11. Also see Cantor, *Wheelin' on Beale*, 64–65.

20. Maurice Hulbert interview, 11–21; Cantor, *Wheelin' on Beale*, 65–66.

21. Maurice Hulbert interview, 14.

22. Ibid., 13.

23. Ibid., 17.

24. Williams, *The Role of Nat D. Williams*, 8–10.

25. Riley "B. B." King, interview by Lex Gillespie, May 1995, Memphis, for *Black Radio: Telling It like It Was*, 5. Also see Cantor, *Wheelin' on Beale*, 77–81.

26. Cantor, *Wheelin' on Beale*, 82–83.

27. Ibid., 70.

28. Ibid., 73.

29. Ibid., 73–75.

30. Ibid., 98–100, 103.

31. Ibid., 100, 103–4.

32. Ibid., 101–2.

33. Ibid., 89–91.

34. Ibid., 91, 118.

35. Martha Jean Steinberg, interview by Jacqui Gales Webb, June 1995, Detroit, for *Black Radio: Telling It like It Was*, 31–33. Also see Cantor, *Wheelin' on Beale*, 91–92.

36. Cantor, *Wheelin' on Beale*, 141–44, 199.

37. Ibid., 174–77.

38. Ibid., 149, 189–216.

39. Martha Jean Steinberg interview, 46.

40. "The Forgotten 15,000,000," *Sponsor* (10 October 1949): 24–25, 54–55.

41. Ibid., 25.

42. "The Forgotten 15,000,000—Part Two," *Sponsor* (26 October 1949): 30–31, 42.

43. Ibid., 42, 44.

44. Ibid., 44, 53.

45. "The Forgotten 15,000,000—Three Years Later," *Sponsor* (25 July 1952): 29–30, 72, 76.

46. Ibid., 36–37, 87.

47. Ibid., 32–33, 78–83, 38–39, 84.

48. Ibid., 29–87.

49. "Negro Radio," *Sponsor* (24 August 1953): 66; 68; (22 October 1962): 7–8; (19 September 1955): 108; (26 September 1959): 5.
50. "Negro Radio," *Sponsor* (24 August 1953): 74.
51. "Negro Radio," *Sponsor* (20 September 1958): 8–9; (9 October 1961): 13–14.
52. "Negro Radio," *Sponsor* (24 August 1953): 63–66.
53. "Negro Radio," *Sponsor* (20 September 1954): 54, 150–52; (17 September 1956): 38–39.
54. "Negro Radio," *Sponsor* (28 September 1957): 10; (26 September 1960): 7, 52.
55. "Negro Radio," *Sponsor* (26 September 1960): 14, 52.
56. "Negro Radio," *Sponsor* (9 October 1961): 15, 25.
57. "Negro Radio," *Sponsor* (20 September 1954): 146.
58. "Negro Radio," *Sponsor* (28 September 1957): 23.

Notes to Chapter 7

1. Martha Jean Steinberg, interview by Jacqui Gales Webb, June 1995, Detroit, for *Black Radio: Telling It like It Was* (Washington, D.C.: Smithsonian Institution, 1996), 35, 40.
2. Ibid., 41.
3. Jack Gibson, interview by the author, February 5, 1986, Washington, D.C.
4. Jack Gibson, interview by Jacqui Gales Webb, July 1995, Washington, D.C., for, *Black Radio: Telling It like It Was,* 8.
5. Ibid., 10.
6. Ibid., 14.
7. Jack Gibson, interview by the author.
8. Ibid.
9. Ibid.
10. Dudley Riley, interview by Portia Maultsby, November 13, 1981, Cincinnati, Ohio, in Indiana University Archives, 1.
11. Jack Gibson, interview by the author.
12. Ibid.
13. *The Beehive* was hosted in 1950 by the "King Bee," Lonnie Rochon, a Cajun from Louisiana. When Rochon left the station, he was replaced by Clifton Smith, an African American who picked up the King Bee moniker. When he moved to Houston's KCOH in 1953, Smith took the King Bee title with him. Joe Howard was Clifton Smith's replacement on KNUZ. See Wes Smith, *The Pied Pipers of Rock 'n' Roll* (Marietta, Ga.: Longstreet Press, 1989), 134.
14. Joe Howard, interview by Portia Maultsby, March 18, 1991, Houston, Texas, in Indiana University Archives, 2–3.
15. Ibid., 4–5.
16. Ibid., 7.
17. Ibid., 9–10.
18. Ibid., 45–46.
19. Douglas, "Jocko" Henderson, aircheck, WLIB, New York City.
20. Douglas, "Jocko" Henderson, interview by Lex Gillespie, July 1995, Philadelphia, for *Black Radio: Telling It like It Was,* 1–2, 22.
21. Ibid., 2.
22. Ibid., 11, 16. Also see Smith, *Pied Pipers of Rock 'n' Roll, 148.*
23. David Hinkley, "The Rhythm, the Blues and the Black Jocks of New York," *Daily News Magazine,* 18 Feb. 1990, 10–12, 14–15; Smith, *Pied Pipers of Rock 'n' Roll,* 158–60.
24. Smith, *Pied Pipers of Rock 'n' Roll,* 158.
25. "Jocko" Henderson interview, 20.

26. Ibid., 15–16.
27. Smith, *Pied Pipers of Rock 'n' Roll,* 144–58.
28. Maurice "Hot Rod" Hulbert, aircheck, WWRL, New York City.
29. Portia Maultsby, interview by Jacqui Gales Webb, April 1995, Washington, D.C., for *Black Radio: Telling It like It Was,* 13–14.
30. J. Fred MacDonald, *Don't Touch That Dial: Radio Programming in American Life from 1920 to 1960* (Chicago: Nelson Hall, 1970), 144–45, 148–50, 231–39, 243–46, 251–52, 265–66, Erik Barnouw, *The Golden Web: A History of Broadcasting in the United States,* vol. 2: *1933–1953* (New York: Oxford University Press, 1968), 6, 99, 155, 193.
31. MacDonald, *Don't Touch That Dial,* 330; John Hope Franklin, *From Slavery to Freedom: A History of Negro Americans* (New York: Vintage Books, 1969), 520–21.
32. See "Negro Radio" series, *Sponsor* (1952–1962), for information on homemaker programs in black appeal radio.
33. "Female Disc Jockey on WHOD," *Ebony* (30 September 1950): 5. Also see "Negro Radio" series, *Sponsor* (1952–1962).
34. Ruth Ellington, interview by Sonja Williams, August 1995, New York City, for *Black Radio: Telling It like It Was* (radio series); Hinkley, "Rhythm, Blues and Black Jocks," 12; "Lou Lutour—the One-Woman Show," *New York Amsterdam News,* 16 April 1955, 23.
35. Gertrude Cooper, interview by Lex Gillespie, June 1995, Chicago, for *Black Radio: Telling It like It Was* (radio series); Norman Spaulding, "History of Black Oriented Radio in Chicago, 1929–1963" (Ph.D. diss., University of Illinois, Urbana, 1981),74, 94.
36. Martha Jean Steinberg interview, 39–40.
37. Ibid., 43.
38. "The Forgotten 15,000,000—Three Years Later," *Sponsor* (28 July 1952): 29.
39. Hattie Leeper, interview by Sonja Williams, April 22, 1995, Charlotte, North Carolina, for *Black Radio: Telling It like It Was,* 39–40.
40. Ibid., 24.
41. Smith, *Pied Pipers of Rock 'n' Roll,* 135; Novella Smith, interview by Portia Maultsby, August 24, 1991, Houston, Texas, in Indiana University Archives.
42. Irene Johnson Ware, interview by Jacqui Gales Webb, July 1995, Mobile, Alabama, for *Black Radio: Telling It like It Was,* 2–3.
43. Hattie Leeper interview, 20.
44. Martha Jean Steinberg interview, 35.

Notes to Chapter 8

1. Al Jarvis pioneered this white swing and pop format on his show *The World's Largest Make-Believe Ballroom,* which debuted on KFWB in Los Angeles in 1932. Martin Block was the swing era's most popular and highly paid DJ; his syndicated show, a direct copy of Jarvis's *Make-Believe Ballroom,* reached an estimated 4 million listeners, and his yearly salary exceeded $100,000. Dave Garroway, Freddie Robbins, and Gene Norman were the first radio disc jockeys to produce and promote pop music concerts in their respective locales. Garroway's popularity as a disc jockey catapulted him into a successful television career, as was the case with Arthur Godfrey. Norman used his celebrity status to launch his own nightclub, record store, and music publishing firm. See Erik Barnouw, *The Golden Web: A History of Broadcasting in the United States,* vol. 2: *1933–1953* (New York: Oxford University Press, 1968), 217–18; Arnold Passman, *The Deejays* (New York: Macmillan Co., 1971), 48–49, 59, 91, 115, 119, 130, 149.
2. Passman, *Deejays,* 67–68, 150.
3. Al "Jazzbo" Collins, interview by Lex Gillespie, June 1995, San Francisco, for *Black Radio:*

Telling It like It Was (Washington, D.C.: Smithsonian Institution, 1996), 7–8, 14–15. Also see Passman, *Deejays,* 122–23.

4. Al "Jazzbo" Collins interview, 10.
5. Margaret McKee and Fred Chisenhall, *Beale Street Black and Blue* (Baton Rouge: Louisiana State University Press, 1981), 35–36.
6. Wes Smith, *The Pied Pipers of Rock 'n' Roll* (Marietta, Ga.: Longstreet Press, 1989), 56.
7. Ibid., 87.
8. Ibid., 82–83, 97.
9. Ibid., 96–98.
10. Steve Chapple and Reebee Garofalo, *Rock 'n' Roll Is Here to Pay: The History and Politics of the Music Industry* (Chicago: Nelson Hall, 1977), 48–49. Also see Smith, *Pied Pipers of Rock 'n' Roll,* 100.
11. Smith, *Pied Pipers of Rock 'n' Roll*, 98–100. William "Hoss" Allen, interview by Lex Gillespie, April 19, 1991, Washington, D.C., for *Black Radio: Telling It like It Was* (audiotape).
12. William "Hoss" Allen interview.
13. Tom Chaffin, "White DJ of Soul Helped America Go Funky in '40s with Black Show," *Atlanta Constitution,* 18 April 1986, M1, M4.
14. Smith, *Pied Pipers of Rock 'n' Roll,* 92–96, 106–16.
15. Chaffin, "White DJ of Soul" M4.
16. Ibid.; William "Hoss" Allen interview.
17. Smith, *Pied Pipers of Rock 'n' Roll,* 108, 111–16. Chaffin, "White DJ of Soul," M4.
18. Ibid.
19. Vernon Winslow, interview by the author, March 25, 1988, New Orleans, Louisiana (audiotape).
20. Ibid. Also see Smith, *Pied Pipers of Rock 'n' Roll,* 121–24.
21. Clarence Harmon, interview by Lex Gillespie, March 1995, New Orleans, for *Black Radio: Telling It like It Was,* 4, 8.
22. Irma Thomas, interview by Lex Gillespie, March 1995, New Orleans, for *Black Radio: Telling It like It Was,* 5.
23. Vernon Winslow interview.
24. "The Forgotten 15,000,000," *Sponsor* (10 October 1949): 31; "The Forgotten 15,000,000—Three Years Later," *Sponsor* (25 July 1952): 35; "Negro Radio," *Sponsor* (19 September 1955): 31; Hamp "Honeyboy" Swain, interview by the author, March 22, 1996, Macon, Georgia (audiotape).
25. Smith, *Pied Pipers of Rock 'n' Roll,* 269–70.
26. Art Neville, interview by Lex Gillespie, March 1955, New Orleans, for *Black Radio: Telling It like It Was,* 4.
27. Joe Howard, interview by Portia Maultsby, March 18, 1991, Houston, Texas, in Indiana University Archives, 3; Hattie Leeper, interview by Sonja Williams, April 22, 1995, Charlotte, North Carolina, for *Black Radio: Telling It like It was,* 10.
28. Smith, *Pied Pipers of Rock 'n' Roll,* 61–64.
29. Ibid., 65.
30. Ibid., 64.
31. Ibid., 67–70, 73.
32. Ibid., 70, 74–75.
33. Ibid., 71–72.
34. Ibid., 75.
35. Hunter Hancock, interview by Lex Gillespie, May 1995, Los Angeles, for *Black Radio: Telling It like It Was,* 1. Also see Smith, *Pied Pipers of Rock 'n' Roll,* 79–80.
36. Hunter Hancock interview, 7.

37. Ibid., 11.
38. Ibid., 2.
39. Johnny Otis, quoted in Arnold Shaw, *Honkers and Shouters: The Golden Years of Rhythm and Blues* (New York: Collier Books, 1978), 159.
40. Ibid., 158–62.
41. Ibid., 162–68.
42. Smith, *Pied Pipers of Rock 'n' Roll*, 78; Passman, *Deejays,* 166.
43. David Hinkley, "The Rhythm, the Blues and the Black Jocks of New York," *Daily News Magazine,* 18 Feb. 1990, 12, 14.
44. Smith, *Pied Pipers of Rock 'n' Roll*, 44, 80–81; Passman, *Deejays,* 61, 246.
45. "Dunaway's Stormy Career," *Billboard* (24 December 1977): 21–22, 27, 34, 38, 45.

Notes to Chapter 9

1. Louis Cantor, *Wheelin' on Beale* (New York: Pharos Books, 1992), 164–69.
2. Gregg Gordon, liner notes to *Red, Hot and Blue: Dewey Phillips Live Radio Broadcasts from 1952–1964* (Memphis, Tenn.: Memphis Archives, 1995).
3. Ibid.
4. Ibid.
5. Ibid.
6. Ibid.
7. Wes Smith, *The Pied Pipers of Rock 'n' Roll* (Marietta, Ga.: Longstreet Press, 1989), 230–31.
8. Ibid., 231–32; Norma Spaulding, "History of Black Oriented Radio in Chicago, 1929–1963" (Ph.D. diss., University of Illinois, Urbana, 1981), 124.
9. Smith, *Pied Pipers of Rock 'n' Roll*, 232.
10. Ibid., 165–68.
11. Ibid., 169–72.
12. Ibid., 173–74, 176.
13. Ibid., 175.
14. Ibid., 180–81.
15. Ibid., 185–89.
16. Robert "Wolfman Jack" Smith interview by Lex Gillespie, January 7, 1995, Washington, D.C., for *Black Music: Telling It like It Was* (Washington, D.C.: Smithsonian Institution, 1996), audiotape.
17. Smith, *Pied Pipers of Rock 'n' Roll*, 254.
18. Robert "Wolfman Jack" Smith interview.
19. Gene Fowler and Bill Crawford, *Border Radio* (Austin, Tex.: Texas Monthly Press, 1987), 7–11.
20. Ibid., 197.
21. Ibid., 202.
22. Robert "Wolfman Jack" Smith interview; Fowler and Crawford, *Border Radio,* 193–204.
23. Steve Chapple and Reebee Garofalo, *Rock 'n' Roll Is Here to Pay: The History and Politics of the Music Industry* (Chicago: Nelson Hall, 1977), 66.
24. Smith, *Pied Pipers of Rock 'n' Roll*, 34–36.
25. Ibid., 38.
26. Ibid., 205–7.
27. Ibid., 188, 192–93.
28. Ibid., 212–18; Peter Fornatale and Joshua E. Mills, *Radio in the Television Age* (Woodstock, N.Y.: Overlook Press, 1980), 51.
29. Chapple and Garofalo, *Rock 'n' Roll Is Here to Pay,* 50–51.

30. Smith, *Pied Pipers of Rock 'n' Roll,* 8.
31. Chapple and Garofalo, *Rock 'n' Roll Is Here to Pay,* 247–48.
32. Smith, *Pied Pipers of Rock 'n' Roll,* 45, 190.
33. Ibid., 8, 44.
34. Fonatale and Mills, *Radio in the Television Age,* 51.
35. Smith, *Pied Pipers of Rock 'n' Roll,* 45–46.

Notes to Chapter 10

1. John Hope Franklin, *From Slavery to Freedom: A History of Negro Americans* (New York: Vintage Books, 1969), 622, 625–26.
2. Ibid., 627.
3. Ibid., 627–33.
4. Arnold Shaw, *The World of Soul* (New York: Cowles Book Co., 1970), 327.
5. Arnold Shaw, *Honkers and Shouters: The Golden Years of Rhythm and Blues* (New York: Collier Books, 1978), 410–15.
6. Nelson George, *The Death of Rhythm and Blues* (New York: E. P. Dutton, 1988), 64–66.
7. Ibid., 86.
8. "Smokey Robinson Interview," *Rolling Stone* (28 September 1968), 14.
9. George, *Death of Rhythm and Blues,* 86–87.
10. Ibid., 79–82. Also see Peter Guralnick, "One Night Stand," liner notes to *Sam Cooke Live at the Harlem Square Club, 1963* (RCA Victor, 1985).
11. Peter Guralnick, *Sweet Soul Music: Rhythm and Blues and the Dream of Southern Freedom* (New York: Harper & Row, 1986), 39–49.
12. George, *Death of Rhythm and Blues,* 82–85. Also see David Nathan, liner notes to *People Get Ready: The Curtis Mayfield Story* (Rhino Records, 1996).
13. Chuck Scruggs, interview by Portia Maultsby, 18.
14. James Spady, *Georgie Woods: I'm Only a Man* (Philadelphia: Snack-Pac Book Division, 1992), 18–19, 51–52, 67, 86–88.
15. Georgie Woods, interview by Jacqui Gales Webb, for *Black Radio: Telling It like It Was* (Washington, D.C.: Smithsonian Institution, 1996), 9–10.
16. Ibid., 11.
17. Ibid., 16–19.
18. Peggy Mitchell, interview by Jacqui Gales Webb, for *Black Radio: Telling It like It Was,* 17–21.
19. The Reverend Erskine Fausch, interview by Jacqui Gales Webb, for *Black Radio: Telling It like It Was,* 8–10.
20. Jack Gibson, interview by Jacqui Gales Webb, July 1995, Washington, D.C., for *Black Radio: Telling It like It Was,* 3.
21. Ibid., 4.
22. Nat D. Williams, interview by the author, Memphis, Tennessee, 1978; Erskine Fausch interview, 10.
23. Maurice Hulbert, interview by Jacqui Gales Webb, May 1995, Baltimore, for *Black Radio: Telling It like It Was,* 15; Douglas "Jocko" Henderson, interview by Lex Gillespie, July 1995, Philadelphia, for *Black Radio: Telling It like It Was,* 14.
24. Martha Jean Steinberg, interview by Jacqui Gales Webb, June 1995, Detroit, for *Black Radio: Telling It like It Was,* 36, 41.
25. Herb Kent, interview by Sonja Williams, September 1995, for *Black Radio: Telling It like It Was,* 34.
26. Roy Woods, interviewed on *America's Black Forum,* PBS, July 29, 1985.

Notes to Chapter 11

1. John Hope Franklin, *From Slavery to Freedom: A History of Negro Americans* (New York: Vintage Books, 1969), 633.
2. Ibid., 643.
3. Douglas "Jocko" Henderson, interview by Lex Gillespie, July 1995, Philadelphia, for *Black Radio: Telling It like It Was* (Washington, D.C.: Smithsonian Institution, 1996), 14.
4. Georgie Woods, interview by Jacqui Gales Webb, June 1995, Philadelphia, for *Black Radio: Telling It like It Was*, 12.
5. James Spady, *Georgie Woods: I'm Only a Man* (Philadelphia: Snack-Pac Book Division, 1992), 136.
6. Georgie Woods interview, 12–13.
7. Larry McCormick, interview by Lex Gillespie, August 1995, Los Angeles, for *Black Radio: Telling It like It Was*, 21.
8. Ibid., 22. Also see Bill Lane, "Montague Signs Off: The Legend of Montague," *KGFJ Soul 2*, 1 (13 April 1969): 1–3.
9. Martha Jean Steinberg, interview by Jacqui Gales Webb, June 1995, Detroit, for *Black Radio: Telling It like It Was*, 44.
10. Del Shields, interview by Sonja Williams, September 1995, New York City, for *Black Radio: Telling It like It Was*, 22.
11. Robert E. Dallas, "Black Radio Stations Send Soul and Service to Millions," *New York Times*, 11 Nov. 1968, L64.
12. Del Shields interview, 24–26.
13. Georgie Woods interview, 14.
14. Purvis Spann, interview by Sonja Williams, June 1995, Chicago, for *Black Radio: Telling It like It Was*, 9.
15. Lucky Cordell, interview by Lex Gillespie, September 1995, Chicago, for *Black Radio: Telling It like It Was*, 42–3.
16. Maurice Hulbert, interview by Jacqui Gales Webb, May 1995, Baltimore, for *Black Radio: Telling It like It Was*, 19.
17. "Black Radio: The Big Rich Sound at the End of the Dial," *Black Enterprise* (November 1970): 34.
18. Jack Gibson, interview by Jacqui Gales Webb, July 1995, Washington, D.C., for *Black Radio: Telling It like It Was*, 18–20. Also see "Where the Negro DJ Stands," *Broadcasting* (19 August 1968): 36–38.
19. Nelson George, *The Death of Rhythm and Blues* (New York: E. P. Dutton, 1988), 112.
20. "The Negro DJ and Civil Rights," *Broadcasting* (31 August 1964): 60.
21. Ibid., 60–61.
22. Ibid., 61–62.
23. Ibid., 62.
24. George, *Death of Rhythm and Blues*, 11–14; Al Bell, interview by the author, March 31, 1979.
25. George, *Death of Rhythm and Blues*, 113.
26. Ibid., 114.
27. Ibid., 114–15; Del Shields interview, 34–35.
28. George, *Death of Rhythm and Blues*, 127–28.
29. "Black Deejays Eye New Course," *New York Amsterdam News*, 26 Aug. 1969, 1, 32.

Notes to Chapter 12

1. Erik Barnouw, *The Golden Web: A History of Broadcasting in the United States,* vol. 2: *1933–1953* (New York: Oxford University Press, 1968), 283–84.
2. Peter Fornatale and Joshua E. Mills, *Radio in the Television Age* (Woodstock, N.Y.: Overlook Press, 1980), 130–35.
3. Susan Krieger, *Hip Capitalism* (Beverly Hills, Calif.: Sage Publications, 1979), 29, 33.
4. Ibid., 30–35, 38.
5. Ibid., 38–54, 71–73.
6. Ibid., 98–103, 136–37, 167.
7. Roland Young, interview by the author, July 1986.
8. Krieger, *Hip Capitalism,* 150–56.
9. Del Shields, interview by Sonja Williams, September 1995, New York City, for *Black Radio: Telling It like It Was* (Washington, D.C.: Smithsonian Institution, 1996), 45.
10. Ibid., 24–25, 46.
11. Ibid., 36–38.
12. Joe Howard, interview by Portia Maultsby, March 18, 1991, Houston, Texas, in Indiana University Archives, 20–22.
13. Ibid., 23–24.
14. Wes Smith, *The Pied Pipers of Rock 'n' Roll* (Marietta, Ga.: Longstreet Press, 1989), 233.
15. "WLIB Returns to the Air after Staff Dispute," *New York Times,* 29 Oct. 1970, A46.
16. Del Shields interview, 46. Also see Nelson George, *The Death of Rhythm and Blues* (New York: E. P. Dutton, 1988), 126–28.
17. George, *Death of Rhythm and Blues,* 129; Frankie Crocker, interview by Sonja Williams, September 1995, New York City, for *Black Radio: Telling It like It Was,* 15–18.
18. James P. Murray, "Lampell Wants to Reach the People," *New York Amsterdam News,* 10 June 1972, D1, D6; Frankie Crocker interview, 22–23; Vi Higginson interview by Sonja Williams, September 1995, New York City, for *Black Radio: Telling It like It Was,* 6, 12–13.
19. Frankie Crocker interview, 26.
20. Georgie Woods, interview by Jacqui Gales Webb, June 1995, Philadelphia, for *Black Radio: Telling It like It Was,* 23.
21. Hollie West, "WHUR: A Refreshing Voice in the Vanguard of Black Media," *Washington Post,* 23 Jan. 1973, L1, L5.
22. Rick Brown, "WHUR-FM Turns on D.C.," *Encore* (spring 1972): 65; Phil Watson, interview by the author, April 30, 1985, Washington, D.C.
23. West, "WHUR," L5.
24. Gil Scott Heron, interview by the author, April 3, 1986, Washington, D.C.
25. George, *Death of Rhythm and Blues,* 132; Hollie West, "Supercharged Soul, Preachers and Prayers: It's All in the Format," *Washington Post,* 23 Jan. 1973, LI, L3.
26. West, "WHUR," L5.
27. Brown, "WHUR-FM Turns on D.C.," 65; Joel Dreyfuss, "WHUR: The Spoils of Success," *Washington Post,* 26 Jan. 1975, F1, F5.
28. Dreyfuss, "WHUR: The Spoils of Success," F5; Phil Watson interview.
29. Dreyfuss, "WHUR: The Spoils of Success," F5.
30. Hector Corporan, interview by the author, September 3, 1996, Washington, D.C.; Dreyfuss, "WHUR: The Spoils of Success," F5.
31. Dreyfuss, "WHUR: The Spoils of Success," F5.

Notes to Chapter 13

1. Fred Ferretti, "The White Captivity of Black Radio," *Columbia Journalism Review* (summer 1970): 35–39.
2. The soul radio chains' stations were on the air in the following locations: Rollins—Chicago (WBEE), Indianapolis (WGEE), Newark, New Jersey (WNJR), and Norfolk, Virginia (WRAP); Rounsaville—Cincinnati (WCIN), Louisville, Kentucky (WLOU), Nashville (WVOL), and New Orleans (WYLD); Sounderling—Oakland, California (KDIA), Memphis (WDIA), Washington, D.C. (WOL), and New York City (WWRL); Speidel—Portsmouth, Virginia (WHIH), Columbia, South Carolina (WOIC), Charleston (WPAL), Savannah (WSOK), Florence, South Carolina (WYNN), and Tampa (WTMP); United—Cleveland (WJMO), Baltimore (WSID), and Washington, D.C. (WOOK). See Ferretti, "White Captivity of Black Radio," 37.
3. Ibid., 38–39.
4. Letter from Dr. Portia Maultsby to the author, May 12, 1994; Jack Gibson, interview by the author, February 5, 1986, Washington, D.C.
5. "New Radio Station: Dentists Build Michigan Broadcasting Firm," *Ebony* (April 1957): 110–13; Mary Bell, wife of Haley Bell, interviewed by the author, April 2, 1988, Atlanta, Georgia; Richard S. Kahlenburg, "Negro Radio," *Negro History Bulletin* (1965): 127–28, 142–43.
6. Ferretti, "White Captivity of Black Radio," 39; Douglas O'Conner and Gayla Cook, "Black Radio: The Soul Sellout," in *Issues and Trends in Afro-American Journalism,* ed. Ralph Tinney and Justina Rector (Washington, D.C.: Third World Press, 1975), 233–46.
7. Ferretti, "White Captivity of Black Radio," 39.
8. "Station WNJR Brings out Realities of Community Control," *African World* (28 October 1970): 10.
9. Del Shields, interview by Sonja Williams, September 1995, New York City, for *Black Radio: Telling It like It Was* (Washington, D.C.: Smithsonian Institution, 1996), 35.
10. Ibid.
11. James Winston, executive director, NABOB, interview by Sonja Williams, for *Black Radio: Telling It like It Was,* 1; "New Broadcasters' Group," *Black Enterprise* (August 1976): 17.
12. See Bishetta Merritt, "A Historical-Critical Study of a Pressure Group in Broadcasting: Black Efforts for Soul in Television" (Ph.D. diss., Ohio State University, 1974) 44–125.
13. Pluria Marshall, interview by Jacqui Gales Webb, June 1995, Washington, D.C., for *Black Radio: Telling It like It Was.*
14. Ibid.
15. Ibid.
16. James Winston interview, 2.
17. Roland Alston, "Black Owned Radio: Taking to the Airways in a Hurry," *Black Enterprise* (July 1978): 24.
18. Ibid., 25.
19. Ibid., 25–26. Also see Les Brown, "Station Ownership by Blacks Lags," *New York Times,* 10 Nov. 1977, C22; Angela Goodman, "The Next Station You Hear May Be Ragan Henry's," *Black Enterprise* (December 1977): 54, 65.
20. Alston, "Black Owned Radio," 20–25.
21. "Away from the Blues," *Newsweek,* 18 Jan. 1954, 51.
22. Hal Bennet and Lew Roberts, "National Black Network: Black Radio's Big Brother," *Black Enterprise* (June 1977): 141–42.
23. Ibid., 143–46.

24. Ibid., 141, 144.
25. N. R. Kleinfield, "Black Radio Network Expands," *New York Times*, 1 Aug. 1980, D1, D4; Lon G. Wells, "NBN and SBN: Network Radio in the Black," *Dollars and Sense* 7, 4 (October–November 1984): 35–39. Also see Marie Moore, "Bob Law: Radio—The Theater of the Mind," *New York Amsterdam News*, 16 Aug. 1980, 33.
26. Ron Davenport, interview by the author, September 1995, Pittsburgh, Pennsylvania; "Black Broadcasting Firm Buys Three Radio Stations in Boston and Buffalo, N.Y.," *Jet*, 7 Sept. 1972, 58.
27. Louis Calta, "Mutual to Begin News for Blacks," *New York Times*, 29 April 1972, D63; William H. Jones, "Black Group Buys Rest of Mutual Network," *Washington Post*, 7 Sept. 1979, E1–2.
28. "Black Group," E2; Wells, "NBN and SBN," 38–39.
29. Ron Davenport interview.
30. Ibid.
31. *American Urban Radio Networks*, promotional brochure, 1996.
32. Ibid.
33. Airchecks, *The Tom Joyner Morning Show*, WHUR-FM, Washington, D.C., July 1998. Also see Jounice L. Nealy, "He's Your Wakeup Call," *St. Petersburg Times*, 6 July 1998, 1D, 4D.
34. Nealy, "He's Your Wakeup Call," 4D.
35. Ibid.
36. Matthew Scott, "Can Black Radio Survive an Industry Shakeout?" *Black Enterprise* (June 1993): 254–60; Tony Saunders, "How Big Can a Superduopoly Be?" *Radio Business* (15 April 1996): 10–11.
37. Melanie Wells, "Hicks, Muse Tunes in American Radio as Next Target," *USA Today*, 26 Aug. 1997, 3B; "Westinghouse Buys Rival Group of Stations," *Washington Post*, 20 Sept. 1997, D1.
38. James Winston interview, 11.
39. Geraldine Fabrikant, "Slow Gains by Minority Broadcasters," *New York Times*, 5 May 1994, D1, D5; Peter Barnes, "Bending the Rules: Investors Use Blacks as Fronts to Obtain Broadcasting Licenses," *Wall Street Journal*, 11 Dec. 1987, 1, 19; Pluria Marshall inteview.
40. Fabrikant, "Slow Gains by Minority Broadcasters," D5; Cathy Hughes, interview by Sonja Williams, June 1995, Baltimore, for *Black Radio: Telling It like It Was*.

Notes to Chapter 14

1. Peter Guralnick, *Sweet Soul Music* (New York: Harper & Row, 1986), 220–45.
2. Del Shields, interview by Sonja Williams, September 1995, New York City, for *Black Radio: Telling It like It Was* (Washington, D.C.: Smithsonian Institution, 1996), 35. Also see Fred Ferretti, "The White Captivity of Black Radio," *Columbia Journalism Review* (summer 1970): 36.
3. James Brown, quoted in Reebee Garafalo, "Crossing Over," in *Split Image: African Americans in Mass Media*, ed. Jannett Dates and William Barlow (Washington, D.C.: Howard University Press, 1993), 98.
4. Guralnick, *Sweet Soul Music*, 243–45; "Brown's Radio Station Sold at Auction in Ga.," *Jet*, 15 May 1980, 18.
5. Percy Sutton, interview by Sonja Williams, September 1995, New York City, for *Black Radio: Telling It like It Was*, 2, 4.
6. Ibid., 6–9; "Percy Sutton: Power Politics New York Style," *Ebony* (November 1972): 170–73.
7. Percy Sutton interview, 10; Leon Lewis, "Harlem's Biggest Black Business: Radio Stations WBLS and WLIB Cost $3.1 Million," *Sepia* (August 1978): 32–36.
8. "Percy Sutton," 172.
9. Lewis, "Harlem's Biggest Black Business," 33–35.

10. Ibid., 32, 35; Percy Sutton interview, 15.
11. "Stevie Wonder Buys $2.2 Million Station," *Jet,* 25 Jan. 1979, 16; Edward Abner, interview by Sonja Williams, August 1995, Los Angeles, for *Black Radio: Telling It like It Was,* 17–18.
12. Karen Slade, interview by Sonja Williams, August 1995, Los Angeles, for *Black Radio: Telling It like It Was,* 10.
13. Ibid., 13. Also see Matthew S. Scott, "Can Black Radio Survive an Industry Shakeout?" *Black Enterprise* (June 1993): 24–25.
14. Karen Slade interview, 16.
15. Cathy Hughes, interview by Sonja Williams, June 1995, Baltimore, for *Black Radio: Telling It like It Was.*
16. Ibid. Also see Marc Fisher, "She's Got the Whole Town Talking: Media Mogul, Radio Host, Rabble Rouser? WOL's Cathy Hughes Answers All Three," *Washington Post,* 6 March 1995, D1–D3.
17. Fisher, "She's Got the Whole Town Talking," D-2; Cathy Hughes interview.
18. Cathy Hughes interview.
19. Ibid.
20. Ibid.
21. Ibid.
22. Ibid.
23. Ibid.
24. Ibid; Dennis John Lewis, "Unorthodox Quiet Storm," *Washington Star,* 18 May 1978, C1–2.
25. Cathy Hughes interview.
26. Ibid.
27. Ibid.
28. Ibid.
29. Ibid.
30. Fisher, "She's Got the Whole Town Talking," D3.
31. Ibid., D2–3; Cathy Hughes interview.
32. Cathy Hughes interview.
33. "One More for Radio One," *Washington Post,* 31 Dec. 1996, D7.

Notes to Chapter 15

1. Ralph Engleman, *Public Radio and Television in America: A Political History* (Beverly Hills, Calif.: Sage Publications, 1996), 143–150.
2. Ibid., 152, 159–60.
3. Lo Jelks, executive director, Black College Radio Association, interview by the author, April 2, 1986, Atlanta, Georgia.
4. Bishetta Merritt, former WSHA-FM faculty adviser, interview by the author, May 5, 1986, Washington, D.C.
5. Rashad Abdul Muhaimin, program director, WSHA-FM, interview by Sonja Williams, August 1995, Durham, N.C., for *Black Radio: Telling It like It Was* (Washington, D.C.: Smithsonian Institution, 1996), 1–14.
6. Howard Myrick, "Programming Philosophy for WCLK," *WCLK Program Guide* (May 1981): 1.
7. Howard Myrick, "Goals for WCLK," *WCLK Program Guide* (May 1981): 1; Howard Myrick, former WCLK general manager, interview by the author, July 15, 1986, Washington, D.C.; *WCLK Program Guide* (April 1986): 1–3.
8. "The Voice of ASU Signs On," *ASU Today,* no. 9 (15 July 1984): 1–2. "There's Something

Going On in the Levi Watkins Learning Center," *ASU Today,* no. 6 (15 March 1985): 3–4.

9. Lo Jelks interview. Also see Glen Gutmacher, "Black College Radio," *College Broadcaster* 2, 6 (March 1990): 8–9, 28–29.

10. "Spotlight on KPUV-FM," *Black College Radio News,* no. 9 (January 1988): 3–4.

11. "WHBC-830 AM, 1996–97 Program Schedule," Howard University, Washington, D.C.; Jennifer Kelly, WHBC operations director, interview by the author, April 1, 1997, Washington, D.C.

12. Gutmacher, "Black College Radio," 9, 28; Lo Jelks interview.

13. Engleman, *Public Radio and Television in America,* 156, 161; Adam Clayton Powell III, quoted in Marc Fisher, "The Soul of the News Machine," *Washington Post Sunday Magazine,* 23 Oct. 1989, 21.

14. Barrington Salmon, "A Leading Radio Personality: President, CEO Delano Lewis Helps to Clear Static at NPR," *Washington Times,* 10 April 1997, C8.

15. Lynn Chadwick, executive director, NFCB, interview by the author, October 16, 1992, Washington, D.C.

16. Obataiye Akinwole, former WAFR station manager, interview by Sonja Williams, August 1995, Durham, North Carolina, for *Black Radio: Telling It like It Was,* 1–4; Donald Baker, former WAFR program director, interview by Sonja Williams, August 1995, Durham, North Carolina, for *Black Radio: Telling It like It Was,* 2–8.

17. Obataiye Akinwole interview, 7–9.

18. Donald Baker interview, 11–13.

19. Joe Rudolph, KPOO station manager, interview by Sonja Williams, September 1995, San Francisco, for *Black Radio: Telling It like It Was.*

20. Paul Mantabane, former WRFG volunteer, interview by the author, July 18, 1992, Washington, D.C.

21. Valerie Lee, former WVSP station manager, interview by the author, August 3, 1986, Raleigh, North Carolina.

22. Engleman, *Public Radio and Television in America,* 71–107.

23. William Barlow, "Pacifica Radio: A Cultural History" (unpublished manuscript, 1991), 57–69.

24. Ibid., 70–78.

25. Ibid., 79–81.

26. Valerie Strauss and Marc Fisher, "UDC to Sell Radio Station: Sale Would Help Close $10.1 Million Deficit," *Washington Post,* 18 June 1997, B6.

27. Ibid.

28. Marc Fisher, "Selling Jazz 90? Not So Fast, CPB Warns," *Washington Post,* 8 July 1977, E1, E7; Marc Fisher, "One Last Request for Jazz 90: NPR Protest Is Unlikely to Halt Station's Sale," *Washington Post,* 1 July 1977, D7.

29. Valerie Strauss, "C-SPAN Buys Radio Station from UDC: Cable Network to Pay $13 Million for Outlet," *Washington Post,* 14 Aug. 1997, D1, D2; Marc Fisher, "From Jazz to Blues: Notes on WDCU's Last Night on the Air," *Washington Post,* 27 Sept. 1997, B1, B2.

Notes to the Afterword

1. John Collins, *West African Pop Roots* (Philadelphia: Temple University Press, 1992), 3.

2. J. H. Kwabena Nketia, *The Music of Africa* (New York: W. W. Norton & Co., 1974), 61, 184; David Locke, *Drum Damba: Talking Drum Lessons* (Crown Point, Ind.: White Cliffs Media Co., 1990), 7, 32–33.

3. See "The Forgotten 15,000,000," *Sponsor* (26 October 1949): 24–25, 54–55.

Index

A & P Gypsies, 21
Abbott, Robert, 41–42
ABC (radio), 76, 158, 259, 260
ABC (television), 144, 190, 254
Abner, Edward, 269–70
Abrahams, Roger, 104
Ace, Johnny, 112
Action Woman, The, 255
Adams, Joe, 129
Adderley, Julian "Cannonball," 287
Adinwole, Obataiye ("Oba"), 286
advertising and radio, 15–16, 26–27, 28, 100–101, 110, 125, 129, 157
African Americans: consumer profiles of, 127–28, 129; demographic shifts in population of, 16, 58, 97, 297–98; in the entertainment industry, 17, 21, 22, 25, 80; expropriation of culture of, 20–22; in radio, 9, 20, 22–26, 27, 30; in radio audiences, 19–20, 26, 28, 34, 52, 108, 110, 114, 125, 126, 127, 195; in radio broadcasting, 9, 20
After Hours, 104
album-oriented rock (AOR), 230
Alexander, J. W., 202
Ali, Muhammad, 237, 266
Allen, Gracie, 147
Allen, William "Hoss," 162, 163, 164
All God's Children, 62
All-Negro Hour, The, 51, 52, 53–54, 55, 57
American Bandstand, 144, 189, 190
American Federation of Labor (AFL), 21

American Federation of Musicians (AFM), 21–22, 27–28
American Federation of Radio Actors (AFRA), 27–28
American Graffiti, 185
American Legionnaires, 185
American Negro Theater, 75
American Society of Composers, Authors and Publishers (ASCAP), 21, 22, 55
American Urban Radio Networks (AURN), 257–59, 282
America's Forum on the Air, 32
America's Town Meeting of the Air, 32, 72
Ammons, Albert, 25
Amos 'n' Andy, 8, 13, 14, 16, 76, 83, 84, 157, 260; African American reactions to, 41–44, 45; audience of, 40; imitations of, 40–41, 46, 54; impact of, 29, 40, 45–46; and racial ventriloquy, 27, 46; sources for, 37, 38; stereotyping in, 27, 36, 40, 42, 44–45, 46, 193; success of, 39–40, 45–46
Anaesthetic and Cerebelum, 40
Anderson, Eddie. See "Rochester"
Anderson, Marian, 72, 86, 112, 147
Andrews Sisters, 33, 147
Anka, Paul, 190
Anthony, Charles, 246
anti-war movement. *See* counterculture/anti-war movement
Apollo Theater, 144–45, 170, 269
Arden, Eve, 147

Index

Armed Forces Radio Service (AFRS), 69, 73, 75
Armstrong, Edwin, 226
Armstrong, Lil Hardin, 25
Armstrong, Louis, 19, 22, 23, 74, 290
Army Hour, The, 73
ASCAP. *See* American Society of Composers, Authors and Publishers
Atlanta University Center Forum, 282
Atlantic Records, 186, 199–200, 224
A-Train, The, 126
Attucks, Crispus, 84, 85, 86, 88
"Aunt Carrie," 122
"Aunt Jemima," 29–30, 76, 88, 112, 147
Aunt Jemima, 41
AURN. *See* American Urban Radio Networks
Avalon, Frankie, 190
Avant, Clarence, 222, 223, 224, 231, 239
Ayler, Albert, 286

Babafine, Adewela ("Baba"), 286
Back to Africa movement, 17
Bailey, Deford, 23
Bailey, Holmes ("Daddy-O Daylie"), 104, 105, 107, 113
Bailey, Mildred, 33
Baker, Donald ("Shango"), 286
Baker, Ed, 9, 94
Baker, Laverne, 122
Bakhtin, Mikhail, 1
Ball, Lucille, 147
Ballad, Hank, 190
"Ballad for Americans" (Latouche and Robinson), 59–61, 62, 63
Bandy, John ("Lord Fauntleroy") 143, 146
Bannister, Frank, 254
Baraka, Amiri, 237
Barrett, Andrew, 262
Barry, Marion, 238–39, 277
Bartlett, Ray ("Groovy Boy"), 167
Basie, Count, 70, 74, 95, 171
Battle of Henry Johnson, The, 70
B-Boyz in a Cipher, 284
Beavers, Rev. E. M., 163–64
bebop, 105, 106
Bechet, Sidney, 19
Beehive, The, 139, 307n. 13
Bell, Al, 222, 224
Bell, Haley, 140, 247, 264
Bell Broadcasting Company, 246, 247
Bensky, Larry, 229, 230
Benson, Al, 98–103, 107, 114, 121, 135, 144; Gibson's apprenticeship with, 135–36, 137; and Vivian Carter, 149
Berg, Gertrude, 147
Bernie, Ben, 22
Bernstein, Leonard, 77

Berry, Chuck, 178, 180
BEST. *See* Black Efforts for Soul Television
Bethune, Mary McCleod, 86, 95, 112, 148
"Beulah," 29, 30, 32, 83, 147
"Big Bird," 218–19, 238, 240
"Big Bopper," 178
"Big Daddy," 174, 191, 227–29, 234
"Big Smith," 183, 184 (*see also* "Wolfman Jack")
Billboard, 76, 192, 199
Bill Haley and the Comets, 180
Birth of a Nation, The, 36, 41, 42, 45
Black Citizens for Media Access, 251
Black College Radio Convention (BCRC), 284–85
Black College Sports Review, 257
Black Efforts for Soul Television (BEST), 250, 251
blackface minstrelsy, 2–8, 52, 133; and radio, 8–9, 20, 26, 27, 29, 35, 76, 77, 78, 157
Black Issues and the Black Press, 254
Black Mafia, 223
Black Muslim Hour, 233
Black Muslims, 237
Black Panthers, 216, 229, 231
Black Power, 219, 224, 229, 231, 248, 265; and FM stations, 10–11, 227, 230, 231, 234, 236, 237, 241
Black View of the Arts, 234
Black World—Third World, 237
Blake, Blind, 19
Blake, Eubie, 23
Bland, Bobby "Blue," 112, 123, 178
Bland, James, 7, 8
Blayton, J. B. Jr., 133, 136, 139, 247, 248, 264
Block, Martin, 158, 308n. 1
blues, 25, 96, 99, 113
Bob Horn's Bandstand, 190
Booker, Sid, 214
Boone, Pat, 161
Boskin, Joseph, 5
Bostic, Joe, 95
Boswell Sisters, 33
Boy Meets Girl, 122
Bracken, Eddie, 150
Bradley, Ed, 272
Bradshaw, Tiny, 74, 75
Bren, Joe, 37, 38
Brewington, Rudolf, 276
Brewster, Herbert, 115
Brinkley, Doc, 184
Broadway Rhythm, 74
Bronze Mike, 132
Brooks, Gwendolyn, 86
Broonzy, Big Bill, 19
Brotherhood of Sleeping Car Porters, 17
Brown, Charles, 163

Brown, Franklin, 70
Brown, Gerry, 122
Brown, H. Rap, 223
Brown, James, 163, 180, 203, 207, 223; as radio entrepreneur, 246, 249, 264, 265–67
Brown, J. Anthony, 259
Brown, Les, 159
Brown, Oscar Jr., 84
Brown, Ruth, 122, 207
Brown, "Snowball" Garrett, 36
Brown, Sterling A., 69
Brown, Tony, 272, 275
Brown, Willie, 264
Brown America Speaks, 115, 117, 209
Brubeck, Dave, 159
Bruce, Ramon, 103, 143
Bryant, "Senator" Bristow, 140
Bryant, Willie, 76, 104, 143, 189
Buck and Wheat, 41
Burke, Jesse "Spider," 103
Burke, Solomon, 199
Burns and Allen, 147
Burt, Ben, 266
Butler, Jerry, 203, 260

Caliver, Ambrose, 69
Callander's Colored Minstrels, 7
Calloway, Cab, 30, 34, 43, 70, 131, 253
Calvin, Floyd J., 24
Cameo/Parkway Records, 190
Cameos of Black Women, 258
Cantor, Eddie, 22
Carmichael, Stokely, 237, 239
Carr, Leroy, 19, 22
Carter, Andrew "Skip," 246–47, 250
Carter, Vivian, 103, 149–50
Carver, George Washington, 70
Casa Loma Orchestra, 33
Castleberry, Ed, 256
Cathings, Tex, 183
CBS, 19, 33, 34, 41, 160; and "Aunt Jemima," 29; "Ballad for Americans" produced by, 59, 60, 61; and black radio after World War II, 76; and commercial advertising, 27; docudrama pioneered by, 79; and Jim Crow policies, 26; progressive radio shows on, 69, 71, 74; and racial issues, 32, 72–73; Robeson appearing on, 62, 63, 303n. 23
Chaney, Lon, 185
Charioteers, 74
Charles, Ray, 123, 163, 170, 199, 202
Check and Double Check, 40, 43
Checker, Chubby, 190
Chedwick, Porky, 174
Cheek, James, 239, 240, 273
Chess Records, 186
Chicago Defender, 17, 83, 84, 112, 149; and the

Amos 'n' Andy controversy, 41, 42, 43; and Cooper, 52, 57
Chicago Tribune, 99
Chick Webb's Orchestra, 34
Children's Radio Workshop, 287
Chisholm, Shirley, 268
"chitlin circuit," 98, 173, 199, 265
Christophe, Henri, 85
Christy Minstrels, 4, 7
civil rights, 77, 86, 197–99, 254, 255, 265; and African American DJs, 204–11, 225, 296; and black radio, 10–11, 264; and crossover DJs, 168, 169, 170, 171, 195; and King's assassination, 219; and NARA, 220, 221–22; and NARTA, 223
Civil Rights Act, 212, 221
Clarence Jones and His Wonder Orchestra, 24
Clark, Bobbie, 190–91
Clark, Dick, 144, 187–88, 189–91, 205
Clay, Tom, 174
Cliff, Jimmy, 237
Cliquot Club Eskimos, 21
Clovers, 122, 205
Coasters, 144, 163, 200, 271
Cobb, Rev. Clarence, 119
Cohen, Octavus Roy, 38–39
cold war, 77, 84, 89; and Robeson, 63, 64, 65, 66
Cole, Nat King, 74, 95, 96, 122, 159, 199; television show hosted by, 144
Collins, Al "Jazzbo," 158–59
Collins, John, 294
Coltrane, John, 230, 237, 286
Columbia Records, 18
Coming Soon, 257, 258
Command Performance, 69
Committee for the Negro in the Arts, 77–78
Communications Brain Trust, 249–50
Communism, 64, 65, 77
Community Radio Workshop, Inc., 286
Community Resource Education Association, 293
Concert Showcase, 149
Congressional Black Caucus, 237, 240, 249, 251, 252, 290
Congress of Industrial Organizations (CIO), 62
Congress of Racial Equality (CORE), 198, 221
Connally, John B. Jr., 106
Connor, Theophilus Eugene "Bull," 198, 207–8
Conrad, Robert, 293
Cooke, Sam, 123, 144, 201–3, 215
Cooper, Gertrude Roberts, 57, 149

Index

Cooper, Jack, 50–58, 99, 101, 135, 149, 157; delivery used by, 9, 51, 57, 93, 94, 135, 136; success of, 114
Cooper and Lamar Music Company, 52
Copeland, Henry, 95
Copland, Aaron, 77
Cordell, Lucky, 103, 218
CORE. *See* Congress of Racial Equality
Corn Cob Pipe Club, The, 40
Corporan, Hector, 240
Corporation for Public Broadcasting (CPB), 279–80, 281, 285, 291, 292; and WAFR, 287, 289–90; and WVSP, 289–90
Correll, Charles, 16; and *Amos 'n' Andy,* 36, 37–39, 40, 42, 43, 45, 45, 46, 51, 54; and racial ventriloquy, 8, 27, 46, 157
Corwin, Norman, 63, 77, 82, 87, 303n. 23; and "Ballad for Americans," 59, 60, 61
Cosby, Bill, 231
Cotton Club, 20
Cotton Makers' Jubilee, 112, 122
counterculture/antiwar movement, 227, 228, 230, 234, 236
Cox, Ida, 17, 19
Cox, Wendell, 247
Cradle Time, 148
"Crazy Blues," 18
Crocker, Frankie, 10, 234, 287
Crosby, Bing, 33, 61, 168
Crosby, Leon, 228–29
Crudup, Arthur "Big Boy," 178
Crump, E. H. "Boss," 109, 110
C-SPAN, 292, 293
Curry, Cathy, 148
Curtis, Craig, 293
Curtis, Peck, 97

"Daddy Jules." *See* "Wolfman Jack"
"Daddy-O Daylie." *See* Bailey, Holmes
Daily Drum, The, 236, 274
Dallas, Stella, 147
Daughters of Africa, 43
Daughters of the American Revolution, 147
Davenport, Ronald, 255, 256, 258, 264
Davis, Angela, 237
Davis, Miles, 230, 286
Dawson, William, 98
Dee, Mary, 148
Defender Newsreel, 57–58
Deff, Lois, 22
Dells, 150
Delta Melodies, 116, 121
Delta Rhythm Boys, 74
Democracy USA, 83
Democratic National Convention, 212, 236
DePriest Oscar, 17
Destination Freedom, 83

Detroit, 70–71, 72, 213, 216
Dewey Phillips' Pop Shop, 178
Dialogue, 237
Diddley, Bo, 178
"Diggie Doo," 152
Dillard, Varetta, 182
DiMaggio, "Joltin'" Joe, 140
disc jockeys, African American, 108, 128, 129, 130, 133, 134–35; and black vernacular, 9–10; early, 93–97; economic situation of, 219; imitating whites, 9, 57, 139; influence of, 219, 296; after World War II, 97; women among, 98, 121–23, 147–53, 232, 234–35, 238
disc jockeys, white: crossover, 9, 133, 157, 158–60, 162–63, 164–75, 176, 186, 193; women as, 147
Dixie Hummingbirds, 163
Dixon, George Washington, 3, 4
Dixon, Larry, 143, 205
"Dizzy Lizzy," 152
"Doctor Blues," 166
"Doctor Hep Cat." *See* Durst, Lavada
docudramas, 79
Domino, Fats, 161, 178, 180, 191
Dominos, 182
Donahue, Tom "Big Daddy," 174, 191, 227–29, 234
Dorsey, Tommy, 74
Dorsey Brothers, 33
Dot Records, 161–62, 186
"Double V" campaign, 62, 65, 68
Doug Henderson Show, The, 142
Douglas, Van, 9, 94
Douglass, Frederick, 6, 84, 85, 86, 88, 111
Drew, Charles, 76, 95
Drifters, 122, 199, 200, 271
Du Bois, W. E. B., 84–85, 86, 87
Dunaway, Chuck, 174–75, 176
Duncan, Todd, 70
duopolies, 261, 262
Durham, "Frantic" Ernie, 140, 146
Durham, Richard, 83–85, 86–89, 135
Durnham, Katherine, 86
Durst, Lavada ("Doctor Hep Cat"), 91, 146; delivery of, 93, 104, 105–6, 107, 113
Dylan, Bob, 167
Dynamic Broadcasting Corporation, 256
Dyson, Leola, 148

Early, James, 103
Ebony, 58, 83, 128, 264, 278, 287
Ebony Moonbeams, 238
Eckstine, Billy, 174
Edwards, Oliver, 57
Election Day: Urban America, 258
Elks, 37, 43

Ellington, Duke, 16, 19, 20, 23–24, 33–34, 43, 149; and *New World a-Coming,* 78; on playlists, 95, 122, 159, 171, 290
Ellington, Ruth, 149
Elliot, Ken "Jack the Cat," 167
Ellison, Bob, 257
Emmett, Dan, 5, 7
Emory, Jake, 117
Emperor Jones, The (O'Neill), 23
End Jim Crow in Baseball Committee, 77
Energy Insight, 255
entertainment industry, 15, 16; African Americans in, 17, 21, 22, 25, 80
Ertegun, Ahmet, 199
Estelle, Delores, 148
Ethel Waters Show, The, 30
Ethiopian Serenaders, 4
Europe, James Reese, 18, 22, 70
Evans, Leonard, 130–31, 253
Evans, Sam, 103
Evers, Medgar, 198

Fabian, 190
Fanon, Frantz, 287
fascism, 50, 68, 72
Fast, Howard, 80
Faulkner, Larry Dean, 140, 209, 210
Fausch, Rev. Erskine, 207–8, 210
Federal Bureau of Investigation (FBI), 44, 65, 77, 102, 231, 277
Federal Communications Act (1934), 26
Federal Communications Commission (FCC), 45, 109, 238, 240, 249, 250, 251, 279, 284, 293; and deregulation of radio ownership, 11, 260–62, 292, 297; and high-power border stations, 184; and radio station ownership, 221, 231, 247, 248, 251–53
Federal Radio Act (1927), 26
Federal Radio Commission (FRC), 43
Federal Radio Education Committee, 69
Ferguson, Bert: and African American DJs, 116, 117, 118; and WDIA's all-black format, 109–10
Ferretti, Fred, 245–46
Fibber McGee and Molly Show, The, 30, 76
Finan, Joe, 191
Fitch Bandwagon, 33
Fitzgerald, Ella, 74, 76, 95, 122, 147, 159
Fitzgerald, F. M., 132
Fitzhugh, McKie, 103
Five Blind Boys of Alabama, 123
Five Songs for Democracy, 62
Fletcher, Louise, 148, 209
Fly, James, 45
FM radio, 226; and Black Power, 10–11, 227, 230, 231, 234, 236, 237, 241; DJ-driven,

black appeal format in, 232–33; economic advantage of, 227; and "free-form deejaying," 228, 241, 283, 286; progressive, 227–30, 233, 236, 241, 283, 286; and radicalization of black radio, 226, 241; and underground format, 235; urban contemporary, 234, 297; and urban rap, 284
Ford, Henry, 44
Ford, Jackie, 148, 149
Foston, Jack, 172
Frankel, Lou, 76–77
Franklin, Aretha, 163, 199, 234
Franklin, John Hope, 84
Franks, Elliott, 250
Frazier, E. Franklin, 69
Freed, Alan "Moon Dog," 9, 144, 179, 180–82, 183, 193; and payola, 187–89, 191; and racial ventriloquy, 9, 181
"Freedom Rides," 198
"Freedom Shows," 205
Freedom's People, 62, 69–70
Freedom's Road, 80
free-form programming, 228, 236, 237, 241, 283
frequency modulation. *See* FM radio
Friday File, 282

Gagarin, Yuri, 145
Gardella, Tess, 29
Garrett, Lee ("Rockin' Mr. G"), 232
Garroway, Dave, 158, 308n. 1
Garvey, Marcus, 17
Gaye, Marvin, 144, 234, 237
George, Nelson, 200
Georgia Minstrels, 7
Gibbons, Floyd, 32
Gibson, "Jockey" Jack, 129–30, 135–38, 140, 146, 151; and Martin Luther King, 208–9; and the NARA, 219, 220; urban contemporary criticized by, 234; and WERD, 136–37, 150, 247
Gillespie, Dizzy, 105, 158
Giovanni, Nikki, 230
Girlfriend, 284
Godfrey, Arthur "Red," 158
Goldbergs, The, 147
Golden Gate Jubilee Quartet, 34, 74
Goode, Mal, 254
Goodman, Benny, 33, 74
Good Neighbors, 115–16
Goodwill, 123
Gordon, Phil "Doctor Jive," 143, 146
Gordy, Berry, 138, 200, 201, 224
Gosden, Freeman, 16; and *Amos 'n' Andy,* 36–38, 39, 40, 42, 43, 45, 46, 51, 54; and racial ventriloquy, 8, 27, 46, 157
gospel music, 119

Index

Gospel Train, 148
Grace, Pattie, 250
Graham, Shirley, 77
Grateful Dead, 174, 228
Grayson, Michael, 77, 78
Green, Eddie, 74
Gregory, Dick, 237, 287
Griffith, D. W., 36, 41, 42, 45
Griffith, Sister Bessie, 148
Gubar, Susan, 2
Gulf Show, The, 41
Gullah Jack, 85

Haight-Ashbury, 227, 228
Haley, Bill, 178, 180
Hall, Gladys, 152
Hall, Juanita, 131
Hallelujah Jubilee, 121
Hamer, Fannie Lou, 237
Hamilton, Colonel West A., 70
Hampton, Lionel, 74, 171
Hancock, Hunter, 133, 171–72, 193
Hand, Rolla, 85
Handy, W. C., 18, 24, 70, 81
Hank Ballad and the Midnighters, 190
Harlem, 16–17
Harlem Broadcasting Corporation, 24
Harlem Echo, 139
Harlem Matinee, 171
Harlem Renaissance, 17
Harlem Salutes Amos 'n' Andy, 43
Harmon, Clarence, 166
Harris, Bass, 9, 94
Harris, Gus, 218
Harris, R. H., 202
Haverly's Colored Minstrels, 7
Hawes, Hampton, 159
Hawkins, Coleman, 19
Hawkins, "Screaming" Jay, 181
Hayes, Isaac, 118, 234
Haylock, Marie, 255
Health Break, 282
Hearst, Patty, 236
Heater, Gabriel, 32
Hellman, Lillian, 77
Henderson, Douglas "Jocko," 141–43,
  144–45, 183, 205, 230; and civil rights,
  209, 210; and race riots, 213
Henderson, Fletcher, 19, 22, 23
Henderson, "Hollywood," 105
Henry, Ragan, 252
Here Comes Tomorrow, 83, 135
Heron, Gil Scott, 237
Hibler, Al, 112
Hicks, Muse, Tate and Furst Holdings, 261
Higginson, Vi, 234
Highway to Heaven, 120

Hill, Big Bill, 103
Hill, John Lamar, 269
Hilliard, David, 229
Hines, Earl "Fatha," 22, 24
Hinzman, Elizabeth, 100
hip-hop, 283, 284, 298
Hip Hop Happy Hour, 284
Hitler, Adolf, 50, 67, 72
Holiday, Billie, 79, 95, 147, 159, 174, 290
Holt, Nora, 149
Home Executive, 148
Homemaker's Holiday, 148
Honesty, Eddie, 9, 94
Honeyboy and Sassafras, 40
Hooker, John Lee, 150
Hooks, Ben, 238–39, 251
Hoover, Herbert, 40, 44
Hoover, J. Edgar, 44
Horn, Bob, 190, 191
Horne, Lena, 74–75, 77, 147
Horseradish and Fertilizer, 54
Hot Line, 211
"Hot Scott," 167–68
"Hotsy Totsy," 152
House of Jive, The, 205
House That Jack Built, The, 95
House Un-American Activities Committee
  (HUAC), 64, 77
Howard, "Joltin'" Joe, 138–41, 146, 167,
  231–32, 307n. 13
Howard University, 95, 254, 272, 277; and
  WHBC-AM, 283–84; and WHUR, 236, 238,
  239, 240, 275
"Howling Wolf," 177, 237
How to Eat to Live, 237
HUAC. *See* House Un-American Activities
  Committee
Hughes, Cathy, 243, 262, 264, 271–78
Hughes, Dewey, 275, 276
Hughes, Langston, 72, 77
Hulbert, Maurice "Hot Rod," 16–18, 120,
  126, 142, 145–46; and civil rights, 209,
  210, 218; and the NARA, 219
Hummert, Frank and Ann, 70
Humphrey, Hubert, 266
Hunter, Alberta, 19
Hunter, Ivory Joe, 113, 161
Hunter, Tab, 161
Hunting with Hunter, 172
Hurt, Marlin, 30

Impressions, 150, 203
In Celebration of Black Mothers, 258
Ingram, Rex, 76
Ink Spots, 74, 76
Inner City Broadcasting, 233, 234, 250, 268,
  269

Inside/Outside, 237
Inside Scoop, 258
Institute for Education by Radio, 76, 87
Institute for Education in Radio and Television, 115
Internal Revenue Service, 187, 189, 191
International Sweethearts of Rhythm, 74, 271
Interpreters, 237
Ipana Troubadours, 21

J., Myra, 259
Jack Benny Show, The, 30, 31, 76
Jackie Robinson Show, The, 76
Jack L. Cooper Advertising Company, 51, 56
Jack L. Cooper Presentations, 51, 56
Jackson, Eugene, 253–54, 257, 264
Jackson, Hal, 95–96, 143, 209, 219, 230, 233
Jackson, Jesse, 202, 210, 211, 277
Jackson, Mahalia, 54, 76, 120
Jackson, Michael, 201
"Jack the Bellboy." See McKenzie, Ed
Jack the Rapper, 138
Jack the Rapper Black Family Affair Convention, 138
James, Harry, 33
James Brown Broadcasting, 266
Jam, Jive and Gumbo, 166
Jarvis, Al, 158, 308n. 1
Jazz Age, 12–26
Jazz from Dad's Pad, 105
Jazz Singer, The, 16
Jefferson, Blind Lemon, 19
Jefferson Airplane, 228
Jelks, Lo, 284
Jewel, James, 31
Jim Crow, 3, 4, 40; policies of, 55, 68, 84; and radio, 9, 10, 27–28, 33–34, 44, 55, 61, 146
"Jim Crow" (Robeson), 81–83
Jimmie Lunceford Orchestra, 159
Jive Master kolb, 146
Jives of Dr. Hep Cat, The, 106
"jive talk," 104, 106
Jocko's Rocket Ship Show, 144
Joe Bren Company, 37
John, Elton, 234
Johnson, Blind Willie, 19
Johnson, Charles, 221, 222
Johnson, Irene, 152–53
Johnson, Jack, 49
Johnson, John H., 128
Johnson, Lonnie, 19, 25
Johnson, Louise, 150
Johnson, Nicholas, 249
Johnson, Pete, 160
Johnson, Robert, 264
Johnson, Roosevelt, 140

Johnson, Russ, 238, 240
Joint II, The, 284
Jolson, Al, 16, 22
Jones, Clarence, 24
Jones, Quincy, 272
Jones, Tom, 239–41, 273
Jordan, Louis, 74, 160
Joyner, Tom, 259
Jubilee, 74–75
Jubilee Roll Call, 121

KAGB-FM, 231, 241
Kallinger, Paul, 183
Kaltenborn, H. V., 32, 301n. 29
Kansas City Rockets, 173
KAOK, 132
KAPP, 222
Karenga, Ron, 231
KBLX-FM, 268
KCIF, 183
KCOH, 251, 307n. 13
KDAY, 252
KDIA, 131, 314n. 2
KDKO, 217
Keepin' It Real, 284
Kennedy, John F., 198
Kennedy, Robert, 198, 266
Kent, Herb, 103, 209, 211
Kersands, Billy, 7, 8
Keystone Broadcasting System (KBS), 130, 131
KFFA, 96–97
KFOX, 173
KFRC, 133
KFVD, 171
KFWB, 158, 221, 308n. 1
KGBC, 138
KGFJ, 171, 172, 214, 215, 217
KGRM-FM, 280
KGW, 40
King, B. B., 112, 120, 163, 177, 207; and WDIA, 118–19, 123
King, Martin Luther Jr., 12, 170, 195, 198, 258, 266; and African American DJs, 10, 206, 207, 208–9, 210, 211, 222, 223, 230, 287, 290; assassination of, 213, 216–17, 218, 219, 223, 253, 266; birthday celebrations of, 258, 270
King, Rodney, 270
KING, 94
King: A Man and His Dream, 258
"King Bee," 146, 307n. 13
King Biscuit Time, 96–97, 108
Kingslow, Janice, 84
Kinnison, William, 57
Kitchen Time, 148
Kitt, Eartha, 121

KJHS, 167
KJLH-FM, 269–70, 296
KKK. *See* Ku Klux Klan
KLAC, 158
KMBR, 173, 174
KMPX-FM, 227–29
Know Your Bible, 57
KNUZ, 139, 167, 307n. 13
KOKY, 222
KOWH, 192
KOWL, 129
KPFA-FM, 236, 290
KPFK-FM, 173, 236, 290
KPFT-FM, 236, 290
KPOO-FM, 287–88
KPPC-FM, 227
KPRS-AM, 132, 246–47, 250
KPVU-FM, 283
Kraft Music Hall, 61
Krupa, Gene, 74
KSAN, 132, 148, 171, 173, 229–30
KSAN-FM, 227
KSAT, 40
KSOL, 204
KUCA-FM, 280
KUET, 93
Ku Klux Klan (KKK), 170, 205, 207, 211
Kuti, Fela Ransome, 286
KVET, 91, 106
KWBR, 171
KWKH, 167
KXLW, 103
KYOK, 139, 152, 250, 251
Kyser, Kay, 33
KYW, 24, 25
KZOK, 152

Ladies Day, 148
Lafayette Players, 24
LaGuardia, Fiorello, 73
Lampell, David, 234
Lance, Major, 203
Lane, Dick "Night Train," 105
Lane, Laura, 148
Lane, Vera, 30
Last Poets, 230, 237, 287
Lathums, Stan, 272
Latin Flavor, 240
Latouche, John, 59
Law, Bob, 255, 258, 282
Leadbelly (Huddie Ledbetter), 74
Leaner, Arthur Bernard. *See* Benson, Al
Leaner, George, 102
Leary, Howard, 214
Lee, Canada, 62, 70, 77; and *New World a-Coming,* 78, 79, 80, 81, 82
Lee, Johnny, 31

Lee, Peggy, 95
Leeper, "Chattie" Hattie, 151–52, 153, 167
Leiber, Jerry, 200
Lenior, J. B., 102
Leonard, Harlen, 173
Lewis, Delano, 285, 292, 293
Lewis, Jerry Lee, 178, 180
Lewis, Sheldon, 256
Lewis, Smiley, 161
Lewis, Stanley, 167
Life Begins at Midnight, 149
Lifeline, 237
Life of Anna Lewis, The, 131, 253
Liggins, Alfred Jr., 278
Liggins, Cathy. *See* Hughes, Cathy Liggins
Light of the World, 119
Lindsey, Melvin, 275
Listen Chicago, 58
Little Richard, 161, 170, 178, 180
Lockwood, Robert "Junior," 96
Loeb, Phillip, 77
Lombardo, Guy, 33
Lone Ranger, The, 31
Long, Huey, 44
Lopez, Vincent, 22
"Lord Fauntleroy." See Bandy, John
Lorenz, George "Hound Dog," 179–80, 183, 193, 232
Lott, Eric, 6
Louis, Joe, 57, 70, 74, 76, 81; versus Schmeling, 47, 49, 50
Louis Armstrong Show, The, 30
Louisiana Weekly, 165
L'Ouverture, Toussaint, 85
Love and Theft (Lott), 6
Lowe, Richard, 79
Lucas, George, 185
Lucas, Sam, 7
Lucky Strike Orchestra, 21
Luke and Timber, 54
Lulu and Leander, 31, 40–41
Lunceford, Jimmy, 74, 122
Lutour, Lou, 149
Lyles, Aubrey, 17, 24, 38, 42
Lymon, Frankie, 189

Mabley, Moms, 103
McCain, Bernie, 276
McCarthy, Glen, 50
McCormick, Larry, 215, 221
McCoy, Sid, 103, 104, 131
McDaniel, Hattie, 30, 74
McDonald, Mary, 287
McKenzie, Ed ("Jack the Bellboy"), 166, 171, 174
McKernan, Phil, 174

McKernan, Rod "Pigpen," 174
McKinney, Star, 122
McLeod, Don, 174, 191
McNeely, Big Jay, 140
McPhatter, Clyde, 144
McQueen, Butterfly, 74
Major League Baseball Notebook, 257
Makeba, Miriam, 286
Malcolm X, 230, 267, 287, 290–91
Malone, Pick, 41
Mammy, 9, 29, 30, 81
Man behind the Gun, 75
"Man with the Goods." See Woods, Georgie
Ma Perkins, 147
March of Time, 79
March on Washington, 198, 203, 210
Markham, Pigmeat, 103
Marley, Bob, 237
Marlin Hurt and Beulah Show, The, 30
Marshall, Pluria, 250–51, 262
Masakela, Hugh, 286–87
Mason, Mary, 209
mass consumption, 15–16
Mauldin, Manny, 57
Maultsby, Portia, 146
Mayfield, Curtis, 201–2, 203, 211, 230, 237
Maynor, Dorothy, 70
MBN. *See* Mutual Black Network
Memphis World, 111–12, 114
Men o' War, 69
Metromedia, 229
Miami Beach DJ convention, 187, 192, 193, 220
Miami Herald, 187
Midnight Ramble, 110, 112
Midnight Special, 161
Milam, Lorenzo, 287–88
Mildred Bailey Show, The, 74
Miller, Flournoy, 17, 24, 38, 39, 42
Miller, Glenn, 33, 160
Miller, Rice. *See* Williamson, Sonny Boy
Mills, Florence, 22, 23
Mills, Irving, 23–24
Mills Brothers, 34, 74
Milton, D. E., 53
Milton, Roy, 160
Minority Business Report, 256
Mintz, Leo, 180–81, 182
Miss Dupree, 259
Mississippi Freedom Party, 212
Mississippi Freedom Summer Project, 195, 211, 255
"Miss Mandy," 152
Mitchell, Parren, 210
Mitchell, Peggy, 207
Mitchell Christian Singers, 19
Mo' Butta fo' Yo' Biscuit, 284

Modern Jazz Quartet, 159
Modern Records, 172
"Molasses and January," 41
Money Smarts, 257
Monroe, Willa, 121–22, 126, 148
Montague, Nathanial ("Montague the Magnificent"), 175, 195, 214–15, 217
Montgomery bus boycott, 197, 198
Moohah's Matinee, 118
Moon Dog House Rock and Roll Party, The, 181
Moon Dog Show, 181
"Moonshine and Sawdust," 41
Moore, Cecil, 205, 206, 213, 238
Moore, Dwight "Gatemouth," 119–20, 146
Moore, Marlene, 150
Moran and Mack, 8
Morning Sound, The, 274
Morton, Ferdinand "Jelly Roll," 19, 22
Moses, Greg, 265, 266
Moss, Carlton, 24
Moten, Bennie, 19, 22
Motown Records, 138, 199, 200, 224, 232
Moulin Rouge Orchestra, 24
Movin' around with Mary Dee, 148
Mundy Choristers, 25
Mush and Clorinda—The Alabama Sunflowers, 54
Mutual Black Network (MBN), 255, 256, 257
Mutual Broadcasting System, 76, 81, 256
My Favorite Husband, 147
My Friend Irma, 147

NAACP. *See* National Association for the Advancement of Colored People
NAB. *See* National Association of Broadcasters
NABOB. *See* National Association of Black Owned Broadcasters
Nambe, Kojo, 237
NARA. *See* National Association of Radio Announcers
NARTA. *See* National Association of Radio and Television Announcers
Nat D.'s Supper Club, 114
National Association for the Advancement of Colored People (NAACP), 33, 198, 207, 209, 233, 267; and radio, 43, 71, 221, 248
National Association of Black Owned Broadcasters (NABOB), 249–50, 251, 252, 261
National Association of Broadcasters (NAB), 21, 45, 249, 250; and radio-station ownership, 221, 231, 248, 252
National Association of Colored Waiters and Hotel Employees, 43
National Association of Radio and Television Announcers (NARTA), 195, 223–25, 248–49, 265

National Association of Radio Announcers (NARA), 133, 219–23
National Baptists Convention, 43
National Black Media Coalition (NBMC), 249–50, 251, 252
National Black Network (NBN), 253–55, 257, 282
National Council of Negro Women, 95
National Federation of Community Broadcasters (NFCB), 286
National Jazz, Rhythm & Blues Disc Jockey Association, 219
National Negro Network (NNN), 130–31, 253
National Negro Newspaper Week, 76
National Public Radio (NPR), 285, 292, 293
Native Son (Wright), 81
Nat King Cole Show, The, 76
NBA Report, 257
NBC, 19, 217, 226; blackface radio shows on, 26, 36, 39–40, 41, 42, 43; in the 1930s, 27, 30, 32–33, 34, 47, 50; during World War II, 62, 70, 72, 73; after World War II, 65, 76, 83, 87–88
NBMC. *See* National Black Media Coalition
NBN. *See* National Black Network
Negro Hour, The, 24, 25
Negro in the War, The, 73
Negro Radio Association (NRA), 130, 131–32
Negro Swing Parade, 94
Nelson, Ford, 119, 120
Nelson, Ozzie, 33
Neville, Art, 167
New Breed, 223, 224, 231, 234, 239, 248–49
Newman, Mark, 54
New World a-Coming, 78–83, 89, 94
New York Times, 145, 245
NFCB. *See* National Federation of Community Broadcasters
NFL Playbook, 257
Niagara, Joe, 174, 191
Night Life, 76
Night Talk, 255, 258, 282
Nisker, Wes "Scoop," 229, 230
Nite Spot, 122
Nixon, Richard, 229, 239, 249, 266
Nkrumah, Kwame, 287
NNN. *See* National Negro Network
Nobles, Gene, 160–61, 162
No Name Jive, 167
Noone, Jimmy, 24
Norfolk Jubilee Singers, 19
Norman, Gene, 158, 308n. 1
Norvo, Red, 74
Novick, Harry, 132, 230, 233, 268
NPR. *See* National Public Radio
NRA. *See* Negro Radio Association

O'Connell, Helen, 33
Office of War Information (OWI), 68–69, 69
Okeh Record Company, 18
"Okey Dokey," 129, 152
OK Group, 132, 139, 152
Olatunji, 286
Oliver, Joseph "King," 16, 19, 22
Oliver North Show, The, 292
O'Neal, Frederick, 31
O'Neill, Eugene, 23
One Man's Opinion, 254
One-Woman Show, 149
One World (Wilkie), 71
On the Avenue, 179
On the Real Side (Watkins), 1
Open Letter on Race Hatred, An, 70–72, 76
Open the Door Richard, 103
oral tradition, black, 135, 143, 146, 294
Original Thirteen, 219
Ory, Kid, 22
Ossie Davis and Ruby Dee Story Hour, The, 254–55
Otis, Johnny, 172–73, 200
Ottley, Roi, 78, 80
Our Community Marches On, 58
Our Gal Sunday, 70
Our Miss Brooks, 147
Owens, Jesse, 50, 57, 70, 103
Oxford, "Jumping" George, 171, 173–74

Pacifica network, 236, 286, 290, 291
Padgett, Pat, 41
Page, Frank "Gatemouth," 167
Paige, Leroy "Satchel," 57
Paley, William, 71
Parade of Stars, 257
Paramount, 18
Parker, Charlie, 158, 290
Parker, Dorothy, 80
Parker, Junior, 177
Parrot Records, 102
Patrick, "Alley Pat," 129, 171
Patterson, E. R., 131
Patterson, Norwood J., 132
Patton, Charlie, 19
Payne, Sonny, 96
payola, 186–88, 219, 220, 222, 227; scandal over, 187, 189, 191, 192, 193
Peabody Award, 72, 79
Pearl Harbor, 70
"Peekskill Riot," 64–65
People's Platform, The, 32, 72–73, 237
Pepper, John, 109, 110, 113–14, 117, 124, 126
Perry, Andre, 238
personality jocks, 146, 297
Pew, Roberta, 143

Phillips, Dewey "Daddy-O," 176–79, 193
Phillips, Jerry, 274
Phillips, Little Esther, 173
Phillips, Sam, 178
Pickard, Charles J., 247
Pickett, Wilson, 199
Pick 'n' Pat, 41
Pinkard, Fred, 84
Pittsburgh Courier, 24, 41, 42–43, 57–58, 112
Planet Black, 284
Plique, Eddie, 57
Polk, Robelia, 148
Ponek, Stefan, 229
Poorhall, Johnny "Jitterbug," 159
"Poppa Stoppa," 146, 165, 167
Potter, Peter, 158
Potts, Eugene ("Genial Gene"), 129, 146, 150, 167
Powell, Adam Clayton, 79
Powell, Adam Clayton III, 285
Powell, Colin, 277
Poyeus, Paul, 85
Prater, George, 138–39
Premium Stuff, 122–23
Presley, Elvis, 112, 123, 178, 180
Price, Lloyd, 271
Prince Omar, 146
product identification, 110, 125, 128
Progressive Party, 63
Prosser, Gabriel, 85
Pryor, Snooky, 102
psychographic programming, 274
Public Broadcasting Act (1967), 279, 280
Purple Grotto, The, 158–59
Pursuit of Happiness, 59

Queen's Throne, The, 284
Quiet Storm, The, 275
Quizzicale, 30

race records, 18–19
racial ventriloquy, 2, 11; and African Americans imitating whites, 139; and blackface minstrelsy, 35–36, 45, 46, 109; and contemporary black vernacular, 9, 10, 135; and crossover DJs, 9, 10, 157, 159–60, 164–65, 175, 181, 183, 193; defined, 1; demise of, 228
racism, 62–63, 65, 67–68
radio: African Americans in, 9, 20, 22–26, 27, 30; audience of, 19–20, 26, 28, 34, 52, 108, 110, 114, 125, 127, 195; golden age of, 34–35; industry growth of, 19–20, 26
Radio One, 241, 262, 278
radio stations: African American nonprofit, 286–91; African American ownership of, 11, 136, 231, 245–46, 291, 294–98; black

appeal, 107, 108, 125–26, 128, 130–33, 134, 147, 148, 149, 157, 166, 170–71, 246, 294–98; black college, 279, 280–85, 291; deregulation of ownership of, 260–63; high-power border, 183–84; ownership of, and gender, 147; ownership of, and race, 133, 152, 219, 221, 225, 245–46, 262–63; and psychographic programming, 274; public, 279–80, 292
Radio Writers Guild (RWG), 27–28
Ragland, John M., 58
Rainey, Ma, 17, 19, 22
Randolf, Lillian, 31
Randolph, A. Philip, 17, 67, 70, 72
Randy's Record Shop, 161, 162, 271
rap, 283, 296
Ravin' Ramon, 103–4, 143, 146
Ravin' with Ramon, 103–4, 143
Rawls, Lou, 202, 257
Ray, Stanley Jr., 132
Rayee, Del, 253–54
RCA Victor, 186, 202
record industry, 220, 221, 224; and payola, 186–87; and race records, 18–19; and shift to FM, 226–27
Red Channels, 77
Redding, Otis, 163, 201, 215, 224
Red, Hot and Blue, 177, 178
Red Skelton Show, The, 31, 73
Reed, Jimmy, 150, 163
reggae, 237
Reid, Ben, 128
Rene, La Mar, 234
Republican Party, 239, 262
Research Company of America, 125
Reverend Ike, 184
Rhodes, Todd, 181
rhyming and signifying, 104, 113, 135, 143, 146
rhythm-and-blues, 100, 159, 169, 175, 199, 296; and civil rights, 168; and crossover DJs, 193
Rice, Thomas "Daddy," 3, 4, 5
Richardson, Dora, 150
Richbourg, John ("John R"), 162–63, 181, 183, 193, 201
"riding the gain," 180
Riley, Dudley, 137
riots, urban race, 212, 213–16, 266, 270, 296
Rise to Culture, A, 24
Roaring Twenties, 20
Robbins, Freddie, 158, 308n. 1
Robeson, Paul, 23, 34, 59–66, 70, 76, 303n. 23; controversy over political views of, 64–66, 77; and *New World a-Coming*, 82–83
Robinson, Bill "Bojangles," 17, 43, 81
Robinson, Earl, 59, 61

Index

Robinson, Edward G., 73
Robinson, Evelyn, 149
Robinson, Jackie, 64, 76
Robinson, Smokey, 144, 201, 275
Robinson, Sugar Ray, 149
Robson, William, 71, 76, 77
"Rochester," 31–32, 74–75, 82
Rochon, "King Bee" Lonnie, 146, 307n. 13
rock and roll, 173, 175, 181, 190, 193
Rocket Ship, 141–42, 143, 144, 145
Rocking in Rhythm, 94
"rocking the pot," 179–80
Rodgers, Jimmie, 16
Rolfe, B. A., 22
Rollins, Inc., 246, 248, 314n. 2
Romance of Helen Trent, The, 70
Roosevelt, Franklin Delano, 44, 63, 68, 71, 82
Ross, Diana, 138, 201
Rounsaville, Robert W., 131–32
Rounsaville Radio Stations, 131–32, 246, 247, 314n. 2
Royal Canadians, 33
Ruby Valentine, 131
Rudy Vallee Show, The, 33
Runnin' Wild, 38
Rushing, Jimmy, 159
Russell, Luis, 25
Russell, Nipsy, 143
Rydell, Bobby, 190

Salem Communications, 292–93
Salem Radio News (SRN), 292
Salute to Great Black Americans, A, 258
Sam 'n' Henry, 39–30, 40
Sambo, 3, 4, 5
Sanders, Pharoah, 274
Santana, 228
"Sapphire," 147
Sarnoff, David, 226
SAR Records, 202
Saturday Night Fish Fry, 118
Savoy, 173
Saxon, Louise "Louisville Lou," 129, 150–51
SBC. *See* Sheridan Broadcasting Corporation
SBN. *See* Sheridan Broadcasting Network
Schmeling, Max, 47, 49–50
SCLC. *See* Southern Christian Leadership Conference
Scott, Hazel, 77, 80
Scottsboro Boys, 32, 301n. 29
Scruggs, Chuck, 204
SDS. *See* Students for a Democratic Society
Search for Missing Persons, 58
Sears, Zenas "Daddy," 168–71, 176, 193, 208
Sehorn, Marshall, 224
Senghor, Leopold, 287
Sepia Serenade, 148

Sepia Swing Club, 116, 118
Shaw, Artie, 33
Shaw, Carolyn, 148
Shaw, George Bernard, 44
Shearing, George, 159
Shell Chateau, 33
Sheridan Broadcasting Corporation (SBC), 255
Sheridan Broadcasting Network (SBN), 253, 255–57, 258, 281
Shields, Del, 234, 239; and Black Power, 230–31, 233, 234; and King's assassination, 216, 217; and NARTA, 22, 223–24, 249, 265
Shiffren, Lalo, 222
Shore, Dinah, 33
Short Cuts, 255
Showboat, 29, 30, 41
Shuffle Along, 23, 38
signifying, 104
Silverstein, Joseph, 52–53
Simmons, Judy, 268
Simms, Hilda, 131, 148
Simone, Nina, 203, 230
Simpkins, John Paul, 239–40
Sinatra, Frank, 33, 76, 159, 160, 238
"Sir Walter Raleigh," 146
Sissle, Noble, 23, 70
Situations Wanted, 58
Slade, Karen, 270
slavery, 2, 20, 84
Slick and Slim Show, The, 31, 40
Sly and the Family Stone, 228
Small, Sidney, 253–54
Smalls, Tommy "Doctor Jive," 143–44, 183, 219
Smiley, Tavis, 259
Smith, Bessie, 16, 17, 19, 22, 23
Smith, Bev, 256, 258
Smith, Clifton, 307n. 13
Smith, Jimmy, 222
Smith, Joe, 191
Smith, Kate, 33, 147
Smith, Mamie, 17, 18, 19
Smith, Novela, 152
Smith, Pinetop, 25
Smith, Robert. *See* "Wolfman Jack"
Smith, Stuff, 74
Smith, Wonderful, 31, 73
Snap Club, The, 205
SNCC. *See* Student Nonviolent Coordinating Committee
soap operas, 70, 72
Social Security for You and Your Family, 58
Sonar Eclipse, 284
Songbirds of the South, 115
Song of Zion, 57

soul music, 199, 200, 203, 204, 237
Soul Stirrers, 120, 123, 202
Sound and Print United, 289
Sounderling, Egmont, 124, 131
Sounderling Broadcasting Corporation, 131, 246, 314n. 2
South, Wesley, 209, 211
Southernaires, 32–33, 34
Southern Christian Leadership Conference (SCLC), 198, 248; and DJs, 170, 195, 208, 209, 222
Southern Fried Flava, 284
Southern Wonders, 115
Southside (Chicago), 16–17
Spaniels, 150
Spann, Purvis, 103, 195, 209, 210–11, 218, 264
Speidel, Joe, 131
Speidel Broadcasting Inc., 131, 246, 247, 314n. 2
Spellman, Charles, 276
"Spinner Joe," 167
Spirit of Memphis, 115, 120, 123
Sponsor, 125, 127, 128, 129–31, 134
Spotlight, 122
Springarn, Major Arthur, 33
Spruill, Robert ("Brother Hussan"), 286
SRN. *See* Salem Radio News
Stafford, Jo, 160
Stage Door, 255
Stams, Richard, 103
Staple Singers, 203, 237
Station, George L., 217
Stax Records, 118, 199, 200, 201
Steinberg, Luther, 122
Steinberg, Martha Jean "the Queen," 122–23, 150, 153, 216; and civil rights, 209, 210
"Stepin Fetchit," 44
stereotyping, 3; in *Amos 'n' Andy*, 40, 42, 44–45, 46; in radio, 29–32, 35, 76–77, 152
Stevenson, Adlai, 87
Stewart, Jim, 201
Stiles, Danny, 174
Stone, Jesse, 199
Storm, Gale, 161
Story of Ruby Valentine, The, 253
Storz, Todd, 192–93
Stowe, Harriet Beecher, 37
Straight Up, 256, 258
Straight Up Philly, 284
Stroller, Mike, 200
Strong Men Getting Stronger, 258
Strother, Miss Susie, 140, 148–49
STRZ Funline, 258
Student Nonviolent Coordinating Committee (SNCC), 197–98, 223, 237, 288

Students for a Democratic Society (SDS), 288
Sullivan, Ed, 144
Sullivan, Maxine, 34
Sultans of Swing, 180
Summer of Love, 228
Sun Ra, 237, 286
Sun Records, 178, 186
Sunshine Orchestra, 22–23
superduopolies, 261, 262, 297
Supremes, 144
Sutton, Percy, 233, 250, 264, 267–69
Sutton, Pierre, 250, 268–69
Sweet Talking Time, 116
swing-band music, 33, 106, 159, 187
Syndicated Communication, 278

Tales from Harlem, 95
"talking drums," 294–96
Talmadge, Herman, 169
"T and Sherry," 232
Tan Town Coffee Club, 114, 120
Tan Town Homemakers, 121–22, 148
Tan Town Jamboree, 113, 114
Tan Town Jubilee, 120
Tate, Erskine, 22, 25
Tatum, Art, 33–34, 79
Taylor, Billy, 143
Taylor, Johnny, 202
Teen Town, 149
Teen Town Jamboree, 118
Teen Town Singers, 118
Telecommunications Act (1996), 261
television, 30, 34, 109, 144, 195, 226; impact on radio of, 89, 108, 157
Temptations, 230
Terkel, Studs, 84
Terrell, Mary Church, 86, 148
Terry, Bob "Nighthawk," 218–19, 238, 240
Terry, Wallace, 239
Tharpe, Sister Rosetta, 120, 129
Theater Owners' Booking Association (TOBA), 17, 25, 52, 54, 98, 133
They Call Me Joe, 73
This Is The Story, 75
Thomas, Carla, 118, 201
Thomas, Henry, 19
Thomas, Irma, 166
Thomas, Robert "Honeyboy," 122, 146, 167
Thomas, Rufus, 112, 123, 201
Thompson, John, 277
Thorpe, Earl, 287
Tilden, Wezlen, 84
Time, 79, 187
Tin Pan Alley, 18, 20, 22, 38, 187
Tiny Bradshaw Orchestra, 74, 75
toasting, 150
Toast of the Town, 144

Index

To Build a Nation, 287
Today's Calendar, 148
Today with Mrs. Roosevelt, 65
Tom Joyner Morning Show, The, 259–60
Too Long, America, 73
"Top Forty," 200, 226, 227, 232, 234, 238; criticized, 228, 246; and Motown, 200; payola rerouted by, 192–93
Torin, "Symphony Sid," 158
To Secure These Rights, 76
Total Black Experience in Sound, The, 217, 230, 231, 233
To Your Health, 257
Travel Line, 282
Trent, Helen, 147
Trower, J. Richard, 128
Truman, President Harry, 76
Truth, Sojourner, 86, 149
Tubman, Harriet, 85, 86, 88, 149
Tucker, Sophie, 16, 18, 22
Tucker, Sterling, 238–39
Tuesday, 131, 253
Twain, Mark, 6
Two Black Crows, The, 8, 41
2 Dope Boyz in a Cadillac, 284

Uncle Tom, 6, 76, 77
Uncle Tom's Cabin (Stowe), 37
underground radio, 227
United Broadcasting Company, 246, 248, 314n. 2
United Daughters of the Confederacy, 37
United Nations, 63, 254, 303n. 23
United Nations Correspondents Association, 254
United Slaves (US), 231
United States Office of Education, 69
Unity Broadcasting Corporation, 253, 254, 255
Universal Negro Improvement Association (UNIA), 17
University of Chicago Roundtable, The, 32
urban contemporary, 234, 297
USA Music Magazine, 258
U.S.S. Booker T. Washington, 75

Vallee, Rudy, 22
Vann, Robert, 41, 42, 43
Van Peebles, Melvin, 272
Van Vechten, Carl, 2
Vaughan, Sarah, 95, 121
Vee-Jay Records, 150
Vesey, Denmark, 85, 86
Victor Records, 18, 29, 61
Virginia Minstrels, 4, 5
Voice of America, 69
Voting Rights Act, 212

WAAF, 56, 101
WABC, 189
WACQ, 222
Wade, Brother Theo "Bless My Bones," 119, 120–21, 123
Wade, Jimmie, 24
WAFR-FM, 286–87, 289–90
WAKE, 139
Wald, Theodore, 77
Walden, Phil, 163, 224
Walker, Jack the "Pear-Shaped Talker," 143, 146
Wallace, George (comedian), 259
Wallace, George (politician), 204
Wallace, Henry, 63
Wallace, Sippie, 19
Waller, Fats, 19, 33–34, 70, 113, 122, 159
Walls, Bishop W. J., 42
WAMF-FM, 280
WAMO AM/FM, 150, 174, 256
WAMU-FM, 292
WAOK, 152, 170, 208
Washington, Dinah, 74, 121, 122
Washington, Freddie, 77
Washington, Grover Jr., 234
Washington, Harold, 211
Washington Post, 95, 191, 236, 239, 273, 277–78
"Watermelon and Cantaloupe," 40
Waters, Ethel, 131, 147, 253
Waters, Muddy, 123, 237
Watkins, Mel, 1, 36
WATL, 168, 169
Watson, Carlotta Stewart ("Aunt Carrie"), 122
Watson, Phil, 236, 237, 239, 241
Watts, Charlene, 238
Watts ghetto, 195, 212, 214, 215
Wave Africa, 287
WBAI-FM, 236, 290
WBBM, 24
WBBW, 179, 180, 183
WBCN-FM, 227
WBEE, 56, 314n. 2
WBHQ, 109
WBIG, 174
WBIV, 150, 167
WBLK-FM, 232–33
WBLS-FM, 233–35, 241, 252
WBNX, 158
WBOK, 129, 132
WCAP, 51, 52
WCHB-AM, 140, 141, 150, 210, 247
WCHD-FM, 247
WCIN, 132, 137, 148, 314n. 2
WCLK-FM, 280, 281–82, 289
WCNW, 94, 95
WCSP-FM, 293

WDAS, 94, 143, 145, 183, 205, 222, 230, 255
WDCU-FM, 282, 291, 292–93
WDIA: black appeal format of, 109–11, 113, 114–15, 126–27, 148, 150, 159, 177, 201, 209, 296; African American DJs on, 110, 111, 116–23; and King's assassination, 217; price escalation of, 227; programs for African American women on, 121–23; and soul, 314n. 2; and Sounderling, 124, 131; sponsors of, 110, 128; success of, 123, 124
WDRE-FM, 278
WEAA-FM, 280, 282
WEAF, 23, 40
WEAS, 126–27, 160, 166
Weather Report, 234
Webb, Chick, 23, 34, 159
WEBB, 266
W. E. B. Du Bois Theater Guild, 84
WEBH, 38
WEDC, 24
WEDR-AM, 120, 128, 148, 207, 209, 210, 256
Welles, Orson, 77
Wells, Ida B., 84, 86, 148
WENN, 207, 210
WERD-AM, 128, 129, 133, 148, 248; and Gibson, 136–37, 139–40, 150, 247
WERQ AM/FM, 278
Westinghouse/CBS, 261
West Oakland Rockers, 173
WESU-FM, 280
WETA-FM, 292, 293
Wexler, Jerry, 199–200, 224
WEZZ, 166, 167
WFIL, 190
WGBS, 24
WGDY, 192
WGEE, 314n. 2
WGES, 98–99, 100, 101, 103, 149
WGIV, 129, 132, 150
WGN, 38, 39
WGOK, 132, 152
WGPR, 141
WGPR-FM, 231–32
WGRY, 149, 150
WHAT, 103, 142, 143, 205, 209, 217
WHB, 192
WHBC (Detroit), 209
WHBC-AM (Howard University), 283–84
WHBI, 174
WHBQ, 159, 177, 178, 179
WHCJ-FM, 280
Wheatley, Phyllis, 149
Wheelin' on Beale, 118
WHFC, 56
WHFS-FM, 227
WHIH, 314n. 2
White, Josh, 70, 77

White, "Rockin'" Leroy, 140, 146
White, "Tall" Paul, 195, 209–10
White, Walter, 71, 72
"White Captivity of Black Radio, The" (Ferretti), 245–46, 247
White House Report, 257
Whiteman, Paul, 16, 22, 74
Whitman, Ernest, 74, 75
Whitman, Walt, 6
WHN, 23, 31, 40
WHOD, 128, 148
WHOM, 143, 149, 158
WHOU, 246
WHOV-FM, 280
WHTA-FM, 278
WHUR-FM, 236–41, 272–75, 290
Widmer, Harriet, 30
WILD-AM, 256
Wiley, Jean, 237, 240
Wiley, Richard, 251
Wilkes, Sybil, 259
Wilkie, Wendell, 71, 72
Williams, A. C. ("Moohah"),116, 118, 123, 126, 146
Williams, Bert, 8, 16, 18, 20, 23, 52
Williams, Dyanna, 238
Williams, Kai, 143
Williams, Mary Lou, 74
Williams, Nat D., 122, 126, 151, 209; and other DJs, 118, 118, 120; and WDIA, 110, 111–16, 117, 118, 123, 124
Williams, Paul, 182
Williams, Wilfred, 74
Williamson, Sonny Boy, 96–97, 118
Willis, Chuck, 170
Wilson, Edith, 30
Wilson, Marie, 147
Wilson, Teddy, 74
Wilson, Woodrow, 45
Winchell, Walter, 32
Wings over Jordan, 34
Winnington, Jimmy, 140
WINS, 182, 183, 188
Winslow, Vernon, 146, 165, 167
Winston, James, 252, 261
WINX, 95, 174
WITH, 117–18, 142, 209, 210
WJAZ, 166
WJBE, 266
WJBK, 94
WJIB, 94, 148
WJIV, 160, 166
WJJD, 99, 101, 135
WJJL, 179
WJLB, 140, 141
WJMO, 314n. 2
WJMR, 160, 165–66

Index

WJOB, 94
WJSV, 158
WJW, 180, 181
WJZ, 23, 24
WKBS-AM, 232
WKSS-FM, 234
WKST, 180
WKTU-FM, 234
WKYS-FM, 278
WLAC, 180, 183, 201; crossover DJs at, 160–61, 162, 164, 166, 181
WLIB, 127, 128, 132, 143, 149, 209
WLIB-AM, 217, 233–34, 268
WLIB-FM, 217, 223, 230, 233, 268
WLOU, 128, 129, 132, 150–51, 314n. 2
WMAQ, 39, 83, 84, 87, 158
WMBM, 129, 130, 132
WMCA, 78, 94, 95, 234
WMDM, 137
WMIL, 175
WMMJ-FM, 278
WMPP, 247
WMRY, 148
WNEW, 158
WNEW-FM, 227, 229
WNJR, 248, 314n. 2
WNTA-TV, 144
WNVB-FM, 282
WOIC, 131, 247, 250, 314n. 2
WOKJ, 148
WOL-AM, 218, 238, 275–78, 314n. 2
Wolf, Sidney J., 131
"Wolfman Jack," 9, 155, 182–86, 271
Womack, Bobby, 202
Woman Speaks, A, 148, 209
women, African American, 25; as DJs, 98, 121–23, 147–53, 232, 234–35, 238; portrayed in radio, 29–30, 147–48
Wonder, Stevie, 138, 144, 201, 232, 234; as radio entrepreneur, 264, 269–71, 287
WOOD, 95
Wooding, Sam, 23
Woods, Georgie, 143, 224, 234, 276; and civil rights, 195, 204–7, 209, 222; and race riots, 213–14, 216
Woods, Randy, 161–62, 164, 167
Woods, Roy, 211, 254, 264
Woodson, Carter G., 84, 85
WOOK, 248, 314n. 2
WOPA, 103, 131, 150
Word from the People, 63
Word Soldiers, 237
WOR-FM, 227
Workers Wanted, 116
world music, 229
World's Largest Make-Believe Ballroom, 308n. 1
World War II, 67–75

WOV, 148, 149, 158
WPAL-AM, 131, 160, 256, 314n. 2
WPFW-FM, 290–91
WQAM, 192
WRAP, 148
WRDW, 265, 266
WRFG-FM, 288–89
Wright, Bill, 250–51
Wright, Ed, 223
Wright, Richard, 72, 81
Wright, Robert, 121
WRNY, 24
WROX, 103
WSB, 23
WSBC, 56, 93; and *The All-Negro Hour,* 25, 51, 52, 53
WSHA-FM, 246, 280, 281
WSID, 142, 148, 314n. 2
WSOK, 128, 140, 148, 209, 246, 314n. 2
WTIX, 192
WTMP, 132, 314n. 2
WTOP-FM, 236
WUFO-AM, 150, 256
WUSN, 126–27
WUSN-TV, 256
WUST, 222
WVAS-FM, 282–83
WVOL, 132, 247, 314n. 2
WVON, 209, 210, 218, 252, 254
WVSP-FM, 289–90
WWAE, 25
WWCA, 129
WWIN AM/FM, 278
WWRL, 143, 183, 205, 234, 255, 314n. 2
WXOK, 132, 152
WXRA, 179
WXYZ, 41, 174
WXZ, 31
WYBC-AM, 275
Wyce, Alice, 148
WYLD, 132, 314n. 2
WYNN, 131, 314n. 2
WYOU, 183

XERB, 155, 185
XERF, 183, 184, 185

Yesterday, Today, Tomorrow, 254
Young, Dale, 174
Young, Ivy, 237, 240
Young, Roland, 229, 230
"Young Widder Brown," 147
Your Legal Rights, 58

Ziegfeld Follies, 16, 23
"Zing Zang," 152
"Zip Coon," 3–4, 8, 9, 31, 40, 44